Political Clientelism, Patronage and Development

Sage Studies in
Contemporary Political Sociology

Trends Toward Corporatist Intermediation
edited by Philippe C. Schmitter and Gerhard Lehmbruch

Political Clientelism, Patronage and Development
edited by S. N. Eisenstadt and R. Lemarchand

Electoral Participation: A Comparative Analysis
edited by Richard Rose

Sponsored by the Committee on Political Sociology,
International Political Science Association
International Sociological Association

Political Clientelism, Patronage and Development

edited by

S. N. Eisenstadt
Hebrew University of Jerusalem

and

René Lemarchand
University of Florida, Gainesville

Contemporary Political Sociology Volume 3
SAGE Publications • Beverly Hills • London

For information address

SAGE Publications Ltd
28 Banner Street
London EC1Y 8QE

SAGE Publications Inc
275 South Beverly Drive
Beverly Hills, California 90212

British Library Cataloguing in Publication Data

Political clientism, patronage and development. —
(Contemporary political sociology; vol. **3**)
1. Political sociology
I. Eisenstadt, Shmuel Noah
II. Lemarchand, Rene   III. Series
306.2   JA76   80-41955

ISBN 0-8039-9794-9
ISBN 0-8039-9795-7 Pbk

First Printing

We acknowledge gratefully the help of the Rockefeller
and Ford foundations who have respectively provided
the facilities at the Villa Serbelloni and the financial
assistance to organize the conference and to the
Truman Research Institute of the Hebrew University
in Jerusalem where the initial theme of the conference
was planned and which supported the work of one of
the editors.

Contents

Introduction

In recent years political clientelism has emerged as a major growth point in social science analysis: no longer is the concept restricted to the field of social anthropology (where it remained consigned, by default as much as by excessive disciplinary purism, until the early 1970s); increasingly efforts are being made by sociologists and political scientists to investigate its empirical roots and theoretical ramifications. The resulting expansion of interdisciplinary research on clientelism has focussed attention on the ancillary concepts of patronage, social exchange and brokerage, and led to more systematic attempts at theory building. The publication in 1977 of two major anthologies on the subject — *Patrons and Clients,* and *Friends, Followers and Factions,* edited, respectively, by E. Gellner and J. Waterbury, and S. Schmidt, J. S. Scott, C. Landé and L. Guasti — and the appearance since then of scores of articles in professional journals, is a measure of the amount of scholarly attention paid to the phenomena explored in the present volume.

The papers collected here attempt to further contribute to this very substantial literature in two complementary directions. One is a further elaboration of the theoretical dimensions of the study of patron-client relations. What is involved here is an explication of two separate aspects of the problem, i.e. first, of the relations between the study of patron-client relations and the recent developments and controversies in sociological and anthropological theory; and, second, of the relations between patron-client relations or the patronage syndrome and those of class and ethnicity, both of which have been implicit in the hitherto available literature on the subject but which have not been fully explicated in it.

The various case studies in this volume complement these theoretical dimensions by stressing and elaborating upon several points made explicit in the discussions authored by the editors.

The first point is the articulation between the analytical core of patron-client relations and its concrete organizational forms. In the earlier literature on patronage great stress was laid on such aspects of patron-client relations as the dyadic relationships between patrons and clients as against corporate groups and it was these organizational structures that were seen as the core of the patron-client syndrome. With the proliferation of studies on patron-client relations more, and more diverse, organizational forms were identified and it naturally became increasingly difficult to identify any of these as the single basic core of patron-client relations.

The theoretical analysis and materials presented here indicate that the way to cope with this problem is by identifying the core of patron-client relations not in any concrete organizational form but in a specific type of exchange relationship — a type of relationship which in principle can become embodied, as it were, in a variety of structural or organizational forms.

The recognition of this fact has far-reaching implications for several other aspects of the comparative study of patron-client relations. The burgeoning literature on patron-client relationships has, of course, recognized that such relationships can be found in many societies and civilizations, on different levels of economic development and social differentiation and in a great variety of cultural traditions. This very fact, when combined with the distinction between the analytical core of the patron-client relations and the variety of its organizational forms, all of which are attested to in the articles presented here from different cultures and societies, raises two interconnected questions.

One question is whether one can identify some common characteristics of the social and cultural setting in which patron-client relations tend to develop. In the existing literature, there is a strong emphasis on such variables as sharp class differences, plantation economy, relations of international dependency, and the like, as conditions under which these relations tend to develop. But these conditions are to some extent presented in a rather ad hoc fashion. The relations among these variables are not fully explored, and, above all, the cultural dimension, that is the characteristics of the cultural traditions in which patron-client relations develop and their relations to existing political structures, is only marginally dealt with.

In the present collection we have attempted to bring all these together in a common systematic framework. Having done this we are able to give appropriate attention to the second question which arises in this context. This is the question of how variations in organizational forms, whether those in Mexico, Peru, France or

Italy, are to be explained. Obviously these variations cannot be explained by the characteristics which are common to all of them but rather by some which cut across common frameworks. The different chapters presented in this book present some indications of the direction in which such systematic exploration can be conducted. They suggest that it is above all such variables as the level of the economy and technology; the structure of the center and its penetration by the periphery; the types of policies undertaken by the center; the structure of the orientation and the internal cohesion of the periphery, which can best explain differences in the organizational structure of patron-client relations.

The last points stressed in the present collection concern both the importance of the international dimension in the analysis of patron-client relations and the necessity to distinguish between two aspects of this dimension.

One such aspect mentioned in the literature and which has yet to be very thoroughly thought through is whether it is possible to apply the concept of client relations between states. The other, which seems to be more fruitful, is to explore whether a situation of dependence between states may give rise within their respective societies to conditions conducive to the development of patron-client relations.

From these various perspectives the papers in this volume attempt to lay the groundwork for a systematic codification and analysis of several crucial dimensions of patron-client relations and at the same time suggest new paths for further research in this field.

To fulfill their obligations to the arts of academic patronage and discernment the editors wish to acknowledge their debt of gratitude to the Rockefeller Foundation for making available to them and their contributors the gracious surroundings of the Bellagio Study and Conference Center: of a more auspicious setting for assessing the merits of clientelism and patronage we cannot think. We are equally indebted to the Ford Foundation for a generous travel grant that made possible the convening of the Conference. The cooperation of the African Studies Center of the University of Florida and the Truman Institute of Jerusalem proved invaluable at various stages in the preparation of the manuscript. So did the typing skills of Hazel Pridgen, Pat Reichert and Marilyn Gordon, whose joint efforts and endless patience enabled us to meet the Publisher's deadline with only minimal delays.

To infer from the foregoing anything even remotely reminiscent of Samuel Johnson's definition of a patron — "One who countenances, supports or protects: commonly a wretch who supports with insolence, and is paid with flattery" — would be clearly inappropriate. Honni soit qui mal y pense.

S. N. Eisenstadt
René Lemarchand

I
Theoretical Perspectives

—————1—————
Comparative Political Clientelism: Structure, Process and Optic

René Lemarchand
University of Florida, USA

Nowhere is the rate of casualty among new concepts higher than in the social sciences. Few survive the scrutiny of critical discourse, and many more end up prematurely fossilized in the pages of esoteric journals. Survival, as has been noted, "is not mainly a function of etymological precision or even clarity of reference . . . but of how much fruitful research a new concept generates. Most concepts new or old are killed not by attack but by neglect" (Goode, 1975: 67).

By these standards the concept of political clientelism seems assured of a comfortable life-expectancy. In the decade or so since it was introduced in the lexicon of political scientists countless books and articles have been devoted to the exploration of clientelistic phenomena in settings as diverse as China and Columbia, Italy and Senegal, Venezuela and Lebanon. Important theoretical insights have emerged from this avalanche of case studies which have added immeasurably to our understanding of developmental issues across national and disciplinary boundaries. It is a measure of its growing popularity, and perhaps symptomatic of what some are prompted to dismiss as an "obsessive concern," that the concept should now be applied to research areas ranging from exchange theory to the dynamics of factional systems, and from processes of class formation to patterns of resource allocation. The list could be further extended. Hardly any dimension of political life seems immune from the contamination of clientelism.

Criticisms of the way in which it has been handled have done little to diminish its attractiveness as a concept. Yet the time has come to recognize its limitations and clarify some of the misunderstandings surrounding the current debate about the merits of clientelistic analysis. For some the concept "has traveled too fast too easily from the anthropological peripheries to developing polities" (Moore, 1977: 257), hence suggesting the need for further refinement before it can be properly used for purposes of comparative analysis. For others "it has become a concept for all seasons" (Gilsenan, 1977: 167), applied uncritically to situational contexts that have little in common beyond their assumed clientelistic properties. More damning still, the concept is said to suffer from an inherent conservative bias, in that "it is part of a functionalist-consensus view of society that obstructs a deeper analysis of social structures in quite fundamental ways" (Gilsenan, 1977: 168).

Since I bear a special responsibility for this unhappy state of affairs — having explored the ramifications of clientelistic circuitry in more ways than one, but always with an almost perverse obduracy — a measure of self-criticism is in order (from which the analytic value of the concept will hopefully emerge unsullied). These expressions of skepticism are, on the whole, salutary because they bring to light a number of conceptual vulnerabilities in earlier formulations of the clientelistic model, including my own, and thus invite us to reexamine a number of enduring questions about its normative implications and the limits of its applicability.

It is impossible within the limits of this chapter to do justice to all aspects of the phenomenon. Rather than to seek maximum coverage of its varied manifestations, I propose to look at the evidence from those perspectives that are most likely to open up new vistas for comparative analysis. We begin with a critical reassessment of the conceptual problems involved in the use of the clientelistic model, focussing primarily on questions of meaning and interpretation; we then move on to a consideration of the several levels of discourse at which the analysis of clientelistic phenomena may conceivably proceed; finally an attempt is made to establish the relevance of the patron-client model to current theories of dependency.

SOME CONCEPTUAL VULNERABILITIES
OF CLIENTELISTIC ANALYSIS

At the root of the disenchantment expressed by various critics of clientelism (both as a concept and a model) lies the suspicion that its analytic value is fatally flawed by (1) its normative implications, (2) its inherent reductionist bias, and (3) the questions it raises as to its applicability to the macro-level, or what is here referred to as the "level of analysis problem." Let us take a closer look at these objections.

1. The Normative Issue:
Clientelism as an "Organicist" Concept

Born and nurtured in the conservative soil of structural anthropology, the concept of clientelism bears the stigma of what some might regard as a predictable birth-defect: its strong conservative bias, reminiscent of "organicist" concepts of society. The vision of society which it conveys is that of a highly cohesive and integrated system in which there is a relatively harmonious interdependence of its component parts. In the varied topography of social formations patron-client sets are generally expected to share "the supposedly spontaneous unity of natural life-forms" (Eagleton, 1976: 103).

Hence the two-fold objection that clientelism unduly restricts the scope of analysis by systematically excluding conflict situations, and that by taking harmony for granted it runs the additional risk of totally distorting social reality. Readers of Maquet, on Rwanda, and David and Audrey Smock, on Lebanon (Maquet, 1961; Smock, 1975) will surely appreciate the validity of this criticism, aware as they must be of the danger of grossly overestimating the capacity of clientelism to promote inter-group equilibrium.

The "organicist" critique poses an obvious challenge to the devotees of clientelistic analysis — but not an insuperable one. To recognize the system-equilibrating functions of clientelism in specific historical situations does not ipso facto imply uncritical endorsement of a teleological-functionalist view of the concept. No serious student of clientelism would deny that the phenomenon has a darker side to it, from which conflict and oppression are not to be excluded. The balance of coercion and voluntary compliance which enters into patron-client ties covers a wide gamut. Not only can reciprocity change to rivalry, but the shifts in the balance of exchange can also lead to various forms of oppression and exploitation. The point hardly deserves elaboration. As has been argued, clientelism is a key element in the "mechanisms of dependency and control" (Flynn, 1974) which help both to legitimate and mask structures of domination. Conflict models, in short, are entirely compatible with the clientelistic mode of analysis.

The crux of the issue, from a methodological standpoint, is to distinguish between social praxis and social values, between the "structural" and "ideological" dimensions of clientelism.[1] Structural forms of dependence, rooted in oppression, may assume all forms of ideological justification, including the notion that the relationship is rooted in the exchange of mutual benefits. What ultimately matters is whether these benefits are real. Establishing this reality, however, is by no means easy, if only because clientelism operates within an ideological framework which carries its own logic. According to this logic some clients may claim contentment in order to avoid retribution; others will feign harassment, but in "their own devotional language," as Donal Cruise O'Brien discovered, they merely wish to "boast" (Cruise O'Brien, 1975: 62); and most patrons will probably exaggerate the extent of their benevolence. Decoding the hidden meanings and rationalizations that lie behind the actual functioning of clientelistic phenomena requires more than a *verstehen* operation. It means that we need to look at the subjective cues, motives and intentions of political actors, and relate them to the cultural matrix and ideological milieu in which they operate. The aim here is not only to achieve understanding, but also "to understand the universe of understanding" (Gadamer, 1974). Thus if we are to deal effectively with the phenomenology of clientelism we need to do more than just refute the "organicist" implications of the concept; one also needs to assess the range of disjunction between structure and ideology. How this can be accomplished is nowhere better demonstrated than in the works of Sydel Silverman on Colleverde (Italy) and Donal Cruise O'Brien on Senegal (Silverman, 1977; Cruise O'Brien, 1975), among the very best efforts at interpretive analysis thus far attempted by any student of clientelism.

What these efforts suggest, for one thing, is the sterility of the "false consciousness" argument when it comes to determining what is structural and what is ideological in any given relationship.

Assuming that there is such a thing as "false consciousness," consciousness is no less real for being false, a point persuasively argued by Kasfir and others, and in this case we need to explain the fact of its existence (Kasfir, 1976). Furthermore, what may be seen by some as tangible proof of "false consciousness" may also be interpreted as a highly rational form of behavior in the face of a situation of social oppression to which there is no alternative other than suicide. Although space limitations preclude a more sustained exploration of these issues, the questions they raise are at least indicative of the perspective from which clientelism needs to be looked at if it is to gain any real analytical leverage.

2. The Reductionist Trap

The objection that clientelism uncritically reduces social phenomena to the same common denominator again raises some important questions of interpretation and meaning. At issue here is not so much the existential reality of the phenomenon as its relationship to class and ethnicity. Should it be viewed as an autonomous, sui generis type of social organization, or a symptom of class oppression? Should it be treated as an integrative device designed to bring different ethnic entities into adaptive equilibrium with each other, or as a thinly disguised form of ethnic domination?

These are evidently complex issues, which can only be dealt with here in the most superficial fashion. However widespread, clientelism is by no means a ubiquitous phenomenon. Nor is its saliency constant. As in the case of class and ethnicity, clientelistic solidarities can be activated at different levels and with varying degrees of intensity depending on the circumstances. Or they may disappear or lapse into a state of suspended animation, as when under the pressure of intensifying class or ethnic hostility patrons and clients are driven into opposing camps, or, alternatively, converted into more or less equal partners within the same group. Again, the fragmentation of the original clientelistic structure may lead to the reformulation of a new one of greater complexity.

Clientelism must be seen as part of the wider social dialectic through which individuals interact with their changing environment. The patron-client nexus does not exist as an entity in itself; it comes into play at a particular historical moment under the pressure of forces which transcend its immediate field of operation. Looked at from this perspective the crux of the issue is not whether ethnic or class analysis has greater explanatory power than clientelistic analysis, but at what point in time, and through what combination of circumstances class or ethnic cleavages are liable to alter, combine with, or supersede patron-client ties. Thus between the sharply contrasting interpretations of the Lebanese political system recently offered by Gilsenan and Khalaf lies more than just a divergence of theoretical perspectives; their disaccord can only be understood in light of the drastic restructuring of group solidarities operated in the crucible of a savage civil war; Gilsenan's case against patron-client ties certainly has considerable validity for an understanding of Lebanon in the mid-1970s; yet the same argument falters when applied to an earlier phase of Lebanese history (Gilsenan, 1977; Khalaf, 1977).

The important issue, then, is not whether class or ethnicity are more "relevant" than clientelism but how they interact with each other. The problem can be approached in one of two ways: either by using clientelism as the independent variable, and in this case attention is inevitably drawn to the way in which patterns of exchange affect the stability of clientelistic nets and their propensity to accelerate the emergence of alternative social formations; or by concentrating on class and ethnicity as the key variables which determine the fate and shape of clientelistic phenomena. In one case the focus is on the transition from a vertical ordering of social relations to one in which horizontal solidarities predominate; in the other attention is drawn to the opposite phenomenon, that is, the resurgence of clientelistic ties in the pursuit of dominant class or ethnic objectives. The latter phenomenon is excellently discussed by Flynn in his analysis of clientelism as a mechanism of internal control. To quote: "Far from being an alternative to class analysis, an approach which . . . emphasizes clientelism can greatly help to understand some of the mechanisms of class control which help to maintain dependency" (Flynn, 1974: 139). Thus to relegate the clientelistic dimension to the status of an epiphenomenon, as some impenitent Marxists tend to do, on the grounds that "the patron-client model obscures the class basis of political action and articulation" (Alavi, 1975: 15) is tantamount to throwing out the baby with the bathwater. As Flynn conclusively shows, clientelistic manipulation is often a necessary condition of class domination.

In short, to the objection that clientelism has become "a concept

for all seasons" one might reply by pointing out that its suscep-
tibility to seasonal change does not necessarily mean that it will
evaporate once and for all. The persistence of the phenomenon
even in the context of industrial societies no longer needs to be
demonstrated; a more urgent and demanding task is to identify the
conditions that are liable to affect its mode of operation and
ultimate impact on society, a question to which we shall return.

3. The Level of Analysis Problem

Which brings us to what is perhaps the toughest issue in discussions
of patron-client relationships: How far above the micro-level can
the concept be stretched if it is to retain its analytical value?

"Climbing the ladder of abstraction," as Sartori reminds us, is
always a risky business. It can easily lead to "conceptual stretching
or conceptual straining, i.e., to vague, amorphous conceptualization"; worse still, it may lead us into "the Hegelian night in which
all cows are black (and eventually the milkman is taken for the
cow)" (Sartori, 1970: 416).   Properly handled, however,
abstractions can also serve as flares to illuminate the social landscape and help us discern who is doing the milking and who is being
treated as the milch cow.

The transition from micro- to macro-analysis, to borrow once
again from Sartori, requires a different kind of logic from the one
generally applied to patrons and clients at the local level, not the
logic of "either-or" but of "more or less"; only by substituting a
"gradualistic" for a "taxonomic" logic can the concept of
clientelism be operationalized for the investigation of supra-local
phenomena.

From this perspective at least two different types of analytic con-
structs need to be considered. The first involves the incorporation
of patron-client ties into the context of nominally modern institutions, and corresponds to what Landé calls "patron-client relations as *addenda*." The assumption here is that, to a greater or
lesser extent, patron-client ties may operate "as additions to institutions whose deficiencies they remedy" (Landé, 1977: xviii) —
or magnify. The grafting operation may produce all kinds of jux-
tapositions and hybridization. Variations range from those semi-
traditional bureaucracies that are thoroughly overlaid with personalized connections — as exemplified by the so-called "ikwa"

phenomenon in Saudi Arabia, consisting of "retainers or compa-
nions . . . who in addition to a variety of specific functions, help
keep their masters in touch with the world" (Hirst, 1977) — to
more modern types, only superficially or intermittently affected by
patron-client ties — for example, the UDR establishment under De
Gaulle — and from parties where clientelistic addenda leave little
room for anything else — as in the case of the Northern Peoples
Congress (NPC) in Northern Nigeria immediately after independence — to those where they occupy a more restricted space.
Although the conceptualization of patron-client ties as addenda has
considerable heuristic validity, not the least of the difficulties confronting the analyst is to establish precisely at what level and to
what extent clientelistic formations in fact penetrate formal institutions.

Another way of resolving the level of analysis problem is to
ascribe to corporate entities the structural characteristics of the
patron-client model: from this standpoint patterns of dependency
at the national or international level are seen as a logical extension
of the basic patron-client dyad. The analogy is not meant to suggest
that parties, bureaucracies, multinationals, or states are to be
treated as faithful replicas of concrete clientelistic structures; the
point, rather, is that as "analytic structures" (to borrow Marion
Levy's phrase) they reveal some of the traits and relationships
derived from the behavior of individual patrons and clients. At this
level of abstraction the range of dependencies "covered" by the
model is almost endless, and the "stretching" operation, once carried to its outer limit, may well become pointless. Yet to dismiss all
attempts at "macro-application" of the clientele concept as sterile
is clearly unwarranted.

A major problem is that "the larger the macro-unit . . . the more
necessary it becomes to introduce into the analysis properties and
assumptions which are not implied by, and cannot be derived from,
the patron-client concept" (Kaufman, 1974: 293). In other words
clientelism cannot be treated both as a paradigm and as a variable,
a point again convincingly argued by Kaufman. Furthermore, the
mere extension of the concept to the macro-level is of relatively
little help to elucidate the nexus of interaction between domestic
and international arenas.

To recognize these weaknesses and vulnerabilities argues for considerable caution in the handling of the patron-client model; the
limitations they suggest are hardly sufficient, however, to disprove

its analytic value. The ultimate test of its usefulness lies in its descriptive and explanatory power. On the strength of these criteria it certainly carries enough plausibility to warrant a further effort to bring its analytic dimensions into still sharper focus.

STRUCTURE, PROCESS AND OPTIC

Only if we recognize the multiple levels of meaning attached to the notion of clientelism can we make the concept operational and cut through the sophistry of definitional purists. Whether one ought to strive for generality at the expense of empirical precision, or vice versa, is not the crux of the issue; the point, rather, is that like all comparative and developmental concepts, clientelism allows us to operate at different levels of discourse depending on whether we choose to emphasize its structural, processual or paradigmatic dimensions.

In its most common social science usage clientelism denotes a specific type of social structure, or mode of social stratification. Here attention is directed to an interstitial social space, lying somewhere between the categories of class and ethnicity, that takes into account those micro-level solidarities, or "quasi-groups," generally referred to as patron-client ties, and whose anatomy has been most extensively studied and dissected by social anthropologists. As has been repeatedly stressed, patron-client ties involve dyadic bonds between individuals of unequal power and socioeconomic status; they exhibit a diffuse, particularistic, face-to-face quality strongly reminiscent of ascriptive solidarities; unlike ascriptive ties, however, they are voluntarily entered into and derive their legitimacy from expectations of mutual benefits. Asymmetry, diffuseness and reciprocity are basic features of the type of social structure that has become associated with political clientelism.

One can appreciate the merits of the structural approach without limiting oneself to the study of small groups, or for that matter without ignoring the social forces that may affect their configurations. All too often, however, an exclusive focus on structural aspects tends to inhibit our perception of the forces of change set in motion by modernization and how these in turn condition the survival (or the extinction) of clientelistic phenomena. Instead attention is generally drawn to (1) the identification of the relevant units of analysis; (2) the structural variables which underlie patron-client relations; and (3) the degree of institutionalization discernible in any such relationship.

These are of course important preliminary steps in any attempt to uncover a broader panorama. Variations in the structure of patron-client roles, ranging from " dyads" to "clusters" and "networks" (Scott, 1977a: 128), invite consideration of what is the most appropriate unit of analysis in any specific situation. Role relationships between clients and patrons can be further differentiated on the basis of the degree of power asymmetry between them, how much diffuseness or specificity enters into their relationships, and the types of trade-offs involved; again, the extent to which normative sanctions underlie the patron-client nexus suggests yet another critical dimension of analysis.

Typologies based on structural differentiation, however, are little more than lists of parts. The vision they convey of society is too static and fragmentary to reveal the full picture of patron-client interactions, the strategies involved in the building of clienteles, or the kinds of conflicts which prompt rural clients to vote with their feet or rise against their landlords. To capture the sense of these phenomena one must move towards the processual aspects of political clientelism.

The emphasis here is on the social processes, strategies and fields of interaction which determine or explain the dynamics of patron-client ties. Rather than clientelism explaining everything else, the phenomenon is viewed as a dependent variable which assumes different forms and degrees of significance in response to the forces at work in the wider environment.

Looked at from this perspective, changes in the scale and structure of patron-client ties are inevitably related to the social and economic processes that modernization sets in motion in specific historical contexts. Bearing in mind Eisenstadt's caveat that "in such situations of change there develops not just one possibility of the restructuring of forces and activities . . . but rather a great variety of possibilities" (Eisenstadt, 1973: 306), it may be useful to consider briefly three basic types of mutations in this overall process of restructuration: (1) the historic shifts that have affected the balance of exchange between patrons and clients at the micro-level, (2) the expansion in scale of clientelistic networks and their incorporation into new institutional frameworks, and (3) the atrophy of these networks in situations where policies of departicipation have been more or less systematically pursued.

1. From "Patrimonial" to "Repressive" Clientelism

The erosion of traditional patron legitimacy and the tendency for rural notables to rely increasingly on coercion to secure compliance is a central aspect of the processes of change that have accompanied the spread of capitalism into the rural sectors of the Third World. As has been shown in a number of recent studies on Latin America, Africa and Southeast Asia, economic and political modernization has radically altered the bargaining relationship between traditional patrons and their clients, thus setting in motion a fundamental process of social dislocation at the grass-roots.

The basic historical trend observable in many colonial and post-colonial societies can be conceptualized in terms of a shift from "patrimonial" to "repressive" forms of clientelism. In the sense in which Anthony Hall uses the term, "patrimonial" ties are characteristic of those rapidly disappearing relationships in which there is "overt acceptance of traditional values by the subordinate," and where "crude physical coercion" is mitigated by the paternalism of the rural patron (Hall, 1977: 511). "Repressive" clientelism, on the other hand, is a coercive response to the assault of modernity on the legitimacy of rural patrons; in this case "cruder forms of repression (play) an increasingly important part in landowners' attempts to resist erosion of the traditional rural class structure and value system in the face of cultural, political and market pressures" (Hall, 1977). In other words, where the traditional context of clientelism no longer serves as the "normative script" of social exchange, what Sahlins calls "negative exchange," that is, "the attempt to get something for nothing with impunity" (Sahlins, 1965) is likely to become the norm.

Nowhere has the shift from "patrimonial" to "repressive" forms of clientelism been more evident than in the colonial environments of Africa and Asia. It is in these transitional settings that we find the clearest evidence of the corrosive impact of the colonial state, to which must be added the wide-ranging dislocations engendered by the spread of commercial agriculture and plantation economies. The expansion of the apparatus of the state into the rural sectors implied a drastic redefinition of patron roles: "Instead of being largely a creature of the locality who dealt with the center, (the patrons) became increasingly creatures of the center who dealt with the local community" (Scott and Kerkvliet, 1977: 454). The backing of the colonial state thus greatly reinforced the security and bargaining position of the patrons while at the same time lessening their dependence on community norms. Moreover, as the extractive capabilities of the state came to depend increasingly on the collaboration of traditional authority figures, the claims they made on the local communities became correspondingly heavier and difficult to reconcile with their traditional roles as benevolent patrons. A further stimulus to coercion came from the spread of market forces, which added new incentives for landlords to extract maximum services from their clients, and put additional pressure on chiefly authorities to help European and "native" capitalists in the recruiting of rural laborers and plantation workers. Despite notable variations in the depth and extent of social corrosion, almost everywhere the result has been to drastically alter the patterns of social exchange to the advantage of the rural notables, and to make the conditions of dependence of their rural clienteles increasingly oppressive. The point has been argued in considerable detail by Scott and Kerkvliet in their excellent analysis of rural class relations in Southeast Asia, but much of what they have to say on the theme of "how traditional rural patrons lose legitimacy" also applies to many parts of Africa and Latin America.

Moving further back into history, the European scene offers many parallels to the situation we have just described. A prime example is the drastic alteration of landlord-tenant relations in the wake of the tremendous disorder and rural unrest caused by the "Black Death" in the 14th century. The so-called "Statutes of Treason" passed in England in 1349 and 1352 directly contributed to strengthening the bargaining position of the landlords, and formed a major element in the background of the rural conflicts that characterized much of the "bastard feudalism" period in English history.

Repressive clientelism represents only a particular epoch, or state of the play, in a more extended process of societal transformation. In the short run rural revolt is, of course, the most obvious alternative to continued oppression, though by no means the most feasible. The history of colonial and post-colonial societies is replete with instances of exploited clients revolting against their traditional landlords, headmen and chiefs, in desperate attempts to make good their "right to subsistence" (Scott, 1976). And so is European history. Behind the Tudor rebellions of 16th century England and the "furies" of 17th century France lies a set of motivations very similar to that which prompted the peasants of Burma and Viet-Nam to rise against their landlords in 1930. The parallel could be extended to Rwanda in 1959, Chad in 1969 and Nigeria in 1968.

Where the historical experience of Third World societies differs fundamentally from that of Europe is that among the former the demands and frustrations of the rural sectors found an outlet in electoral channels long before their social identities were allowed to crystallize along class lines. The result has been a process of fragmented restructuration which offered ample scope for the reemergence of patron-client ties in the guise of nominally modern institutions.

2. Patterns of Incorporation: Clientelistic Aspects of Machine Politics

It is primarily where social change has lagged substantially behind political modernization that clientelistic forms of dependency have been most resilient. Unlike what we find in most of Western Europe (with the qualified exception of Mediterranean countries), where class formation preceded the introduction of universal suffrage, making it possible for parties and trade unions to organize themselves and articulate their demands in class terms, in much of the Third World electoral processes took place in an environment saturated with ethnic and clientelistic loyalties, with only scattered evidence of incipient class formation. In these conditions the obvious way to contain societal fragmentation was through the organization of political machines. These, however, took on radically different characteristics depending on the extent of political participation allowed at any given time, the settings in which they developed and the strategies pursued by political entrepreneurs.

As has often been emphasized, electoral competition affects the dynamics of patron-client interactions in two fundamental ways: It enables the clients to use the vote as a lever to shift the balance of exchange to their advantage, and through a proces of pyramiding of patron-client ties it promotes the expansion of local or regional reciprocities on a more inclusive scale. Both are critical aspects of the conditions that have led to the emergence of clientelistic machines.

Contrary to what is generally assumed, however, elections do not automatically give the clients a meaningful option. For if in theory the vote enables them to improve their bargaining position, in practice there are numerous and severe limitations on their ability to do so. Where electoral practices fit into the general pattern of "election without choice" (Hermet et al., 1978) — where the vote is neither free nor extensive, where competition is non-existent and the ultimate impact on government policies negligible — the suffrage offers very little in the way of an alternative. "Faggot" votes[2] in 18th century Scotland were hardly more of a "resource" for local peasants than were the *votos de cabrestas* ("cattle votes") in Imperial Brazil, or what Rouquié calls "gregarious votes" in other parts of Latin America (Rouquié, 1978: 24). In each case the prime beneficiaries were the rural notables, the great county families (like the Dundas in Scotland), the *coroneis* and *caciques*.

Equally significant in restricting political options at the grassroots are the "the indirect social pressures exerted upon voters, especially by a dominant culture or ideology" (Hermet, 1978: 3). Without resorting to the crude cultural determinism characteristic of explanations based on the alleged "dependency syndrome" of "primitive peoples" a convincing case can be made for the view that traditional deference patterns may have a decisive influence on the electoral choices of rural clienteles. More important still are the constraints arising from local power structures, as when the dice (and the guns) are so heavily loaded in favor of the dominant cliques as to leave no other option to the clients but to vote as they are told.

Conditions of extreme economic insecurity, social uprootedness and rapid impoverishment are just as instrumental in forcing urban and rural clienteles into the fold of a clientelistic apparatus. What may be referred to as the "marginalization syndrome" is indeed an essential ingredient of machine politics. The phenomenon is particularly evident in rural areas where rising demographic pressures and the spread of capitalist farming have caused serious land shortages and a sharp decline in rural employment. It is also found in those urban sectors where squatter settlements and "bidonvilles" are a conspicuous element of the social landscape. In these conditions marginalization provides a fertile ground for the restructuring of dependency relations through the selective allocation of patronage resources and the extension of special favors. Unemployment, however, though clearly a concomitant of marginalization, is not enough to account for the presence of clientelistic control; the important factor is the sociopolitical context of unemployment, including whether or not there exist meaningful alternatives to the use of clientelistic channels for coping with problems of economic survival.

In the absence of such alternatives machine politics tend to fit into two distinctive patterns: One is what I have described elsewhere as the "neo-traditional" pattern, in which clientelistic solidarities of a traditional type are incorporated into a broader institutional framework, usually a party; the other is the "orthodox machine" type, held together not by the persistence of traditional ties of deference but by expectations of concrete, short-run benefits (Lemarchand, 1977). These are, of course, "ideal types"; in practice they each allow for countless variations.

Neo-traditional patterns include such typically archaic phenomena as the Liberal and Conservative machines in 19th century Brazil, both equally captive of the whims of traditional rural bosses (*coroneis*); the Union Progressiste Senegalaise (UPS) in post-independence Senegal, which to this day remains heavily dependent, politically, on the support of the Mouride brotherhoods; and the curiously paternalistic links established between President Odria and the squatter settlements in Lima from 1948 to 1956, which reveal "a striking parallel between certain features of the organization of the haciendas of traditional agriculture in the highlands of Peru and the nature of Odria's relationship with the squatter settlements" (Collier, 1976: 60). Depending on the kinds of traditional subsystems encapsulated into the machine, the manner in which the "nexus function" is being performed, and the scope of the networks, a variety of different "neo-traditional" subtypes suggest themselves for analysis.

The same is true of the "orthodox" machine, but here a more sustained effort is required to differentiate the classical machine model (best exemplified by the American urban machine) from what may be called the mass patronage machine. Although both are highly responsive to concrete, particularistic rewards, the latter is much more in the nature of a mass organization, its resources are far more diversified (and so is its clientele), and its ramifications in-

to the state bureaucracy are considerably more complex and extensive. In this sense the Daley machine in Chicago has a great deal
more in common with the Radical machine of Argentina in the
1920s (Rock, 1972) than they each have with the Christian
Democratic (DC) machine in contemporary Italy. The difference is
nicely captured in the words of a Sicilian observer (Graziano, 1976:
149):

> What we have here is mass clientelism, organized and efficient, which consists in
> laws, extraordinary provisions, emergency measures and concessions granted no
> longer to the individual, but to favored groups. In order to put this powerful
> machine to work, through time the Christian Democrats have had to place party
> men at every level of power, in each key position . . . Today clientelism is a rela-
> tionship between large groups and public power.

What distinguishes the Christian Democratic Party of Italy from
more classical types of machines is both the diversity of its
clienteles (ranging from entrepreneurial middle classes to public
employees and urban poor) and the combination of monetary and
non-monetary rewards at its disposal. Yet another characteristic of
the mass patronage machine lies in its ability to intervene, directly
or indirectly, into the workings of the bureaucratic machinery of
the state. As Judith Chubb shows in her study of patronage in
Palermo in this volume, it is not just public spending, subsidies or
its control of access to credit which enter the flow of patronage
resources, but also, and more importantly, "discretionary implementation of the powers of licensing and interdiction of local
government, particularly in the areas of urban planning, construction licenses and enforcement of zoning and building codes."
This is a type of resource which is not only characteristic of an advanced state of "bureaucratization" and entrepreneurial development, but which allows the machine to operate at a remarkably
cheap rate of exchange. Trading votes for ways of circumventing
legal procedure, or for simply greasing the wheels of a normally
slow and unresponsive bureaucracy, is a basic feature of mass
patronage.

Monetary inducements are not the only ingredient in the reward
system of orthodox machines, at least not of the mass clientele
type. Their stability, as Judith Chubb demonstrates, lies not only in
their discretionary use of public spending but also in their ability to
create obligations through a host of favors that are no less critical

for being of a non-monetary nature.

What makes the case of Italy of particular interest for students of clientelism is that, perhaps better than any other society, it brings into relief different strategies associated with clientelistic control.

As a strategic response to conditions of expanding political participation, clientelism can be viewed in one of two ways: (1) as a strategy designed to maximize parliamentary influence at the center in order to better insulate the peripheries from "adverse" public policies, or (2) as a strategy aiming at maximizing the local vote-getting capabilities of the "peripheral" machine so as to enhance its parliamentary influence at the center. These processes are by no means unrelated. In a number of instances the quest for influence at the center is the normal consequence of a less than optimal vote-catching ability at the local level.

The first type of strategy finds a specially apt illustration in the phenomenon of *trasformismo* in post-Risorgimento Italy. The alliance of the landed elites of the Mezzogiorno with the liberal bourgeoisie of the north had as its major objective the preservation of their powerful clientelistic base in the south. The nature of the quid pro quo is excellently phrased by Graziano (Graziano, 1978: 300):

> What the southern bourgeoisie asked from the new regime was essentially a recognition of their landholding to protect themselves against both the old barons, whose land they had usurped, and the peasants . . . They renounced any claim to control of the state and unconditionally accepted the policy of the dominant classes in the north. The mechanism by which the southern elites were coopted into the national system of power as subordinate partners was called *trasformismo*.

What is involved here is an attempt to forge a coalition of ruling classes at the center so as to thwart or devitalize incipient class conflicts on the periphery — or, as Doro puts it, an attempt "to castrate the revolution through personal transactions with the (national) leaders" (Graziano, 1978: 299). A similar type of surgery was conducted in Lebanon in the years following the second world war: the parliamentary alliances built through various compromises and quid pro quos among "bosses" (*zu'ama*) were a precondition of their continued hegemony in the countryside (Hottinger, 1966).

The second is of course the standard strategy employed by political entrepreneurs to gain access to and control over the institutions of the state, including parliamentary institutions. Colonial and post-colonial societies offer countless examples of encapsulation and cooptation for purposes of "state-building." The emergence of dominant, multi-ethnic machines in Africa and Asia shows how effective the distribution of material rewards at the local level can be in enhancing their electoral strength and ultimately in facilitating their control of parliamentary institutions. India's Congress Party and Ghana's Convention People's Party (CPP) are cases in point. Yet, as these examples suggest, the incorporation of local networks may in time generate bitter factional struggles. Moreover, where alternative political structures are available, in the form of class-based parties and trade unions, and where social mobilization is more than a surface phenomenon, the detachment of clientelistic networks may lead to very different patterns of incorporation. Thus with the emergence of peasant leagues (*ligas camponesas*) and rural trade unions (*sindicatos rurais*) in the northeast of Brazil in the mid-1950s, the old "patron-dependent" relationship associated with *coronelismo* gave way to what some have described as "revolutionary agrarianism," and others as "a major breakthrough into non-traditional, class-oriented patterns" (de Kadt, 1970: 24). This description also fits the losses suffered by the Congress Party to the Communists in Kerala and other states over the last decade, and, even more appropriately, the defeat of the Christian Democratic machine in Naples by the Communists in the 1975 elections. In each case the breakdown of the machine pattern is traceable to the skillful exploitation of a local distributive crisis by an alternative, non-clientelistic political structure.

Where the machine is unable to cope with the threats posed to its existence by the volatility of the electoral process — when it can neither accommodate the individual or sectional demands of its clientele, nor institutionalize the clientelistic linkage structure through a fairly stable set of expectations as to what it can and cannot deliver — one possible solution is for the political system to reconstruct itself along corporatist lines. Whether in "exclusionary" or "inclusionary" form, to borrow Stepan's distinction (Stepan, 1978: 73), the corporatist formula implies the elaboration of functional dependencies. Clientelistic networks in this case reach out into the periphery through functional associations, segregating clienteles on the basis of occupational or class affiliations. Elections merely serve to institutionalize a type of control in which coercion figures at least as prominently as material inducements in the overall process of social exchange. Portugal under Salazar is a classic example of how dependency relationships may survive into the framework of corporatist associational organizations, and indeed of the basic principle which insures their survival: *Para os amigos pao, para os inimigos pau* (for friends, bread; for enemies, the stick) (Cutileiro, 1971).

Another solution is to do away with the electoral process altogether and restrict the scope of patron-client ties to the strict minimum compatible with the maintenance in office of the ruling cliques. Only the briefest mention of the phenomenon will suffice to illustrate its effect on clientelistic nets.

3. The Atrophy of Clientelistic Nets

What has been referred to as "the pervasive spread of departicipation" (Kasfir, 1976: 267) is a central feature of political life in many states of Africa, Asia and the Middle East. With the elimination of the electoral process and the removal of participatory structures, a new type of clientelism sets in, primarily focussed on armies and bureaucracies. The "shrinking of the political arena" leads to a similar atrophy of clientelistic nets; social exchange takes the form of unrestrained corruption and extortion; insofar as one can speak of a "nexus function" it operates among highly personalized cliques, and is primarily used in the form of an exploitative monopoly of public resources. What the system fails to accomplish through its anarchic reward system it does by way of periodic purges of the army and the civil service (as in Uganda), by the indiscriminate slaughter of anyone suspected of opposition (as in the Central African Empire under Bokassa), and by political assassination (as in Pakistan, Bangla Desh, Chad, etc.).

In these conditions clientelistic nets are understandably fragile and constantly in a state of flux. The calculation of costs and benefits is a never ending process, and there is little or no incentive to operate a redistribution of public resources below the charmed circle of intimates who happen to be on the receiving end of the line. Despite valiant attempts to identify a "managerial brokerage" modality in military regimes like those of Togo and Zaire, to describe them as being endowed with a high capability to satisfy group demands clearly strains credulity (Decalo, 1976: 251). Because the patron-client nets are so fluid and limited in scope, and because politics is thereby reduced to "shadowy behind-the-scenes appeals on the basis of personal influence'' (Kasfir, 1976: 267), it is a question whether clientelistic patterns can be identified otherwise than in the most tentative fashion.

As the foregoing suggests, the patron-client model can be used not only to identify particular structures and processes but also as an "optic" which enables us to locate and explore some critical dimensions in the analysis of political systems. Although economic and political modernization makes possible the mobilization of new resources, the really important issues lie elsewhere: Exactly what kinds of resources are made available to whom, through what channels and within what kinds of economic and political constraints? Rephrased in these terms, the classic Lasswellian question — Who gets what, when and how? — is at least suggestive of the contribution which a clientelistic perspective can make to our understanding of the political process.

The clientelistic "optic" helps illuminate a still larger segment of political life, which transcends the local and national arenas and forces us to reexamine some important aspects of center-periphery relations at the international level.

CLIENTELISM AND DEPENDENCY:
THE INTERNATIONAL DIMENSION

Conceptualizing international actors in terms of patrons and clients does little more than provide a "script" for different kinds of historical scenarios. The relationships of ancient Rome to the Hellenistic world after the second Macedonian war,[3] the complex tributary system of the *orbis sinarum* under the Tang dynasty, and the neo-colonial ties forged between France and her former colonies are all amenable in one way or another to this type of conceptualization. The most familiar of such scenarios is of course that of the former colonial state whose "clientele sovereignty" masks the continuing control exercised by the metropolitan power. What is involved here, to quote from Kwame Nkrumah, is perhaps best described as "the practice of granting a sort of independence by the metropolitan power with the concealed intention of making the liberated country a client-state and controlling it effectively by means other than political ones" (Good, 1962: 49).

From this perspective the patron-client model lends considerable plausibility to the central argument set forth by *dependentistas*, i.e., that dependency is the inevitable concomitant of the international division of labor which accompanies the expansion of capitalism into Third World peripheries. In its most perverse form clientelism serves as the mechanism through which subordinate states are converted into satellites of the metropolitan centers: "Clientele classes . . . carry out certain functions on behalf of foreign interests; in return they enjoy a privileged and increasingly dominant hegemonic position within their own societies, based largely on economic, political or military support from abroad" (Bodenheimer, 1971: 337). Domestic forms of clientelism thus ramify beyond national boundaries to serve as a bridge-head for the penetration of foreign capitalist interests.

Dependency theory in this sense assumes an auxiliary role similar to that played by class analysis at the domestic level, pointing to the more fundamental forces underlying clientelistic phenomena. This role can easily be reversed, however, with clientelism serving as the auxiliary tool that enables us to identify some basic shortcomings in dependency theory.

A major flaw in dependency theory, as some have recently stressed (Smith, 1979) is that it tends to treat the client-state as an object of international economic and political forces, and thus greatly underestimates its capacity to shift the balance of exchange to its advantage. Much of course depends on the nature of the resources at the disposal of the client, and his ability to work out effective bargaining strategies. What can be achieved through the oligopolistic control of a vital resource like oil can hardly be accomplished by a cartelization of peanuts. Yet to argue that client states are by definition powerless and therefore permanently pliable is to deflect attention from what is after all the central issue in clientelistic analysis, that is, the extent to which a given resource-base offers any opportunity for renegotiating the terms of exchange.

Nor is dependency everywhere reducible to the expansion of world capitalism into Third World peripheries. As recent events in Cambodia, Viet Nam and Afghanistan clearly demonstrate, a client-state system may also flourish in a non-capitalist environment, and produce patterns of competition which fall somewhat short of the ideal of international socialist solidarity. Capitalism is evidently not a sine qua non of clientele classes, nor is it the only force which impels them to seek patron support. Power asymmetries may develop independently of the "international division of labor" and the "international feudal structure." Again, asymmetries may also develop among clients on such a scale as to provide the basis for a major restructuring of dependency relationships, as when client-states increasingly seek to cast themselves in the role of patrons towards lesser states.

Such is indeed the global trend observable in the emergent "nightmare of world order" (Hoffmann, 1978: 105). The bipolar client-state system which flourished at the height of the Cold War is coming to an end, ushering in patterns of far greater complexity. Within the periphery new centers of power are emerging which are increasingly asserting themselves as the dominant partners in a wide variety of regional sub-systems. As the number of potential patrons increases, so does the range of opportunities for new partnerships. The result has been to inject an unprecedented fluidity into the structure of international dependency relationships.

Further contributing to the complexity of the situation is the changing style and tenor of world politics. Not only are distributive isues taking precedence over issues of "high politics," such as security and power, but "distributive political activities on the international and national levels have become intermingled" (Hanrieder, 1978: 50). Access rather than acquisition is emphasized; penetration rather than possession; control rather than coercion. As the patterns of dependency are becoming more subtle and diversified, so are the mechanisms through which they operate. The analogy which suggests itself is that of the multiple dependencies which at the domestic level tend to arise in the wake of greater social differentiation and modernization. Dependence, however, is no less real for being more widely distributed, or more functionally structured.

Granted that there is room for greater flexibility at the international level than most *dependentistas* would be prepared to recognize, this leaves unanswered the question of whether international gains have any perceptible impact at the domestic level. The evidence on this score is highly ambiguous. International gains do not ipso facto lessen the costs of dependency within nations. It is one thing for a client-state to shift the balance of international exchange to its advantage so as to gain more effective control over investment policies, equity capital, credit facilities, and so forth; whether this will in fact lead to a more equitable *internal* distribution of resources is an entirely different matter. The logic of clientelism acts as a deterrent against equity-oriented policies. To give in to the distributive pressures of rural and working class elements is seen by most Third World governments as tantamount to sowing the seeds of their own destruction. The preferred alternative is to use external resources to further solidify patron-alliances at the top while at the same time retarding by every conceivable means, including force, the advent or resurgence of mass politics. There is unfortunately considerable validity to Fagen's dismal assessment: "Changes in dependence relationships internationally, to the extent that they result in larger shares for peripheral economies, in the main serve to strengthen peripheral elites who typically have little autonomy from anti-equity class forces at home" (Fagen, 1978: 295).

The questions raised by power asymmetries within and among nations lie at the heart of the "development of underdevelopment" syndrome. To frame these questions in clientelistic terms is not meant to minimize the contribution of dependency theory to our understanding of modern economic imperialism, but merely to suggest an alternative perspective from which to look at the relationship of Third World elites to the international system. So far from being antithetical to the theoretical concerns explored in the following chapters such an optic might conceivably serve as a logical supplement to them.

NOTES

1. The argument in this paragraph owes much to Bernd Baldus, of the University of Toronto, who was kind enough to share with me his insights into the structural and ideological aspects of clientelism, and to Sydel Silverman's penetrating analysis of clientelism in central Italy (Silverman, 1970).

2. "Faggot" votes in 18th century Scotland were created at the discretion of county notables generally in total violation of the rules governing the exercise of the franchise, and awarded to lesser notables who for all intents and purposes acted as their trusted and obedient clients. According to Holden Furber, "When Dundas entered political life, every Scotchman knew that a very large number of the votes in each county were fictitious. Scotland being a land of large proprietors and great

estates, it was most natural that her leading nobles and the heads of the great county families should take advantage of the opportunities afforded by the outworn feudal law to create votes for persons who would implicitly do their bidding at election meetings. Such votes were colloquially termed 'faggot' votes.'' (Holden Furber, 1931: 180-81).

3. The projection of clientship into the sphere of "hegemonic" relations between Ancient Rome and her imperial dependencies has been discussed by one scholar as follows: "Inevitably these (clientele) relations spread beyond the city of Rome and its territory as Rome came in contact with places and people more and more remote . . . Both collectively and as individuals, men abroad owed *officia* to the Roman aristocrats who had conferred *beneficia* on them, e.g. by governing them, by sparing them after victory, by looking after their interests in Rome. It was a natural consequence that Roman aristocrats, accustomed to seeing personal relationships, both within the community and outside, in these terms of moral relationships and duties based ultimately on the facts of power, should transfer these attitudes to their political thinking: that Rome in fact should appear as the patron city, claiming the officia both of actual allies and subjects and of 'free' kings and cities with which she had come in contact." (Badian, 1967: 14).

REFERENCES

ALAVI, H. (1975), *Dependence, Autonomy and the Articulation of Power.* Working Paper No. 7, Centre for Developing Area Studies, McGill University, Montreal.

BADIAN, E. (1967). *Roman Imperialism in the Late Republic.* Oxford: Blackwell.

BODENHEIMER, S. (1971). "Dependency and Imperialism: The Roots of Latin American Underdevelopment," *Politics and Society*, 1(3): 327-58.

COLLIER, D. (1976). *Squatters and Oligarchs: Authoritarian Rule and Policy Change in Peru.* Baltimore and London: Johns Hopkins University Press.

CRUISE O'BRIEN, D. (1975). *Saints and Politicians: Essays in the Organization of a Senegalese Peasant Society.* London: Cambridge University Press.

CUTILEIRO, J. (1971). *A Portuguese Rural Society.* Oxford: University Press.

DECALO, S. (1976). *Coups and Army Rule in Africa: Studies in Military Style.* New Haven: Yale University Press.

DeKADT, E. (1970). *Catholic Radicals in Brazil.* London: Oxford University Press.

EAGLETON, T. (1976). *Criticism and Ideology.* London: Verso Editions.

EISENSTADT, S. (1973). *Tradition, Change and Modernity.* New York: Wiley.

FAGEN, R. (1978). "A Funny Thing Happened on the Way to the Market: Thoughts on Extending Dependency Ideas," *International Organization*, 32(1): 287-300.

FLYNN, P. (1974). "Class, Clientelism and Coercion: Some Mechanisms of Internal Dependency and Control," *Journal of Commonwealth and Comparative Politics*, 12(2): 138-56.

FURBER, H. (1931). *Henry Dundas First Viscount of Melville, 1742-1811.* Oxford: University Press.

GADAMER, H. G. (1974). *Truth and Method.* New York: Seabury Press.

GILSENAN, M. (1977). "Against Patron-Client relations," pp. 167-84, in Ernest Gellner and John Waterbury, eds., *Patrons and Clients.* London: Duckworth.

GOOD, C. (1962). "The Congo Crisis," pp. 34-63, in Laurence W. Martin, ed., *Neutralism and Non-Alignment.* New York: Praeger.

GOODE, J. (1975). "Homans' and Merton's Structural Approach," pp. 66-75, in Peter Blau, ed., *Approaches to the Study of Social Structure.* New York: Free Press.

GRAZIANO, L. (1976). "A Conceptual Framework for the Study of Clientelistic Behavior," *European Journal of Political Research*, 4(2): 149-74.

GRAZIANO, L. (1978). "Center-Periphery Relations and the Italian Crisis: The Problem of Clientelism," pp. 290-325, in Sidney Tarrow et al., eds., *Territorial Politics in Industrial Nations.* New York: Praeger.

HALL, A. (1977). "Patron-Client Relations: Concepts and Terms," pp. 510-12, in Steffen W. Schmidt et al., eds., *Friends, Followers and Factions.* Berkeley and Los Angeles: University of California Press.

HANRIEDER, W. F. (1978). "Coordinating Foreign Policies," pp. 45-60, in Werner Link and Werner Feld, eds., *The New Nationalism.* New York: Pergamon.

HERMET, G. (1978). "State-Controlled Elections: A Framework," pp. 1-18, in Guy Hermet, Richard Rose and Alain Rouquié, eds., *Elections Without Choice.* New York: Wiley.

HIRST, D. (1977). "Saudi Arabia: A Sense of Fraternity," the *Guardian* (weekly edition), 10 July.

HOFFMAN, S. (1978). *Primacy of World Order.* New York: McGraw Hill.

HOTTINGER, A. (1966). "Zu'ama in Historical Perspective," pp. 85-106, in Leonard Binder, ed., *Politics in Lebanon.* New York: Wiley.

KASFIR, N. (1976). *The Shrinking Political Arena.* Berkeley and Los Angeles: University of California Press.

KAUFMAN, R. (1974). "The Patron-Client Concept and Macro-Politics: Prospects and Problems," *Comparative Studies in Society and History*, 16(3): 290-320.

KHALAF, S. (1977). "Changing Forms of Political Patronage in Lebanon," pp. 185-206, in Ernest Gellner and John Waterbury, eds., *Patrons and Clients.* London: Duckworth.

LANDE, C. (1977). "Introduction," pp. xiii-xxxviii, in Steffen Schmidt et al., eds., *Friends, Followers and Factions.* Los Angeles and Berkeley: University of California Press.

LEMARCHAND, R. (1977). "Political Clientelism and Ethnicity in Tropical Africa: Competing Solidarities in Nation-Building," pp. 100-22, in ibid.

MAQUET, J. (1961). *The Premise of Inequality in Rwanda.* Oxford: University Press.

MOORE, H. C. (1977). "Clientelist Ideology and Political Change," pp. 255-74, in Ernest Gellner and John Waterbury, eds., *Patrons and Clients.* London: Duckworth.

ROCK, D. (1972). "Machine Politics in Buenos Aires and the Argentine Radical Party, 1912-30," *Journal of Latin American Studies*, 4(2): 233-56.

ROUQUIÉ, A. (1978). "Clientelist Control and Authoritarian Contents," in Guy Hermet, Richard Rose and Alain Rouquié, eds., *Elections Without Choice*. New York: Wiley.

SAHLINS, M. D. (1965). "On the Sociology of Primitive Exchange," pp. 139-227, in M. Banton, ed., *The Relevance of Models for Social Anthropology*. New York: Praeger.

SARTORI, G. (1970). "Concept Misformation in Comparative Politics," *American Political Science Review*, 64(4): 413-28.

SCOTT, J. (1976). *The Moral Economy of the Peasant*. Yale University Press.

SCOTT, J. (1977a). "Patron-Client Politics and Political Change in South-East Asia," pp. 123-46, in Steffen Schmidt et al., eds., *Friends, Followers and Factions*. Los Angeles and Berkeley: University of California Press.

SCOTT, J. (1977b). "Revolution in the Revolution: Peasants and Commissars," *Theory and Society*, 7 (1 and 2): 97-134.

SCOTT, J. and KERKVLIET, B. (1977). "How Rural Patrons Lose Legitimacy," pp. 439-57, in Steffen Schmidt et al., eds., *Friends, Followers and Factions*. Berkeley and Los Angeles: University of California Press.

SILVERMAN, S. (1970). "Exploitation in Rural Central Italy: Structure and Ideology in Stratification Study," *Comparative Studies in Society and History*, 12(3): 327-39.

SILVERMAN, S. (1977). "Patronage as Myth," pp. 7-20, in Ernest Gellner and John Waterbury, eds., *Patrons and Clients*. London: Duckworth.

SMITH, T. (1979). "The Underdevelopment of Development Literature: The Case of Dependency Theory," *World Politics*, 32(2): 247-88.

SMOCK, D. and A. (1975). *The Politics of Pluralism: A Comparative Study of Lebanon and Ghana*. New York: Elsevier.

STEPAN, A. (1978). *The State and Society: Peru in Comparative Perspective*. Princeton: University Press.

II

The European Context:
Italy, France and Poland

—————2—————

The "New" Clientelism in Southern Italy: The Christian Democratic Party in Catania

Mario Caciagli
University of Catania, Italy

and

Frank P. Belloni
Virginia Commonwealth University, USA

Political clientelism can assume two distinct types: the clientelism of the notables and that of the modern mass party (or bureaucratic clientelism).[1] Alex Weingrod was first to offer a definition of party-based clientelism, and Sidney Tarrow the first to apply this model to the analysis of Christian Democracy (DC) in southern Italy (Weingrod, 1968; Tarrow, 1967). But perhaps the best explanation for the shift from one type of clientelism to another is that advanced by a Sicilian politician (cited in Graziano, 1976: 149):

"Clientelism" . . . is by now an old word and needs to be replaced before long. It evokes, in fact, the letter of recommendation from the notable, a practice still in existence and still frequent in Sicily, though less and less so. For at least fifteen years clientelism has been changing in nature and instead of being a vertical tie as it was before, descending from the notable to the postulant, it has become a horizontal one; it now concerns entire (social) categories, coalitions of interests,

groups of (private) employees, employees of public office or of regional enterprises. It is mass clientelism, organized and efficient, which consists in laws, *leg-
gine* (laws made by parliamentary committees), extraordinary provisions,
emergency measures and concessions granted no longer to the individual, but to
favored groups. In order to put this powerful machine to work, through time the
Christian Democrats have had to place party men at every level of power, in each
key position . . . (Today clientelism) is a relationship between large groups and
public power.

I. OLD AND NEW CLIENTELISM

Various studies have noted the transformation that occurs in
clientelist forms in sociopolitical systems undergoing major
changes, such as rapid urbanization, the shift of the work force
from agricultural to other economic activity, and widespread
popular exposure to mass media. In such periods of transition, the
old forms of clientelism, which relied on important "notables" and
traditional patronage, are displaced by a clientelism deriving support from a patron organization of a mass clientele.

This process occurred in the Catania DC during the period from
1954 to 1960, and it had a lasting effect upon the character of the
existing system of Christian Democratic power.[2] During this period
a new type of leadership emerged within the DC, its power resting
precisely upon the modern form of clientelism they invented. Thus,
two things, intimately related, occurred at the same moment: (1) a
modern, mass-based party was created; and (2) a different system
of power was formed in Catania, under the control and direction of
a new political elite.

These developments were facilitated by several factors: the
establishment of the DC as the predominant party in the Italian
political system; the DC's efforts to organize itself in the Mezzogiorno as a mass party; the enlargement of the functions of the
state and its public entities; and the launching of a major development program for the Mezzogiorno. These last two have special
significance for the DC in Catania for they involved the allocation
of large amounts of public monies and other state resources obviously of great value to those engaged in the construction of a new
clientelistic system.

The "old" clientelism, as it existed in Catania, was the
clientelism of the true "notables," characterized by great inequalities between patron and client. The deference enjoyed by such
notables derived from their status as aristocrats, or large landowners or professionals (judges, lawyers, university professors).

Their status as notables — together with the deference they received — was taken for granted by them, and accepted by their followers, as an established and more or less permanent fact, unrelated to any political position that they might choose to accept. Furthermore, what resources they controlled, including economic resources, had little to do with the exercise of public power, but flowed instead from their personal wealth, social standing, and prestige — all highly permanent resources which could be utilized in an autonomous and discretionary fashion. Finally the old clientelism of notables could flourish even where organization was lacking or very weak.

The new clientelism, on the other hand, rests upon organization in the most fundamental sense. It is the clientism of the apparatus of the Christian Democratic Party, sustained by the support it is able to purchase from its clients in exchange for its distribution of benefits to them. The *apparatichi*, the men who constructed the modern, mass-based party (whose characteristics will be discussed below), are the new patrons. Their survival as patrons, as well as the survival of the party apparatus, depends upon the votes and consensus of their clients. The latter is obtained only in exchange for the tangible benefits dispensed by the party. And it is precisely in this new system of exchanges that the explanation lies of why and how the professional party politicians came to replace the old notables in the patronage function. Not only does the type of personnel change, however; so do the very rules of clientele exchange as well as the nature of the mediating instrument.

The new clientelism is inherently tied to the modern, conservative, mass-based party (the DC in Catania). It is a clientelism deriving from, or resting upon, the judicious use of the party organization and public resources. The new clientelist form was necessary because the resources of the old notables were insufficient for the needs of a mass society: the society of the towns and cities experiencing rapid, sometimes explosive, urbanization within the space of a few years. The new clientelism is connected, therefore, to the steady enlargement of the scope of state activities, which has occurred in response to the increase in volume and character of demands which have accompanied major societal changes. And the principal instrument through which public resources may be obtained is the apparatus of the Christian Democratic Party. The DC is the dominant force in the central government. As such, it enjoys control over public agencies and state resources. The distribution of these resources, however, has been largely a function of the dynamics of internal party politics: public resources are distributed throughout the country in accordance with the competitive positions of subnational units of the DC.

Thus emerged a new type of patron in the Catania DC, different from the old notables both in terms of class origins and in orientation towards politics. The new dispensors of patronage are of lower-middle and middle-class backgrounds who, in contrast to the avocational approach to politics of their partisan forebears, embark upon politics as a professional career. Involvement in party politics, so far from being an occasional activity, is a way of life; they truly live *for* politics and *by* politics.

1. The Strengths and Weaknesses of the New Clientelism

The new clientelism clearly has a greater capacity to provide benefits to its clients, benefits which it extracts from the center, i.e., from the state. But this does not mean that the position of the new patrons (in relation to their clients) is more secure than that which characterized the old notable in his relations with his clients. In certain respects, in fact, the position of the new patron is more vulnerable.

One thing is clear, however: the initial status of the new patron is less important in the clientelism of today. The modern patron's ultimate standing now depends on (and changes with) the fortunes of his political party career. Beginning without the resources of the traditional patron, the success of the party professional and would-be patron appears to depend above all on personal initiative. Yet there is considerable competition, for the number of persons who turn to politics as a means of acquiring power and status has increased markedly. Consequently, the shift in the base of clientelism from the notable to the party organization man constitutes a veritable "democratization" (at least partial) of the patron class: anyone with some talent, a party connection, and a great deal of initiative can aspire to "patronship."

2. Escalation of Costs

This situation, in turn, is responsible for another characteristic of the new clientelism: the perpetual escalation of its costs. The factors which account for this escalation are not hard to grasp: since there are limits to the Christian Democratic pool of potential clients, and since the number of persons aspiring to patronship has increased notably, competition for control of the client market has heightened considerably. This, in turn, has engendered a type of competitive bidding for support, as each patron attempts to offer more than his patron competitors. Nor does the cause-and-effect chain end here. The open, often crass, bidding for the support of followers has contributed significantly to undermining client respect for the patron class. And with the passage of popular deference towards the patron, the days of the inextinguishable debt — the eternal gratitude — on the part of the client are largely gone. In the absence of such intangible reinforcements of the patron-client relationship, the new patron is obliged to rely more and more on the distribution of tangible benefits as a means of retaining his following. This renders him more dependent upon the party apparatus (and his own patrons within it), as well as upon his clients. And nowhere are these facts better appreciated than among the ranks of the new clients themselves.

Apart from the above, the costs of the new clientelism have been inflated also by the absolute increase in explicit demands of the clients. This occurs because of three factors: the simple fact that the patron cannot continue as a patron without clients, the increase in the number of and competition among patrons, and the growth of client "political consciousness" (i.e., his awareness of the first two facts). The increase in client demands partially reflects, therefore, the psychological change in the condition under which the clientelistic exchange now occurs. Thus, despite the marked increase in tangible resources available to the new patrons, their status is less secure than that of the old notables, for it rests upon their continued ability to deal with the ever-increasing demands of their followers. Unfortunately, there is no inexhaustible source of funds; and large-scale debits have begun to accumulate, producing unhappy consequences for everyone involved.

As a consequence of the foregoing, the overall terms of exchange in the new clientele system have changed. The dispensation of patronage now depends upon access to public resources, for which the party serves as the principal channel. Thus, the new technicians of the party apparatus have become the new patrons; but (as we noted) with the steady rise in their numbers, the entire patronage market was democratized. This represents a qualitative as well as quantitative development, for once patrons began to compete for client support the factors of deference and respect were minimized, thereby altering the psychological character of the patron-client relationship. The terms of the contract between patron and client under the new clientelism now rest upon an implicit element of bargaining: they are subject to negotiation and renegotiation. The new clients, furthermore, have acquired a capacity for measuring the benefits offered by and received from the patrons, and if there is no objective standard of what ought to be received in exchange for support rendered, it is certainly possible to make comparisons with what other patrons offer and what they demand in return. The patron can no longer play the role of gate-keeper, of the exclusive holder of information on many aspects of political and administrative life, which was so fundamental for the perpetuation of a strongly asymmetrical type of exchange, the type necessary to establish the perennial obligation of the client.

For all the foregoing reasons, therefore, the distributive pressures on the patrons exceed their traditional boundaries, and so do the costs of keeping a clientele. While the process of competitive price increases guaranteed the initial success of the party-technician patrons, it also constitutes an element of weakness in the new power structure, the effects of which weigh progressively heavier as the inflationary process continues.

The principal problem for the new patrons is finding funds to meet the cost of the growing demands. As we noted, given the social origin of the new patron, he does not have private resources which he can pour into the clientele distribution process. The resources of the new patron must be, therefore, all public, and in fact there has been a notable increase in the spending of public agencies. Consequently, as is well-known, the deficits of both national and local public agencies have increased notably in recent years. In some cases we have studied, deficits have reached such dimensions that the annual input of revenues now serves only to pay the interest on accumulated debts.

The inflationary effect is endemic to the new clientelism. The latter engenders an inflationary spiral which is self-expanding and self-perpetuating. It produces pressures for increased distribution of goods, it undermines the solidity of the position of the patrons, and it increases the competition among them for the votes they need to survive. The inflationary costs of clientelism have thus contributed directly and significantly to a similar inflationary process in the Italian economy as a whole.[3]

The roots of all this lie in the different matrix and type of political activity of the new patrons. When the party technicians began to act in the late 1950s the local power structure was controlled by the old notables. Thus, for those of the new patrons who hoped to manage some resources it was necessary to create them. And the party men did just that: drawing upon resources acquired from the national government they created a system of benefits with which the old notables could not compete.

3. New Clientele Relations

The traditional forms of clientelism, as we noted, were very asymmetrical, rich in loyalty and deference, and tended to commit the client for life. These have been replaced by the present forms, which are characterized by a continual renegotiation of the terms of exchange, and by often successful attempts on the part of clients at increasing the price of fidelity. Thus, from the patron's viewpoint, the present situation is one in which it is of fundamental importance to secure the greatest number of votes possible, while spending the minimum amount of resources; for the client, instead, it is necessary to know how to sell one's "allegiance" in the best way possible. Put in other words, the patron aims at securing in a lasting manner the dependency of the clients, while the client, in contrast, seeks to avoid any permanent commitment to the patron, so as to be able to play the game of periodically upping the ante.

The clients are not completely at the mercy of their patrons. In an effort to protect themselves and to advance their own interests, clients can exert themselves either as individuals or as a collectivity. For the individual the vote is the principal resource. As a mechanism of blackmail it can be used to impose new demands on the patron. The client's goal may be the regularization of his work position, an increase in his stipend, the bettering of his work status, or a promotion. The client's method is the threat to withhold his vote (and perhaps those of his family in the event they were included as part of the original clientele exchange) either in the public elections or in the intraparty elections, where the competition for power among groups and factions is continual. The loss of client preference votes in the public elections may threaten the patron's reelection; within the party a similar loss may weaken the patron's position in the assembly of the section, commune, or province, etc., vis-à-vis his patron adversaries. The threat is more effective, of course, if it appears that the client intends to switch his support to a direct adversary of his patron.

The collective weapons of the clients include strikes, occupations and other forms of mass action aimed at obstructing the activity of a public agency. Indeed, one of the distinctive characteristics of the new clientelism is its departure from transactions limited to individual patron-client relations to those involving a patron and a category of clients. The novelty here is the capacity of the new clients to effect collective action against the patron; however, while the action is collective, the goals sought continue to be particularistic. Thus, corporative associations, especially those with close ties to the DC leadership, often assume the role of transmitting and supporting the demands of the client-workers. Such associations may supplant the face-to-face transaction (or negotiation) typical of traditional clientelism, playing the role of intermediaries between patron and clients. This mediation may be desired both by the patron, who may not wish to expose himself to the dangers of umpopularity and perhaps the defection of clients, and the client-dependents, who wish to avoid exposing themselves to reprisals.

This aspect of the new clientelism affords some decided advantages for the client. No longer completely isolated in his state of dependency vis-à-vis his patron, the asymmetry of the exchange is somewhat minimized. In some cases the result has been a marked increase in the economic benefits clients are able to extract from their patron. For with the introduction of categorical affiliations — and here the trade union is of notable importance — the clients' contractual (or blackmail) power is increased.

II. THE MASS CLIENTELE PARTY:
THE INSTRUMENT OF THE NEW CLIENTELISM

It is our contention that the Catania DC has been transformed from a party of representation collectively led by "notables" to a modern type of party under the direction of a new class of party professionals. The question remains as to what type of modern party the Catania DC represents. Having compared it with the classic "machine party"[4] and the "mass party"[5] of Michels and Duverger, we have concluded that neither of these models satisfactorily characterizes the Catania DC.

The new party of Catania does bear some similarities to the classic machine party: both have a type of "boss" or manager, both are concerned primarily with the survival of their own local power structure, and both rely heavily on a system of reciprocal exchanges of benefits as a means of sustaining the "machine." Yet the Catania DC differs from the machine party in very significant respects. In contrast to the latter, the Catania party is definitely integrated into the power structure of its national counterpart, it is conditioned by the ideological and policy postures assumed by the leadership of the central party, and it has an abiding concern with the formal enrollment of members into a complex of partisan base structures (the sections). Thus, the Catania DC appears to deviate significantly from the classic machine party.

On the other hand, the Catania party bears some striking resemblances (ignoring differences for the moment) to the mass party: viz., its large number of formally registered members organized into a multiplicity of base structures, its dependence on and integration in a national party apparatus, its control of ancillary organizations, its recruitment and internal development of new leadership elements, and its role as a mechanism for the transmission of demands arising from the supporting base of members.

The Catania DC's recruitment of a mass membership and its creation of an extensive number of sections at the base of the party are foremost among its mass party properties. The party's growth in membership over the past 30 years[6] has given it an unquestioned mass following. Indeed, at its 1959 peak, the DC in Catania province had one of the highest membership levels in Italy, inferior only to those of Rome and Naples. Within the province, the greatest increases occurred in the capital city, thus indicating the growing importance of Catania in the local party apparatus, as well as the steady urbanization of this peripheral party.[7]

The basic explanation for the massive recruitment of members must be seen in relation to the local party's interest in seizing control of its immediate external environment — to serve its own ends. Thus, the mass party *appearance* of the Catania DC is the product of its effort at dominating its local environment. This particular use of the party's mass membership (and the *use* explains the mass recruitment itself), and more significantly, its employment of the instrument of clientelism as the principal means for achieving its goal, is what distinguishes the Catania party from the mass party model proper. And it is this particular combination of purpose (political dominion) and means (clientelism) that results in our characterization of the Catania DC as a *mass clientele party*.

1. The Model of the Mass Clientele Party

In many respects, the DC in Catania has become a mass party. Besides the high number of members (which remains high even after having taken account of the incidence of false memberships), it exhibits, as we have noted, various other characteristics attributed to the mass party model in the extant literature (keeping in mind, first, the model of Duverger). The DC of Catania depends upon a national center with which it is notably integrated; it tends to control the collateral associations that gather around it; it promotes within itself new leadership cadres; and it receives (and perhaps accommodates) the demands (even if particularistic, individualistic, and/or intermittent) of the base. On the other hand, the DC simultaneously lacks other mass party features and contains some which are extraneous to it. These include its failure to develop any permanent activity in the sections at its organizational base; the tendency of the leadership of the apparatus to be disinterested in the political growth of the ordinary members of the party or in their mobilization in a politically conscious way; the almost exclusive preoccupation of the party with electoral activity and the management of power and, as a consequence of the latter, its tendency to serve mainly as a channel for the distribution of benefits; and finally, the fact that mass recruitment is a function mainly of the ongoing competition for the control of the party's apparatus.

With these limitations, however, there remains in Catania a party which succeeds in involving a significant mass of citizens, and which permits, particularly in comparison to the party of notables which preceded it, or even to a machine party, a greater volume of contact at various levels between the elite and followers. This contact occurs, however, through a series of structured exchanges and mediations according to which the mass base concedes to the directors of the party apparatus a permanent "power of delegation," so long, that is, as the benefits claimed by the base or promised to it by the patron-leaders are forthcoming. Thus the party enlarges itself and rules on the basis of the extended chain of interests and fidelity conferred upon it by its most fundamental attribute: clientelism. And this attrribute, extraneous as it is to the mass party model, serves to distinguish the Catania DC from the mass party. Thus, as we noted earlier, while the Catania DC shares some characteristics with the mass party model, the clientelistic aspect of the party is definitely its most salient characteristic. And in labeling it a mass clientele party, our emphasis is far more on the "clientele" than on the "mass" attribute.

Three components — clientelism, a mass-based structure, and public resources — were used to transform the Catania DC into a mass clientele party. The mass clientele party, in turn, is the instrument for advancing the interests of the new political-administrative class. This new class uses the mass clientele apparatus to gain and maintain control over public agencies, which then provide the resources and control needed to perpetuate the party apparatus. Thus, the entire process becomes circular and (for the managers of the apparatus) self-serving.

The bureaucratic clientelism of the DC is realized not only through the public offices and agencies, but also through the administration of the communes and provinces and — especially in the South — with the control that the men of the party have over the flow of public money and other resources. The flow of these resources is assured by the direct ties the local party men have with their party's leaders in the central government. The intervention of the state cancelled the distinction — in the South more than in the rest of the country — between the political sphere and the socio-economic sheres of society. Furthermore, since the Christian Democratic Party has for so long served as the government of the state, the latter is in many respects the instrument of the party; and this instrument "allows" the party to serve as the privileged mediator between public institutions and society. In any event, it is precisely the availability of resources coming from the center that appears to explain the extraordinary growth of the force and the power of the DC in Catania.

If the criteria of management are primarily of a clientelist type, then it is possible to assume that the party satisfies demands of an individualist or corporative character (not those of a collective nature), whose referents belong to a wide variety of social classes — including the "popular" classes. If, however, clientelism is viewed as an instrument for the conservation and exercise of power, which tends to consolidate a mass consensus to the end of facilitating the self-perpetuation of that system, the next step is to determine in whose favor this system really is maintained, and who reaps the greatest profit. The first hypothesis is that the party uses its power as a means of procuring advantages for those who immediately represent it — above all, those who make up its apparatus and those who are nominated and elected under its aegis. The second is that it uses its power to protect the interests of certain dominant classes. These in turn are seen by the men of the apparatus as powerful *supportive* allies, whom they are willing to protect for reasons of self-interest. Our thesis is that the party apparatus in Catania has responded to both of these sets of interests. The Catania DC together with the dominant classes of the city has constituted an integrated *bloc of interests*, i.e., an alliance system that joins economic interests with the interest of political privilege and dominion. Recent research on Catania permits us to identify the classes which have been involved in this process over the past 30 years, the nature of the exchange that has occurred among them, and what type of relations were established within the bloc.

2. The Structure and Operation of the Mass Clientele Party

At the national level the DC organizes and incorporates into its fold a mass body of Italian citizens of widely differing social classes. Once recruited into the party, however, participation by the masses is restricted mainly to electoral activity. In the performance of this activity the members are guided by the party apparatus and by faction leaders. There is little scope for effective mass-member participation. These characteristics the DC shares wholly or in part with other Italian parties. The specificity of the DC derives in part from its own structural features and in part from those characteristics which it arrogates to itself within the Italian political system: i.e., its quasi-monopolistic claim to the representation of the Catholics, its mediating role among and between dominant and subordinate classes, its location at the center of the party spectrum, its uninterrupted functioning as a participant in government. These same elements, and especially the first two, have accentuated its apparent lack of interest in the base of the party (recognizing, of course, that the attitude of the DC on these two points has varied in accordance with the exigencies of historical periods and according to different zones of the country).

The model of the apparatus of the mass clientele party takes the form of a *pyramid*, which includes the mass membership, the so-called *capi-tessera*, the section secretaries, and the "manager." The base of the pyramid consists of the million and a half (more or less) *members* of the party who do not participate and who therefore can be easily manipulated. The second level is composed of the *capi-tessera* (membership heads), whose main task is to artificially stimulate enrollment in the party and subsequently to assure that the new members "give" their support to the appropriate group or faction — i.e., the one to which the *capi-tessera* belong. These *capi-tessera* may succeed in recruiting family or tenement clusters of new members and in attaching them to their faction. It is precisely the activism of these recruiters, in fact, which accounts for the enlargement, both real and artificial, of the mass base of the DC. Yet the specific objective of such recruitment is always the reinforcement of one's own power group or faction — and within it one's own personal following, thus making clientele leaders, albeit on a small scale, of the *capi-tessera* themselves. Since the number of members, real or fictitious, determines the "power of delegation" of those men who, through the sections, ultimately control the party apparatus, the role and activity of the *capi-tessera* militants assume considerable importance in the pyramidal power structure. In the case of the Catania DC, for example, control of membership recruitment and section development, and of those immediately responsible for directing the sections and representing them (and thus their members) in the provincial congresses, constituted an essential aspect of the new political class' conquest of the direction of the party and then of public power. Ultimately, this control, extending to the very bottom, serves as the principal instrument of power for the "manager" and his men.

Our analysis shows that the principal factors which negatively condition the life of the DC section in Catania are: (1) a pattern of recruitment which greatly facilitates the control of the apparatus over the base and which involves criteria and techniques that hamper the emergence of a politically knowledgeable following; (2) a base participation which is reduced to a sporadic activism tied exclusively to electoral schedules; and (3) a retarded level of political development among lower-ranking party cadres, due to the particularistic ties between them and their leaders. Such is the basis on which loyalty to the party rests.

It is evident that those who direct and control the section are the most immediately responsible and, equally, are those who extract the greatest advantages from this negative state of affairs at the base of the party. The most important intermediate structure in the pyramid of the mass clientele party is the *section secretary*, for control of the sections is critical to the power of the "manager." Here the section secretary must be singled out, for it is around this party office that the entire life of the section revolves.

In a party such as the Catania DC, the section secretary assumes full responsibility for representing hundreds and hundreds of members, and he uses it to support the faction to which he belongs. To this end he attempts to control the choice of section delegates to the provincial congresses and to secure preference votes for specific candidates in the administrative and political elections. Furthermore, he acts as a key intermediary in the management of administrative and political interactions between the base and the superordinate structures of the party and vice versa. This gives him the opportunity to oversee or block any initiative originating from below, especially those aimed at altering, both in minuscule and more significant ways, the internal power relations of the section.

The image of extreme personalization and apparent fragmentation which emerges from an analysis of the DC party organization in Catania is in a way recomposed and given order by the provincial directing organs. It is through the latter that the development of the sections, the activity of the section secretaries, and the contrasts that exist in the intermediate strata are bent to the design and purpose of the apparatus.

This pyramidal structure of Demochristian power succeeds in bringing together, both within and outside the party, a large constellation of interests. The mass clientele party, which constitutes its center, is thus subject by its nature to the pressure of varied and often conflicting interests which threaten to pull it apart. To constrain these conflicting thrusts and still function, its organization requires strong guidance from the top and the articulation of rigid roles with specific functions, carried out by those who control and manage the clientele channels. The roles are ordered hierarchically and men are assigned to them at different levels of the pyramid in accordance with the type of dependency relation that ties them to the top.

At the top there is the "manager," the leader of the group which creates the power apparatus that gains control of the party. The "manager" is that person who, with the assistance of his "clan" (those in the direction and the intermediary structures of the party who are most loyal to him), succeeds in retaining firm control of the entire party for a long period. We have called him a "manager" because his capacity must be that of *managing* the diverse and particularistic interests in such a way as to insure that interest which is common: the preservation of the apparatus and its power. It is only the "manager," with his centralized decision-making, skillful use of controls, and close regulation of the distribution of benefits, who can mediate the conflicting interests and hold the mass clientele party together. He must, therefore, direct like a business enterprise both the party apparatus and the system of power. Using the party apparatus, its electoral force, and the resources that flow from his party's control of the government at the local (and the national) level, the "manager" of the local party gradually extends his influence to all decisive sectors of the political, administrative and social life of the city. In this manner, his party becomes part of a complex power apparatus that extends well beyond its own organization limits.

3. Conditions and Functions of the Mass Clientele Party in the Periphery and within the National Framework

Three principal sets of social, economic and political conditions appear to contribute to the emergence of a mass clientele party and to its ability to acquire a position of dominance. First, such a party appears to emerge within the context of a "marginal area"; i.e., an

area characterized by the survival of precontractual social relations, undergoing an accentuated urbanization, and in a largely
non-industrialized economic framework which is dependent on and
in need of intervention by the national government. The second
condition is the existence of a disaggregated social mass which has
not developed an awareness of any collective interest and thus is incapable of expressing collective political demands, and which the
party succeeds in dominating and manipulating. The final condition is the existence of certain "interests" in the environment
(financial and building speculators, "subsidized" building contractors, professionals, public bureaucrats) which the party by virtue of
its self-assigned role of representation ties together in a "managed"
equilibrium in order to promote its *own* interests, while
simultaneously maintaining (again motivated by its own self-
interest) the disaggregation of the wider society.

   In a situation such as this, the mass clientele party assumes the
structure of a pyramid and serves as the single channel through
which resources from the center flow. The selection and distribution of these resources (as well as those locally available) must be
accomplished with the aim of conserving the equilibrium of the existing social system. The latter is and must remain a system of in-
equalities. Accordingly, the party itself becomes the expression of
this inequality. Its leadership must know how to perpetuate it and,
if possible, create new inequalities by emphasizing particularistic
interests and by ignoring needs of a collective type. This can be carried out only under the direction of a single authoritative and
authoritarian leader. By exercising a centralized and arbitrary control, and by the judicious doling-out of benefits, the "manager"
can maintain the difficult equilibrium (or disequilibrium). Any
slackening in this type of management will subject the apparatus to
multifaceted and continuing conflict, with disastrous consequences
for the power position of the party.

   The mass clientele party which is described above characterizes
the DC as it evolved and operated in Catania from the 1950s to the
early 1970s. The party has been inserted in a solid and deeply-
rooted "system of power" which, while created by the party and
guided by the *Dorotei*, is much larger than both. It is our conviction, moreover, that during the past two decades the DC has
assumed similar structures and functions in other Mezzogiorno
zones, those where pronounced social distances and a particularistic fragmentation of interests favor a mass clientele-type

party guided by a "manager" and his "clan." Examples would include the clientele mechanisms constructed by Gava in Naples, De Mita at Avellino, Gioia in Palermo, or Gulloti in Messina. In entire southern provinces, if not whole regions, DC power during the 1960s has been identified with a single important leader capable of dominating his zone and of negotiating with his equals at the national level. Thus, in discussing the DC system of power, especially in the southern regions, reference is often made to its "feudal" or at least "federal" structure; and to "barons" who dominate the political territories reserved to them. Unfortunately, we lack the empirical evidence to determine the extent to which the origins of these "barons" and their techniques of control conform to the model described here.

III. NEW CLIENTELISM AND DEVELOPMENT

The political culture of the Mezzogiorno is clearly congenial to the survival of political clientelism and its multiple derivations. And the DC, in terms of its organization and operation in Catania, has been deeply influenced by this tradition. The techniques the party has used to create a consensus and solidly establish its power base have been efficacious because the subjects involved were culturally receptive to such techniques. The political party, however, could have been the historical instrument committed to and capable of changing the political culture and the customs which are so hospitable to clientelism. For the mass of DC members and voters the party could have served as a guide in their search for a more fruitful type of political association and activity. Instead, the DC adapted itself to the preexisting sociocultural fabric. And in so doing it has contributed to further accentuate the corruptive potential of the existing culture. Rather than being an innovative element of civil organization, the DC contented itself with being a mere bureaucratic "machine." And in its operation the party machine has accelerated the Mezzogiorno's social and political disaggregation, modifying only in the most limited respects the backwardness of the masses, and preferring instead to keep them divided and fragmented.

Thus, the modernity of the DC — its mass party properties — is a superficial phenomenon. It failed to promote the growth of civil society and it never succeeded in exercising a true leadership over its popular following. Consequently, when the masses do rise up at times of economic and political crisis, they express only anger and protest, never having been taught how to express their political needs in a positive form. And because the mass clientele party has neglected the opportunity to transform its mass following into a modern and democratic force, there is a possibility that this following under pressing circumstances could carry itself and the entire country backward.

The mass clientele party has, nevertheless, proved itself capable of governing a large southern Italian city which has experienced an accelerated urbanization without industrialization, a tumultuous immigration of social strata coming from the country and without prospect of employment, an increase of unproductive middle classes, a reduction of the active population, and a persistence of pockets of poverty and marginality. And while the activity of the clientele party has weighed heavily on the changing economy, its guidance of political change has responded almost entirely to the dictate of preserving the equilibrium of the national system. Accordingly, it has promoted economic activities and an unemployment structure which have actually contributed to maintaining Catania (like all of the Mezzogiorno) in a condition of dependency and subordination to the centers of economic power. Yet at the same time it has succeeded in containing social tensions by either composing or postponing the explosion of conflicts, or transforming them into corporative conflicts or into individual competitions. In this fashion the DC in Catania has made its contribution to the overall stability of the Italian system and to the dominance of certain classes within it. Thus, control of the Italian southern society appears to have been the historical task of the mass clientele party in the postwar period. This indeed has been, at least up until recently, "the chief political work of the DC."[8]

In the framework of the unequal development of capitalism and of the changes which it has provoked throughout Italy, the mass clientele party has been assigned the task of administering those dependent and peripheral areas such as Catania. The more prevalent these areas (like the over-urbanized city of Catania), the more necessary is the presence of a party like the Catania DC — no longer a local organizational expression, but instead a political structure which must be placed at an intermediate level on the periphery-center scale. The Catania DC thus stands as a necessary intermediate layer bound to the center by strong ties, such as those forged with the national faction leaders or with the centers of decision-making in the national government and bureaucracy. With the resources and the authority that come from its control of the central government, the DC governs and controls the southern zones as a function of capitalistic development.

We have gathered a volume of data on the existence of bureaucratic clientelism in Catania, and on the basis of our reflections we offer the following general considerations on the way this system functions in the Italian political system. Those who examine clientelism as a mode of exercising power and of aggregating consensus, and as a means of integrating new subjects into a sociopolitical system, often express a positive judgment about it. What impresses them is the ability of clientelism to limit conflicts and thus regulate and stabilize a society in change. Certainly, in an environment whose economic and social conditions make it susceptible to such type of behavior, the practice of clientelism can be an effective regulatory mechanism. By controlling latent tensions it can reinforce the power of a ruling class and contribute to the equilibrium of the system (and not only the local system). We grant that this view of clientelism finds verification in Catania, and most likely in other parts of Mezzogiorno. But it is worth noting that the new clientelism has not yet been in operation all that long, nor has it assured a lasting stability. For while it has for many years cemented Christian Democratic power, it has almost never legitimized it in the eyes of its presumed beneficiaries. Above all, it carries within itself conflictual and inflationary thrusts which in turn have had a strong and lasting destabilizing effect on the Italian political system at several levels.

What is important to understand about clientelism, then, is not its efficiency, but the crises that have attended its operation over the past decade. The reasons for the latter are not difficult to find. On the level of political and civil relations clientelism continues to exclude too many "subjects" who could become active citizens. However, in the interest of preserving the exclusive positions of the political patron class, clientelism prefers to stymie every attempt at meaningful participation. Thus, impeding the self-assertion of genuinely modern political behavior, the new clientelism devitalizes civil society and makes it pay an exorbitant price to the dominant classes.

By perpetuating a style of politics which contains many socially non-productive featues, and by multiplying the divisions that exist in an already fragmented society, clientelism serves mainly to preserve the rule and privileges of the dominant classes, both local and national. Clientelism is most useful to those who control the economic and political levers of command both in the dependent periphery and in the national center. There is no doubt that through clientele politics the individuals, groups, and classes that make up the mass base of the DC obtain at least partial satisfaction of their immediate and particular interests (employment, an increase in remuneration, the commercial license, the construction permit, access to public housing, etc.) But these interests are secured by means of a process that puts individuals and groups among the masses in opposition to one another, without ever bringing them together in support of interests which they share in general. In any event, those interests which are catered to through the system of clientelism are clearly subordinate to the interests of the dominant classes. The new clientelism has generated a type of corporatization of civil society which divides the workers and favors the local and national bourgeoisie.

The management of local power by the DC is not just a matter of clientele plotting. It is simply a question of directly satisfying the interests of a power bloc, which we perceive as the combination of groups and social classes which in the local context have a position of dominance. From its very inception the DC tied itself to the dominant classes of Catania, choosing to serve them — and be served by them.

NOTES

1. Research for this paper was carried out under the direction of Professor Mario Caciagli of the University of Catania with the collaboration of Dr. Anastasi, Dr. R. D'Amico, Dr. M. R. Gentile, Dr. N. Gori, Dr. L. Mattina and Dr. D. E. Nocifera. For a more elaborate version of the results of our enquiry, see Caciagli et al. (1977).

2. In the same historical period the process would apply to the whole of southern Italy; for the case of Naples, see Allum (1973).

3. On the whole, the causes of the clientele-inflationistic process in Catania appear to be no different from those at the base of the inflationistic character of the clientele democracy singled out in the research of J. C. Scott on the politics of Southeast Asia. See, "La Natura e Dinamica del Politico Clientelismo nel Asia Sudest," and "Corruzione, 'Macchine Politiche' e Mutamento Politico" in L. Graziano, ed. (1974); Scott (1977).

4. By a "machine party" we refer to a stable partisan apparatus led by a local "boss" who is capable of mobilizing voters at election time, and of controlling political decisions and economic activity in his area of influence to the extent necessary to sustain the "machine" and, hence, his own power. Since the concern of the party-machine (which existed in a number of American cities and some states in the late 19th and early 20th centuries) was mainly the perpetuation of the boss' power structure, it traded largely in the distribution of benefits (positions, goods, and services), and lacked any concern for ideology. Nor was it concerned with the autonomous growth or meaningful participation of its supporters, who were mobilized to act only at election time.

5. The "mass party" is defined here as a structure for the integration (with auxiliary organizations) and the mobilization (including ideological) of large strata of citizens belonging to different, and above all, popular classes; and, which is organized stably (by means of cells or sections) for the pursuit of collective goals.

6. In its first recruitment phase (1946-53), membership in the Catanese DC grew in the province from less than 9,000 to about 25,000 or nearly three-fold in eight years. From the beginning to the end of its second phase (1954-59), membership doubled to its all-time high of 53,229. In the last phase, which began in 1960, membership dropped to settle at about 45,000. Even allowing for the undoubted inflation of membership (not peculiar to Catania) through various falsifications, these figures document significant real increases.

7. Party membership in the city of Catania, as a proportion of the entire province, increased from an average of 21% for the years of the first period (1954-59) to a 39% average for those of the final period (1960-71).

8. For further information, see Vianello (1975).

REFERENCES

ALLUM, P. (1973). *Power and Society in Postwar Naples*. Cambridge: University Press.

CAGIAGLI, M. et al. (1977). *Democrazia Cristiania e Potere Nel Mezzogiorno: Il Sistema Democrastiano a Catania*. Florence: Guaraldi Editore.

GRAZIANO, L. (1976). "A Conceptual Framework for the Study of Clientelistic Behavior," *European Journal of Political Research*, 4(2): 149-74.

GRAZIANO, L. (ed.) (1974). *Clientelismo e Mutamento Politico*. Milan: Franco Angeli Editore.

SALADINO, G. (1973). "Guardando dentro la DC siciliana," *L'Ora*, 23 July.

SCOTT, J.C. (1977). "Patron-Client Politics and Political Change in Southeast Asia," *American Political Science Review*, 66 (2): 91-113.

TARROW, S. (1967). *Peasant Communism in Southern Italy*. New Haven: Yale University Press.

VIANELLO, F. (1975). "La DC e lo sviluppo capitalistico in Italia dal dopoguerra a oggi," in Autori Vari, *Tuto il potere della DC*. Rome: Coines.

WEINGROD, A. (1968). "Patrons, Patronage and Political Parties," *Comparative Studies in Society and History*, 10 (3): 377-400.

————————— *3* —————————

The Social Bases of an Urban Political Machine: The Christian Democratic Party in Palermo

Judith Chubb
College of the Holy Cross, USA

The Italian South (the Mezzogiorno) constitutes an ideal terrain for studying the relationship between a dominant system of clientelistic power and the processes of economic and political development, within the context of a national political system characterized by a high level of state intervention in the economy and in civil society. This chapter and the following one will examine the linkages between clientelism and development through detailed case studies of the two historic capitals of the Mezzogiorno, Palermo and Naples, both of which have, throughout the postwar period, sustained powerful political machines in the hands of Italy's dominant Christian Democratic Party (DC). The chapter on Palermo will focus on the specific patronage mechanisms linking the party to its mass base and, on the basis of this empirical evidence, will reconsider theories about the resource base necessary for maintaining consensus through clientelistic means. The conclusions of the Palermo study will then be confronted with the experience of Naples where, after 25 years of clientelistic power identical in its essentials to that described for Palermo, the Left succeeded in 1975 in taking over local government. By comparing the experiences of these two cities, we will attempt to formulate some more general propositions regarding the strengths and weaknesses

This chapter is reprinted with the permission of *Political Science Quarterly*. A shorter version appeared in Volume 96 (Spring 1981).

of clientelism as a method of organizing political support, the impact of economic crisis on clientelistic systems of power, and the scope for political and social change at the local level in a situation like that of southern Italy.

Many students of clientelism and political machines (see Chapter 1 in this volume) have emphasized the eventual inflationary consequence of such methods of mobilizing political consent, concluding that clientelistic political systems can be sustained over time only in the presence of a constantly expanding resource base. In the Italian context, observers (Allum, 1973; Caciagli et al., 1977; Tarrow, 1967) have emphasized the massive transfer of resources from the national government to the underdeveloped South; this influx of public resources from the center, it is held, has, by substituting for local resource scarcity, provided the economic underpinning for clientelistic power at the local level. This approach focusses on the role of the dominant Christian Democratic Party as a mediator between the resources of the center and the needs of a resource-scarce periphery. While not denying the importance of the resources of the state in sustaining positions of local power in the South, this chapter will attempt, on the basis of an in-depth case study of the DC machine in Palermo, to demonstrate that such an emphasis on the inflationary aspects of machine politics seriously underestimates critical *local* patronage mechanisms which depend only minimally upon expenditure of public resources. This evidence suggests that, contrary to the predictions of the resource-based model, economic crisis need not necessarily spell the demise of clientelistic systems of power; the case of Palermo demonstrates instead that the machine has substantial non-monetary levels of power at the local level which can sustain it even in the absence of substantial external resource flows. Finally, the chapter will question the validity of a typology of political parties which sees patronage-based parties, like the DC in southern Italy, as a transitional stage of political development between traditional patron-client ties and modern mass ideological or interest-based parties (Allum, 1973; Graziano, 1973; Scott, 1969). The experience of southern Italy demonstrates instead the ability of clientelistic systems of power to perpetuate the conditions of poverty and socioeconomic fragmentation upon which they thrive. Far from being progressively undermined by inevitable processes of social and economic development, machine-based elites have proved capable, through their links to national power and their consequent control over critical resources, to impede indefinitely precisely those processes of development which would transform the nature of political organization.

THE FAILURE OF DEVELOPMENT IN THE SOUTH

In order to understand contemporary politics in southern Italy, it is necessary first to give a brief overview of the so-called "Southern Question" and the reasons for the dramatic gap — economic, social, and political — which continues to separate North and South over 100 years after Italian unification. The economic and social dualism between a modernizing, industrializing North and a largely feudal, agricultural South, already in existence at the time of unification in 1860, was further exacerbated rather than reduced by the subsequent process of national economic and political integration. The political underpinning of liberal democracy in unified Italy was an alliance between the northern industrial bourgeoisie and the southern landed aristocracy, one of the conditions of which was the preservation of the social and economic status quo in the South.[1] The developmental choices implicit in this alliance, reinforced subsequently by the logic of market forces, meant that, by the beginning of the postwar period, the dualism between North and South had become so consolidated that the only possibility of reversing it lay in the adoption of a deliberate policy of state intervention to promote and sustain economic development in the South.

Such a policy of state intervention was initiated in 1950 with the establishment of the Cassa per il Mezzogiorno, set up as an autonomous arm of the government, independent of the regular ministries, in order to facilitate rapid and effective action in the South.[2] After 25 years of "extraordinary" intervention by the Cassa, the face of the South has indeed changed. A massive exodus from agriculture has nourished a migratory flow of about four million people from the South to northern cities and to the industrial nations of Western Europe between 1951 and 1971. Modern industrial giants (refineries, steel mills, automobile factories and chemical plants) have sprung up where recently one encountered only impoverished peasants and flocks of sheep.[3] Both income per capita and the share of total income produced by industry have increased substantially. Yet, after 25 years of activity and approximately 10,000 billion lire invested in the South, even government spokesmen have been compelled to judge the Cassa a failure: the gap between North and South has widened rather than narrowed, industrial employment has grown at rates far below those anticipated, and overall employment has actually decreased (see Table 1).

Table 1
Indicators of Regional Differences, 1951-71

| | All Italy = 100 | | | | 1951 = 100 | |
| | South | | Center-North | | South | Center-North |
	1951	1971	1951	1971	1971	
Per capita income	67.9	64.3	119.0	19.6	253.7	270.4
GDP at factor cost	24.5	22.9	75.5	77.1	272.2	298.5
Agriculture	38.6	42.6	61.4	57.4	174.8	148.1
Industry	17.0	16.6	83.0	83.4	380.7	391.9
Services	22.7	23.5	77.3	76.5	299.1	285.2
Employment	33.0	34.3	66.7	65.7	91.8	101.8
Agriculture	42.6	50.4	57.4	49.6	50.0	36.5
Industry	22.5	23.2	77.5	76.8	145.2	139.3
Manufacturing	19.5	17.6	80.5	89.4	122.0	138.0
Construction	32.3	40.0	67.7	60.0	209.5	149.7
Services	27.4	27.8	72.6	72.2	142.2	138.8
Public administration	33.3	34.3	66.7	65.7	163.4	156.3
Industrial investment outlays	15.1	35.4	84.9	64.6	732.3	239.2

Source: Data from Comitato dei Ministri per il Mezzogiorno; table reproduced from Gisele Podbielski, *Italy: Development and Crisis in the Post-War Economy* (Oxford: Clarendon Press, 1974), p. 137.

Given such a massive state commitment, how can the failure of economic development in the South be explained? While the poverty and backwardness of the South may once have been attributable to objective natural factors and subsequently to the workings of the market in a unified economy, such arguments are less persuasive after 25 years of deliberate public intervention aimed at eliminating at least the most glaring disparities between Italy's "two nations."

To understand the contemporary gap between North and South, one must in the first place analyze the strategy guiding Cassa investment. After an initial period of concentration upon the creation of infrastructures, in 1957 the orientation of the Cassa shifted to a new strategy of providing direct incentives to public and private industrial investment in the South. These investment incentives were concentrated in "development poles" (*poli di sviluppo*), the majority of which were sited in the vicinity of the large coastal cities, and, although originally intended to favor small- and medium-scale, relatively labor-intensive industries, were increasingly granted instead to large public and private firms in precisely those sectors — steel, chemicals and petrochemicals — in which the ratio of labor to capital is lowest. Thus began the process of what has become known as "industrialization without development."[4] Because of the priority accorded to the creation of "cathedrals in the desert" (industrial giants, often subsidiaries of northern monopolies or state-controlled firms, artificially implanted in the South without linkages to the local economy and with little propulsive capacity in terms either of employment or the creation of a supportive network of small and medium firms), industrial employment actually fell in many areas as the new industries undermined the traditional artisanal firms without creating sufficient new jobs to absorb the labor thereby displaced (not to mention the massive outpouring of manpower from agriculture). Enormous public investment thus had the paradoxical effect of encouraging rather than restraining the ever-swelling migratory flows from the South.

Political as well as economic factors, however, lie behind the failure of the Cassa in the South. Designed as a special streamlined instrument to channel state funds into carefully chosen economic development projects, the Cassa was soon transformed into a political bandwagon for the maintenance of local clienteles: in numerous cases the selection and siting of public works and development projects was determined not by criteria of economic rationality but rather by the political needs of local Christian Democratic bosses. The linkages between the management of the Cassa and the exigencies of local clientelistic politics, however, may have implications going beyond the particularistic distribution of state funds. An argument has been made (Collidà, 1972) that the fundamental choices concerning the strategy of public intervention in the South have been conditioned from the outset by the necessity of the dominant Christian Democratic Party to maintain a certain type of power base in the South. Local party leaders, it is held, saw industrialization as a long-term threat to their power and therefore, often in alliance with the leaders of the Cassa itself, exercised a continual rearguard action against the concrete realization of such initiatives. At a certain point, however, when outright local resistance to industrialization became incompatible with increasing national pressures to avoid total stagnation of the southern economy, a compromise solution was reached:

> The compromise solution . . . was to direct to the South industrial complexes not likely, because of their organizational characteristics, to promote integration with the pre-existing economic base. In this way clientelistic control . . . remained substantially guaranteed, and the new industrial investments served only in a very indirect and marginal way to promote the further development of the area in which they were located (Collidà, 1972: 186).

Thus we return once again to the theme of "industrialization without development." Seen from this perspective, the investment activity of the Cassa, while failing in its proclaimed objective of industrializing the South, did perform important political functions — on the one hand, it undermined the opposition through a massive program of industrial investment in the South, while on the other it preserved in large part the traditional economic and social structure of the South upon which the DC's clientelistic local power bases depended and, not coincidentally, sustained a flow of low-cost migrant labor to northern factories.

Because of the failure of 25 years of state intervention to reduce the North-South gap and the still further disintegration of the already fragile economic structure of the South under the impact of the current economic crisis, the "Southern Question" has re-emerged in recent years as a major topic of political debate in Italy. Few attempts have been made, however, to document the bases of DC power in the South through in-depth empirical studies at the local level. Until recently most research on the South consisted of anthropological studies of peasant communities, dealing with clientelism, if at all, exclusively in terms of the traditional patron-client bond between the landowner and the peasant. Since the mid-1950s, however, the real focus of DC power has shifted to the cities, in which both the southern population and the most striking contradictions of the model of development which has subordinated the economy of the South to the needs of the industrial

North have come to be increasingly concentrated. With the partial exception of Naples (which will be examined in the following chapter), the city in southern Italy is emblematic of the phenomenon of "urbanization without industrialization" — i.e., rapid population growth without a concomitant expansion of the productive base of the urban economy. On the one hand, then, the local economy is characterized by extreme resource constraints and, for the individual, extreme economic insecurity; on the other, as a consequence of the above, the local economy is sustained primarily by external public intervention (e.g., the salaries of public employees, transfer payments, funds for public works and state-financed development projects, grants and subsidies to local firms).

THE STRUCTURE OF THE URBAN ECONOMY

In order to understand the bases of DC power in Palermo, we must take as our point of departure a more detailed examination of the structure of the local economy. Without entering into a lengthy discussion of the available statistical data (see Table 2),[5] there are four essential points to be made about the nature of the urban economy in a situation of "urbanization without industrialization." (1) The rate of formal labor force participation is extremely low, only 26% as compared to a national average of 34.8% and a figure of 40.5% for a northern industrial city like Milan. The official unemployment rate as of June 1979 was about 12%,[6] but this figure seriously understates the gravity of the actual situation, since it does not take into account either the vast "marginal" workforce (see below) or those unemployed who have withdrawn in discouragement from the formal labor market. (2) The overwhelming majority of firms included in the industrial sector by the Italian census are "industrial" in name only. The construction industry, noted for its cyclical instability and for the precarious nature of the employment which it provides, alone accounts for one third of the "industrial" workforce in Palermo; the bulk of these workers are unskilled laborers drawn from the seemingly endless ranks of the city's unemployed, hired on short-term contracts and returning to unemployment as soon as the project is completed. The manufacturing sector, usually considered the index of industrial development, is polarized between a handful of large and medium-sized firms sustained predominantly by public capital (there are only four firms in Palermo employing over 500 workers) and a myriad of traditional artisanal shops and small family firms (see Table 3). Since the onset of the current economic crisis in 1973-74, this already fragile industrial structure has been still further devastated by growing numbers of layoffs and bankruptcies. (3) Reflecting the weakness of the local economy, the public sector embraces over 30% of the urban labor force (keeping in mind that in Italy the "public sector" includes not only civil servants in the offices of the national, regional, provincial and municipal governments, but also workers in public services like garbage collection and public transportation, teachers and other employees of the public school system, and employees in the state social-security and health-insurance systems, in most banks and hospitals, as well as in a myriad of public and semi-public agencies or *enti*[7] and state-controlled enterprises). (4) The urban economy is heavily weighted toward the tertiary sector, but, apart from the public administration, the nature and functions of this sector are very different in southern Italy to those in other European or North American cities. Here the tertiary sector, like industry, is dominated by petty commercial and service activities (from family-run food shops to hawkers and street vendors of every conceivable variety) which, in the absence of alternative employment possibilities, serve primarily as a "refuge" sector for the urban poor (see Table 3). As one observer (*L'Ora,* 1973) has put it, Palermo, like many large Third World cities, "is not a city but a huge bazaar." The character of the urban poor or *sottoproletariato* in large southern cities like Palermo or Naples is best defined by the classic figure of the *"mille mestieri"* (literally, "a thousand professions"). Without a fixed profession, changing their trade from day to day as the vagaries of the city's "marginal economy" dictate, the *mille mestieri* in Palermo have been estimated at around 200,000, or one quarter to one third of the total urban population (Rochefort, 1961).[8] Their way of life, vividly described by Renée Rochefort in the late 1950s, remains little changed today:

> The rhythms of work appear even more characteristic than its forms. Just as the normal state of a river in North Africa is to be without water, the almost normal condition here is to be without work. In the course of a day as in the course of a life-time, work lasts much less than does unemployment . . . Furthermore, professional mobility is extreme. Not only is the rate of change rapid, but the successive transformations may appear surprising to one who comes from an industrialized country. The bricklayer becomes a shoemaker, the hairdresser a

bricklayer, the blacksmith a tripe-seller. The original trade, if it ever existed, in the end counts much less than the successive substitutions: porter, bootblack, vendor of parsley or prickly pears, stevedore, car-washer. There is neither specialization nor fragmentation of tasks . . . The artisan sells, the vendor manufactures, the herb-gatherer proceeds to cook and sell his own herbs, the candy-seller makes up his product for the next day, and the exploited each attempt to exploit in turn (Rochefort, 1961: 312).

In this jungle of great and small powers, everyone tries to sell to everyone else. An economy of recuperation dominates the city. It is the sordid recuperation of the city's wastes and the gathering up of the meager offerings of nature — gatherers of snails, pickers of lavender, young children who pick up cigarette butts or orange peels from the streets, collectors of garbage who spend half the night filling their baskets, stealing waste from the city government in order to sell it directly to the peasants in the rural suburbs (Rochefort, 1958: 352).

One of the most characteristic aspects of life in the slums of Palermo is the widespread dependence, of the individual family as well as of the local economy, on the exploitation of child labor. Although, given the nature of the problem, there are no exact figures as to the number of children involved, unofficial estimates run as high as 8,000-10,000 (*L'Ora,* 1969), and even a casual visitor to the city cannot help but be struck by the veritable army of children between eight and sixteen years of age employed in bars and restaurants, shops, warehouses, and all manner of small-scale manufacturing — at the most meager wages and without even a minimum of benefits or legal protection. The extent of child labor is a horrifying index of the stark poverty of the Palermo slums, where a child can find work more easily than an adult and where, as a result, entire families eke out a bare subsistence on the wages of several children.

THE SOCIAL BASES OF THE MACHINE

The remainder of this chapter will examine the linkages between the Christian Democratic Party and its mass base in Palermo. Since 1956 the DC has ruled Palermo through a formidable party machine which has extended its control into virtually every sphere of the social, economic and political life of the city. (It should be noted that Palermo alone resisted the swing to the left which led to Communist-Socialist administrations in every other major Italian city in 1975.) Through in-depth examination of the specific patronage mechanisms linking the DC to key social groups in

Table 2
Occupational Distribution of the Labor Force by Sector,
Palermo and Milan, 1971

	Palermo	Milan	Italy
Total population	642,814	1,732,000	54,136,547
Active population	168,319	701,744	18,831,127
	(26.2%)	(40.5%)	(34.8%)
Agriculture	9,756	1,945	3,242,621
	(5.8%)	(0.3%)	(17.2%)
Industry	58,972	329,762	8,350,061
	(35.0%)	(47.0%)	(44.3%)
Construction			
(as % of industry)	18,787	32,381	2,026,265
	(31.9%)	(9.8%)	(24.3%)
Tertiary (total)	99,591	370,037	7,238,445
	(59.2%)	(52.7%)	(38.4%)
Public administra-			
tion	21,935	34,584	1,216,065
	(13.0%)	(4.9%)	(6.5%)

Source: ISTAT, *11° Censimento generale della populazione,* 1971.

Palermo, this chapter will challenge theories of clientelism based on undifferentiated concepts of "patronage" and "resource flow." It will demonstrate instead the importance of a variety of patronage resources, many of which are non-monetary in nature, that can be used to generate and maintain consensus among distinct client groups. Such an analysis points, as indicated in the introduction, to the weakness of theories premised on the need for an ever-increasing resource base to sustain political machines and demonstrates the possibility of maintaining a high level of clientelistic consensus depending only in part upon large-scale patronage expenditures of public resources.

The above description of the urban economy highlighted the three major components of Palermo's social structure: (1) the white-collar middle classes, for the most part public employees, (2) the local entrepreneurial class, concentrated in the construction industry, and (3) the urban poor. Each of these key social groups will now be examined in turn, focussing on the specific type of

Table 3
Distribution of Commercial and Industrial Firms by Size, Palermo and Milan (1971)

Size of firm	Industry[1]				Commerce			
	No. of firms		Total employees		No. of firms		Total employees	
	Palermo	Milan	Palermo	Milan	Palermo	Milan	Palermo	Milan
0-9 employees	4,935 (91.8%)	25,579 (83.5%)	10,122 (26.8%)	65,876 (16.3%)	10,897 (97.6%)	41,350 (93.8%)	21,168 (73.9%)	95,296 (52.3%)
10-49 employees	356 (6.6%)	3,964 (12.9%)	7,364 (19.5%)	79,720 (19.7%)	232 (2.1%)	2,398 (5.4%)	4,213 (14.7%)	45,612 (25.1%)
50 employees and over	83 (1.5%)	1,076 (3.5%)	20,290 (53.7%)	258,411 (64.0%)	35 (0.3%)	340 (0.8%)	3,267 (11.4%)	41,114 (22.6%)
TOTAL	5,374 (100%)	30,619 (100%)	37,776 (100%)	404,007 (100%)	11,164 (100%)	44,088 (100%)	28,648 (100%)	182,022 (100%)

Source: ISTAT, *5° Censimento dell'industria e del commercio, 25 ottobre 1971.*

1. The Italian census does not break this data down into specific industrial sectors at the city level. Since the majority of industrial firms are found in the manufacturing sector, however, these figures give a fairly accurate picture of the structure of the sector. They are reinforced by data showing the average manufacturing firm in Palermo to have only 5.3 employees.

patronage relationship linking them with the holders of local power.

Public Employees

The case of public employees is that which conforms most fully to the "resource theory" of clientelism, the theory, that is, which sees the key to the success of the machine in its control of the public treasury and its large-scale distribution of public resources, primarily in the form of job patronage, for political ends. It is undeniable that job patronage has played a fundamental role in the system of power built up by the DC in Palermo over the past 30 years, although, as we shall see, its significance goes far beyond the simple exchange of a job for a vote. In an economic context like that of Palermo, where a stable job is a rare commodity, employment in the public sector, however lowly, has become a universal aspiration — the dream, so fleeting in Sicily, of stable and dignified employment, of a regular salary and fringe benefits, in sum, of security. As a result, for a large part of the population, politics revolves around the *posto* (job or position) and, when all is said and done, "a job signifies a vote and vice versa." (*L'Ora,* 1967). While this is undoubtedly an exaggeration, its common acceptance conveys the political atmosphere of a city where politics is widely perceived as the only road to obtaining secure employment. The reality of massive hiring on the basis of political "recommendations" which underlies such a perception can be documented in the uncontrolled expansion, from the mid-1950s until the early 1970s, of local government bureaucracies (in particular the Commune and the Region) to elephantine proportions.[9]

The mechanisms by which patronage hiring has taken place are in themselves a fascinating object of study.[10] Because, since the mid-1960s, public competitions (*concorsi*) have been required for almost all public-sector jobs, the techniques of patronage hiring have become more refined. Apart from rigging the *concorsi,* which remains commonplace, the foremost instrument at the disposal of local political leaders has been that of *assunzioni fuori ruolo* — the hiring of persons on short-term contracts (usually six months) and outside regularly defined bureaucratic positions since their employment was allegedly temporary; in this way the *concorsi* required for all permanent administrative personnel could be circumvented.

Once hired, however, the contracts would be regularly renewed until, under the pressure of hundreds of "precarious" employees (the contingents mounting at the approach of every election), the public-sector unions would be compelled to demand their incorporation into the permanent bureaucratic structure. From the viewpoint of the unions, anxious to justify their presence and to recruit support in a traditionally hostile environment, support for such pressures, eminently just insofar as the individual employee was concerned, was unavoidable. The overall effect of such actions, however, has been to draw the unions as well as the opposition parties into objective collusion with the very system of clientelistic power which they are ostensibly seeking to overthrow.

Another tactic by which the unions have been drawn into legitimation of clientelistic hiring is known in bureaucratic jargon as *"svolgimento di mansioni superiori"* (performance of a job superior in rank to that for which one has been hired). The key to the usefulness of this concept is the requirement of *concorsi* only for persons filling administrative positions, while for all other positions (clerks, typists, ushers[11] and doormen, janitors, laborers, etc.) personnel can still be hired on a direct personal basis. (Of 3,056 positions in the city government in 1976, 2,514 were of the latter type as opposed to only 542 requiring *concorsi*.)[12] This has *not* meant, in general, that the DC has used these positions to link significant sectors of the city's low-income population to the party. Instead, what often happens is that, in order to circumvent the *concorso,* persons with high-school and even university degrees are hired as typists, ushers and janitors. Since such individuals, however, could hardly be expected to perform tasks so far beneath their dignity and qualifications, they are rapidly assigned appropriate functions, while continuing to be paid for the lower-ranking job. Eventually, as in the case of the *assunzioni fuori ruolo,* the unions are obliged to protest such blatant exploitation, putting pressure on the administration to promote these people to positions commensurate with the duties which they are in fact performing. As might be expected, the impact of such a system of hiring on the functioning of public offices is disastrous: despite continual hiring for subordinate positions, many offices suffer such an acute shortage of clerical and maintenance personnel that they find it difficult to maintain even a minimal level of services.

Another highly successful technique of job patronage has grown out of national legislation requiring all public offices or agencies to set aside 15% of all positions for the disabled. Since this legislation provides that a person certified as disabled can be hired without the normal *concorso,* the potential for political speculation, particularly in a context like that of Palermo where anything is possible with the proper "recommendation," is extremely high. At the approach of every election, large numbers of "disabled" persons are hired on short notice, providing hundreds or even thousands of dependable votes for certain well-placed candidates. The key to this operation is the medical commission of the city government's Office of Hygiene, which examines applicants and provides the required certificate of disability. With the same party controlling both the certification of disability and subsequent hiring, the prospect of political gain from the hiring of the "disabled" can hardly help but prove tempting.

The ramifications of clientelistic hiring and the network of political obligation created, however, go far beyond the mere act of placing a person on the public payroll. Otherwise, it might be objected, how can the continuity of the patron-client bond be guaranteed once the original vote-for-job exchange is consummated, and the client is securely installed in a public-sector job from which he cannot, for all intents and purposes, ever be removed? The "recommendation" by which the public employee accedes to the object of his aspirations is only the first link in a chain of reciprocal obligation which will progressively bind him ever more irrevocably to his patron and protector. If he wishes to further his own career as well as to insure the possibility of future employment for other family members, the public employee can ill afford to neglect his obligations to his patron once he has secured his job. Within the bureaucracy, for example, promotions and pay raises proceed almost exclusively on the basis of political favoritism. In a highly competitive situation for both hiring and promotion, with virtually everyone recommended by one prominent politician or another, the weight of the recommendation is directly proportional to the power of the patron, which in turn is closely linked to the number of personal preference votes received in the preceding election. The employee's fate, as well as his chances of placing other family members, are thus directly dependent on the continued electoral success of the patron, with loyalty and its rewards being measured in the currency of an ever-increasing number of personal preference votes.

A final consideration about patronage hiring in Palermo is that, even though the staffs of the numerous government offices and public agencies in the city are swollen far out of proportion to their effective personnel needs, the demand for public-sector jobs continues to exceed supply by a ratio of at least 30:1 — an example is a 1976 *concorso* for 1,000 positions in the city government for which over 35,000 persons applied. Such figures underline an essential qualification to an analysis of the problem focussing entirely on the expenditure of public resources for patronage jobs. In the last analysis, the system works less through the mass distribution of benefits to all comers than through the astute management of *scarcity* and, above all, the critical element of hope. The key to the successful politician is not mass patronage but the maintenance of the maximum clientele with the minimum payoff in terms of actual concrete benefits.

In conclusion, the overwhelming consensus for the DC among public-sector employees is based on a complex interlocking of short-term material incentives (or at least the promise thereof) with a broader sense of self-interest, both individual and corporative. It is beyond question that, more than in any other social class, support for the DC among this sector of the middle classes is directly linked to the large-scale expenditure of public resources in the form of patronage jobs, politically-based promotions, and a system of compensation which creates entrenched positions of privilege, both for individuals and for the category of public employees as a whole.[13] In this case, however, consensus implies more than just the buying of votes with patronage; it implies a deeper unity of interest or ideology. The instrument of such consensus has been the ideology of individualism and social privilege which pervades the middle classes in southern Italy, an ideology based on two fundamental elements: (1) the conviction that one can get ahead only on an individual rather than a collective basis and that to do so "it is necessary to have saints in heaven" — i.e., one can rely only on an immediate and personalized relationship with an influential patron; and (2) the very real sense of privilege, in southern Italy, conferred by public-sector employment, not merely in terms of material benefits (which may be substantial), but above all in terms of stability and security. There are thus two distinct components — the ideological and the material — at work producing support for the DC machine among public employees. The former is probably the primary factor in producing the general party vote for the DC, which is attributable at least as much to a perceived identity of class interest as to any specific clientelistic exchange; where the latter is expressed is above all in the preference vote for individual DC candidates, in which the conception of the vote as a direct expression of the patron-client bond predominates.

The Local Entrepreneurial Class

In turning to the linkages between the Christian Democratic Party and the local entrepreneurial class, we are dealing with an issue which has long engaged political scientists, Marxist and non-Marxist alike — the relationship between political and economic elites. In contrast to American theories of the "power elite," which posit the domination of politics by business interests, what we find in Palermo is the opposite extreme — the subordination of the entrepreneur to the politician and of the profit logic to the exigencies of party and factional struggle. The causes of this dependency relationship lie in three interrelated factors: (1) the nature of the southern bourgeoisie, (2) the model of postwar Italian development, which has perpetuated the subordination of the South to the needs of northern industry, and (3) the expanding role of the state in the economy since 1945, particularly pronounced in the South because of the weakness of the private sector.

Since the latter two points have been discussed previously, we will focus here on the problem of the southern bourgeoisie. The new bourgeois class which came into existence in the South in the decades just before 1860 was in its outlook more closely wedded to the conservatism of the landed aristocracy than to the independent initiative and propensity for risk characteristic of the entrepreneurial spirit, tendencies which have continued to mark the southern bourgeoisie until this day. Loath to invest without a maximum guarantee against losses, this class has preferred investment in sectors producing rapid, short-term gains (in particular construction and real-estate speculation) to more productive, but riskier, uses of their capital. As a result, productive investment in the South has been disproportionately the result of external, predominantly public, intervention. Even those firms which are formally part of the private sector are in most cases dependent for their survival upon some form of political support, so that a truly private sector can be said to be virtually nonexistent.

What, then, has been the nature of the linkage between the DC and the local entrepreneurs? Lacking the resources for autonomous development, the southern economy has become increasingly dependent upon public intervention, in the form both of direct public investment and of various programs of incentives and subsidies for private investors. In each case, the intermediary role of the local political elite has been a central factor. This does not necessarily imply the absence of entrepreneurship in the South, but rather the weakness of an entrepreneurial class sufficiently autonomous to bargain on an equal basis with political elites. In the last analysis, the entrepreneurial function in the South has been assumed by the politician, who controls the access to all forms of public resources and who thereby holds the power to determine the success or failure of the individual economic actor. As a result, a solid bond of reciprocal obligation is formed between the political intermediary and the entrepreneur, a confluence of interests having more to do with political power than with economic development:

> The criterion of maximization is not the productive efficiency of the credit conceded, but rather the solidity of the bond of gratitude established and the type of service which will be made available in return . . . Economic credit, that is, generates a political debt (Pizzorno, 1974: 330).

The end result of this interaction is to further reinforce the marginal nature of the local economy. Empirical studies (Bonazzi, Bagnasco and Casillo, 1972) have shown that political contacts are proportionately stronger for the marginal firm which, because of its weakness, is less able to resist pressures to provide patronage jobs in return for the requests for special credit, subsidies, tax reductions, building licenses, etc., which are essential to its survival. As a result of such exchanges, the small firm with the requisite political contacts is protected and sustained, but at a substantial cost to the economy as a whole, because of the sacrifice of criteria of economic rationality and profitability in the distribution of benefits. In the end, then, where the goal of economic development has been subordinated to the interests of local power, political intervention, rather than breaking the vicious circle of underdevelopment, serves instead to reinforce it:

> The goals of development end up by coinciding with the creation of an industrial apparatus capable of absorbing labor, but in no way efficient and rational with regard to production . . . In sum, the allocation of public funds serves latent functions of a welfare nature as well as sustaining local entrepreneurial groups for political ends, rather than promoting economic development (Catanzaro, 1975: 291-92).

The result is a self-perpetuating process by which marginality, and with it the bases of clientelistic power, are continually re-created.

Public intervention in the southern economy has taken three general forms, which correspond to three distinct types of linkages between the Christian Democratic Party and the local entrepreneurial class: (1) direct public spending by national and regional governments, in the form of incentives and subsidies as well as special industrial salvage programs, on the one hand, and favoritism and corruption in the awarding of the highly lucrative public works contracts of the Cassa and the regional government, as well as concessions let out by city governments for certain public services (e.g. garbage collection, public transport, maintenance of streets and sewer lines) on the other; (2) control of access to credit, both public and private, through special publicly-financed programs of low-cost credit and through DC intermediation with commercial banks and credit institutions, the majority of which are controlled by party representatives;[14] (3) discretionary implementation of the "powers of licensing and interdiction"[15] of local government, particularly in the areas of urban planning, the issuing of construction licenses, and enforcement of zoning and building codes.

This last aspect assumes particular importance in a city like Palermo where, as we have seen, the local entrepreneurial class is made up predominantly of building contractors. The process of postwar urban development in Palermo has been one of chaotic, unregulated expansion in which the logic of speculation has reigned supreme. One of the outstanding characteristics of local politics in Palermo from the mid-1950s until the early 1970s, the period of the building boom, was the manifest collusion between the competent organs of the DC-controlled city administration and powerful speculative interests, in this case represented disproportionately by the mafia (a distinctive kind of entrepreneurship, to be sure, but entrepreneurship all the same!).[16] The result of this collusion has been the almost total destruction of the city's once rich agricultural hinterland and its replacement by endless waves of high-rise towers, an entire "new city" constructed in abeyance of any public control and of even minimal standards of public service provision, a cement and asphalt desert. Palermo has become a national symbol of the ravages of uncontrolled speculative development, but in the meantime immense fortunes, both economic and political, have been accumulated.

This privileging of speculative interests, which initially took the form of episodic operations of favoritism on the part of the old DC notables, undertaken without any broader strategic vision and limited to a restricted social elite, was transformed by the 1960s into a comprehensive strategy of urban expansion and of DC power, managed directly from key posts of power within the city administration. In one way or another, almost every social and economic group in the city found it had something to gain from the tumultuous expansion which completely transformed the face of the city in the space of a decade. The "power bloc" (*blocco di potere*) consolidated by the DC in these years around the politics of speculative expansion represented a broad cross-section of the major social and economic forces of the city: (1) the great speculative interests — landowners, real-estate brokers, contractors (in the ranks of all of which the mafia held a dominant position), plus the banking interests which financed them; (2) the myriad of artisans and small manufacturing firms which supported the construction industry; (3) firms dealing in the production and commerce of all types of home furnishings; (4) an important sector of the professional and technical middle classes (engineers, architects, surveyors, etc.); (5) the white-collar middle classes, in particular the new class of public employees created by the tremendous expansion of local government bureaucracies in the 1950s and 1960s, for whom the speculative boom provided the means, through the acquisition of a modern apartment, of materializing their newly-found social status; (6) the working class proper and the thousands of *sottoproletari* who found employment in construction in the years of the boom, as well as the building-trades unions whose self-interest, despite their connection to left-wing political parties, clearly coincided with that of the industry in stimulating maximum construction activity with little concern for the long-term consequences of such chaotic expansion; (7) the masses of low-income residents of the old city, abandoned to total neglect and decay in the rush for suburban expansion, who were brought into the "grand design" through endless promises of public intervention to restore the old city on the one hand and to create huge model housing projects on the city's periphery on the other. The latter, totally inadequate for the massive low-income housing needs of the city, quickly became new ghettoes, isolated from the city itself and deprived of the most basic infrastructures and of even minimal social services, while promises of the former continue to lie at the heart of political debate in the city, but without producing as yet the slightest concrete result.[17]

While alike in their generation of consensus on the basis of short-term material benefits, the three instruments of patronage politics discussed above — distribution of public funds in the form of subsidies, contracts, etc., access to credit, and discretionary use of the regulatory powers of local government — imply very different relationships between the dominant political party and public resources. While the first constitutes a direct and substantial outlay of government expenditure, conforming to the traditional wisdom as to the effects of machine politics in squandering public resources for political ends, the second, control of access to credit, while confirming the critical intermediary role of the party, concerns resources which emanate only in part from governmental sources. Finally, the third category, as demonstrated in the case of the construction industry in Palermo, provides a striking example of the creation of a solid clientelistic bond between a critical sector of the local entrepreneurial class and the Christian Democratic Party which depends only in small part on any direct expenditure of public funds and therefore constitutes only a very minimal drain on party or public treasuries. Yet it is precisely this final category which has provided one of the most solid pillars of DC power in Palermo over the past twenty years.

As this example demonstrates, city governments possess a wide range of powers which, while conferring significant advantages or disadvantages of an economic nature, do not impose any *monetary* costs on the bestower. In contrast to those studies which emphasize the inherently inflationary, and hence eventually self-defeating, characteristics of a political system dependent for support on short-term material incentives, this evidence shows instead how, through manipulation of the substantial regulatory powers of local government, a high level of clientelistic support can be maintained over an extended period of time, and in a context of severe resource constraints, without such inflationary consequences. Naturally the long-term social costs of such a policy — the sacrifice of broader social interests and policies to immediate individual benefits — are very high, but this is not a constraint imposed by the exhaustion of available public resources through patronage spending, nor does it necessarily imply the imminent collapse of the DC machine. In conclusion, it can be argued that the primary linkage between the DC and the local entrepreneurial class has not been the outright expenditure of public resources for political ends, but rather the critical intermediary role of the party as an obligatory middleman between the individual entrepreneur and a variety of benefits, only a portion of which imply a direct outlay of a monetary nature.

The Traditional Middle Classes and the Urban Poor

A third and final pillar of DC power in Palmero is constituted by the traditional middle classes (small shopkeepers and artisans) and the *sottoproletariato* or urban poor. Probably the most fascinating aspect of the DC machine in Palmero is its solid electoral base in the poorest neighborhoods of the city, in particular the slums of the old city, where, given the incredible poverty and squalor, the crumbling housing, overcrowding, and sanitary and health conditions reminiscent of Third World cities,[18] one might expect instead substantial support for the Left. Unlike public employees and industrialists, these people have received remarkably few material benefits from the machine; yet, since the collapse of the Monarchist Right in the late 1950s, they have provided a stable reservoir of votes for local DC notables.

Why, then, do the city's low-income residents support the DC machine? Although in class terms the traditional middle classes and the urban poor constitute two distinct groups, they will be considered together here for two reasons: (1) the economy of the center-city slums revolves around small commercial and artisanal shops, together with all the petty vending and service activities associated with the traditional open markets which are the heart of each neighborhood's economic structure; (2) in the absence of alternative employment possibilities, small shops, street vending and petty services serve as critical "refuge" activities for a substantial portion of the urban *sottoproletariato*. As a result, there is in reality considerable overlap between these two analytically distinct components of the urban population. As in the case of the local entrepreneurial class, a major linkage between the DC machine and these groups is the exercise of the regulatory and bureaucratic functions of local government. The difference is that the benefits in question are at a very different level — on the one hand, the millions of dollars which may be at stake from a public contract, a building license, or a variation to the city plan; on the other, the seemingly petty favors involved in granting a street vendor's license, voiding a fine for a minor violation of commercial regulations, or helping a low-income resident to obtain a document or pension.

In the case of the traditional middle classes (including street vendors and hawkers for our present purposes), the regulatory and police powers of local government form the basis of DC consensus. Within the city government the department responsible for the distribution of commercial and vending licenses has traditionally constituted a major center of clientelistic power, and thus an important object of dispute among ambitious DC politicians. Equally important, however, and particularly fascinating as an illustration of the concrete ways in which the patronage bond is forged, is the exercise, or better yet the *non-exercise,* of the surveillance and enforcement powers of the city police. By what means, one might ask, can an ordinary city policeman become a powerful political figure? On closer examination, it becomes clear that, in the course of his daily rounds, there are literally thousands of ways in which a vigilant police officer can either perform a favor or make life miserable for a shopkeeper or street vendor:

> If a policeman wants to be fussy, he can ruin a shopkeeper. He can slap him with a fine of 30,000 or 40,000 lire if he lowers his grill five minutes after the official closing time. He can levy another 50,000 lire fine if the price tag has fallen off the crate of oranges. And if the shopkeeper is very careful and commits neither of these infractions, the policeman always has an ace up his sleeve: he needs only express a doubt as to the sanitary conditions of the shop and its merchandise, and the merchant will never re-emerge from the troubles which will beset him — controls, inspections, months of closing, endless expenses (Sottile, 1972).

Each of the above examples is, in and of itself, a relatively trivial matter — but one which can take on vital importance for the individual shopkeeper should the policeman decide to enforce the letter of the law. In practice the power of the policeman derives less from the controls which he effects than from those which he *omits* (failing to denounce, for example, an unauthorized shop or vendor, of which there are thousands in Palermo), in return for an immediate payoff or, more often, a debt of gratitude which will be repaid on a future, preferably electoral, occasion. One reason such a system of control over the individual shopkeeper or artisan has been so effective is that, as noted above, a large proportion of these persons — especially at the level of neighborhood food shops, market stalls, and street vendors — themselves come from the ranks of the *sottoproletariato*. Their ignorance of the law is compounded by an inbred fear of and deference toward the powerful, particularly if they wear a uniform. An able administrator can thus transform an automatic bureaucratic procedure (such as concession of a commercial license under the pre-1971 laws or a permit for the occupation of public soil in the open markets) into a personal favor, just as the policeman can exploit the slightest infraction of the law, real or imagined, to create a network of personal obligation which he can then use as a bargaining arm with the holders of local power. For a policeman only the function of traffic control offers no potential for political exploitation — perhaps this explains why a recent mayor assigned only 50 out of the 500 men on the police force to direct the city's absolutely chaotic traffic!

For the urban poor in general, however, the most important linkage mechanism is the role of bureaucratic intermediation performed by the party. To some extent this is an extension of the preceding discussion of the utilization of public offices for the purpose of petty clientelism. The difference is that here we are dealing not with the discretionary distribution of public funds or the selective implementation of certain regulatory codes, but rather with intervention in the processes of ordinary administration. This is by its nature a much more continuous relationship than that produced by the dispensation of subsidies or "favors" just prior to elections, which is the aspect of patronage politics among the poor most often pointed to in studies of political machines. The possibility of such intervention in normal bureaucratic procedures for political ends can be explained by the failure of the Weberian ideal of impartial bureaucracy to take root in Italy. In contrast to Weber's rational, impartial model of bureaucratic conduct, all relationships are highly personalized and politicized, even those regarding the most trivial administrative procedures. As a result, the citizen's legal right is transformed into a personal favor and used as an instrument of pressure to obtain votes.

One reason this system functions so well is that the bureaucracy in Italy, and particularly in the South, is such an inefficient, slow-moving apparatus, bogged down in endless red tape, that it is often indeed only by the personal intervention of an influential intermediary that one can obtain any immediate result. Thus, what strikes the observer as a pathological disfunction of the bureaucracy serves in effect as a highly efficacious instrument for generating and maintaining political support. For practically every necessity of day-to-day life — the innumerable documents required for even the most trivial public act in Italy; eligibility for a welfare benefit, pension, or family allowance; admission of a family member to a day-care center, hospital, or other public institution; application for public housing or a public-sector job — the individual citizen finds himself confronted with an impersonal and unresponsive bureaucracy. In such a situation ordinary citizens, and in particular the poor, disadvantaged by their illiteracy and lack of experience in dealing with bureaucratic institutions, are constrained to seek assistance from a higher-status "patron" who can intervene directly on their behalf. In a system where the functioning of the public bureaucracy has been so entirely subordinated to the logic of personal political gain, the individual simply has no alternative but to seek a particularistic solution to his problems. Thus, once again, consensus is rooted in the critical intermediary role of the party or the individual politician in every transaction between the citizen and the state.

A final type of linkage between the DC and its electorate in the low-income neighborhoods of the city depends upon a different kind of intermediary network within each neighborhood, one which functions independently of any direct personal relationship between the party or candidate and the individual voter. The superficial version of such linkage mechanisms can be seen in the case of petty electoral corruption, where votes are essentially sold to the highest bidder, without the slightest regard for the individual candidate, his party, or the political positions, if any, which he represents; because of the system of preference voting in Italian elections, many people in fact vote only for a number, with no idea of the actual person to whom it corresponds. The real networks of electoral influence within these neighborhoods, however, are of a quite different nature: they are based on the ties linking a person of influence within a given neighborhood — the local *capo-mafia,* the parish priest, a doctor or prominent merchant — to a particular party or candidate. The nature of the bond — friendship, *clientela,* or an outright exchange of cash — varies according to the case. What is important is that the local "boss" is capable of mobilizing blocks of votes through his personal influence alone, an influence which may be based equally on respect or fear, without any exchange of benefits between the candidate and the individual voter. These votes, which depend entirely on the prestige of the local influence broker, are thus, in their pure form at least, independent not only of the individual candidate and the party but also, and most importantly, of all the traditional patronage levels of local power.

A critical factor for understanding the nature of political behavior in the low-income neighborhoods of the city is their extreme social and economic fragmentation and the absence of any associative structures which could serve as poles of aggregation for the population. This fragmentation stems above all from the lack of stable employment among the *sottoproletariato*. With the disintegration of the traditional economy of the old city, the social and cultural fabric associated with it largely disappeared as well, leaving behind entire neighborhoods cut off from the mainstream of the city's economic life and relegated to abandonment and decay, both physical and moral. Those economic activities which remain are, as we have seen, dispersed in thousands of individual expedients for day-to-day survival. The absence of centers of employment within these neighborhoods or of any form of occupational aggregation outside them (e.g., stable factory employment) deprives the residents not only of any sense of collective economic interests but also of one of the primary aggregative structures through which political and other organizations can gain access to a mass base.

In the absence of alternative structures to aggregate and mobilize collective interests, every individual seeks to resolve his problems on his own, through whatever personal channels are open to him. People are convinced, on the basis less of cultural conditioning than of direct experience, that nothing can be obtained from the existing power structure without direct personal intervention by an influential patron. As there are no structures for collective organization, there is no sense of collective efficacy. Even in those collective organizations which do exist, for example unions, the cohesion of the membership in many cases is due less to the ideology or programmatic goals of the organization than to a series of parallel individual ties to the leader, who carries this personal following with him even if he changes party or union organization.

While, in all the cases which we have examined, the essence of the clientelistic bond is the direct personal relationship with a more powerful or prestigious figure, the maintenance of this relationship is not necessarily contingent upon continual repetition of specific acts of material exchange. Although success in obtaining one's goals depends on the individual patron-client tie, the personal bond which is created may ultimately transcend the specific act of exchange. It has been argued that the critical element for understanding the strength of clientelism, at least in the southern Italian context, is less the concrete exchange relationship than this more generalized personal bond which underlies it.[19] The relationship assumes a value in and of itself, independent of any specific act of exchange which, while serving to reinforce it, is not essential to the survival of the relationship. In this view, the crucial factor is rather that of access — i.e., it is less the immediate benefit received which maintains the relationship than the constant anticipation of possible future favors as a result of the personal tie to an individual in a position of power. Such an analysis, by pointing to the ability of the clientelistic relationship to endure over time without continual reinforcement by concrete acts of exchange, underlines once again the central importance of the element of hope in sustaining a clientelistic system of power in a context of limited resource availability.

CONCLUSION

The image which emerges from the preceding pages is one of a stagnant, immobile political system, in which political control is so complete as to make stimulation of change from within almost impossible. Such a conclusion, pessimistic though it may be, is, I believe, the only one possible on the basis of the evidence presented here and any reasonable projection of developments in national politics in the foreseeable future. The justification for such a conclusion is to be found in the particular strengths of clientelism as an instrument of political mobilization and in its relationship to fundamental economic and social structural variables.

The strength of the machine as an organizer of consensus lies above all in its incentive structure which, because of the direct particularistic bond linking the machine to its electorate, maximizes the incentive to individual participation. Essential to discussion of the incentive structure of the machine is the question of the resource base required to support clientelistic systems of power. As we have seen, many studies have argued that, because its support is based on the distribution of short-term material benefits, such a political system requires access to an expanding resource base in order to sustain its power over time. These inevitable inflationary tendencies are seen as posing an inherent limit to the scope and duration of systems of political support based on clientelistic incentives, a limit to be found either in the restricted resource base of the economy (the case in most developing countries) or in the impact of economic crisis. This argument has been heard with increasing frequency in recent years with regard to the case of southern Italy. Its proponents maintain that, while until the present a flow of resources from the state — in terms both of local government spending and of development funds from national agencies like the Cassa per il Mezzogiorno — has compensated for the severe resource constraints of the southern economy, the current economic crisis, by shrinking the resource base available for patronage politics, will progressively undermine the local political machines which dominate much of the South.

The evidence presented in this chapter with regard to the bases of support for the Christian Democratic Party in Palermo demonstrates that such an analysis is only partially valid. Because of the severe resource constraints under which local government operates and the broad-based consensus generated by the DC, Palermo can be viewed as a kind of test case for a theory of clientelism which links sustained support to an expanding resource base. That there has been a tremendous expenditure of public resources for patronage purposes in Palermo cannot be denied. The beneficiaries of this patronage spending, which has drained resources which might otherwise have been invested in public services or economic development projects, have been above all the white-collar middle classes and certain sectors of the local entrepreneurial class, the latter through public contracts, publicly guaranteed low-cost credit, and regional programs of industrial salvage. By contrast, the limitations of the resource argument become manifest when we consider the cases of building contractors, the traditional middle classes, and the urban poor. Each of these groups has constituted a major pillar of DC power in Palermo and yet, in terms of direct patronage spending, has received practically nothing.

The key to the strength and durability of the DC machine in Palermo, I would maintain, lies in the nature of the linkages between the DC and these latter groups. Here, as in the case of public employees, we are speaking of a direct exchange of short-term particularistic benefits, but in this case the benefits, while implying significant economic advantages or disadvantages for the individual recipient, are not necessarily *monetary,* and therefore do not require any expenditure of public resources. Patronage mechanisms like the issuing of construction and commercial licenses, variations to the city plan, the wide range of police powers of local government, and bureaucratic intervention on behalf of the urban poor are central to the maintenance of Christian Democratic power, but, in terms of direct public spending, cost nothing. (This is not to say, of course, that they may not imply a high social cost in the long run, because of the favoring of individual benefits at the expense of substantive social policy and of private interests at the expense of collective services, but this is another issue.)

Looked at from this perspective, it is clear that the essence of DC power lies not in the quantity of resources which it is able to distribute, but rather in its monopoly hold on all resources, whatever their level, and in its control over all the critical interstices of society — political, economic, and social — so that the party becomes an obligatory intermediary in all transactions between the individual and public power. Given such a monopoly of resources in the hands of the dominant party, combined with the important non-monetary sources of clientelistic support which we have examined — the regulatory powers of local government, the function of bureaucratic intermediation, and the enduring nature of the patron-client bond — not only is an expanding resource base not essential to the survival of a political machine, but economic crisis alone is not a sufficient condition for the disintegration of a system of political support based on clientelistic bonds. In fact, in the short term at any rate, just the opposite may be the case; as economic crisis shrinks even further the already restricted resource base of the society, the role of the party as the privileged channel of access to the few remaining resources may actually be enhanced.

A second crucial element explaining the solidity of DC power in Palermo, one which distinguishes it from the experience of big-city machines in the US, is the relationship between local and national power. As those who emphasize the importance of resource transfers from the center to the periphery in maintaining local machines rightly point out, the monopoly of power in the hands of the Christian Democratic Party at both the national and the local level has provided the holders of local power with privileged access to the resources of the state. Given the weakness of the local resource base, such access has unquestionably played a central role in sustaining local positions of power (see below). A second critical factor in this regard is the logic of factional politics *within* the DC. While we have argued here that the sources of electoral support for the machine in Palermo are primarily local, the domination of the party organization and of all levers of local power by a single faction within the party would not be possible without the protection of the local bosses by the national party leadership. This protection continues, despite national scandals involving prominent DC personalities in Palermo, because of the logic of intra-party factional struggle. So long as the votes which local bosses can carry to the national congress are critical to the success of their respective "patrons" within the national leadership, meaningful change from within the DC at the local level is unlikely.

In the final analysis, however, the perpetuation of a clientelistic system of power in Palermo is dependent upon national power and policy in an even more fundamental way. The key variable underlying DC power in Palermo is, in my opinion, the economic structure of the city and the social fragmentation associated with it, which impede the aggregation of political demand and the organization of collective interests necessary for the emergence of an alternative model of political behavior. The monopolization of economic resources in the hands of the DC is possible, as we have seen, because of the absence of an autonomous resource base at the local level and the consequent dependence of the local economy on the resources of the state. Once all centers of both local and extra-local power are concentrated in the hands of one party, however, an expanding stock of resources is no longer necessary; indeed, the power of the party rests rather on the manipulation of *scarcity,* on maintaining large numbers of people in competition for scarce resources, all of which are channeled through the party. In such a situation, there is little incentive on the part of the party to create new jobs; it is in fact economic development rather than economic crisis which presents the greater threat to such a clientelistic regime, since it offers the possibility of the creation of alternative sources of economic goods which could eventually elude strict political control, as well as the creation of an industrial working class which, even if subject to clientelistic control in the short run, provides a potential focus for alternative models of political aggregation and mobilization. While the possibility for a clientelistic model of politics to take root at the end of the war was clearly closely related to a pre-existing state of underdevelopment, the situation since then can be described as one of a mutually reinforcing bond between the structure of political power and the economic base upon which it rests — i.e., through its political control the DC has succeeded in perpetuating the very conditions of resource shortage and social disaggregation upon which the survival of the system of power which it has created depends. Thus, far from being a transitional form of political organization, a mass-based clientelistic party, once having established control over key economic resources, can block precisely that process of economic development which is seen as bringing about its eventual demise, thereby perpetuating the structural base of its own power.

What, then, are the possibilities for political change in a situation like that of Palermo? Having minimized the probability of change from within the DC, the only alternative would appear to be the Left. The critical issue here is what kinds of incentives the Left has to offer as an alternative to the existing structure of power. On the one hand, it has no access to alternative resources, either public or private, to offer in place of those controlled by the DC machine. On the other hand, as the experience of Communist administration in Naples since 1975 clearly demonstrates (see Chapter 4), even should the Left succeed in gaining power at the local level, the fundamental structural constraints underlying the system of DC power in the South cannot be changed through control of local levers of power alone. If the critical variables determining the shape of the economy and thereby of politics are outside local control, then the only way left to effect change is through external intervention to transform the basic structural variables. This means concretely, given the centralized character of the Italian political system and the nature of the "Southern Question," a serious national commitment to the economic development of the South. Although not necessarily sufficient in and of itself (the experience of the Cassa demonstrates the capacity of the DC to exert effective control over certain kinds of investment), economic development is an essential precondition for political change, because only through stimulation of a process of autonomous development will it be possible to create alternatives to the existing resource monopoly of the DC. The success of such a policy, however, clearly depends, as we have seen, on changes in the structure of power at the national level, in terms both of the DC monopoly over the critical levers of state power and of factional politics within the DC. So long as the DC continues to control the major centers of state economic power and so long as national faction chiefs continue to rely upon the votes provided by local machine bosses to retain their power, even economic crisis is unlikely to seriously challenge the bases of clientelistic power in southern Italy.

NOTES

1. For a good historical discussion of the development of clientelism in southern Italy, see Graziano (1973).

2. For a more detailed description of the Cassa's structure and its development policies, see Podbielski (1974: 131-44).

3. For an excellent description of the effects of state-induced industrialization on the southern economy, see Hytten and Marchioni (1970).

4. From the title of the above-cited book by Hytten and Marchioni.

5. The state of economic statistics at the communal level in Italy is near disastrous. The only official sources are the *Census of the Population,* which breaks down the labor force into broad economic categories (agriculture; extractive industries; manufacturing; construction; electricity, gas and water; commerce; transportation and communications; services; and public administration) and the *Census of Industry and Commerce,* which reports the number of firms and employees for each of the above sectors and their sub-divisions. The *Census of Industry and Commerce* also gives figures on the distribution of firms by size, but this data is reported only for the generic categories of "industry," "commerce," and "other"; this information broken down by economic sector exists only for the provincial level. In both cases the categories used are so general as to be of little assistance in providing a detailed understanding of the occupational structure of the city.

6. This figure was calculated using unemployment data for June 1979, but labor force statistics from the 1971 census, since no more recent figures are available. For the province of Palermo, official unemployment as of June 1979 was 52,532, an increase of almost 10,000 from June 1978.

7. The numerous *enti* operating under the tutelage of the various levels of government in Italy are referred to in Italian as *"sottogoverno."* The presidencies and administrative councils of these bodies are strictly divided up among the parties making up the majority coalition in the city, regional or national government. Control of these *enti* is so important for patronage purposes that government crises are often protracted for weeks or even months before the parties can agree on the division of these critical levers of power.

8. Although Rochefort's study was completed in the late 1950s, there is no evidence to suggest that the economic situation of the city has changed radically since then; if anything, it has worsened.

9. As of the 1971 census, the labor force in Palermo was 168,319. Although

reliable earlier figures for city employees are not available, they numbered about 9,500 (including the *aziende municipalizzate* — garbage collection, public transport, gas and water) at the end of 1976. For the regional government, whose bureaucratic apparatus is overwhelmingly concentrated in Palermo, we have more exact figures. The first law regulating the regional bureaucracy was passed in 1953, limiting its size to 1,474 employees and prohibiting any subsequent hiring except by *concorso*. Clientelistic hiring continued unabated, however, so that by 1958 a new law was required, expanding the bureaucracy to 3,567 positions. Only in 1962 were *concorsi* for the regional government finally instituted, with 500-600 persons entering by this means between 1962 and 1971, since which time all new hiring has been blocked in accordance with new legislation aimed at a complete reorganization of the regional administration. Despite this hiring ban, the effective strength of the regional bureaucracy at the end of 1976 was 6,149, an excess of 2,500 employees over the legal ceiling. This figure does not include the approximately 7,000 employees of the special economic agencies run by the regional government.

10. The information on techniques of patronage hiring contained in the following paragraphs is based on personal interviews with leaders of the public-sector unions of city and regional employees of the CGIL.

11. The figure of the usher or *usciere* is fundamental to an understanding of the functioning of public bureaucracies in Italy and, in particular, of a clientelistic system of power like that of Palermo. The *usciere* is a ubiquitous figure in every public office (there are 82 in the offices of the city government alone), but his precise functions are difficult to discern. First and foremost, the position of *usciere* represents the epitome of job patronage, requiring no other quality but physical presence. The *usciere* does, however, perform an important — and to the public often exasperating — function, that of controlling access to public offices and in particular to persons in high positions. This role of "guardian of the sanctuary" has symbolic as well as functional aspects: the *usciere* personifies the social and political gap between the official and the individual citizen, who is instilled with appropriate awe as he is shuttled from one *usciere* to another before finally gaining access to the "inner chamber." Finally, the *usciere* serves an important communications function, carrying messages and documents from one office or department to another in a bureaucracy with no institutional links between different departments.

12. Data from the Office of Personnel of the Commune of Palermo.

13. For discussion of the substantial material privileges of public employees, particularly at the higher levels, and of the corporatist policies of public-employee unions, see Chubb (1978: 192-208).

14. The presidency of a major bank is such an important political prize that it is bitterly contested among competing factions within the DC. In some cases, like that of the Banco di Sicilia, the factional struggle is so intense that years may pass before the party succeeds in agreeing upon a candidate; the term of the current president of the Banco di Sicilia expired in 1968, and, as of the end of 1978, his successor had yet to be nominated.

15. The phrase is Pizzorno's (1974: 329).

16. A fascinating chapter in any analysis of the Christian Democratic Party in Sicily is the history of the party's relationship with the mafia. In the immediate postwar period the mafia was allied predominantly with traditional right-wing notables (for the most part large landowners). As DC control over the national government was consolidated, however, *mafiosi* (whose power had always depended

upon a symbiotic relationship with the holders of political power) progressively deployed their impressive vote-gathering capabilities under the banner of Christian Democracy. Until the end of the second world war, the influence of the mafia was confined largely to the latifundial zones of the interior of western Sicily, where the typical *mafioso* served as an intermediary between the absentee owners of the large estates and the peasant workforce, as well as a guarantor of social peace in the countryside. By the mid-1950s, however, it had become clear to the rural elite, landowners and *mafiosi* alike, that the real potential for economic gain no longer lay in the countryside, already witnessing the beginnings of the mass exodus which would drain it of its most vital forces during the next decade, but instead in the large coastal cities, whose tremendous population explosion since the war had opened vast new possibilities for enrichment, particularly in the areas of real-estate speculation and control of urban produce markets. In this process of transferral to the city, the mafia's ties to political power underwent an important transformation — no longer just the traditional exchange of votes for protection, but increasingly a concrete co-involvement in lucrative speculative deals and business affairs linked to public contracts. The extent of such collusion between the mafia and DC-controlled local administrations during the 1960s, reflected in an unending series of scandals accompanying the city's rapid and chaotic expansion, was such as to provoke the formation of a national parliamentary commission of inquiry on the mafia, of which a large portion of the investigation was focussed on the activities of the DC administration of the city of Palermo. For a good general account of the relationship between the mafia and the DC in western Sicily, see Pantaleone (1966). For a detailed discussion of the process of postwar urban expansion in Palermo and the collusion between the city administration and the mafia, see Chubb (1978: 231-70). Extensive documentation of this question can be found in the reports of the Antimafia Commission of the Italian Parliament (1973).

17. The debate which continues to rage over the issue of the reconstruction *risanamento* of the old city is described in detail in Chubb (1978: 270-76). Although funding to initiate the project has been available from the national and regional governments since May 1976, implementation has been indefinitely stalled by fierce political battles over the nature of the reconstruction (luxury vs. low-income) and the firms to which the lucrative public contracts would go.

18. A survey conducted in four low-income neighborhoods of the city in 1975-76 by students of the Faculty of Medecine of the University of Palermo found that stable employment among adult males (ages 15-55) ranged from a low of 24.0% to a high of only 57.5%. There are at least 100,000 persons in the city living in substandard housing, without adequate sanitary facilities and often without heat, sunlight or fresh air; mean population density in the slums of the old city and peripheral shanty-towns is 2.5-3.5 inhabitants per room, with numerous reported cases of ten-fifteen persons crowded into a single-room dwelling. Since the 1968 earthquake, collapses of buildings in the old city have become so commonplace as to scarcely attract any notice. Running water and garbage collection are both sporadic. Given the above conditions, it is not surprising that digestive disorders, infectious diseases like typhus and hepatitis, and respiratory ailments caused by the extreme humidity of the winter months are rampant. In some of the worst neighborhoods of the city, infant mortality rates approximate those of Third World countries (69-134 deaths/1,000 in the first year of life in contrast to a national average of about 30).

19. This argument was made by Alessandro Pizzorno in a private conversation with the author.

REFERENCES

ALLUM, P. (1973). *Politics and Society in Post-War Naples*. Cambridge: University Press.

ANTIMAFIA COMMISSION (1973). *Testo integrale della relazione della commissione parlamentare d'inchiesta sul fenomeno della mafia*, 3 vols. Rome: Cooperativa Scrittori.

BONAZZI, S., BAGNASCO, A. and CASILLO, S. (1972). *Industria e potere in una provincia meridionale*. Turin: L'impresa edizioni.

CACIAGLI, M. et al. (1977). *Democrazia Cristiana e potere nel Mezzogiorno*. Florence: Guaraldi.

CATANZARO, R. (1975). "Potere e politica locale in Italia," *Quaderni di Sociologia*, 24(4): 273-322.

CHUBB, J. (1978). "The Organization of Consensus in a Large Southern Italian City." Unpublished PhD dissertation, Massachusetts Institute of Technology.

COLLIDA, A. (1972). "Aspetti clientelari dell'intervento straordinario nel Mezzogiorno," pp. 182-87, in L. Marelli, ed., *Sviluppo e sottosviluppo nel Mezzogiorno d'Italia dal 1945 agli anni '70*. Naples: Morano Editore.

GRAZIANO, L. (1973). "Patron-Client Relationships in Southern Italy," *European Journal of Political Research*, 1(1): 3-34.

HYTTEN, E. and MARCHIONI, M. (1970). *L'Industrializzazione senza sviluppo*. Milan: Franco Angeli.

L'ORA (1967). 28 September.

L'ORA (1969). 6 May.

L'ORA (1973). 20 November.

PANTALEONE, M. (1966). *The Mafia and Politics*. New York: Coward-McCann.

PIZZORNO, A. (1974). "I ceti medi nei meccanismi del consenso," pp. 315-38, in F. L. Cavazza and S. Graubard, eds., *Il caso italiano*, Vol. 2. Milan: Garzanti.

PODBIELSKI, G. (1974). *Italy: Development and Crisis in the Post-War Economy*. Oxford: Clarendon Press.

ROCHEFORT, R. (1958). "Les bas-fonds de Palerme," *Annales, Economies, Sociétés, Civilisations* (April-June): 349-58.

ROCHEFORT, R. (1961). *Le travail en Sicile*. Paris: Presses Universitaires de France.

SCOTT, J. C. (1969). "Corruption, Machine Politics and Political Change," *American Political Science Review*, 63(4): 1142-58.

SOTTILE, G. (1972). "Ecco come un vigile può essere trasformato in grande elettore," *L'Ora*, 13 November.

TARROW, S. (1967). *Peasant Communism in Southern Italy*. New Haven: Yale University Press.

Naples Under the Left: The Limits of Local Change

Judith Chubb
College of the Holy Cross, USA

The conclusion of the previous chapter, an in-depth examination of the specific patronage mechanisms linking the Christian Democratic Party in Palermo to different social groups in the city, was that it is virtually impossible to change clientelistic systems of power like those which dominate much of southern Italy through political action at the local level. Meaningful change, it was held, can come only through a national commitment to an autonomous process of economic development in the South which could create alternative resources to those currently monopolized by the Christian Democratic Party. The case of Naples, however, appears at first sight to dramatically contradict such an argument. In local elections in June 1975 the Communist Party defeated the incumbent Christian Democrats, who had ruled Naples in a manner virtually identical to that described in the preceding chapter on Palermo, and went on to form, for the first time in Naples' history, a left-wing city government together with the Socialists.

How was the Communist Party able to come to power in Naples, Italy's third largest city (pop. 1,200,000) and traditionally one of the country's major strongholds of machine-style politics, what difference has Communist-led local government made for the city,

This paper is reprinted with the kind permission of the editor of *Comparative Politics*.

and why did the party, particularly in the period 1976-79 face increasing difficulties in maintaining its mass electoral base? These are the questions which this chapter will attempt to answer. In so doing, it will argue that, contrary to appearances, closer examination of the experience of Naples since 1975 actually reinforces the conclusions drawn from the Palermo study. The example of Communist power in Naples provides an ideal case study of the critical linkages between local and national power to which we have pointed in Palermo and of the limits which they impose on change at the local level in a situation, like that of Italy, where the Communists are not yet in a position to impose their own goals and priorities upon the national government. This has been a particularly important issue for the Italian Communists since 1975, when they won control of local government in virtually all the country's major cities, most of which had left-wing majorities for the first time.[1]

Thus, analysis of the experience of the left-wing administration in Naples, though to some extent unique because of the magnitude of the problems confronting the city, can provide important insights into similar dilemmas faced by the Communists in taking over the administrations of other major cities like Rome and Turin.[2] The experience of these cities is part of a more general trend throughout Latin Europe (Italy, France, Spain), with the most recent local elections in each country showing clear evidence of a growing political dualism between national governments controlled by centrist coalitions and major urban centers dominated by the Left; by examining the Neapolitan experience, we may be able to illuminate as well some of the broader issues raised by this phenomenon. Finally, the evolution of the political and social situation in Naples since 1975 provides an illustration of both the resiliency and the limitations of clientelistic forms of political organization under precisely those conditions of severe economic crisis and resource scarcity in which a theory of clientelism focussing on the need for an expanding resource base would lead one to expect instead their rapid disintegration. Thus, not only does Naples constitute a fascinating case study in its own right, but its experience can also yield significant insights into the strengths and weaknesses of two very different models of urban government — on the one hand, attempts to create a left-wing alternative at the local level, on the other, the more traditional model of the urban political machine.

THE PAST — THE REIGN OF THE MACHINE

To understand Naples under the Left, we must first examine briefly the nature of Neapolitan politics before 1975. Throughout the postwar period Naples constituted a major stronghold of right-wing strength in Italy. In the institutional referendum of 1946, 80% of Neapolitans voted for the monarchy (in contrast to a national figure of only 46%), and from 1952 until 1958 the city gave overwhelming support to the Monarchist administrations of the shipping magnate Achille Lauro, whose appeal was based on a combination of populist anti-statism and petty clientelism. Only when Lauro's administration was dissolved in 1958 by prefectural decree, after a long history of scandals and corruption, were the Monarchists displaced as the city's leading party by the Christian Democrats, who have dominated national politics in Italy since 1945. From the early 1960s until 1975, both the local Christian Democratic Party (DC) and the city and provincial administrations were dominated by a powerful "machine" in the hands of the Gava family, local representatives of the *doroteo* faction of the DC.[3] At its peak the Gava machine seemed omnipotent, extending its control into every aspect of social, political and economic life and monopolizing the levers of political and economic power in the city.[4] Like the DC machine in Palermo (see preceding chapter), the Gavas consolidated their power through manipulation of the resources of local government and control over the local labor market, creating a far-reaching network of patronage linking virtually every major social group in the city (with the partial exclusion of the industrial working class) to the party. Under both the Monarchists and the Christian Democrats, unrestrained building speculation ravaged the city, burying its famed panoramas under tons of cement as it created economic fortunes overnight for an emerging class of unscrupulous local entrepeneurs and political fortunes for their accomplices in local government. At the same time, the creation of thousands of patronage jobs in the city and provincial bureaucracies wedded a vast new class of white-collar civil servants to the party machine. The support of the masses of the urban poor (*sottoproletariato*) was insured by the time-honored techniques of the wardheeler (Lauro's distribution of one shoe before the election and one after has become proverbial) and by the increasingly important role of the DC politician as intermediary between the individual citizen and the bureaucratic apparatus of the state which, in a country like Italy, plays such a major role in everyday life.

In case of the Gavas, these traditional levers of power at the local level were reinforced by the family's close ties to national power to create a machine of a scope and power far surpassing that of a Lauro, whose power, even at the peak of his popularity, was confined to the local level. Silvio Gava, the "patriarch," one of the founders of the DC in 1943, has been a member of the party's national directorate since 1944, a Senator since 1948, and a high-ranking member of almost every government from 1949 until 1973; his son, who runs the family's affairs at the local level, was recently named to head the DC's national office for local government affairs. This direct access to centers of national power and thereby to channels of state spending gave the Gavas control over critical sectors of the urban economy, in particular banking and credit, public works, and state-controlled industries. Given the weight of the public sector in the Neapolitan economy (see below), the Gavas' political empire seemed virtually unassailable.

And yet, in June 1975 the Gava machine suffered a stunning defeat, losing control of one of the principal pillars of its power, the municipal and provincial administrations. The Communist Party became the city's first party, winning almost 33% of the vote and, after three months of bitter and inconclusive negotiations with the DC and its former coalition partners, formed a minority administration with the Socialist Party (PSI), later joined by the Republicans (PRI) and Social Democrats (PSDI), in order to save the city from total administrative paralysis. In the parliamentary elections of June 1976, after less than a year in office, the Communists went on to reap an astonishing 41% of the vote in Naples, a figure heretofore reserved for traditional Communist strongholds like Bologna and, to many observers, inconceivable in this city notorious for its steadfast support first of Monarchist and then of Christian Democratic bosses. (See Table 1 for electoral results.)

How can such a rapid and radical shift in the political orientation of a city like Naples be explained? At the most obvious level, one could point to the scandals and misgovernment of the previous DC administrations, to the crisis of local finance in Italy which, combined with the more general economic crisis, has narrowed the margins for the politics of mass patronage upon which the city's rulers had relied for the past 30 years, and to the growing discontent provoked by the impact of the worsening economic crisis on

Table 1
Electoral Results for the City of Naples, 1956-79 (% of vote by party)

	PCI[1]	PSI	Radicals and New Left	DC	Small lay parties (PSDI, PRI, PLI)	Monarchists	MSI-DN
1956 (municipal)	19.2	4.5	—	16.4	5.1	51.8	3.2
1960 (municipal)	23.4	6.0	—	26.2	5.7	35.0	4.1
1962 (municipal)	20.9	8.4	—	27.8	6.4	31.0	5.6
1963 (national)	25.0	11.5	—	30.2	13.9	11.0	8.4
1968 (national)	28.1	10.1[2]	3.0	29.2	8.3	9.2	10.3
1970 (municipal)	26.0	7.4	1.8	34.0	14.3	3.8	12.0
1972 (national)	27.8	5.6	2.1	28.4	9.2		26.3
1975 (municipal)	32.3	6.9	1.5[3]	28.4	12.0		18.5
1976 (national)	40.8	4.8	3.1	29.9	5.8		15.5
1979 (national)	30.7	5.9	8.1	30.5	8.2		16.4
1980 (municipal)	31.7	7.7	1.6[3]	25.3	11.3		22.3

1. Note to party abbreviations: PCI — Partito Comunista Italiano, PSI — Partito Socialista Italiano, DC — Democrazia Cristiana, PSDI — Partito Socialdemocratico Italiano, PRI — Partito Repubblicano Italiano, PLI — Partito Liberale Italiano, MSI-DN — Movimento Sociale Italiano-Destra Nazionale.

2. In the 1968 election the Socialist Party (PSI) and the Social Democratic Party (PSDI) were unified under the name PSU (Partito Socialista Unificato).

3. The Radical Party did not present a list for the municipal elections of 1975 and 1980.

Sources: Bollettino di Statistica (Naples, 1977) and *Corriere della Sera* (6 June 1979; 11 June 1980).

the already fragile economic structure of the city. None of these factors can be entirely disregarded, but their explanatory value is undermined by the example of Palermo, where each of these factors weighs at least as heavily, if not more so, than in Naples, and where the local DC machine actually strengthened its position in the 1975 elections. Why, then, did such an unexpected political upheaval occur in Naples? Why in Naples, contrary to Palermo, was the DC monopoly over the centers of political and economic power no longer sufficient to guarantee the party's electoral success?

THE ECONOMIC STRUCTURE OF THE CITY

Any attempt to understand Neapolitan politics must begin with an examination of the economic structure of the city. A vivid example of "urbanization without industrialization," the economy of Naples, like that of Palermo, is disproportionately weighted toward the tertiary sector, a tertiary sector dominated by two profoundly different forms of economic activity — on the one hand, a massive public sector (including banks, hospitals and a wide range of semi-public agencies, as well as government offices and city services like garbage collection, public transportation, gas and water), and on the other, a myriad of small shopkeepers, street vendors and providers of petty services of every imaginable kind (see Table 2 for comparison of the occupational structure of Naples to that of a major northern Italian city). The industrial sector in Naples is dominated by the construction industry and composed, like commerce and services, primarily of small family firms or artisan shops; in Naples firms employing fewer than ten workers account for 92% of all "industrial" enterprises and 26% of industrial employment (ISTAT, 1972). In the absence of a solid industrial backbone, the outstanding characteristic of the Neapolitan economy is its inability to provide steady employment for a large proportion of the city's population. One-quarter of all unemployment in Italy is concentrated in the region of Campania, of which Naples is the capital. In the city proper, official figures (notoriously low in Italy), place unemployment at about 25%, or circa 120,000-130,000 persons (*Bollettino di Statistica*, 1978: 728-29) while unofficial sources estimate at least half the city's labor force to be either unemployed or underemployed.[5] This vast "marginal" labor force, based on the one hand, as in Palermo, on the traditional *mille mestieri* ("a thousand professions"), who literally invent their trade from one day to the next (as day laborers, street vendors, contrabandeers, etc.), and on the other on a growing army of unemployed young people, is the most characteristic feature of the Neapolitan economy.

Table 2
Occupational Distribution of the Labor Force
by Sector, 1971 (percent)

	Naples	Milan	Italy
Rate of labor force participation	25.8	40.5	34.8
Agriculture	1.8	0.3	17.2
Industry	39.0	47.0	44.3
Construction (as % of industry)	17.9	9.8	24.3
Commerce and services	49.1	47.8	32.0
Public administration[1]	10.0	4.9	6.5

1. The true weight of the public sector is understated by Italian census figures, which include only administrative personnel of various levels of government. All other public employees are recorded under the specific sector in which they work.

Source: ISTAT, *11° Censimento generale della popolazione* (Rome, 1971).

As in the rest of southern Italy, economic development in Naples has been impeded by severe resource constraints and the weakness of entrepreneurial initiative at the local level. As a result, the economy is sustained primarily by external public intervention (the administrative costs of maintaining a vast public bureaucracy, public works projects, special economic development programs financed by the state, public subsidies and credits to stimulate private enterprise, transfer payments in the form of pensions, unemployment compensation, etc.). The weakness of local stimuli for economic development has been compounded by the failure of 25 years of deliberate state intervention aimed at the industrialization of the South. Despite massive public investment in the South between 1950 and 1975 (the last year for which official data are available), even government spokesmen have been compelled to judge the program a failure: the gap between North and South has widened rather than narrowed, industrial employment has grown at rates far below those anticipated, and oveɪall employment in the South has actually decreased.[6]

Thus far, the description of the Neapolitan economy is similar to that of most other southern Italian cities — if anything, because of the city's size and importance, the distortions provoked by "urbanization without industrialization" are even more accentuated in Naples. What makes Naples unique is that, backward as its economy appears when compared with that of a modern industrial city, what limited industrial investment *has* occurred in the South has been concentrated disproportionately in the Neapolitan area. Some 60%-70% of the entire industrial apparatus of the South is located in the region of Campania (the majority within the metropolitan area of Naples); of this industry, approximately 70% is accounted for by public enterprise, primarily in the sectors of metalworking and steel (Geremicca, 1977: 106). To a certain extent this reflects the weight of the Gavas at the national level (for several years the elder Gava was Minister of Industry), illustrating another face of the machine, its capacity through its connections to national power to stimulate development — but only insofar as such development, and the jobs resulting from it, can be kept under control of the dominant party. As a result, in comparison to other southern cities, Naples can boast a substantial industrial base, dominated by huge publicly-sustained firms like the Italsider steelworks (8,000 workers) and the Alfa Sud automobile factory (15,000 workers). Although they remain isolated islands in the vast sea of artisan workshops and the seemingly endless waves of the unemployed, these large, highly unionized complexes (particularly Italsider) have provided Naples with a compact and combative working-class nucleus, a focal point for left-wing political organization which is missing in a more purely tertiary city like Palermo. Because of this organized working-class base, the PCI has throughout the postwar period maintained a stronger grassroots organization in Naples than in other southern cities. Although before 1975, the DC and the Right dominated all local administrations, the PCI vote has since 1960 approximated the national average (23%-28%);[7] in addition, because of the continuing strength of the Right in Naples, the gap between the PCI and the DC has been narrower than in other southern cities.

THE TURN TO THE LEFT

Although, as we have seen, the PCI already had a substantial mass base in Naples even before 1975, the gain of 6.3% over the previous administrative elections and of 4.5% over the parliamentary elections of 1972 was an unprecedented advance, putting the party at almost one-third of the vote in the local elections and a year later at almost 41%, an increase of 13 percentage points in only four years.[8] The gains of the PCI in Naples must, of course, be seen within the context of the broader swing to the Left which swept Italy in 1975. To a certain extent, the 1975 and 1976 votes in Naples reflected the broader national trend, itself the result of two converging factors: (1) a shift to the Left of a significant part of the Italian bourgeoisie (in particular professionals and intellectuals) and (2) an increasing bipolarization of Italian politics, as a large proportion of the vote previously going to the minor parties of the Right and Left was absorbed into the two major mass parties, the DC and the PCI.[9] This trend was particularly noticeable with regard to the Left in Naples, where the Socialists, reduced to less than 5% of the vote in 1976, have been completely eclipsed by the Communists. The conformity of the Neapolitan vote to the general outlines of the national results was welcomed by many observers as evidence that, 100 years after Italian unification, the political unity of North and South had finally been achieved.

However, while transformations in the social and political climate at the national level clearly played a part in the Neapolitan vote, a full understanding of the causes of the PCI victory requires a closer analysis of the local situation after 1970. Although, already by 1970, there were growing signs of division and discontent within the local Christian Democratic organization, there was little reason to believe that the DC (with 34% of the vote in the 1970 administrative elections) would not easily retain the relative majority in 1975. Observers on both sides of the political fence agree that the "moment of truth" arrived in August-September 1973, when Naples was struck by a sudden outbreak of cholera and, for a few agonizing weeks, the threat of a major epidemic loomed over the city. The crisis situation created by the cholera outbreak, in its exposure of the shocking degradation of the city's sanitary structures (for example, Naples' sewer system is still that of 1888, even though the city's inhabited area has doubled just since the second world war), laid brutally bare the consequences of 20 years of clientelistic power. Between the 1950s and the beginning of the 1970s the already precarious sanitary situation of the city was further exacerbated by wave after wave of uncontrolled speculation, with entire neighborhoods the size of small cities springing up on the periphery without the most basic urban infrastructures. At the same time the slums of the *centro storico* (the old city), already infamous 100 years ago for their crumbling housing, extreme overcrowding and deplorable conditions of health and hygiene, were abandoned to ever more rapid decay. Even before the cholera outbreak, Naples registered levels of infant mortality and infectious diseases rivalling those of Third World cities.[10] From this perspective, what was surprising about the cholera outbreak was not its occurrence, but rather its failure to develop into a full-blown epidemic.

Above all, the crisis exposed the total incapacity of the incumbent DC administration. In the face of an emergency situation, the "establishment" was paralyzed. Into the void stepped the PCI, rising to the occasion with an impressive demonstration of organizational capacity and administrative efficiency. As the total disorganization of the authorities became evident, the party mobilized both the Provincial Federation and the neighborhood sections to maintain calm among a panicked population, set up innoculation centers, and organize special precautionary hygienic measures. Throughout the PCI projected the image of a "party of government," a party capable of honest and efficient administration in contrast to the incompetence and immobility of the established power structure. As the Secretary of the PCI Federation at that time put it, "In those critical days we *were* the government of the city. Even the Prefect was calling the Federation to ask what to do" (Geremicca interview, 1978).

In terms of the local situation 1973 was clearly a turning point, even if the magnitude of the changes in public opinion which had occurred was not revealed until June 1975. The key social groups behind the electoral shift of 1975 in Naples were, on the one hand, the white-collar and professional middle classes and, on the other, the urban poor.[11] A warning of the changing attitudes of the bourgeoisie, always a moderate and highly traditional force in Italian politics, particularly in the South, came in the 1974 referendum on divorce. The DC, which had campaigned vigorously in favor of repeal of the existing legislation, was shocked by the outcome — 59% of Italians in favor of divorce and over 60% in Naples which, because of its reputation as a stronghold of the

Right, had been looked to by the anti-divorce forces for especially strong support. These results demonstrated the increasing autonomy of the traditional Catholic electorate, which had heretofore constituted one of the principal pillars of DC power. Among a significant segment of the Italian middle classes, this new-found autonomy was fed by a growing disgust with DC corruption and inefficiency and, correspondingly, a growing openness to the possibility of a PCI alternative. As for the Neapolitan bourgeoisie, these tendencies had been reinforced by the vivid example of the cholera crisis, in terms both of the demonstrated incapacity of the DC administration to protect them from the threat of epidemic and of the contrasting display of organization and efficiency on the part of the PCI. So long as the degradation of the urban fabric had been perceived as primarily a matter of the center-city slums, the political outlook of the middle classes had been little affected by scandals over speculation, substandard housing, and inadequate water and sewerage facilities. When such conditions threatened to set off a city-wide epidemic, however, the fruits of misgovernment became much more immediate and the prospect of an alternative more attractive.

The case of the urban poor, the second major pillar of the PCI victory, provides a fascinating example of the potential for crisis within a deeply-rooted system of clientelistic power. A critical factor for the understanding of Neapolitan politics after 1970 is the changing relationship between the working class and the *sottoproletariato*. Traditionally, Naples' vast "marginal" labor force had constituted a reservoir of votes for demagogic right-wing movements and unscrupulous machine bosses. However, in the wake of the intense workers' struggles of Italy's "Hot Autumn" of 1969 (struggles bitterly fought by Naples' working-class nucleus as well), a part of the *sottoproletariato* began to become politicized. An explanation for such politicization must be sought in the neighborhood structure of the city. Within the low-income neighborhoods of Naples, whether the slums of the old city or the new public-housing projects of the periphery, it is often difficult to make a clear distinction between the stable industrial working class and the "marginal" labor force; within the same neighborhood and often within the same family, one finds the steel or automobile worker side by side with the street vendor or unemployed day laborer. After 1969 the effect of contagion, which had traditionally been one of hegemony of the attitudes of the *sottoproletariato* upon the working class, began to work in the opposite direction; the lesson of organization learned from the successful workers' struggles began to make inroads upon the traditional cynicism and individualism of the Neapolitan slum. These changes were hastened by the fact that, with the onset of the economic crisis, increasing numbers of the unemployed were no longer the traditional *mille mestieri*, but rather ex-factory workers or youth with high-school or even college diplomas, who brought with them a very different attitude toward and experience of collective action.

Here too, however, the real turning point came in 1973 in the wake of the cholera outbreak. The economic damage inflicted by the crisis was immense and struck directly at the heart of the city's "marginal" economy. Since, according to official reports, the virus had been brought into the city by contaminated shellfish, one of the few initiatives taken by the authorities was a series of dramatic police actions against the fishermen and the hundreds of street vendors and owners of small bars and restaurants who could not demonstrate compliance with official standards of hygiene. The effect was to drastically reduce the margins of subsistence for thousands of the Neapolitan poor. The immediate reaction was desperate, but doomed, mass resistance to the police actions. Subsequently, however, the unemployed and the underemployed, under the leadership of student groups of the "extraparliamentary Left," began to organize a new movement, the *disoccupati organizzati* (the organized unemployed), which within a few years would revolutionize the face of Neapolitan politics.[12]

Heretofore the very heart of politics in Naples had been the ability of the dominant party to exert an almost iron-clad control over the local labor market. In a situation of mass unemployment, the need for a political patron in order to obtain a job had provided a large and reliable mass base for the DC and its centrist allies (in southern Italy the small lay parties — PSDI, PRI, PLI — are generally deeply involved in clientelistic politics at the local level). The creation of an organized movement of the unemployed challenged the very foundations of this clientelistic structure of power in Naples. Boasting 10,000-15,000 active members at its peak (1975-1976), the movement was based upon a radically different conception of the *posto di lavoro* (job or position), no longer regarded as an individual favor to be conceded by the powerful but rather as a fundamental right to be conquered through collective struggle. The unemployed imposed their own "lists of struggle" upon the state employment office, insisting that those who actively participated in the protest demonstrations which soon became a daily and increasingly violent fact of life in Naples should have first priority when jobs became available. This entrance of collective organization into a sector of society previously characterized above all by its lack of any poles of social or political aggregation marked a first critical breach in the old structure of power.

THE LEFT IN POWER

Thus, on the crest of two different but converging movements, the shift to the left of important sectors of the bourgeoisie and the birth of new forms of mass struggle among the urban poor, two important pillars of DC power in Naples were seriously weakened, and the PCI became the city's first party, forming a minority administration with the Socialists. The record of left-wing power in Naples is very mixed. Naples is a city with problems of phenomenal proportions. Apart from its chronic economic problems, the city boasts the highest population and traffic density, the largest number of rats, the highest concentration of substandard dwellings, the highest levels of atmospheric and noise pollution, and the highest levels of infant mortality and infectious diseases of all Italian cities (Caprara, 1975: 124). In addition, the new administration inherited the fruits of 30 years of misgovernment and corruption, exemplified by the ravages of unrestrained speculation and the decay of the old city.

The catastrophic problems facing the city were compounded by yet another catastrophe — the state of local finances. The clientelistic politics of the "old regime," together with the inability of local governments in Italy to levy their own taxes, had brought the city to the verge of bankruptcy. The first year of the new administration, until passage of national legislation to reform local finances, was marked by continual confrontation with the state simply to obtain funds to meet monthly payrolls. As a result, one of the first priorities of the new administration was to put local finances in order. Although this necessarily meant extreme austerity during the first few years, this goal has been achieved. From a situation of total financial chaos, with Naples the most indebted city in Italy, unable to pay either its creditors or its employees, not only has the budget been balanced, but for the 1980 fiscal year provides for 12% of expenditure in the form of new capital investment, as opposed to only 1% under the previous center-left administrations.

Upon moving into the city offices, the would-be reformers found a bureaucratic machine swelled by successive waves of patronage hiring (over 34,000 employees), a bureaucracy built up over a period of 30 years not for the purpose of honest and efficient administration, but rather as an electoral machine for party bosses, first Monarchist and then Christian Democratic. A large percentage of the city employees were not only unqualified for the task of administering the city, but strongly organized as well in defense of corporatist privilege (in addition to the three national labor confederations, eight distinct "autonomous" unions are present among city employees, each dedicated to preserving and extending the privileges of its narrow constituency).

Faced with such a situation, the first task of the PCI and its allies was an attempt to put some order into the administrative chaos around them, to inaugurate a new style of rigor and morality in the public sphere. Among the first initiatives were a clampdown on all nonessential costs (e.g., the widespread private use of city cars and telephones), distribution of former patronage plums like commercial and construction licenses with strict impartiality, and, of particular symbolic value after 20 years of public collusion with speculation, the demolition of several edifices built in violation of the city plan. An attempt to enforce new standards of work upon the city's civil servants, however, illustrates the difficulties against which the initial moralizing and rationalizing impulse of the new administration all too frequently ran aground. Contrary to the practice of previous administrations, which had looked the other way not only at employee lateness but at outright absence as well, the new junta immediately announced a crackdown on lateness and began deducting a half hour's pay from the check of every late employee. The guilty employees, rather than accept the payroll deduction, retaliated by taking the *entire* day off as sick leave, for which they received full pay. The attempt to enforce punctuality soon provoked absentee rates of up to 35%, and the junta was forced to back down. Although seemingly trivial, this case symbolizes the difficulty even of insuring more rational and efficient administration with a bureaucratic structure built on patronage and privilege, let alone attempting to inaugurate any more radical policy changes.

In terms of substantive policy issues, unemployment has clearly been the most critical problem facing the administration, even though, in a highly centralized political system like that of Italy, the formal powers of local government in this sphere are quite limited. In a situation like that of Naples, this problem lies at the very center of political attention and mobilization, as well as providing an accurate mirror of the changing relationship between the PCI and mass protest movements like the "organized unemployed" as the party moves from a role of opposition to a role of government. Although the PCI itself never directly organized the unemployed, the movement (like the housing struggles of the early 1970s), breaking as it did with the traditional bond between the DC/Right and the urban poor, clearly played a fundamental role in the Communist advances of 1975 and 1976. Among the unemployed the formation of the left-wing administration was greeted with intense joy and expectation, reflected in the oft-repeated slogan of those first enthusiastic days, "Finally we will go to work."

Once the new administration took office, however, the relationship between the party and the unemployed became strained rather quickly. This is because, in the absence of any concrete prospects for the creation of new industrial jobs, the "organized unemployed" set as their immediate goal a position, however humble, in the public administration. Given the weakness of the private sector in the South, economic demands are focussed directly on the organs of the state, symbolized at the local level by the City Hall. Thus, from leadership of the struggles of the unemployed when in the opposition, the PCI, as the dominant force in the new administration, suddenly found itself manning the other side of the barricades.

In this city where the promise of a patronage job in the public sector has constituted the very essence of politics for decades, one point PCI leaders emphasize with pride is that they have eliminated hiring by political recommendation. Although to a certain extent this is true, the reality of the situation is more complex. With local finance in shambles and the bureaucracy already overinflated, the number of jobs which the city government could provide was derisory in relation to the magnitude of the unemployment problem; on the other hand, the desperation of the unemployed, with nowhere else to turn, expressed itself in increasingly vocal and at times violent demonstrations against the administration and the PCI.[13] With regard to those jobs which *are* available, the PCI and the unemployed have clashed over the criteria by which they should be assigned. While the "organized unemployed" insist that jobs be assigned on the basis of their own "lists of struggle," the PCI and the unions counter that hiring must take place strictly in accordance with the lists of the state employment office. Our struggle, insist the Communists, must not be, as in the past, to procure a position for the individual, but rather to promote new investment so as to create jobs for all the unemployed. Thus the PCI denounced the position of the "organized unemployed" as narrowly corporatist, as acceptance of a "welfare logic" in contrast to a broader strategy of struggle to expand the productive base of the local economy. While such a position clearly has its merits, it does little to resolve the immediate problem of those who are unemployed *today*. As a result, representatives of the DC as well as of the neo-Fascist Right have stepped into the widening gap between the PCI and the "organized unemployed," organizing competing lists of the unemployed — a kind of mass clientelism as opposed to the individual clientelism of the past — which they have used to maintain social tensions at a fever pitch and to channel the discontent of the unemployed against the left-wing administration.

In the face of this situation, and in the absence of any serious initiative on the part of the regional and national governments with regard to the employment problem, the local administration has, particularly in the last year, increasingly come to terms with the necessity, in the short term at least, of using the city government as an instrument of "assistance" to absorb unemployment. Thus, since 1979 over 6,000 young people have been hired by the city government (under the aegis of national legislation for youth employment)[14] for such tasks as garbage collection, park maintenance, restoration of monuments, various programs of assistance for children and the elderly, or else have been admitted into "courses of professional formation" whose purpose, in the absence of eventual occupational outlets, has more to do with welfare than with job training. This example illustrates the extent to which, in a context like that of Naples, the Left as well has found itself constrained, in order to maintain consensus, to use local government institutions for what its opponents have not hesitated to define as clientelistic ends. Another good example of the ways in which the structural weaknesses of the local economy have limited the potential reforming instincts of the left-wing administration concerns the city's thriving black market in contraband cigarettes.

An estimated 50,000 Neapolitans make a living from contraband, with their boats docked openly along the waterfront, in full view of the customs police. The authorities watch and do nothing, not because they condone contraband, but because they know only too well that any attempt to move against it would deprive tens of thousands of families of their only means of subsistence. Given the overwhelming nature of the problems facing Naples, and the limited power and resources available to local government to deal with them, the new administration came increasingly to be accused of immobilism; despite the generally unquestioned honesty and dedication of the Communist administrators, the PCI's attempt to inaugurate a "new way of governing" in Naples had by 1978-79 produced few concrete results.

THE TIDE TURNS BACK

The record of the local administrations under its control has become increasingly critical to the PCI in the last few years. Beginning with the results of the partial administrative elections of May 1977, in which the Communists suffered significant losses in several important southern centers, the "wind from the South" seemed once again to have changed direction. The 1977 results, already cause for concern among PCI leaders, were followed a year later by still further setbacks for the Communists and substantial gains for the DC in a second round of administrative elections, again concentrated disproportionately in the South.[15] The progressive erosion of the PCI's electoral base in the South was further underlined by the results of a June 1978 national referendum for the repeal of two laws — one a measure to provide public financing for political parties, the other the so-called *Legge Reale*, a law-and-order bill originally pushed through by the DC but, in the wake of Italy's rising terrorist wave, supported by the Communist and Socialist parties as well. Repeal of the two laws was opposed by all the major parties (including the PCI, which supported the governing coalition from 1976 to 1979); only the neo-Fascist MSI, the tiny Radical Party (which had initiated the referendum), and the groups of the extraparliamentary Left were in favor of repeal. The parties opposing repeal thus represented over 90% of the Italian electorate (on the basis of parliamentary seats), as well as all the power and prestige of the Italian political establishment.

Yet, despite a heavy-handed campaign dominated by the PCI, which accused opponents of the laws of favoring terrorism on the one hand and of attempting to undermine Italian democracy on the other, the outcome was the following:

	Public financing	Legge Reale
Against repeal	56.3%	76.7%
In favor of repeal	43.7%	23.3%

Although neither of the laws was repealed, turnout was very low by Italian standards (81.4%), and the final result, even on the *Legge Reale*, was closer than anyone, including the sponsors of the referendum, had expected. In Naples, where the PCI alone had won 40.8% of the vote in 1976, throughout the South, and in major northern cities like Rome, Milan and Turin, a majority actually voted to repeal the law on public financing of parties; the gravity of such results is reinforced by the figures on turnout, which fall sharply as one moves from North to South (see Table 3). The outcome of the referendum was unmistakably a slap in the face for Italy's major parties, above all the PCI, which had assumed the burden of the electoral campaign. The outcome on the law for party financing was particularly alarming, both because of its symbolic value as an indicator of public attitudes toward the parties and

Table 3
Results of the June 1978 Referendum (percent)

	Public Financing		Legge Reale		Turnout	
	In favor of repeal	Against repeal	In favor of repeal	Against repeal		
Italy	43.7	56.3	23.3	76.7	81.4	
North	39.9	60.1	20.2	79.8	87.3	
Center	41.0	59.0	20.9	79.1	85.9	
South	52.7	47.3	30.7	69.3	70.2	
Naples	59.7	40.3	30.1	69.9	(Campania,	69.8)
Palermo	64.0	36.0	36.0	64.0	(Sicily,	67.8)
Rome	54.9	45.1	26.9	73.1	(Lazio,	83.3)
Turin	51.2	48.8	26.5	73.5	(Piedmont,	84.3)

Source: Corriere della Sera (13, 14 June 1978).

because of the magnitude of the gap which it revealed between the leaders of Italy's major parties and their mass base.[16]

The June 1979 Elections

The danger signals for the PCI implicit in the 1977-78 returns were amply confirmed by the results of the June 1979 parliamentary elections. These elections, held two years in advance of the normal date, were precipitated by Communist withdrawal of support for the Andreotti government in January 1979. When all attempts to resolve the ensuing governmental crisis failed, early elections were called to break the impasse. The PCI hoped through these elections to reinforce its claim to full governmental participation, while the DC appealed to the electorate to return a clear centrist majority, eliminating the need to deal with the Communists by returning them to a role of permanent opposition. The results of the elections fulfilled neither of these hopes, but rather reconfirmed the political stalemate which has paralyzed successive Italian governments throughout the 1970s. Contrary to most predictions, the DC failed to increase its share of the vote beyond the 38% reached in the 1972 and 1976 elections. While the small center parties (PSDI and PLI) did make gains (reversing the trend toward bipolarization of the Italian electorate which had characterized the 1976 elections), these

Table 4
National Electoral Results (Camera dei Deputati),
1972-79 (percent)

	1972	1976	1979 (regional elections)	1980
New Left	2.9	1.5	2.2	2.1
Radicals	—	1.1	3.4	—
PCI	27.2	34.4	30.4	31.5
PSI	9.6	9.7	9.8	12.7
PSDI	5.2	3.4	3.8	5.0
PRI	2.9	3.1	3.0	3.0
DC	38.8	38.8	38.3	36.8
PLI	3.9	1.3	1.9	2.7
MSI-DN	8.7	6.1	5.3	5.9
Abstention Rate	6.8	6.6	10.1	12.3

were insufficient to provide a clear centrist majority. Substantial voting shifts took place instead on the Left, with the loss by the PCI of about 4% of its vote with respect to 1976 and the meteoric rise of the Radical Party, which tripled its 1976 vote (see Table 4).

While most commentary, particularly on this side of the Atlantic, focussed on the PCI losses, the first setback for the party in national elections in the postwar period, these losses must be seen in the proper perspective. First, although the PCI did lose a significant portion of its extraordinary 1976 gains, its share of the vote still remains higher than in 1972; despite its losses, the party continues to represent over 30% of the electorate and thus remains a critical force to be dealt with in the formation of any future government. Second, the balance between the forces of the Left and the Center-Right at the national level has remained virtually unaltered by these elections. What changes took place were primarily *within* the Left — gains by the Radicals (a relatively new political force focussing primarily on civil libertarian issues), and to a lesser extent the Socialists and the New Left, at the expense of the Communists. Analyses of PCI losses in the North, for example, show that the party retained most of the middle-class votes conquered in 1976, its losses coming instead primarily among young voters and, in large industrial cities, among the party's traditional working-class base — i.e., among those sectors of the electorate critical of PCI policies from the *left*. The PCI's failure to attract young voters in this election is particularly serious since, in 1976, about half of the party's gains came from new young voters (18 to 21 year olds).

A final important feature of the 1979 elections was the abstention rate of over 10%, a heretofore unheard of figure in a country where voting has always been considered virtually obligatory. This figure underlined the pervasive climate of apathy and disillusionment among many Italian voters, reconfirming the earlier signals of discontent expressed in the referenda of June 1978.

Perhaps the most striking aspect of these elections, however, was the disintegration of the political unity of North and South which had been hailed as one of the most important outcomes of the 1976 elections. In 1979 what we see instead are two very different political processes taking place in the North and the South. In the North both the PCI and the DC suffered substantial losses, particularly in large cities, with the PCI losing young voters and many workers either to the Radicals or through abstention, while the DC lost a significant portion of its middle-class electorate to the small lay parties of the center. If we focus instead on the South, the image which emerges from the electoral data is quite a different one. Abstention rates rise dramatically as one moves from North to South, PCI losses are substantially higher than in the North, and the DC increases its share of the vote almost everywhere (while the DC lost votes in every region of the North, it gained in seven out of nine southern regions). Communist losses in the South are not fully compensated for by the gains of other leftist parties; unlike the North, there is evidence of a direct transfer of votes from the PCI to the DC and the small lay parties.

In Naples the collapse of the PCI between 1976 and 1979 is extraordinary (10 percentage points), the largest loss for the party in any major Italian city, even though the Communists remain, by a hair, the city's leading party (see Table 1). Although, as elsewhere, the PCI lost substantially both to other left-wing parties and through abstention, there remains a significant percentage of the Communist losses which can be accounted for only by a shift of left-wing votes to the DC, the small lay parties, and the Right. Analyses of the Neapolitan vote by the party's own spokesmen emphasize the widespread disillusionment with the left-wing administration, above all among youth and the urban poor, both pillars of the Communists' 1975 and 1976 victories (Bassolino, 1979: 12-13). It is interesting to note that in Naples, like many northern cities, PCI losses were heavier in the slums of the old city and in the low-income neighborhoods of the periphery than among middle-class voters won over to the party in 1975 and 1976, with some of the most serious losses coming precisely in the party's traditional strongholds, like certain public-housing projects where the party has long reaped over 40% of the vote.[17] Although these results are for national parliamentary elections, they clearly reflected the prevailing mood of Neapolitan politics as well. Consequently, they were interpreted by both the PCI and its adversaries as sounding a clear and present danger for the future of left-wing rule in Naples, to be decided in administrative elections in June 1980.

WHAT WENT WRONG?
THE LIMITS OF LEFT-WING RULE IN NAPLES

How can we explain such a massive vote of no-confidence on the part of Neapolitan voters? What had happened since 1975-76 when over 40% of the electorate had placed its hopes for change in the Communist Party? The electoral results of 1977-79, combined with a renewed flare-up of social tensions in Naples, belie a growing disillusionment with the PCI among those social groups — the middle classes and the *sottoproletariato* — whose support was pivotal for the party's earlier victories, as well as among growing sectors of its traditional electorate. In many cases the support for the Communists in 1975-76 from groups outside the party's traditional working-class base had been more a vote of protest against the "old regime" than an expression of a stable alliance with the PCI. Particularly in the case of the "organized unemployed," the PCI had supported the movement for electoral purposes, but without fully integrating these new voters into the party's organizational structure. It could also be plausibly argued that many new PCI voters, especially among the urban poor (and probably including some grassroots party activists as well), saw a vote for the Communists in terms less of a coherent program of social change than of a new clientelism of the Left, changing the beneficiaries but not the basic style of local government. Less ideological and less organizationally molded, the allegiance of these new Communist voters (among the middle classes as well as the urban poor) was thus more contingent on concrete results than was that of long-time party militants and, as a result, potentially more subject to fluctuation. The Communist electoral successes in Naples in 1975 and 1976 provoked a tremendous wave of popular enthusiasm and almost mythical expectations. Four years later it was not the desire for change which had faded, but rather its credibility.

Why was the PCI unable to deliver on the promises of change which had brought it within the "area of power" at both the local and national level? To understand the situation in which the PCI found itself from 1976 on, we must first examine the national political context. From 1973 on, the PCI's national strategy was based on the formula of the "historic compromise" — collaboration among the country's three mass parties, the Communists, the Socialists and the Christian Democrats. In line with this strategy the PCI consistently rejected the idea of a left-wing alternative, insisting instead on a government of national unity including all the major political forces. From the summer of 1976 until January 1979 the PCI participated in the government majority (first through abstention and then through direct support), but without sharing executive responsibility. The Communists were caught in the dilemma of responsibility without control — while participating publicly in the formation of government policies, the PCI, excluded from ministerial responsibility, had no power over their implementation. In the eyes of the masses the Communist Party had become a full participant in government, yet many, including a growing number of longtime party militants, increasingly came to feel that nothing had changed but the political formulas. The failure of Communist participation in government to produce any immediate concrete results thus reinforced the attitude, particularly pervasive in the South, that "all the parties are the same — they make fine promises but nothing ever changes."

In Naples as in Rome, Communist strategy was, until the beginning of 1979, determined by the goal of the "historic compromise." Although the Communists agreed to form a minority left-wing administration after the failure of months of fruitless negotiations with the DC, their goal remained that of an eventual re-entry of the DC into the majority. (An agreement to this end was finally reached in June 1978, where the DC would support the majority but without participation in the junta, essentially the reverse of the national situation.)[18] The justification for such a policy, at both the local and the national level, was (1) that the problems facing the city (or the country) are so critical that they can be resolved only through a unified effort of all the major political forces and (2) that to exclude the DC would allow it to avoid its responsibility for the current state of affairs and to engage in demagogical opposition. In both cases this strategy meant endless negotiations and extreme caution on the part of the PCI to prevent any actions which might threaten the goal of collaboration. Collaboration with the DC became the Communists' top priority, to which the demands for change coming from below were subordinated; as a result, party activity became increasingly dominated by top-level inter-party negotiations. This policy provoked growing friction between the PCI leadership and the party's mass base, many of whom felt that their vote for the Communists in 1975-76 had been a call for a political alternative, not for compromise with the old ruling parties.

The DC in Naples took advantage of this situation to play the game on both sides. While proclaiming its availability for a "programmatic accord" with the PCI, the DC engaged the Communists in lengthy and exasperating negotiations, at the same time conducting an obstructionist policy with regard to the concrete activities of the left-wing administration. Having, from the unaccustomed perspective of opposition, "rediscovered its ties with the masses," the DC (or, more accurately, its conservative wing — the Gavas) organized groups of the unemployed to protest against the administration's failure to provide jobs, supported corporatist unions in extravagant demands on the already bankrupt city treasury, and promoted strikes by essential city services in an attempt to discredit the administration. The PCI thus found itself caught between the increasing mobilization of social tensions and corporatist pressures by its opponents and its own commitment to seek unity with these same opponents. As a result, the administration found it increasingly difficult even to insure normal administration, while initiatives for change were to a large extent blocked by the search for compromise with the DC. Once again, one of the consequences was a widening gap between the PCI and those sectors of the population which had brought it to power.

The relationship between the party apparatus and its mass base is a critical issue for a party like the PCI when — with its history, organizational structure, and *raison d'être*, as it were, all those of an "anti-system" opposition party — it suddenly finds itself called upon to assume governmental responsibility within a capitalist state. The PCI defines itself as a "party of government and of struggle," but the two roles are not easy to reconcile, either in the party's activities or in the minds of its supporters and activists. A serious problem where, as in Naples, the PCI directly participates in power has been the identification of the party with the institutions which it administers, greatly limiting its capacity to mobilize the masses against these institutions and transforming the role of the party apparatus into a passive support structure, organizing grassroots consensus for the left-wing administration. This situation was aggravated in those cases, like Naples, where the party's sudden electoral success was out of proportion to its organizational strength. On the one hand, this meant that the party faced a serious shortage of qualified administrators to fill the top positions in local government; on the other hand, as a result, the best cadres were funneled into the administration, leaving little time, energy or talent left to attend to purely party concerns. In a sense, the party was absorbed into the administration.

As might have been expected, the "party of struggle" became increasingly difficult to realize when it became a question of organizing protest against the PCI-dominated administration. Motivated by fear of creating additional troubles for the administration in a difficult moment or of placing obstacles in the path of compromise with the DC, PCI organizers in many cases either abandoned mobilization of the masses altogether or, at the very least, attempted to contain protest within limits not threatening to the city's delicate political equilibrium. The party's caution in this sphere provoked growing frustration among grassroots activists, as well as a move by other political forces to fill the void left by the PCI's organizational absence. This trend has been most obvious in the case of the "organized unemployed," who, as we have seen, constituted a major source of support for the new administration in its early days. Since early 1977, however, the movement has become increasingly fragmented and anti-Communist, as the weakening of the PCI's organizational hegemony has opened the door to an escalation of protest against City Hall by competing groups of the unemployed under the leadership not only of extremist groups to the left of the PCI, but of neo-Fascists and displaced DC notables as well.

A related but distinct problem is the issue of grassroots participation in local government. The PCI's promise of a "new way of governing" included not only a commitment to honest and efficient administration, but also the inauguration of a new relationship between governmental institutions and their constituents, one based on direct citizen involvement in decision-making. Translated into a far-reaching program of decentralization of the functions of city government to neighborhood councils, this idea was first introduced by Communist administrators in Bologna and has since become a keystone of PCI urban policy. Such a "democratization" of local government was seen as especially important for the South, where the state has long been perceived by the populace as an alien entity, foreign to its needs and aspirations. The PCI saw its participation in power as a break in this tradition — the beginning of a new kind of organization of the endemic protest of the southern masses, no longer to be directed *against* the state as such, but aimed instead at a *transformation* of the state. Attempts at implementing decentralization, however, ran up against serious political resistance, with direct election of neighborhood councils, passage from purely consultative to deliberative powers, and effective decentralization of municipal services scheduled to take place only in 1980. Consequently, the left-wing administration in Naples found itself caught in the traditional pattern — i.e., delegation of responsibility by the citizenry to the PCI and the junta and continued perception of City Hall not as an instrument of the people's will, open to the participation of all, but rather as the seat of *power*, where one goes only to petition or to protest. A leading PCI spokesman and administrator depicted the party's dilemma in the following terms:

> At the institutional level we have overemphasized the element of "good government" and "clean hands," of efficiency based on the rigor and spirit of sacrifice of our administrators (even if this is decisive in the South), without giving top priority to the question of participation and popular control . . . This has generated a new form of delegation of responsibility and passive expectation on the part of the citizenry vis-à-vis those local institutions where our presence is determining . . . (Geremicca, 1977: 142-43). The city government is a sort of island under seige, at the center of all the social and economic tensions of the city, but without the capacity to give the responses which the people expect. In this way are created attitudes of extreme trust, which are then followed by extreme disillusionment (cited in Giustolisi, 1977: 24).

If the PCI does not succeed in building a new kind of relationship between the masses and the state, he goes on, "the traditional rebelliousness of the South may re-emerge, but this time directed against the Left" (Geremicca interview, 1978).

A RETURN TO CLIENTELISM?

The difficulties encountered by the PCI in its attempt to initiate social change through control of local government underline some more general considerations about the limits of local power in a country like Italy, as well as reinforcing the conclusions of the previous chapter with regard to strengths of clientelism in a socioeconomic context like that of the South. Underlying all the myriad and pressing demands bombarding Naples' Communist administrators is one fundamental and overriding problem — the economic structure of the city. The weakness of the local economy, which makes the city's very survival revolve around the state, has been compounded by the institutional limits of local power and by the crisis of local finance. These are basic structural problems which *political* power at the local level, regardless of the party which controls it, is simply not in a position to resolve. At the heart of this issue is the interpenetration of political and economic power in Italy and the ways in which the Christian Democratic Party, in its 30 years of political domination, has monopolized key sectors of the economy and shaped them into solid pillars of its own hegemony. In the South, where the economy depends overwhelmingly on the public sector, this aspect of DC power has been — and remains — of central importance. As the Communist mayor of Naples, Maurizio Valenzi, put it:

> It must be made clear that, just because the Left controls local government, this does not mean that it "holds power" in Naples. The left-wing parties participate in the city and provincial administration, it is true, but the decisive aspect of power — i.e., the levers of economic power, still remain in the hands of the DC (Valenzi, 1978: 141).

In Naples all major centers of *economic* power — the Ministry of State-Controlled Industry (which controls 75% of Neapolitan industry), the Bank of Naples and other credit institutions, ISVEIMER (the regional agency for publicly subsidized credit), the Cassa per il Mezzogiorno (the state economic development agency), the Port Authority, the Consortium for Industrial Development, the Chamber of Commerce, and the Union of Industrialists — as well as the regional government of Campania, continue to be controlled by the DC.[19] The combination of continued DC domination of the state apparatus and the DC monopoly of local economic power has made it virtually impossible for the PCI to transform the fundamental structural constraints of the Neapolitan situation. Without a serious *national* commitment to economic development in the South, a commitment which Communist participation in the national government from 1976 to 1979 proved incapable of producing, left-wing control of local government in Naples has been able to do little to affect the most critical problems facing the city (unemployment, housing, etc.); the most it can do is to attempt to use local institutions as levers of pressure to extract resources from the state and the regional government. Under these circumstances, the left-wing administration has had little alternative, as we have seen, but to fall back on normal administration — undoubtedly more honest and somewhat more efficient than that of its predecessors, but normal administration nonetheless (and even that rendered precarious at times by the colossal problems facing the city, the inexperience of many Communist administrators, and the continued obstructionism of certain sectors of the DC). In the meantime, the social and economic conditions of the city push it ever closer to the edge of the abyss.

The growing gap between the needs of the population and the resources available to local government to deal with them risks, as recent elections have shown, provoking a dangerous schism between the citizen and the state, a schism which recent events in the South indicate could well be exploited by subversive right-wing movements. The electoral results of 1977-79 can be interpreted as signalling not only a growing protest against the state, however, but also indications of a resurgence of clientelism in the South. The roots of such a resurgence lie in the economic crisis, the effects of which upon the South have been devastating. Although many students of clientelism have predicted that economic crisis, by shrinking the resource basis available for patronage politics, would undermine political machines like that of the DC in southern Italy,[20] the outcome could be just the opposite; in the short run at least, economic crisis may lead to a reinforcement of clientelism rather than to its disintegration.

The reason why is not hard to grasp. The southern vote for the PCI in 1975-76 was in large part a vote for change, a protest against decades of neglect by the national government and corruption in local politics and a demand for new priorities and new policies to transform the South from an eternally assisted area into a productive component of the national economy. Instead, the southern economy has deteriorated still further since 1975,[21] and national politics and policies seemed little affected by the Communist presence in the "governmental area". As a result, confidence in the changes promised by the PCI had turned by 1979 to frustration and despair. Not only the inability of the Communists to initiate broad social change but their unwillingness, in its absence, to offer people at least the prospect of an individual solution, left the door open to a return of the forces of the "old regime," more than willing to exploit the resulting disillusionment. If the PCI proves unable to fulfill the expectations which it has created, one Communist explained, southerners may turn back to the "traditional image of the city government as a 'mediator' of assistance and favors between a South in need of everything and a distant and hostile state." If that happens, he concludes, "who better than a certain sector of the

Christian Democratic Party, with the formidable apparatus of party and state behind it, can perform such a function?'' (Geremicca,
1977: 144).

Thus, as the economic crisis reduces available resources, privileged access to the few remaining resources — concentrated, as we
have seen, in the hands of the DC and its allies — becomes more
important than ever. More concretely, when the prospect of work
for all begins to fade, many turn back to the desperate search for a
patron, in order to insure at least an *individual* solution. People
begin to look back with nostalgia on the "good old days" when,
with the proper connections, one could at least obtain *something*.
As one observer (Balbi, 1977) put it, "Better a clientelistic system
than no system at all." The key to the enduring strength of
clientelism in an area like southern Italy is the element of hope, and
it is precisely on this terrain that the Communists have been unable,
or at least for the moment unwilling, to compete with their opponents. Mayor Valenzi recounts the following episode as a symbol
of the dilemma of the PCI in Naples. He was approached by a
middle-aged woman who explained that she had shifted her vote
from the DC to the Communists because, after years of electoral
promises by the DC, her son was still unemployed. "You Communists are good people," she said, "and I know that you can find
my son a job." The Mayor patiently explained that he personally
could do nothing, that her son would have to go to the state
employment office and there go through regular channels. The
woman turned away in anger and dismay — "But then you want to
take even *hope* away from us!" The tragedy for the PCI, Valenzi
notes bitterly, is that "if you deny them hope, the old patron is
right there ready to extend it, because *his* game revolves around
hope." (Valenzi, 1978: 166).

1980 — WHITHER NAPLES?

In the wake of the 1979 electoral results, the prognosis for reconfir-
mation of the municipal and regional governments conquered by
the Left in 1975 was, as we have seen, far from optimistic, with
Naples clearly at the top of the danger list; the thesis of a return to
clientelism, in Naples in particular and in the South more generally,
was thus an issue of foremost concern for both the PCI and the DC

as they prepared for the administrative elections of June 1980. During the campaign national attention was centered on Naples as a symbol of the counter-offensive mounted by the DC and the Right against left-wing rule in Italy's major cities. Not only did the DC focus its hopes for victory on Naples, but the neo-Fascist MSI, counting on a broad-based wave of protest against the left-wing administration, mounted a massive campaign to make its national secretary, Giorgio Almirante, the next mayor of Naples. The results confirmed neither the optimistic hopes of the DC and the Right nor the worst fears of the Communists. In Naples the PCI managed to hold its own with regard to the local and regional elections of 1975 and to reverse slightly the disastrous losses of 1979, but fell one seat short of obtaining an absolute majority for the left-wing coalition which had governed the city since 1975. On the other hand, the Neapolitan DC suffered one of the worst losses in the entire country (-5.3% with respect to 1979), while the MSI, although failing in its promise to make Almirante mayor of Naples, increased its vote from 18.7% in 1975 to 22.3% in 1980. At the national level, the PCI lost 1.9% over 1975 but stabilized its vote at the level of 1979 (31.5%), while the DC (36.8%) gained over 1975 but lost with respect to 1979, thus reversing the tendency which had emerged in the 1979 political elections and which had led to predictions of an irreversible electoral decline for the Communists. On the basis of these results, it is likely that, as in the other major cities administered by the Left since 1975, in Naples as well the Left will continue to govern for another five years.[22]

Given the above analysis of the dilemmas confronting the PCI in local government and the thesis of a return to clientelism, how can these results be explained? With regard to the Communists, the party underwent a profound process of self-criticism after the 1979 elections, with respect not only to its strategy vis-à-vis the DC, but to the larger question of the relationship among institutions, party and mass base as well. Having resumed a role of opposition at the national level and concomitantly abandoned its fixation on agreement with the DC at the local level, the PCI in Naples proved able to revitalize the energies of its grassroots activists, to begin to restore its ties with local struggles (particularly in the fields of housing and youth unemployment), and to promote a series of new initiatives on the part of the city government during the last year (e.g., a program of free cultural events in the summer of 1979, new programs of assistance for the elderly, approval of a far-reaching plan for the redevelopment of the urban periphery, as well as the hiring of the over 6,000 young people noted above). The Communists themselves admit that these first five years of left-wing rule must be seen more as an indication of direction than as a record of concrete accomplishments.[23] However, as a result of the new wave of dynamism evident in the past year, they seem to have convinced Neapolitans that a "new way of governing" is perhaps indeed possible.

With regard to the DC and the Right, the analysis is more complicated. The electoral results of 1980 indicate a clear-cut distinction between Naples and the rest of the South. On the one hand, the PCI vote in Naples is in sharp contrast to the substantial losses suffered by the party throughout the rest of the South; on the other, the DC, which loses badly to the neo-Fascist Right in Naples, advances significantly elsewhere in the South, as well as in the region of Campania outside the province of Naples. The Neapolitan vote (like that of the other major cities administered by the Left since 1975 and in contrast to a city like Palermo where, having controlled local government uninterruptedly for 30 years, the DC advanced still further in 1980) seems to indicate that, despite disillusionment with the leftist administration, the traditional DC system of power has been seriously undermined by the party's loss of control over a major lever of patronage like the city government. A second and related peculiarity of the Neapolitan situation lies in the capacity of the MSI, rather than the DC, to attract those sectors of the population dissatisfied with the Left. With regard to the two traditional models of southern political behavior outlined above — the spontaneous protest against the state and the search for individual solutions through clientelistic channels — the Neapolitan vote (combined with an abstention rate of almost 15%) seems to indicate less a resurgence of clientelism than of the right-wing populist anti-statism so deeply rooted in certain sectors of the middle classes and the urban *sottoproletariato*, an expression of frustration and alienation from democratic institutions even more alarming in its implications than a revival of the machine politics of the Gavas.

Thus while, for the South as a whole, the thesis of a return to clientelism is amply confirmed by the results of the 1980 elections, in Naples the Gavas seem to have lost their hold on the city, which more than ever is polarized between Left and Right. With regard to the prospects for the left-wing administration in Naples during the next five years, the renewed dynamism of the PCI and its allies

since the electoral disaster of June 1979 has for the moment succeeded in stemming, at least temporarily, the wave of scepticism
and frustration which seemed about to engulf the Left. The question which remains open, however, is whether, in a situation like
that of Naples, even the most dynamic program of cultural and
welfare initiatives is enough. The crux of the issue — both for
Naples and for the South — remains the linkages between local and
national politics and between political and economic power. Given
the continued absence at the national level of both the political will
and the necessary resources to seriously confront the ever more
dramatic problems of Naples and the South, there is little reason to
expect that the social and political tensions underlying the electoral
results of the past three years will be alleviated in the foreseeable
future. As a result, the political gap between North and South may
well continue to widen, with incalculable consequences for Italian
democracy.

NOTES

1. After 1975 of the ten largest Italian cities, only Palermo and Bari were not administered by the Left. Apart from Red Belt cities like Bologna, which have had left-
wing local governments throughout the postwar period, the other major cities with
left-wing majorities in 1975 had previously been administered by center or center-
left coalitions.

2. For an account of Communist local government in Turin, see Hellman
(1979).

3. The *doroteo* faction represents a center-right position within the DC.

4. Good in-depth accounts of the Gava machine can be found in Allum (1973)
and Caprara (1975).

5. Estimate by members of left-wing factions of the Neapolitan DC (1975).

6. For data on North-South differences, see Table 1 in preceding chapter on
Palermo.

7. This is contrary to the general pattern in the South, where Communist
strength has tended to be concentrated in the countryside and weakest in urban
centers.

8. Before 1975 Italian voting patterns had been so stable that even advances of
1% in the PCI vote were hailed by the party as major victories.

9. For an in-depth analysis of the 1975 and 1976 votes in Italy, see Parisi and
Pasquino (1977).

10. In 1970 Naples registered 23.6/1,000 still births and 58.9/1,000 deaths in the
first year of life, in contrast to national averages of 15.3 and 29.2 respectively; in the
same year infectious diseases reached a level of 33.8/1,000 in contrast to a national
average of 8.3/1,000.

11. While the PCI advanced substantially in all neighborhoods of the city, surpassing 60% of the vote in some working-class strongholds, a breakdown by neighborhood shows the most substantial increases in 1975 and 1976 in middle-class neighborhoods and in the slums of the old city.

12. For a detailed account of the movement of the "organized unemployed," based on first-hand accounts by participants, see Ramondino (1977).

13. Beginning with protest demonstrations against the city and regional governments, the unemployed have since engaged in attempts to block major arteries and in occupations first of the state employment office and, recently, of the local offices of the major political parties, including the PCI. Such an unprecedented move demonstrates the extent to which the unemployed no longer distinguish in their protest between the Communist Party and the state.

14. Special legislation to promote youth employment was passed with the support of the PCI in 1976. Of the 28,000 jobs created in all of Italy on the basis of this legislation, 6,668 were in the city government of Naples.

15. In 1977 the PCI lost control of two medium-sized cities in the Neapolitan area, Castellammare and Capua, to the DC. The loss of Castellammare was particularly painful for the PCI, which had won 42% of the vote in the previous elections, because this is the home base of the Gavas; the result was widely interpreted as a warning of a possible Gava comeback in Naples itself. In those towns and cities which voted in May 1978, the PCI lost 9% with respect to 1976, while the DC gained 3.6%.

16. A prominent Italian political scientist has calculated that 1,000,000-1,500,000 of the PCI's 1976 voters went against the party's orders in the June 1978 referendum (see Galli, 1978).

17. The pro-repeal vote in June 1978 was strongest in many of the same neighborhoods which had swung the elections for the PCI in 1975 and 1976 (i.e., the middle-class neighborhoods and the old city), while the anti-repeal forces prevailed in the party's traditional strongholds. In 1979, on the contrary, PCI losses were heavy throughout the city, but were concentrated most heavily in the low-income neighborhoods, both working-class and *sottoproletariato*, while the middle-class vote, relatively speaking, remained more loyal.

18. Although the June 1978 agreement alleviated some of the pressures on the administration, the DC's formal support of the junta did not prevent certain sectors of the party from continuing to use their leverage to obstruct the left-wing administration wherever possible. The objective of the DC, in the words of the ex-mayor, Bruno Milanesi, was "to cook the PCI over a slow fire."

19. According to Ugo Grippo, head of the DC delegation to the Regional Assembly, of 88 positions of economic power in Naples, all continue to be held by the DC and 65% are concentrated in the hands of the *dorotei* (cited in Valenzi, 1978: 141).

20. See, for example, Caciagli et al. (1977) and Scott (1969).

21. The impact of the economic crisis on the South is evidenced by the following data: investment by publicly-owned industries in the South declined 35% between 1976 and 1978 (*Rapporto Saraceno*, 1978: 30); the 1978 unemployment rate in the South was 10.1%, as opposed to a national figure of 7.1% (*Rapporto Saraceno*, 1978: 36); in the region of Campania alone official unemployment increased by 45,000 between June 1977 and June 1978 (Giustolisi, 1977: 51), while in the city of Naples over 8,000 workers in small and medium firms were laid off during the same year (Valenzi, 1978: 148).

22. As in the period 1975-80 the absence of an absolute majority for the leftist coalition will require external support from the DC on critical votes like approval of the budget. Although numerically speaking the only possible junta is a PCI-PSI-PSDI-PRI coalition, the ambiguous position of the Socialists, currently participating in the national government with the DC, has given rise to concern over the PSI's eventual position with regard to the local juntas. Thus, there is a possibility that, if the Socialists prove unwilling to cooperate, the city council will be dissolved and a prefectural commissar appointed to administer the city.

23. During the electoral campaign some of the concrete though less visible achievements of the left-wing administration were made public for the first time (for example, reduction of infant mortality by one-half between 1975 and 1980, construction of 333 kindergarten classrooms in five years as opposed to the 210 constructed during the previous 30).

REFERENCES

ALLUM, P. (1973). *Politics and Society in Post-War Naples*. Cambridge: University Press.

BALBI, R. (1977). "Dove soffia il vento del Sud," *La Repubblica*, 22 June, p. 6.

BASSOLINO, A. (1979). "Per capire torniamo al 20 giugno," *Rinascita*, 22 June, pp. 12-13.

Bollettino di Statistica, 1977 (1978). Naples: Comune di Napoli.

CACIAGLI, M. et al. (1977). *Democrazia Cristiana e potere nel Mezzogiorno*. Florence: Guaraldi.

CAPRARA, M. (1975). *I Gava*. Milan: Feltrinelli.

GALLI, G. (1978). "Analisi del voto," *La Repubblica*, 14 June, p. 6.

GEREMICCA, A. (1977). *Dentro la città: Napoli angoscia e speranza*. Naples: Guida Editori.

GEREMICCA, A. (1978.) Interview with Andrea Geremicca, PCI Assessor of Economic Planning in the City Government, 26 June.

GIUSTOLISI, F. (1977). "Napoli è in provincia di Castellammare," *L'Espresso*, 1 May, pp. 22-24.

HELLMAN, S. (1979). "'A New Style of Governing': Italian Communism and the Dilemmas of Transition in Turin, 1975-1978." Unpublished manuscript.

ISTAT (1972). *5° censimento generale dell'industria e del commercio, 25 ottobre 1971*. Rome: Author.

NEAPOLITAN DC (1975). "La necessità di un impegno politico e sociale a Napoli" (Open letter to the Provincial Secretary of the DC). Mimeograph.

PARISI, A. and PASQUINO, G. (eds.) (1977). *Continuità e mutamento elettorale in Italia*. Bologna: Il Mulino.

RAMONDINO, F. (ed.) (1977). *I disoccupati organizzati*. Milan: Feltrinelli.

Rapporto Saraceno (1978). Annual report of the Cassa per il Mezzogiorno, 25 June. Mimeograph.

SCOTT, J. C. (1969). "Corruption, Machine Politics and Political Change," *American Political Science Review*, 63 (4): 1142-58.

VALENZI, M. (1978). *Sindaco a Napoli*. Rome: Editori Riuniti.

5

Political Clientelism in France:
The Center-Periphery Nexus Reexamined

Jean-François Médard
Institut d'Etudes Politiques, Bordeaux, France

Students of French politics have shown surprisingly little interest in the systematic exploration of patron-client ties: could it be that there is no such thing as "political clientelism" in French politics? This is the crux of the argument advanced by Sidney Tarrow in a recent comparative survey of French and Italian mayors (Tarrow, 1977). After contrasting the "political entrepreneurship" of the Italian mayor who acts through party structures, and the "administrative activism" of his French counterpart who works primarily through bureaucratic channels, the author goes on to analyze two different models, i.e. the French model of *"dirigiste political integration"* and the Italian model of "clientelistic political integration." Compelling as the argument may seem in the light of the evidence supplied by the author, the validity of Tarrow's dichotomy is open to debate. Such a model rests on two questionable assumptions: (1) that administrative activism of the kind attributed to French mayors is by definition incompatible with political clientelism, and (2) that party structures play only a marginal role in the overall context of French mayoral politics and therefore can safely be left out of the picture. The point we wish to emphasize at the outset is that although political clientelism may operate even in the absence of strong party structures, such structures are of crucial importance for an understanding of center-periphery relations in contemporary France.

Our knowledge of local politics in France has improved considerably over the last fifteen years. For this much of the credit goes to the pioneering efforts of a school of organization theory associated with the names of Michel Crozier, Pierre Worms, Jean-Pierre Grémion and Jean-Claude Thoenig. Each in his own way has contributed significantly to the reinterpretation of the French local government system. Until then the local administration was viewed not only as centralized (which is true) but as almost entirely controlled by the center (which is far more debatable). It was commonly assumed that Paris governed France with only slight intervention from elected local officials. There was no local government in France, only local administration. In recognizing the strategic role of elected notables they unequivocally laid bare the political dimension of the "political-administrative" system. They correctly argued that the influence of Paris had to be mediated by the notables as trustees of the local communities, while at the same time stressing their dependence on the decisions of the civil servants, including those at the center. From their strategic position on the periphery the notables can build a *"pouvoir periphérique,"* as Grémion calls it, a power which has both an internal dimension based on their relationship to their local communities, and an external one based on their links with the central bureaucracy and its peripheral ramifications (Grémion, 1976).

On the whole their analysis relies heavily on the use of concepts reminiscent of "political clientelism,"[1] including terms like 'dyads', 'networks', 'exchange', etc. There is indeed an implicit recognition of the significance of clientelistic phenomena, which, had it been translated into a more explicit framework might have added an important heuristic and comparative dimension to their work. In this connection let us note at the outset two major limitations inherent in their approach: the first has to do with the use of a specific "ideal typical" model; the second stems from their operational definition of the notable as "a relay of the administration."[2] The use of the "ideal type" approach conveys an impression of uniformity which seems at variance with the "real life" situations encountered at the grass roots, so much so that the reader is often tempted to forget the importance of the exceptions to the model. Indeed, these exceptions, which the authors are prepared to recognize, are so numerous that it is a question whether they can be treated as exceptions. Furthermore, to define the notable as the "relay of administration" has several unfortunate consequences.

By focussing attention almost exclusively in center-periphery relations it is easy to lose sight of the horizontal dimension of local level "politicking." The notable's sociological background, his relationship to the class structure, the factors determining his access to power tend to be neglected. Moreover, this vertical approach combined with the use of a somewhat abstract model masks the rich variety of situations found at the local level. This is because the same kind of organizational format has been applied to a variety of regions, cultures and societies, whose diversity has been noted time and again. If "notabilism" as a concept is bound to the local government system, the nature of the notables varies according to their social, political and cultural background, and with the region and type of community (Mendras, 1977).

Another drawback of this "administrative relay" bias is a relative neglect of the national political dimension. It tends to play down the role of the members of parliament, particularly the deputies, the political parties and the coalition in power, and to overestimate the autonomy of the local government in relation to the national government.

The notable is not only the relay of the administration, he is the mediator between the center and the periphery, which suggests the need for a greater emphasis on the relations between the notable and his community, and more sustained attention to the sociological dimension of this relationship. Nor can we accept the idea that local government functions in a kind of political vacuum. Its autonomy varies with the political conjuncture. Let us, then, begin this discussion by drawing an analytical distinction among three dimensions: the political-administrative, the sociological, and the political-partisan dimensions. It is the interaction among these three dimensions that shapes the contours of clientelistic relations in specific places, at specific points in time.

The political-administrative dimension is related to the organizational approach. The local government system created by the Third Republic is based, ultimately, on the dependency of the periphery on the center. Permeating such a system and at the same time constituting its armature, complex networks of personal dependency and exchange ramify across administrative boundaries. What is meant by "notabilist system" or notabilism,[3] is a form of clientelism which permeates local government institutions. Because of the uniformity of the organization, there is uniformity in the system itself; it spreads across the whole of France from the Third to the

Fifth Republics. But if these notables are the product of local institutions, they are also the product of the communities in which they live; they have their own sociological specificity.

From a sociological point of view, the notables are part of a given socioeconomic culture and historical environment. Some originate from noble or well-known families; others from the landed gentry; others still are identified with the professional bourgeoisie. The classical type of notable has disappeared almost everywhere. In certain cases he has been replaced by his descendants, and these descendants are still considered notables even though their basis of power has changed. The persistence of a social class through adaptation is indeed a common phenomeon. In most cases the notables are no longer recruited from the landed gentry but from the professional bourgeoisie. It is important to note, however, that although individuals come and go the system remains. Further, the same organizational system applied to different environments cannot give birth to the same political reality; the very idea of a *"pouvoir périphérique"* implies that it can accommodate itself in some degree to these variations.

To properly grasp the political-partisan dimension we must try to relate the notable to the national political system. Admittedly there is a tension between the political-administrative kind of clientelism which is based on ideological and partisan neutrality and the intermittent pressures of the political system. These pressures are related to changes in political regimes, changes in the majority in power, the nature of parties in power, and so on. Not only the parties, but the members of parliament need to be taken into account. The deputies in this respect have been woefully neglected by students of local government, which is perhaps not too surprising since they are most often considered as a part of the national system, and until they become actors in the local system they are seldom taken into account.

Broadly speaking, we can distinguish two types of clientelism that are relevant to this discussion: the clientelism of the notables and the clientelism of the political parties. The former involves a combination of political-administrative and sociological dimensions. It is the product of the local government system and its interaction, or lack of interaction, with local clientelistic traditions. This type of clientelism involves mostly mayors and *conseillers généraux* interacting with local representatives of the central administration.

Party-based clientelism must be understood in a broader sense than "party-directed patronage" which has a connotation of bossism and machine politics (Graziano, 1973). We take "party" to also include loose, ideologically-based coalitions, such as that of the Republicans at the beginning of the Third Republic. These national groups, whether designated "mass parties" or "cadre parties," must find their own "fit" between the local notables and the national ideological tendencies.[4] The "cadre parties" are parties of notables, but they are also related to the national ideologies. The Radical-Socialists are a good example. On the other hand, the "mass parties" may be pervaded by notabilism, as is the case for the Socialists (SFIO) in some places; or they may even use the resources of the municipality as a source of patronage while fighting against notabilism. Thus the clientelism of the notables and the clientelism of the parties are not always and inevitably exclusive of one another.

I. THE LOCAL POLITICO-ADMINISTRATIVE SYSTEM AND THE CLIENTELISM OF THE NOTABLES

Local politics in France must be seen in the light of a continuous interaction between the citizens, the notables and the civil servants in both the center (Paris) and the periphery (*"la Province"*). As mediators between the Administration and the citizens, the notables hold a strategic position in the system. Although French organization theory does not explicitly use the notion of clientelism in its analysis, it uses some very closely related notions. This gives the approach a quasi-clientelistic coloration which ought to be brought to light before attempting to show that a more explicit use of the notion of clientelism is relevant to the study of the French local politico-administrative system.

1. The "Quasi-Clientelism" of the French School of Organization Theory

Worms, Grémion and Thoenig all base their analyses on the notions of dyads and networks, reciprocity and exchange (Worms, 1966; Grémion, 1976; Thoenig, 1973).

The dyad constitutes the primary unit of their analysis: the dyad is composed of the Prefect and the notable, or the mayor and the bureaucrat of the department. The Prefect-notable partnership has been said to involve a kind of complicity based on an exchange of favors. Each is dependent on the action of the other. The notable, as the legitimate and recognized representative of the population, can use his influence to guarantee public order. The Prefect can by-pass the law in favor of the notable. This is not clientelism since no question of equality or inequality between the partners arises, and yet the relationship between them is asymmetrical. The notables compete for favors from the Prefect, but the reverse is not true. Although the Prefect is moved from one department to another precisely to prevent him from acting as a patron in the usual sense of the word, the dyadic partnership analyzed by Worms is very close to a clientelistic relationship.

Thoenig refers explicitly to clientelism in his description of the relation between a *Ponts et Chaussées* civil servant and the mayor:

> la compétence principale requise pour un responsable d'une cellule territoriale réside dans son sens des relations avec les représentants de la société locale de son aire . . . Ces fonctionnaires vont jusqu'à enserrer les représentants politiques et économiques dan un faisceau de services rendus et d'échanges qui transforment la relation entre le fonctionnaire et l'administration en un rapport complexe de clientèle (Thoenig, 1973: 28).

He goes on to quote a bureaucrat who describes his clientelistic strategy as follows:

> savoir se rendre utile par tous les moyens petits et grands, c'est la meilleure façon de travailler de près une commune. Pour cela, un maire doit être reconnaissant au moins autant que si vous lui faites un prix avantageux pour des travaux (Thoenig, 1973: 29).

Each of these dyads is a part of a larger network. Neither the Prefect nor the department officials can afford to disregard the basic requirement of an efficient administration, i.e. create, nurture and preserve personal networks of influence. In Grémion's words,

> le comportement du fonctionnaire s'explique autant par sa position dans un territoire constitué de clients et ou d'administrés que par sa position sur l'échelle hiérarchique de l'organisation (Grémion, 1976: 180).

Just as the local civil servant is likely to invest considerable time and energy in setting up and lubricating his network, the same is true of the notable: "arrondir son réseau" — rounding out one's connections — is indeed a crucial aspect of his social role. Again to quote from Grémion:

> le notable se fraie un réseau de relations dans l'appareil de l'Etat. La capacité d'interconnection bureaucratique ne dépend pas seulement de la position des individus dans la structure formelle des institutions représentatives départementales, elle devint progressivement une propriété personelle non substituable et non transmissible. Le notable se définit progressivement par son réseau de relations et d'interventions dans l'appareil administratif de l'Etat (Grémion, 1976: 213).

In the description of the networks sketched by Grémion and others there is sometimes an allusion to clientelism, but not in any systematic sense. Grémion, for instance, mentions that the political relationship, being de-ideologized, becomes a clientele relationship; but he does not show just how asymmetrical the relation between civil servant and notable, or between notable and citizens, really is. This is perhaps because his point is to demonstrate the existence of a power in the periphery, but this in turn tends to de-emphasize the power of the center. Yet, he does recognize the subordination of the peripheral institutions and shows that the power of the notables over the local society is an "answer to a domination which introduces another domination" (Grémion, 1976: 266).

In his study of the *Ponts et Chaussées*, Thoenig seems to go further in the direction of expliciting clientelism. In his paper on the relations between the center and the periphery in France, he describes the situation of divide and rule which is typical of clientelism:

> un partenaire a le pouvoir parce qu'il est le seul à pouvoir traiter avec une collection d'individus. Chacun de ceux-ci agit par lui même indépendament des autres, sans chercher à offrir un refus collectif contre l'intervention d'un élément étranger à la situation (Thoenig, 1975: 81).

He shows that the direct relationship between the mayor and the civil servant reinforces the isolation of the communes and the competition for favors of the state between the mayors. His description of the resulting partnership is strikingly reminiscent of clientelism:

La relation est inégale car un partenaire domine l'autre. Cependant en même temps elle suscite l'interdépendance entre eux. Celui qui domine prend en charge les intérêts vitaux de celui qu'il domine, et notamment le besoin que ce dernier a vis à vis du monde extérieur, d'apparaitre comme le véritable responsable. Celui que est dominé s'acquiert un appui décisif pour sa propre réussite et obtient des faveurs qu'il ne pourrait pas obtenir aussi aisément par d'autres moyens . . . L'infériorité dans l'un des jeux est acceptée pour autant que l'autre jeu lui assure une position dominante (Thoenig, 1975 : 83).

He concludes that in such a relation between center and periphery there is, in spite of the inequality, some kind of interdependence between partners. From our point of view, this is precisely the combination of inequality and interdependence which is at the heart of the patron-client relationship.

Surprisingly, however, Thoenig rejects the idea that his analysis should be confused with clientelism: "le réseau de relation est davantage que la somme des couples qui le dessinent, il ne peut être analysé comme une association de clientèle telle que la définit Graziano" (Thoenig, 1975 : 96).

In order to clarify this point we have to go a bit further in the analysis of notabilism and clientelism in the French local politico-administrative system. For in actuality, even if it is true that the network of relations is more than the sum of the dyads which comprise it, this does not mean that it cannot be analyzed as clientele association; there is, in fact, an overall institutional mode of organization of the system which lies at the root of the various clientele networks. The organization is more than the addition of the dyads, because the dyads proceed from the system and not the system from the dyads.

2. Notabilism, Brokerage and Clientelism in the Local Politico-Administrative System

The title of "notable" implies a particular kind of local leader, yet there is no agreement on the definition of the concept. This ambiguity is due to the fact that over the years the notables' background, recruitment and resources have changed. However, the "système notabilaire," as Grémion calls it, persists. Although the definition of the notable may vary, all notables are intermediaries between the local society and the wider environment and hence function as mediators; in addition they are also the clients of the Administration and the patrons of their constituents.

Historians were the first to give systematic attention to notables. Tudesq defines them in terms of their sociological characteristics, that is their ability to accumulate economic, political and social power at the local level (Tudesq, 1973). The *Grands Notables* accumulated these powers at both the local and the national levels. This is the traditional definition of the notable. However, these notables are historical figures. They were recruited from the *Noblesse* and the *Grande Bourgeoisie*, they were the ruling class in 19th century France from the Restoration to the beginning of the Third Republic. Although they survived the advent of universal suffrage, they emerged essentially during the period of limited suffrage (*"suffrage censitaire"*). The notables were then largely replaced by the middle classes, called the *"nouvelles couches"* by Gambetta. These *"nouvelles couches"* did not have the economic power of the notables:

> alors que le pouvoir politique des notables n'était qu'une conséquence de leurs autres pouvoirs, le pouvoir politique local sous la Troisième République est l'élément prioritaire pour les nouvelles couches qui occupent les mairies et peu à peu les conseils généraux; c'est à partir de ce pouvoir politique qu'elles peuvent acquérir le pouvoir social (Tudesq, 1973 : 3).

Lagroye in his recent study of machine politics in Bordeaux still uses the traditional notion of the notable, but he also introduces the notion of *notabilité*: the latter lacks the economic power of the notable and is generally recruited from the professional classes (Lagroye, 1973).

Grémion, on the other hand, begins his analysis with the idea that any attempt to define notables by their attributes is "essentialist" as it were and leads nowhere. For the purpose of his analysis he prefers to adopt a functional definition — the notable is the "privileged relay" of the Administration.

> on peut discuter longuement pour énumérer les attributs des notables et fixer les contours de l'espèce. Mais ce débat essentiliste conduit à une impasse. Seule une définition fonctionelle liée à la position des individus concernés dans le système des rapports entre les structures territoriales de l'Etat et leur environnement permet de progresser. Le notable dans cette perspective est un homme qui dispose d'un certain pouvoir pour agir sur l'appareil de l'Etat à certains niveaux privilégiés, et qui par effet de retour, voit son pouvoir renforcé par le privilège que lui confèrent ces contacts pour autant qu'ils soient sanctionnés par des résultats (Grémion, 1976: 166).

This definition introduces the idea of the notable as a mediator between the Administration and the citizen. The traditional notable was also a mediator due to his monopoly of power; in Grémion's definition, however, it is the fact that he is a relay of the Administration which makes him a notable. In either case, the notable can be considered a mediator.

(a) The Notable as a Mediator

Grémion reduces the mediating function of the notable to the relationships between the Administration and the citizen. Basically, the notable is a local leader who, because of his role as representative, performs a mediating function between the center and the periphery, between the state and society, between the Administration and the citizen. Centralization essentially means the uniformity of the universal rule, which is elaborated at the center but applied at the periphery by the territorial administration. The lower levels of the administration are expected to apply the law in a quasi-mechanical way. But the higher levels of the administration have the informal power to adapt the law to particular situations. According to Grémion, the notables are precisely those who can bargain for a modified application of rules and regulations:

> le notable est un individu qui dispose d'une représentativité suffisante pour obtenir de l'administration locale une transgression de l'universalisme de la règle centrale, et qui occupe de ce fait une position médiatrice stratégique entre l'Etat et la société civile (Grémion, 1976 : 212).

This mediating power is based on the representativeness of the notable: the notable is the man who can speak for the population. Why? Not so much because of his personal as because of his institutional representativeness:

> Cette médiation toutefois, avant d'être fondée sur la représentativité personnelle est juridiquement determinée par la structure des institutions de représentation du régime politique et administratif (Grémion, 1976 : 212).

Grémion seems to imply that the notables are such because they are elected to the institutions which are in charge of representing the population at the local level: it is by virtue of this politico-administrative position that they become notables. We agree fundamentally with this method of defining the notable as both mediator and relay. But as Jeanne Becquart-Leclercq has noticed, this approach suffers from an excessive administrative bias and ignores the problem of recruitment: "leur rôle de relais se surajoute après coup à une position de base d'abord acquise dans les rapports sociaux locaux, magnifiée ensuite par l'accès aux 'ils' et aux puissants au regard des besoins" (Becquart-Leclercq, 1976: 11).

For all its merits, Grémion's approach is overly biased towards the Administration, in that it emphasizes the relations between the Administration and the notables more than the relation of the notables with their local environment. The organizational postulate leads to a neglect of both national and local sociological factors: the politico-administrative system appears to operate in a kind of sociological vacuum. Paradoxically, while Grémion discovers a power in the periphery, this periphery remains somewhat abstract, undifferentiated and without any specificity of its own. Might not the "personal representativeness of the notable" account for his institutional representiveness? Hence the need to concentrate on the sociological and economic forces at the local and supra-local levels. Danielle Bleitrach and Alain Chenu have attempted to do just that from a neo-marxist point of view (Bleitrach and Chenu, 1974).

They observe that the notables have two characteristics which are common to all elected local leaders. They act in the capacity of relays between local and global society and they are well-known public figures. Local notoriety is a psychological and sociological phenomenon through which an individual is recognized and distinguished by the population. This can best be achieved by rendering services to the community and to individuals, and through symbolic identification with the local community. In addition, the notable has a specific characteristic: he is part of the dominant class or acts in alliance with it. In this way the authors consider the notables as a fraction of the bourgeoisie and orient their analysis towards the contradiction between this fraction of the bourgeoisie and the monopolist bourgeoisie related to the central state and the multinationals, as other marxists do. Retaining the idea of mediation, introducing implicitly the idea of legitimacy, and suggesting some kind of quasi-clientelism, they finally characterize the notable by his class. Useful though it is to introduce here a class perspective, the notables' relation to the dominant class does not constitute the specificity of the notable.

In the end it is Mendras who gives us the most comprehensive definition of the notable. He characterizes the notable by his marginal position between the peasant collectivity and the global society. The notable is a mediator who possesses a power both internal and external:

> le médiateur doit disposer d'une au moins des ressources de pouvoir interne à la collectivité (possession d'une bien rare, contrôle ideologique . . .) mais l'essentiel de son pouvoir nait de sa capacité de jouer de son rôle de médiateur pour renforcer l'un par l'autre son pouvoir interne et externe (Mendras, 1972 : 135).

In fact, for Mendras, the notable is not strictly a French phenomenon. He is an element of all rural societies and even a part of Mendras' definition of rural societies. His perspective of the relation between the rural collectivity and the global society encompasses more than the politico-administrative facet. He distinguishes global and sectorial dimensions, and attempts to relate the change in the recruitment of the notables to changes in the relation between the village and the global society. His analysis is in fact more complementary to than in contradiction with Grémion's. The main difference is that Grémion focusses on the local politico-administrative system at the level of the relations between the notables and the Administration; Mendras, as might be expected of a rural sociologist, is more concerned with the relations between the notable and rural society.

The existence of urban notables must also be brought into the picture. Notabilism is neither a purely administrative nor a purely rural phenomenon. Mediators exist also in an urban environment, at least in France. This is central to an understanding of the opposition between center and periphery, an opposition not only between the rural sectors and the global society but between Paris and "*la Province*," and the latter includes urban as well as rural areas.

In short, the idea of mediation is at the heart of the concept of the notable; there is no notable without mediation. But not all mediators are notables. There is, in addition, another element, which involves reputation, prestige, or some kind of locally rooted legitimacy (Graziano, 1976: 164). This legitimacy is often based on traditional claims later sanctioned by election. But in the election process, tradition still plays a role. Even when the elected official is an outsider, he must still participate in patronage relations with local notables in order to be accepted and become a notable himself.

(b) The Notable as Patron and Client

Local government in France is remarkably uniform: the framework of communes and departments covers the whole national territory and the rules are basically the same whether the communes are rural or urban. Nevertheless, the various forms of administrative cooperation between the communes (*syndicats de communes, communautés urbaines*), complicate the picture. To properly grasp the roles of patron and client assumed by elected notables at the local level, the communes must be kept analytically separate from the departments. It is important to keep in mind, however, that a notable can be elected at both levels: he may be both mayor and *conseiller général* (i.e., member of a departmental council). Furthermore, there is a strong interaction between local and national politics: although the deputy elected to the National Assembly does not have any formal responsibility in the local system, he is by no means insulated from it. This is even more true when he serves both as mayor or *conseiller général*, and deputy: this accumulation of offices (*cumul de mandat*) is not uncommon. For the moment, we will analyze separately the role of the mayors in the commune and of the *conseiller général* in the department.

(i) The Mayor in the Commune

The mayor is the key figure in his commune. Even if he does not possess the traditional characteristics of a notable, the expectations of his constituents and the logic of his position conspire to make him the prominent notable of his commune. He is the source of all authority, even though he delegates some of it to his assistants (*adjoints*). He controls all relations and interactions with civil servants. He thus claims both internal and external power. But the basis of his power has changed over the years: whereas he used to have the right to choose the public employees of the commune, today his patronage is extremely limited. Under the pressure of the trade unions, parliament has imposed strict regulations on the recruitment of public employees at the municipal level. The status of public employees at the local level is now similar to that of civil servants. The mayor still controls some resources of his own, but his role as a patron depends more and more on his capacity to act as a broker. Only by creating and cultivating his connections within the Administration can he acquire "clout"; he has to become a client not only to be a patron but even to be a good manager of his commune.

Before going any further some attention needs to be paid to the distinction between the rural and urban communes.

The rural commune. In many parts of rural France the mayor used to be recruited among the nobility or *Grand Bourgeoisie*: he was the *"châtelain."* This phenomenon still persists in some places in western France, but only in a marginal sense. Today the majority of mayors come from the professional bourgeoisie, the so-called *bourgeoisie libérale.* They include medical doctors, veterinarians, pharmacists, lawyers and other occupations based on a private practice (*professions à clientèle*) (See Becquart-Leclercq, 1976: 38; Souchon, 1968; 1976). These career lines imply not only a wide range of supra-local relationships but, at the community level, pave the way for the building of an extra-professional clientele. The small peasants rarely become mayors. With the increasing importance of management and the socioeconomic development of the local communities, a third category of notables appears: the civil servants, who claim both technical experience and supra-local connections. Whatever the basis of his recruitment as a notable, the mayor of the village is expected to behave both as "father" and manager of the commune (Kesselman, 1967). Conflicts may arise between the two roles; depending on the subculture of the village and the personality of the mayor, the latter may lean in one direction or another. But the fact remains that he is perceived as being much more than a simple administrator by the citizens of his commune. His role of patron and broker is related to this fatherly image.

As has been repeatedly stressed, the rural mayor spends a good deal of his time on non-administrative matters. On the one hand, he is expected to play an active and supportive role in the daily life of his constituents — which often means combining the qualities of social worker, trouble shooter and benevolent jack-of-all-trades. On the other hand, he is the key mediator with the Administration, and as such he is seen by his constituents as their only recourse against the byzantine ways of the civil servants — as their only hope in the face of a growing volume of bureaucratic red tape.

Inasmuch as he often goes beyond the call of administrative duty in helping his constituents, the mayor, consciously or not, builds for himself a personal clientele of *"obligés"* which he adds to his professional clientele. He is then a kind of patron even though he controls no jobs. As a broker vis-à-vis the bureaucracy, he also becomes a client who seeks bureaucratic favors. In the performance of his managerial role, he cannot avoid soliciting favors from civil servants. To set up his budget correctly, he often asks the help of the tax collector; to get collective goods like paved roads, he needs to make friends among the *Ponts et Chaussées* and so on. For any kind of equipment he must look for state grants (*subventions*). Even if these grants are a right and not a favor, the whole process of negotiation involves favors at the level of the department or above. His main task is to develop connections and relations in order to build clientelistic networks. As has been shown, just how much a commune gets in the form of equipment is closely correlated to the scale of mayoral networks (Becquart-Leclercq, 1976: 160).

In his relations with the local population the mayor is often perceived as the "father" of the commune; the commune constitutes a large family which must not be disrupted by political conflict, and hence whatever favors the mayor happens to dispense his attitude must be seen as politically neutral. He must at all cost preserve his reputation of not playing favorites with anyone. Much the same situation characterizes the relations between civil servants or Prefects and the mayor. On closer inspection, however, the political neutrality ascribed to such favors is often more apparent than real: one must not forget that the main role of the Prefect and of his superior, the Minister of Interior, is to win elections for the government. The Prefect is caught in a role conflict: for the sake of his reputation as a "good administrator" he must remain politically neutral, and yet at the same time he has to help the government win the elections, which means that he has to help the "right" candidates without showing it. The larger the commune the more difficult it becomes to stay out of politics. In the smaller communes, there is often a single municipal ticket labeled *"intérêt communal"*; elsewhere, however, electoral competition sometimes generates a civil war atmosphere. These conflicts, though often rooted in local issues, are easily translated into the language of competing ideologies.

As the communes increase in size and become more urbanized, the role of the mayor as patron and client still survives but is significantly modified.

The urban commune. With the spread of urbanization we should expect the gradual disappearance of clientelism, but we know from the example of American machine politics that things are not always so simple. It is true, however, that the social trends which accompany the process of urbanization tend to militate against clientelism.

The basic trend which mitigates the saliency of clientelism is the decline of personal relations in an urban environment. But this does not imply the disappearance of all personal relationships. Since there are obvious limitations to the range of personal connections a mayor can hope to establish, he will tend to rely increasingly on relays and mediators in order to consolidate his position at the top of the clientelist pyramid. Although the exploration of these phenomena has just begun, the data available from Toulouse and Bordeaux confirm this impression.

A recent study on the Radical Socialist municipality of Toulouse from 1880 to 1906, for example, reveals the existence of a genuinely clientelistic system, based on the participation of a relatively small group of notabilities. Recruited among the petty bourgeoisie, their influence stemmed from their social status and reputation within their own neighborhood, and from their personal connections with personalities outside their immediate environment. They were not notables in the traditional sense, but rather "notabilities." When selected by the mayor to appear on his ticket, they brought in the votes of their clienteles. The mayor returned the favor through patronage jobs. Because of the competition between these personalities and their factions, these clienteles were very unstable, however.

The overall picture conveyed by Toulouse at the turn of the century is that of a true municipal spoils system (Nevers, 1975). With every election there occurred a "purge" of municipal employees and the recruitment of new ones. Thus in the 1880 elections almost 50% of the city employees hired by the previous mayor lost their jobs. When in 1906 the Socialist Party won the city election (partly because of its anti-clientelistic platform) the old-style clientelism of the Radical notables gave way to a party-based clientelism; from then on it was the party as such, and not the notables, who managed the municipal resources. Furthermore, with the new statutory limitations on the recruitment of municipal employees the mayor eventually lost his power of patronage and the municipal spoils system largely disappeared. Clientelism, meanwhile, reappeared in a new guise. This phenomenon is perhaps best illustrated by the case of Bordeaux during the Fourth and Fifth Republics.

Municipal politics in Bordeaux hinges to a very large extent around the meteoric rise — and fall — of its illustrious mayor (since 1947), Jacques Chaban Delmas. His *cursus honorum* is as impressive as any among French politicians. He served as deputy during the Fourth and Fifth Republics, Minister in the Fourth Republic, Chairman of the National Assembly during the first part of the Fifth Republic, Prime Minister under Georges Pompidou; his star might have risen higher still had not his candidacy to the Elysée been defeated by Valéry Giscard d'Estaing in the 1974 presidential election. His local career and his national career were built on each other. His power is based, in part, on a skillful use of both local and national resources through quasi-clientelistic ties at both levels. Although he came into politics as an outsider, he was immediately seized upon by the local establishment and supported by the Catholic Church. In return for their help he offered them his national connections, and his prestigious image of a Resistance hero. If at the beginning the relationship between Chaban Delmas and the local establishment seemed to work to the latter's advantage, with the consolidation of his local power base and the development of his national connections this relationship was reversed.

The important point at any rate is that the joint support of the Bordeaux notables and of the Catholic Church has been highly instrumental in helping him "sell" his image to the electorate. In addition, he succeeded in establishing a clientele among the wholesale dealers of the *marché des Capucins* and, more importantly, among the elderly. Bordeaux is an aging city where the vote of the senior citizens is crucial. Backed by the philanthropic wing of the local bourgeoisie and by the Catholic Church he developed a progressive social policy toward the aged in creating social centers (*foyers sociaux*) for them. In that task he was assisted by a very popular *adjoint* in charge of the social sector, herself a former social worker. This cannot, strictly speaking, be considered as a form of political clientelism since it is aimed at a social category and not at a specific person or persons; and yet there is no gainsaying the significance of the *adjoint*, whose role as a go-between is inseparable from his close personal ties with the elderly and the notables. In addition, there is Chaban Delmas' own style, which consists as much as possible in multiplying personal contacts, making public appearances, attending local events, so as to give a distinctive personal twist to his actions. In so doing Chaban Delmas is able to transform a quasi-clientelistic relationship into straightforward clientelism. But the importance of his popular clientele must not be over-estimated. What is more significant is that it reveals an all-around strategy which is used whenever the circumstances permit. In the course of his career Jacques Chaban Delmas has had the opportunity to help many people personally, including his opponents at the local level. This is what Jacques Lagroye calls the "vassalisation" of the opposition. In Bordeaux, for example, he skillfully coopted his political rivals by recruiting them as municipal councillors on his campaign ticket, thus endeavoring to create a kind of patron-client relationship with them, a relationship all the more valued since they in turn, as spokesmen of local interest groups, may have a clientele of their own.

Around Bordeaux, at the level of the metropolitan area, the department and the region, he has similarly vassalized his opponents by the means of an informal agreement, a kind of non-aggression pact with the leaders of the Socialist Party. This has led to the creation of what we have described elsewhere as the *"système politique Bordelais,"* a system which became quasi-institutionalized through the creation of the so-called *communauté urbaine* as a form of metropolitan government (Médard, 1971). The system is based not only on non-aggression, but also on various exchanges of favors including the support of the mayor in case of external threats: its acid test came with the defeat of Jean-Jacques Servan-Schreiber, resulting from his inability to detach more than a marginal fraction of the electorate from the Chaban machine. This system has recently survived a more serious crisis when the Socialist Party gained the majority within the *communauté urbaine*. The crisis was eventually resolved through the time-honored practice of *partage d'influence* — "horse trading" — whereby the leading Socialist candidate was allowed to retain the chairmanship of the *communauté urbaine* and the Chaban supporters the majority of seats in the *communauté urbaine de Bordeaux*. All these compromises and "deals" are based on trade-offs and quasi clientelistic ties which cut across party cleavages.

This still strong but declining position of Chaban Delmas in and around Bordeaux cannot be understood unless some attention is paid to the clientelistic ties he was able to create and cultivate within the Administration and the "political class" of both Republics, first as a Minister, and then as Prime Minister. As will be seen, the accumulation of offices on top of a large urban mayorship completely transforms the mayor's relation with the local administration: the big mayor may become the "boss" of the Prefect. This is also true of the chairman of the *conseil général* when he is a national political leader.[5]

(ii) The Conseiller Général in the Department

At the department level, the key notable is the *conseiller général*. Elected by the population within the canton, he exercises the legislative functions in the *conseil général*, whose executive arm is the government-appointed Prefect. His formal status within the canton or the department is inferior to that of the mayor in his community, the reason being that executive power in the department is in the hands of the Prefect who is neither elected nor controlled by the *conseillers généraux*. However, the *conseiller général* is still a notable in the rural areas. Since he does not control any resources directly, as the mayor does, he is more of a broker than a patron. One third of the *conseillers généraux* come from liberal professions and especially the medical profession.

M. H. Marchand describes the relationship of the *conseiller général* with his electors as that of a broker who translates the language of the administration to the people, as well as that of a "protector" to whom his electors turn whenever they need help. But much depends on the social background of his electors: the more educated or wealthy look upon him as an administrator and when the circumstances require they generally seek the help of the deputy. But the ordinary people tend to treat him as their mediator:

les interventions qu'il fait sont multiples, diverses selon l'activité de la population, les traits principaux du canton, ses charactéristiques économiques et sociales: elles vont du permis de chasse, à une demande de pose de téléphone dans une ferme, d'aide médicale gratuite etc. . . . Le conseiller est celui qui défend le dossier à la Commission cantonale d'assistance, qui passe à la préfecture pour hâter la solution d'un problème ou le versement d'une allocation, qui peut intervenir à tout propos pour tout le monde" (Marchand, 1970: 151).

In addition, not unlike the mayor, he is always ready to offer his counsel to those in need:

sa fonction rappelle les moeurs de l'Antiquité: c'est le "patron" entouré de ses "clients." Il crée effectivement autour de lui un réseau de relations qui rappellent à certains égards les protecteurs d'autrefois et d'où la politique, malgré sa discretion, n'est pas absente (Marchand, 1970: 152).

It seems that on the whole there is a relative decline of the influence of the *conseiller général* in comparison with the mayor; as Longepierre remarks: "une vraie substitution s'opère qui voit remplacer le conseiller général dans le salon d'attente du Préfet" (Longepierre, 1971: 21).

If we now try to figure out the structure of power in the departmental system, the notable emerges as the official who can bargain with the Prefect, that is, obtain from the Prefect exceptions to the rule. From that point of view, Grémion distinguishes two different systems: the urban departmental system based on the interaction between the Prefect and the mayor of the big city, and the rural departmental system based on the interaction between the Prefect and the Chairman of the *Conseil Général*.

We have seen in both the case of the mayor or of the *conseiller général*, how important the brokerage and patronage functions of the elected notables are. These functions are related to the position and the status they have: they are positional notables. But they have been elected as positional notables because, in many cases, they already were sociological notables or "notabilities." The nature of clientelism may vary depending on local traditions and regional subcultures.

3. The Peripheries and Local Clientelistic Traditions

The uniformity of the French local government system masks the variety of the 36,000 municipal systems. Only recently has this diversity been explored. Thanks to Pierre Barral and to the *Groupe de Sociologie Rurale* (GSR) directed by Henri Mendras, we are just beginning to gain some insight into these rural arenas (Barral, 1968;

Mendras, 1977). Some tentative regional classifications have been proposed.

Using mainly data collected by the GSR Pierre Barral offers a classification of the rural sectors on the basis of three criteria. The first criterion is the class system of the village. This leads to a basic tension between the "rural democracies" and the "hierarchies." The former's social structure is characterized by a majority of small, independent and egalitarian landowners; the latter's by the domination of small peasants by large landowners. Barral's second criterion takes into account the basic mode of social relations of the village community, including its ties to the wider society and the existence of the clientele nexus:

> Nous y ajouterons le phénomène trop peu connu de la clientèle, c'est à dire la dépendance consentie à un pouvoir extérieur en échange d'une protection avantageuse. Certaines régions se montrent favorables au développement de cet esprit qui, soit consolide la hiérarchie, soit encadre la démocratie, (Barral, 1968: 54).

The third criterion reflects an ideological cleavage. The religious factor (clericalism versus anticlericalism) is directly related to the choice of political camps: the Left (*mouvement*) vs. the Right (*ordre établi*).

Henri Mendras has recently proposed a classification of rural local political systems which is focussed more on political power. He distinguishes among the so-called "Mediterranean oligarchies," the "mountain democracies," the "federalism of Rouergue and Limousin," the "hereditary monarchy" and the "*principat electif*" (Mendras, 1977: 137).

Such classifications, though tentative in character, draw our attention to an important facet of the local politico-administrative systems.

The relationships between notables and the administration have been much more extensively studied than the relations between the notables and their local environment. Just how salient local clientelistic traditions are in any given setting helps us understand the persistence of apparently archaic and anachronistic forms of political behavior. Such traditions merely reinforce the clientelism which is already inherent to the system as a whole: the notables, then, are not only electoral notables, they are also sociological notables.

On the basis of data available from these studies, we would suggest three types of clientelistic tradition: the Mediterranean model,

146   *Political Clientelism, Patronage and Development*

which is characteristic of only part of the French Mediterranean area: i.e., Corsica and Nice; the Western model which is usually presented as typical of traditional *notabilism* rather than of clientelism; and what might be referred to as the pro-government clientelistic model, found in many different regions and based on a non-ideological exchange between the electors, the notables and civil servants.

Whether or not it is proper to speak of a Mediterranean model of clientelism, the fact is that clientelism flourishes all around the Mediterranean area. In the case of Mediterranean France, it is only found, however, in a traditional form in Nice and in Corsica. There used to exist some form of clientelism before 1848 in Provence, for instance, but it has disappeared. Both Nice and Corsica share a peripheral status in terms of geography, culture and economics. Both have been rather recently attached to France; the weight of Italian history and cultural influences persists. But Nice is on the continent and Corsica is an island; Nice is a city and Corsica is predominantly rural.

Nice is a kind of paradox: a buoyant center of cosmopolitan tourism and advanced technology which claims the second largest international airport in France, and yet a city with an archaic political system which seems to belong to the 18th century. It has been described as "elective monarchy in the middle of the 20th century" (Amiot and Fontmichel, 1971).

Jean Médecin, father of the incumbent mayor, Jacques, was elected to office in 1928 in circumstances which revealed the strength of his personal following. He became a member of the *Conseil Général*, and was then elected deputy and finally senator. But he always gave priority to his municipal role. He used to make up his own slate of candidates to the municipal council by picking out one or two representatives from each influential interest group. He carefully selected his municipal employees among people who were personally loyal to him, and even had some of them elected as mayors in municipalities of the department. He knew everyone personally, and every civil servant, from the lowest ranks up to the highest, could talk to him.

A l'intérieur même de l'administration municipale certains fonctionnaires subalternes connaissaient le maire comme un vassal connait son suzerain et sont craints par leurs supérieurs hiérarchiques (la hiérarchie fonctionnelle de la compétence technique entrant parfois en conflit avec la hiérarchie des statuts définis par le rapport personnel au maire) (Amiot and Fontmichel, 1971: 50).

When he died in 1965, some old women at the funeral were crying and asking in the local dialect: "and now who is going to protect us?". He was then replaced by his son through "a kind of posthumous cooptation organized by his friends, thus paving the way for a hereditary and dynastic monarchy reminiscent of the Italian Republics of Genoa and Pisa . . ." (Amiot and Fontmichel, 1971: 53). As Amiot and Fontmichel note, national ideologies must not be taken at face value in Nice. If the Médecins had reasonably good relations with the Communists it is because local politics were based on personalities more than on programs; this is not to be explained in terms of a survival of an aristocratic power but of a new personal power which uses traditional norms, including clientele relations and a communal and particularistic ideology in order to consolidate its hold over the local community. The example of Nice illustrates the usefulness of an approach which does not consider the periphery as a simple projection of the center, but instead argues that the periphery can sometimes accommodate and absorb impulsions from the center. The dependency of the periphery in relation to the center does not exclude a relative autonomy of the periphery in relation to the center. This holds true of Corsica as well (Pomponi, 1976).

The general features of Corsican politics can be summarized as follows: Corsican politics are patrimonial politics: "en Corse la politique et les affaires ne font qu'un" (Ravis-Giordani, 1976). The mayor manages his municipality as his own patrimony, combining private and public interests. A private home was once used as the city hall. Corsicans make a distinction between what they call "*bassa politica*" and "*alta politica.*" *Bassa politica* is about purely local affairs, spoils and *combinazzioni. Alta politica* has to do with what they call the "*matrimoine,*" that is, the favors which can be extracted from the "*mère patrie.*"

Corsican politics is quintessentially clientelistic in nature. The mayor is a patron. He is usually the head of a relatively wealthy family of landowners. His parental ties are the core of a clientele:

> en dehors de la parenté, le noyau s'élargit en clientèle où l'on relève principalement ceux qui sont sous la dépendance du chef de parti, ses bergers, ses métayers, ses journaliers ou ceux d'une manière générale qui attendent quelque chose de lui (Pomponi, 1976: 156).

Corsican politics are dominated by factions ("*politique des clans*"). The style of politics is conflictual, but the sources of conflict are purely local. National ideologies are irrelevant, even if the patrons have a national political affliliation. Conflicts between clans are a constant of village politics. Normally there are two clans fighting each other, each led by a *capi partitu*. In the past, these conflicts led to private wars, feuds and vendettas; recently they have been incorporated into electoral competition: "autrefois, ils nous auraient suivi à la guerre, aujourd'hui ils nous suivent au scrutin" (Ravis-Giordani, 1976: 173).

Corsican politics is thus marked by the persistence of a strong and original subculture based on the traditional Mediterranean sense of honor. The result is that the mayor behaves as a despot, a tyrant, a "little Caesar" against those who are not members of his clan. And the law of the Republic is powerless against the endemic character of electoral fraud:

> le moindre acte officiel délivré, la moindre demande agrée, sont reçues comme une faveur, comme un service, rarement comme un droit: c'est la différence de comportement entre un citoyen et un client. Les partisans attendent satisfaction du chef indépendamment des règles et des limites imposées par la loi à son pouvoir (Pomponi, 1976: 158).

The *bassa politica* is based on two different kinds of clientelist resources. In some parts of the island (Balagne, Cap Corse, Sartenais) the resources are land ownership; elsewhere, in the center of the island, the resources are found in municipal land control.

The first case corresponds to classic clientelism. Although every Corsican owns a piece of land, most of them cannot live off the land. Because of the small size of their holdings, they have little choice but to enter into a quasi-clientelistic relationship vis-à-vis the large landowners. The latter are wealthy only in comparison with their clients; they are not motivated by economic rationality but by political amibition: "Un de mes frères gère nos propriétés; moi, en qualité d'aîné, j'ai la direction politique. Je donne ma vie et je pourrai dire ma fortune à nos clients et nos clients nous donnet leurs voix" (Ravis-Giordani, 1976: 172). Here the finality of clientelism is the prestige and honor of the family more than the pursuit of material interest.

In the second type of clientelism, the key political resource lies in control over municipal land. The mayor uses land for his own profit and the profit of his clients, and withholds it from his enemies; the mayor can play this game because of his law enforcement prerogatives; the mayor, after all, is the head of the municipal police in France.

These two kinds of clientelism illustrate how economic resources can be used for building political resources. In both cases, the relations between wealth and power are fundamental.

The dominant trend recently has been for the *alta politica* to replace the *bassa politica*. The former involves access to the national "*matrimoine*". The patrons, through relations and connections both in the island and in Paris, seek out jobs for their friends on the mainland or overseas. Many Corsicans have indeed found jobs in the metropolitan civil service. Other favors like pensions, welfare benefits and the like, can be distributed locally through the mediation of the mayor; and many jobs on the island depend on the local influence of the patron. It is typical, that at the level of the *Conseil Général*, between 50 and 60% of the councillors come from the medical professions — pharmacy and civil service, the very same professions from which mediators are drawn. The *alta politica* has become more and more the business of the elected patrons at the supra-municipal level. The *capi partitu* of the village is the mediator between his clients and the political or professional levels; he is both an intermediary and a screen. He is himself part of a larger clan in which he bargains for the voices he controls.

This political system generates conflict among patrons who belong to the same class and thus conceals the class cleavages between patrons and clients, and inhibits the manifestation of class conflict. In a way it also serves as a mechanism for ensuring a measure of regional integration — but only up to a point. The regionalist movement in Corsica is today directly related to a crisis in the system of center-periphery relations. A similar crisis also exists in western France.

Western France is traditionally conceived of as the land of "notabilism," another word to describe a particular kind of clientelism. No one has portrayed the regional subcultures of western France better than André Siegfried (Siegfried, 1913). He was primarily interested in explaining electoral behavior in the light of geographical or regional variables; specifically, he wanted to explain why some parts of Brittany traditionally voted for parties of the Right. In spite of his mastery of the subject, he could not find a convincing answer, as Paul Bois demonstrated (Bois, 1971). Nevertheless, his brilliant analysis of voting patterns is directly relevant to this discussion. For Anjou, Maine and *"Bretagne bretonnante,"* he shows the extent to which ties of personal dependency linked rural population to the landowner (the *châtelain* of noble descent) and to the priest. The first type of dependency is essentially material, the second more spiritual, but both have material and ideological dimensions. The power and influence of the Right is at its maximum when there is a convergence of pressures from the Church and the nobles. The large landowner in effect controls all those who are dependent on him for their livelihood — servants, gardeners, farmers, day laborers. But at the same time, these *châtelains* enjoy legitimacy, in the sense that the population feels that it is "natural" to vote for them. As for the Church, it controls all the women and almost all of the men; they obey the priest out of religious conviction, but the priest indirectly controls other resources which can be used as a deterrent against nonconformism: "du château, on tient le paysan par l'intérêt matériel, du presbytère par un épouvantail terrible, la peur de l'enfer" (Siegfried, 1915: 189).

Even if Siegfried has overemphasized the influence of the rural notables and of the Church, this two-fold influence is nevertheless important. A recent study by Susan Berger shows that the traditional hierarchical subculture of Brittany has been significantly reinforced by the strategy of the social and economic elites; despite the threats posed to their traditional power base some of these elites were remarkably successful in controlling the organizational leadership of the peasantry. Her study of the *Office Central de Landernau* illustrates the originality of their strategy: the key to their success lay in their ability to set up peasant unions outside the realm of governmental control with a view to providing goods and services directly to the peasant (Berger, 1972). In so doing, they unwittingly contributed to the persistence of a closed regional subculture. This phenomenon is reminiscent of the strategies of the Communist Party in other regions among the municipalities it controls. This operational style is clearly very different from that of the notables of Corsica who, on the contrary, have survived through the use of their connections with the center. In both cases, the notable still acts as the mediator between the center and the periphery, but in Brittany he is more of a protective screen than an intermediary.

The clientelism of the notables is a by-product of the institutional system within which relations between the center and periphery have developed. We have seen that in some regions and in some localities, it was congruent with cultural traditions of clientelism. This clientelism of the notables has not been replaced by party-directed patronage like in Italy; it conflicts or combines with a party clientelism which manifests itself intermittently depending on the political conjuncture.

II. THE FRENCH POLITICAL ADMINISTRATIVE SYSTEM AND PARTY CLIENTELISM

We have considered the French politico-administrative system without paying much attention to the influence of the political parties both at the local and national levels. At the local level, the nature of the party in power is not a key determinant: the policy outputs are fairly stable whether the party in power is Socialist or Gaullist. However, the Communist municipalities have a more coherent social policy; the tenor of municipal life is very different in Communist communes; it is controlled by the party through many associations which in turn makes for the persistence of a sort of closed subculture. Communist office holders have a good reputation as administrators, and if they hold any grudges against the Administration or the government, this is not because they feel discriminated against (Montaldo, 1977).

Whatever the nature of the competition among parties at the national level, this, it would seem, does not have much of an impact on local government. And yet, if local politics can indeed be conceptualized in terms of a relatively autonomous subsystem, this does not mean that national party politics have no influence whatsoever on the local scene. In spite of the rhetoric of *apolitisme* local elections are political contests which involve overt or covert political competition between the local branches of national parties. The capture of power at the communal or departmental levels is an important stake. Even if local politics are not reducible to a mere projection of national politics into the local arena, there are significant interactions between the two. A fundamental aspect of this interplay between center and periphery has to do with the existence (or nonexistence) of a majority in power. When government rests on a stable majority, that is in most instances when one party controls the exercise of executive power for a long period of time, the autonomy of local government declines and a party-based clientelism tends to develop. This phenomenon finds expression in party-based patronage in a particularist, partisan-oriented mode of resource allocation whereby party members and their followers receive the lion's share of municipal resources. This party-based clientelism is an intermittent phenomenon: its intensity and scope vary with the winds of political change at the center.

During the Third Republic, the conflict between Right and Left expressed a conflict between traditional and "new" notables, the latter backed by the republican state. With the advent of the Fourth Republic after the second world war, control over the state was exercised by the three mass-based parties of the so-called tripartite government coalition; the result was a temporary eclipse of the notables. No sooner did the tripartite coalition break down than the system moved back into the old notabilist mold of the Third Republic. The ruling parties became *partis de cadres*, and the notables reappeared.

1. Party-based Clientelism in the Third Republic

During the 19th century most of the peasantry remained under the influence of rural notables. It took no less than a century for the ideas of the Revolution to finally penetrate the rural population. At the beginning of the Third Republic the majority of the peasants voted for the Right; ten years later, in the 1880s, the majority voted for the Republic (Gouault, 1954). In order to consolidate the new Republic, its supporters on the Left used a typically clientelistic strategy. The Right did basically the same thing, keeping alive its traditional patron-client nets while at the same time trying to generate new ones.

After their victory following the crisis of 16 May 1876, the Republicans (first the *Opportunistes*, then the Radical Socialists) worked to strengthen their position and spread their influence by mobilizing all the resources in the state for their own use and that of their supporters. Meanwhile, through legislative action, they created an institutional base for their political action. In addition, the republican bourgeoisie, looking for popular political support, resorted to what is generally known as "the republican synthesis," that is a political and class-based coalition founded on the support of the small urban bourgeoisie and the peasantry. This populist strategy designed to take the wind out of the sails of both anti-republican and working-class elements succeeded in many places in replacing the former traditional notables by new ones, i.e., the *nouvelles couches* heralded by Gambetta (Halévy, 1930). These new notables, as we have seen, were recruited from among the liberal professions. In short, the clientelistic strategy of the republicans involved a combination of three phenomena: the capture of power at the center by a new political movement; the setting up of new institutional structures; and a certain type of class coalition based on the influence of the new notables on the peasantry.

The villages were a key target for the Republicans: not only did they develop new means of communication, thus bringing to an end the traditional isolation of the countryside, but they paved the way for a mass education system via the *école communale* (communal school); in each commune, therefore, the teacher emerged as a new notable as well as the spokesman of republican ideas. The well-known tug of war between the rural school master (*instituteur*) and the rural priest has long been part of the political landscape of many villages. The Republicans understood that the Republic must first win control of the villages. That is why they felt the need for a local government reform and in time introduced a special administrative framework to implement their rural policy.

The new local government system has a long history. Two dates must be noted: in 1871 the new package of laws on the departments and the communes was introduced along with universal suffrage for the election of the *conseil général* and *conseils municipaux*. By 1882 provision was made for the mayors to be elected by the *conseil municipal*. We have seen that this system was based on collaboration between elected notables and civil servants, the latter dependent on the central government. We have shown how the institutional dependency of local government on the central government resulted in the personal dependency of the mayors on the favors of the civil servants and of the Prefect. As political representative of the central government, however, the Prefect's first responsibility was to insure the electoral victories of the incumbents.

Political favoritism on the part of the Prefect was a common occurrence. This exchange process was greatly facilitated by the creation, in November 1881, of a Ministry of Agriculture. Together with the Ministry of Interior, the Ministry of Agriculture was soon converted into a powerful political tool in the hands of the Radical

Socialists under the Third and Fourth Republics. So much so that it became one of the most thoroughly politicized ministries of the Third Republic.

> Maires, conseillers généraux, députés, sénateurs, préfects, notables, devinrent autant de canaux par lesquels remontaient justqu'à Paris les doléances de la paysannerie. Les faveurs obtenues permettaient de consolider la position des élus locaux, et par contre coup celle de la République. Le mouvement s'amplifia à un tel point que le Ministère de l'Agriculture, ministère mineur, devint un ministère "politique," grace auquel on pouvait asseoir solidement une influence dans une circonscription éléctorale . . . Les milieux agricoles ne demandaient pas autre chose à l'Etat que ce qui lui était accordé. Parallèlement, l'Etat et les partis profitaient de cet heureux concours de circonstances pour faire accepter le régime républicain à une paysannerie qui représentait près de 50% de l'electorat (Faure, 1966: 163).

Further increasing the efficiency of this political machine, about half of the peasant organizations came under the control of Radical Socialists. In reaction to the creation of conservative peasant unions (*syndicalisme des ducs*), Republican-led peasant unions were organized (*syndicalisme jacobin*):

> Le syndicalisme jacobin voit dans le syndicat agricole un moyen de consolider la République, et les notables opportunistes ou radicaux qui le dirigèrent, souvent issus des milieux ruraux, pouvaient compter sur l'Etat, sur l'Administration et les Préfets, sur un corps de fonctionnaires dévoués, depuis l'instituteur rival de curé, jusqu'aux professeurs départementaux d'agriculture et aux professeurs spéciaux d'arrondissement (Estier, 1976).

This penetration of rural society by the Republican state began with the electoral victory of the Republicans in 1879. This led to Republican control of the Senate, otherwise known as *"le grand conseil des communes de France"*. In 1889 the *scrutin d'arrondissement* was adopted for elections to the Chamber of Deputies which had the effect of personalizing the relation between deputies and electors; but since the Republican candidate was generally backed by the government, the result was a system of "official candidates" reminiscent of the Second Empire and the "monarchist" period of the Third Republic. This electoral system, which put a premium on both the notability of the candidate and his political backing, played first into the hands of the *Opportunistes*, and ultimately in favor of the Radical Socialists. The Parti Radical, typically a cadre party based on the support of local notables and their clienteles, emerged as the dominant party of the Third Republic. It became a participant in every ministerial coalition. Through the Radical Socialists and the Freemasons, who were very closely tied to each other, the clientelism of the notables and party clientelism emerged as two sides of the same coin. But other parties of the Third Republic, mostly parties of the Right, were playing the same game; irrespective of his party affiliations the deputy was the central figure in the political system of the Third Republic. With strong roots in his electoral "fiefdom," he was, above all, a broker, the mediator between his electors and the Administration. We are reminded of Alain's words: "la lettre du député saute par dessus tous les obstacles; elle marque un intérêt direct; elle se risque; elle réveille les bureaux; elle exige une réponse; c'est la Province qui parle, telle province tel coin de France . . . " (Alain, 1952).

The mobilization of state resources in order to win over the peasants to the cause of the Republic has been described by André Siegfried who suggests that it is more because the Republic was the state, rather than just the Republic, that it conquered Brittany:

En Bretagne, l'Etat français pèse de tout son poids pour le Breton: un gendarme, en même temps qu'un protecteur, un employeur; pour tous enfin, c'est le deus ex machina, dont l'intervention souveraine est sollicitée dès que quelque difficulté menace, c'est l'arbitre qu'on appelle au moindre conflit, c'est le protecteur riche et puissant qui apporte l'argent dont on a besoin. A tous égards, le prestige de l'Etat est énorme, énorme est l'autorité de ceux qui en sont ou apparaissent ses représentants, préfets, sous préfets, et aussi, ne l'oublions pas, le député de la majorité . . . Ici l'Etat, ou si vous voulez le gouvernement républicain qui l'incarne, est puissament outillé; par les places dont il dispose, par les pensions, par les faveurs, les secours qu'il octroie, c'est pour ainsi dire dans toutes les familles qu'il pénètre, car il est bien rare qu'à un moment donné de son existence, un Breton n'ait pas quelque chose à solliciter de lui. Le voilà, donc, mieux armé que le noble au domaine démantibulé, mieux armé souvent que le prêtre, lorsque celui ci cesse d'être craint. Ne nous y trompons pas, c'est non seulement parce qu'elle est la république mais aussi parce qu'elle est l'Etat que la République a peu à peu conquis la Bretagne. Il est plus d'une circonscription qui peut-être ne voterait pas avec la gauche si son député n'était pas considéré par l'opinion, comme ayant une part pour ses protégés dans la répartition des faveurs. De ce coté-ci l'état republicaine assied son pourvoir par des arguments matériels puissants, où dans l'appui censé populaire, le bienfait s'unit à la force (Siegfried, 1915: 223).

But in spite of this systematic use of the resources of the state, certain regions resisted its influence and refused to accept Republican ideas for a long time. These were the regions where the traditional notables were most solidly entrenched.

The notables preserved their influence not only in their traditional role of notables but with a new weapon: the organizational weapon. They were the first to take advantage of the new law of 1884 on unionism to create farmers' unions and organizations which they controlled both at the local and national levels. It was in reaction to the success of their efforts that the Republicans, in turn, created other organizations. But if both strategies were clientelistic in their inspiration of distributing material favors in exchange for political support, they involved radically different tactics. While the Republican farmers' unions were backed by the state, the unions of the "dukes," to the contrary, were aiming at isolating the peasant from the state by substituting their own organization and leadership for those of the Republican state. In her study of the *Office de Landernau*, Suzanne Berger has excellently described this strategy which was both corporatist and paternalist at the same time: the main function of the so-called *"syndicats boutiques"* was to meet the needs of the population in a way that would insulate it from the "nefarious" influences of the cities and the state.

As a consequence of the strategies pursued by both the Right and the Left, the peasantry ended up politically divided. Not until recently did they learn to fight for themselves instead of passively following their notables on the Right or the Left. Not until the Fourth Republic was an attempt made to change the rules of the game.

2. Party Clientelism in the Fourth Republic

The advent of the Fourth Republic expressed a widespread desire for political renewal. The resulting political formula at first played against the old parties of the Third Republic (like the Radical Socialists and the parties of the Right), but after the collapse of *tripartisme* one notices an irresistible tendency to return to the practices of the Third Republic.

Tripartisme brought together into the fold of a fragile coalition Communists, Socialists (SFIO) and members of the *Mouvement Républicain Populaire* (MRP). The Third Republic notables were swept away; the new political class was recruited mostly from among the war *"résistants."* This marked the end of the clientelism of the notables; instead emerged a "partitocracy" which de Gaulle promptly condemned as the *"régime des partis."* The three major parties shared control of the state along vertical lines, each party controlling some ministries and "colonizing" them as in a spoils system; they did the same for the new nationalized enterprises.

The tripartite alliance did not last long, since the Communists were forced to leave the government in 1947. With the end of *tripartisme* the Fourth Republic tended to look more and more like the Third.

Although ministries were no longer considered as the exclusive "fiefdom" of a party, there were still some exceptions: Interior and National Education were reserved primarily for the Radicals and the Socialists, and Foreign Affairs for the MRP. In 1956, when the Socialists were back in the government after five years of absence, they returned largely to the old practice of appointing party members to ministerial cabinets and to the "commanding heights" of the civil service. This had the consequence of provoking a counter-colonization of the party by the administration: many policemen, for example, became members of the party, at a time when the police were a decisive factor in French political life.

With the end of *tripartisme* we also note a trend toward the electoral practices of the Third Republic. In spite of changes in the electoral law, the personality of the candidate assumed increasing significance. The introduction of *"apparentement"*, in 1951, brought some exceptions to the logic of proportional representation, so that even in the case of the more centralized parties it became important to take into consideration the personality of the candidate. What this meant in practice is perhaps best shown by the transformation of the SFIO from a mass party into a party of notables and by its success in replacing the Radical Socialists in their former local strongholds. In fact, the electors continued to vote for individuals, and in some departments local personalities appeared who dominated their party at the local level and could dispose of considerable autonomy vis-à-vis the central party headquarters. As in the Third Republic, the deputies viewed themselves as "social workers" among their constituents. For instance, Philip Williams mentions that in 1949 the Ministry of Justice received 11,700 demands from parliamentarians; in 1957, the Minister of the Interior discovered that 600 out of 800 candidates in a police examination were backed by a letter of recommendation from their deputy (Williams, 1971: 589). Although such practices were seldom brought to the attention of the public they are revealing of the image of the deputy in the minds of his constituents.

At the end of the Fourth Republic a new political class had come into existence. Recruited from the parties which made up the various coalitions, it had strong local roots at the municipal and departmental levels and maintained strong connections with the Administration. But the influence of the deputy was no longer the same as during the Third Republic:

> Infiniment plus anonyme qu'autrefois, inconnu à Paris, il est loin d'avoir la puissance départmentale d'un député de la troisième République. Sa correspondance personelle écrasante, est celle d'un redresseur de torts, d'un personnage qu'on voudrait dispensateur de faveurs, mais il a perdu sinon le pouvoir d'intervention et de recommandation, du moins le pouvoir de nomination et de promotion dont le syndicat des fonctionnaires s'est emparé (Siegfried, 1956: 219).

During its short life, the Fourth Republic brought to light a combination of party clientelism and a clientelism of notables rather similar to that of the Third Republic. All this was based on a multiparty system with no clear majority and no dominant party. With the Fifth Republic, the existence of a stable majority and of a dominant Gaullist party made for the development of a strong tendency toward party clientelism.

3. Party Clientelism and the Fifth Republic

At first glance, Gaullist ideology seems hardly conducive to the development of clientelism: its mixture of nationalism and statism, its jacobinism, its anti-party bias and anti-parliamentarianism, its *"certaine idée de la France"* and of the *"République pure et dure"* are the opposite of what we would expect from a clientelist party. There is nothing in the character of General de Gaulle and his faithful followers (like Michel Debré) which reminds one of the image of a political boss or patron.

And yet from the very beginning of the Gaullist movement the bonds which tied de Gaulle to his *"compagnons"* had something personal and affective. What was involved here was a relation based on personal loyalty, more evocative of a kind of feudal homage than of clientelism. At the time of the Resistance or during the "crossing of the desert," when de Gaulle temporarily retired from public life, to be faithful to de Gaulle was to be faithful to an ideal, not to personal favors. This disinterested aspect of Gaullism did not survive the establishment of the Fifth Republic.

(a) The Neo-Radicalism of the Gaullist Majority

The institutions of the Fifth Republic do not seem to particularly favor clientelism. The basic nature of the regime is made plain by the emasculation of parliament and the emergence of the presidency as the central fulcrum of power. All this goes directly against the grain of clientelism. However, the system can only perform adequately if there is a majority for the President in the National Assembly, since the Prime Minister, named by the President, is responsible to the Assembly. Ironically, "anti-party" Gaullism had to rely on a party, and the Gaullist Party eventually became the most important party of the majority. The Gaullist brand of clientelism was born of the conjunction of a stable majority party and of the unintended consequences of the *scrutin d'arrondissement*. The most interesting effect of this electoral reform, as Giles Martinet suggests, was a renewal of electoral clientelism:

> Un député élu au scrutin uninominal dans le cadre d'une circonscription, a davantage d'obligations personnelles, que n'en avait sous la Quatrième République un député élu à la proportionnelle sur une liste départementale. Il sera sollicité d'une manière beaucoup plus directe et constante par ceux de ses élécteurs qui ont besoin d'un service ou d'une recommandation. Il se constitua ainsi, par la force des choses, une clientèle plus sensible à ses interventions auprès des pouvoirs publics qu'à ses votes au Parlement. Dans un pays aussi centralisé que le nôtre, la France, où toutes les décisions importantes se prennent à Paris, une telle sensibilisation favorise de toute évidence, les membres du parti gouvernemental, dont les démarches passent, même si ce n'est pas toujours vrai, pour plus efficaces que celles des membres de l'opposition. C'est ce qui permet aujourd'hui de comprendre la relative solidité de l'UDR . . . Ainsi le parti Gaulliste qui a été d'abord le parti d'un homme, est devenu progressivement un parti de clientèle. Le député de la cinquième République est avant tout une assistante sociale (Martinet, 1973: 63).

The clientelist strategy of the Fifth Republic developed in response a double exigency: the necessity for the parties of the majority and, above all, the Gaullist party, to consolidate and expand their bases of support; the necessity for each individual deputy of the majority to take advantage of his political affiliation to strengthen his personal position among his constituents.

The first elections held under the Fifth Republic brought a large infusion of new blood into the National Assembly. These new deputies were for the most part unknown to their electors; they owed their election only to de Gaulle's name and personal prestige. This fragile and uncomfortable position explains the strong discipline of the Gaullist group in the National Assembly. Although most of them were in favor of *Algérie française,* they finally accepted the independence of Algeria. At that time, public opinion considered de Gaulle as a temporary phenomenon; he had been elected solely to bring peace to Algeria. Thus in order to ensure his survival in office the average deputy felt it was imperative that he become personally known and appreciated by his constituents. From the point of view of the majority and of the Gaullist Party, if Gaullism was to survive de Gaulle, it had no choice but to sink its roots in the rural soil of French society.

Thus it came that ministerial cabinets, particularly at election time, served as patronage agencies to hand out favors to the representatives of the majority party so as to facilitate their election. This almost open mobilization of the Administration in favor of the majority recalls the *candidatures officielles* during the Second Empire and the early days of the Third Republic; in fact, because of the resemblance to the practices of the Third Republic, some observers talked of *"néoradicalisme"* (Pini, 1971: 73). The "neoradicalization" of the Gaullist Party became more and more manifest as time went on, to reach its full flowering under Pompidou. As one observer put it:

> . . . aussi le Gaullisme, ou plus profondément le Pompidolisme, s'est il présenté en cette terre qui demeure profondément républicaine, sous des traits tranquilles, le "Gaullisme rondouillard", juge un élu, adoptant un style Troisième République. De plus, gouvernant seul et sans interruption, le régime a repris dans une région pauvre, (comme l'avait fait le radicalisme), les méthodes propres aux partis au pouvoir (subvention, crédits à ceux qui votent bien): il s'est ainsi constitué une clientèle. Clientèle d'ailleurs ambigüe, elle reste sensible à la non contrainte, au libéralisme politique, à la primauté de l'individu; c'est pourquoi elle est républicaine, mais elle n'ignore pas sur le plan économique, le pouvoir du pouvoir (Schiffres, 1973).

However, in its efforts to consolidate its position at the local level the new national political class found the former notables still firmly entrenched in the communes and departments. The local bases of support of the old parties of the Fourth Republic had been weakened but never really eliminated. Whether they liked it or not the Gaullists often had to find some kind of *modus vivendi*. Let us recall in this connection that it was de Gaulle's underestimation of the power of the notables in the countryside which brought his own downfall on the issue of regional and senatorial reform. The Senate, elected by these notables, was one of the most tangible manifestations of their power at the national level. Just how powerful they were became clear when they successfully mobilized the majority of the French population against de Gaulle's reforms.

The various attempts at regional reform were directed against the notables; and they failed because of the continuing influence of the notables. The Gaullists had to find new ways of overcoming these obstacles. This led to some compromises: one such compromise was to choose Gaullist candidates who had strong local roots and looked like notables; another, as we have seen, was to consolidate their fragile local position through national patronage. A third is what has been called *"le phenomène des jeunes loups"* — the "young wolves phenomenon."

(b) "Les Jeunes Loups"

Who is, or what is, a "young wolf"? The term usually refers to a young, ambitious, high-ranking civil servant recently graduated from the Ecole Nationale d'Administration (ENA), who has begun a political career within the orbit of the majority with the hope of at least becoming Minister. Their first motivation is power and they will build their political career on the strength of mutually supportive interactions between administration and politics. Their most valued resource is their technical expertise: they are first and foremost technocrats and are recruited as such into the networks of ministerial cabinets. If in addition they demonstrate sufficient skill at bargaining, manipulation, etc. their strategic importance within and outside the cabinet may increase to the point where they will acquire dozens of friends who, in turn, will help them when they run for election.

Their second major resource is indeed their "connections": in order to be recruited into the cabinet, they must have connections in the first place but in time they must demonstrate the quality of such ties. The real test here is their ability to reach out into national and local structures, into business, administration and politics.

At first de Gaulle chose many of his ministers among higher civil servants who had already established reputable careers in the civil service; they eventually were expected to run for election in order to gain democratic legitimation. Being ministers, they were easily elected. The "young wolves" appeared on the scene for the first time in the 1967 legislative elections: they tried to build their political careers first and then ran for legislative office after having accumulated political resources at the cabinet level. As Paris-based technocrats they would promise to use their access to national resources to help their constituents, but they risked being seen as strangers: there is still a strong prejudice in France against the candidate who is *parachuté* from Paris. In some cases, the "young wolves" were faced with hostility from the old notables, so much so that the majority refused to endorse them for election.

The case of Jacques Chirac, however, is clearly a success story (Clessis et al., 1972). His first patron was Marcel Dassault, the well known aircraft manufacturer and one of the most influential financial supporters of Gaullism. Marcel Dassault, long-time friend of Chirac's family, was from the start one of the most efficient of Chirac's supporters. It was Pompidou, however, who was directly responsible for launching his political career. A graduate of ENA, Chirac was admitted into Pompidou's cabinet when the latter was Prime Minister. Pompidou appreciated Chirac's ability and helped him to be elected and then to begin a career as a Minister. Very close to Pompidou, Chirac was considered to be the *"poulain,"* the *"homme lige,"* the *"vassal"* of Pompidou, all metaphors evoking the idea of a client:

> les journalistes ne se trompent pas, Jacques Chirac s'est fait de la fidèlité à Georges Pompidou une spécialité, il est son vassal au sens strict du terme; sa carrière dépend du Chef de l'Etat qui l'a tiré des brumes technocratiques pour le rejeter vers la lumière du pouvoir (Clessis et al., 1972: 12).

When Chirac was in the cabinet he had the opportunity to make several friends by distributing favors. For example, he helped Mazeaud in his attempt to be elected in Limoges:

> pour les municipales de Limoges, Jacques m'avait donné un sérieux coup de pouce, il plaidait tous mes dossiers, décrochait des décisions en faveur de ma région: l'aérodrome, le Center Universitaire Hospitaler, l'Université, c'est à lui que je les dois. Les alpinistes savent renvoyer l'ascenseur (Clessis et al., 1972: 82).

This is why, when Chirac chose Ussel district as his electoral constituency, Mazeaud returned the favor by introducing him to one of his friends from Ussel, who, in turn, presented Chirac to the local notables. Although Chirac had already been elected municipal councilor in the village of Corrèze, he was not a notable. He had to be patronized by the local bigwigs. He thus took a local notable (Belcourt) as an alternative on his own ticket, and then tried to prove the usefulness of his connections by distributing favors. The Chirac-Belcourt tandem seemed unbeatable: "l'un apporte en dot le modernisme, l'efficacité, l'appui des hautes sphères du pouvoir, l'autre la caution locale" (Clessis et al., 1972: 84). In addition, he got the support of a former political leader who was still quite influential even though his political career had been broken by the war: Lespinasse. All of which amounted to an impressive collection of assets:

> Résumons nous: l'appui logistique du cabinet de Matignon, les conseils de Juillet, et l'argent de Dassault; l'héritage du père Queuille et la bénediction de Spinasse; le soutien des familles usseloises commes les Belcour, Mazeaud ou Limoujoux et leurs clientèle. Chirac ne se parachute pas sans biscuits (Deligny, 1977: 86).

Not only could Chirac accumulate an exceptional number of assets, but he could use them productively as well. Although he is a technocrat, he knows instinctively how to talk to the people of Corrèze: he calls them by their first names; he flatters the cook, asking her for her recipes; he asks about the health of the grandfather; not only does he bring favors, but he knows how to make each favor a personal one. His local popularity in his fiefdom, *"la Chiraquie,"* is personal, not ideological; he even succeeds in securing the vote of some Communists. In addition, he could count on the help of the local administration, especially after he became Minister:

> . . . la tournée au café et la claque dans le dos ne suffisent pas pour que se réparent les routes et que courent les lignes téléphoniques. Avec l'autorité du ministre, M. Chirac dispose de l'administration. Le préfet ou plus souvent le sous-préfet, l'accompagne dans ses déplacements. Une doléance est-elle émise? "Prenez note". Et M. le Sous-Préfet s'empresse de consigner. Dans le fief electoral, c'est le Sous-Préfet qui règle les détails des déplacements. Il trace l'itinéraire, fixe les rendez vous, apporte les médailles, rédige les éléments de réponse aux questions qui seront posées . . . (Deligny, 1977: 70).

The case of Jacques Chirac is a classic example of a successful combination of the clientelism of the notable and party clientelism. For he is not a notable in the usual sociological meaning of the term but in the organizational sense. In fact, he illustrates a third generation of notables. The first notables were brokers because they were sociological notables and patrons. The second generation, the professionals, were natural brokers who became patrons. This new generation of civil servants is composed of outsiders who are not local notables. Their resources are strictly national. But they progressively transform their national resources into local resources and they build themselves into real brokers and notables.

Giscard's accession to the presidency introduced an important change in the political formula of the Fifth Republic: in the Gaullist period, the President could rely on a stable majority; the heart of the majority was the Gaullist Party which at first was the "majority of the majority" and then the majority itself. Giscard is not a Gaullist, yet he had to take into account the Gaullist Party in order to win a majority: this is why he chose Jacques Chirac, the inheritor of Gaullist legitimacy, as his Prime Minister. When Chirac broke with Giscard and left the government, however, he lost his direct access to patronage, leaving Giscard with no other choice but to replace Chirac's friends with his own supporters. The *"Etat UDR"* may well give way to an *"Etat UDF"*[6] But whatever the change from Pompidou to Giscard, and in spite of the decline of parliament, the electoral clientelism of the deputy remains a permanent characteristic of the Fifth Republic.

(c) The Electoral Clientelism of the Deputies
under the Fifth Republic

Despite appearances to the contrary, legislative elections are still very important in the Fifth Republic: there must be a majority in parliament. We have noticed the congruence of the individual electoral strategy of the candidate of the majority and the electoral strategy of the majority parties. Both the personal and partisan variables impinge on the choice of candidates. On the one hand, the monopoly of the parties in the selection of candidates is increasing; on the other hand, the personal qualities of the candidates are taken more and more into consideration.

During the Fourth Republic, the electoral tickets were made up by the parties and proportional representation gave the party a monopoly in the selection process. With the return to the *"scrutin majoritaire à deux tours"* we could have expected a decline of the role of the party in the selection process. This did not happen. The dependency of the individual candidate is still very great; without the endorsement of a party, he has very little chance of being elected.

However, the behavior of the deputy is more than ever oriented toward personal action in favor of his electors. Before being a member of parliament, the deputy works for his electors as a broker. In addition, he often accumulates offices in order to increase his local influence: the increasing importance of accumulation of offices at the national and local levels as criteria for the selection of the candidates is a striking phenomenon.

(i) The Deputy as a Broker

The deputy is considered by his electors as their personal representative. They expect him to assist them in their relations with the Administration: "Que voulez vous? Opposants ou pas les électeurs considèrent l'intervention comme un dû. Le député pour eux, c'est le représentant du gouvernment. C'est l'homme qui est le plus près du manche . . ." (Denis, 1979: 26). The image which the deputies have of their role corresponds to the expectations of the electors. This is why the most important part of their time is spent in procuring favors for their electors. As Robert Buron says:

> en bref, l'activité première du parlementaire n'a que des rapports très lointains avec la politique proprement dite. L'élu est d'abord et avant tout un avocat rémunéré au salaire mensuel, un interprète, un démarcheur infatigable. C'est aussi une assistante sociale . . . la plus efficace de son département (Buron, 1963: 32).

What is the degree of efficiency of such a strategy? The polls do not give us much information. To the question "what importance do you give to the personality of the candidate in the choice of deputy?" 37% of the respondents said a very great importance and 28% a great importance. But we know little of the sources of the candidate's personal attraction. The image of the candidate is also a product of the mass media and this can be totally at variance with his personal actions. We do not know how many electors have been helped by the deputy and among them, what proportion voted for him. The deputy has no means of checking whether the electors are paying back their debt. Yet the deputies admit the importance of their personal action in favor of the electors. When asked about their role as a deputy, 28% emphasized their national role, 10% their local role, and 37% stressed both roles. When asked whether it is their legislative function which is more important to them, or their position as intermediary between their electors and the administration, they responded thus: 36.8% — their legislative function; 27.8% — their work as mediators; and 32.5% — both (Cayrol et al., 1971).

The examination of the deputies' mail sheds a most revealing light on electoral clientelism. Escarras, on the basis of some 2,000 letters seeking a deputy's intercession, noticed that 86.7% concerned personal matters, 10% local matters, and 2.6% national problems. Roughly 50% of the personal letters dealt with relations with the Administration. Pini notes that 90% of the letters sent to deputies were written by individual citizens and only 4.1% refer to the role of the deputy as a legislator. Robert Buron emphasizes the work of the deputy in relation to his electors; he estimates that, out of ten letters, one is about political action and doctrine, two about local problems, and seven about personal problems (Buron, 1963; Pini, 1971).

In order to give satisfaction to these demands, the deputy needs to get in touch with the civil service, influential politicians, the ministers and their cabinets. According to Grémion, the influence of the deputy at the local level is generally weak unless he is the mayor of an important city; but many of the demands made by the deputy at the local level reflect the personal demands presented to him by his electors, they do not involve the local decision-making system as such. The Administration in Paris will take the deputy seriously only if he is also a mayor. This is why the deputies from the majority prefer to contact ministerial cabinets, which are the real distributors of favors.

In short, the personal dimension of the deputy's role has increased while at the same time his relation to his party has become stronger. Only through the accumulation of offices can the deputy acquire a relatively independent source of power.

(ii) The Accumulation of Offices

The accumulation of offices has always existed in the French system, but under the Fifth Republic the phenomenon has become extraordinarily widespread. It cannot be considered an exception in the mode of regulation between the center and the periphery, but as an essential part of it. The result has been to increase the interdependence of local and national government, that is of the clientelism of notables and party clientelism.

Two thirds of the deputies hold office as mayors or *conseillers généraux*. This proportion is much higher than in the Third and Fourth Republics; it reached its peak in 1973 when 71.88% of the deputies held a local office. This phenomenon is even more apparent in the case of the mayors of large towns: in 64 out of 158 cities with a population of 30,000 or more, the mayors also hold office as deputies. The larger the town, the greater the chances of the mayor "doubling" as deputy (Médard, 1972).

Another innovation of the Fifth Republic has been the reversal of the usual *cursus honorum*. Under the Third Republic the normal itinerary was the following: mayor, *conseiller général*, deputy, senator, and eventually Minister, in that order. Under the Fifth Republic many political careers began first at the national level and next at the local level. In the one case local office serves as a springboard for a national career; in the other it is a way of consolidating one's position at the center.

This accumulation of local and national offices conforms to a double logic, both functional and electoral. From an organizational and functional point of view the "cumulant", instead of simply adding to his networks, multiplies their efficiency. For the mayor to become a deputy is a way of strengthening his connections with Paris so as to depend less on the Prefect. For the deputy to become mayor is a way of opening administrative doors in Paris. The result is that the "cumulant" often becomes the political leader of his department because he has built a quasi-monopoly of networks: it is what Grémion calls the "*verrouillage*" (Grémion, 1976: 222). Most of the holders of political "fiefdoms" are "cumulants." In the rural departments the best strategy is to be at the same time President of the *Conseil Général* and deputy. Some big city mayors still refuse to contemplate a national political career but they are the exception. But when the local mandate is that of big city mayor and the national mandate that of deputy the former is the one that really counts. The mayor as such becomes a national figure.

Through the accumulation of offices the "cumulant" is able to control a wide range of resources necessary for the building of clienteles. The more networks they control the more influence they accumulate, and hence the greater their ability to bring favors to a growing number of friends and clients. Accumulation works both ways: the popularity one acquires as mayor can be transformed into electoral capital and vice versa.

CONCLUSION

The paradox and the originality of the French system lie in its unique way of combining and articulating two logically contradictory principles, i.e., universalism and particularism. The French political culture is universalistic, but the internalized cultural norms of the citizens are not those of a civic culture. The expectations of French citizens are particularistic, focussed on their own individual interests. This strange combination of universalism and particularism expresses their uneasy coexistence.

Viewed from a historical perspective, we can say that clientelism has been on the decline since the beginning of the Third Republic up to the present time. But this trend is not simple: it is associated with the phenomenon of persistence and even rebirth, and this is what needs to be explained.

This overall decline is both quantitative and qualitative. Quantitatively the frequency of clientelism in French has decreased; qualitatively, clientelism is less global and more functionally specific along the politico-administrative dimension. This is shown by the changes in the bases of recruitment of the notables. Clientelism is not only less important in society as a whole but also in the private life of individuals. The socioeconomic trends which accompany modernization, such as the acceleration of rural exodus and the concomitant expansion of urbanization, tend to lessen the incidence of clientelistic phenomena.

But this trend has slowed down and is being transformed by a counter current. If the socioeconomic basis of clientelism is disappearing, the culture, as usual, is lagging behind. This should not be interpreted only as a cultural lag. The persistence of clientelism at the cultural level is related to institutional and structural problems. From a cultural point of view, the clientelistic expectations of the electors in their dealings with notables and elected officials are striking; this is encouraged but not created by the way in which officials are elected. These expectations must be seen in the light of the problems raised by the relation of the individual to the Administration. Clientelism, therefore, is a response to the institutional dependence of local government on the whole politico-administrative system. This institutional dependency is only one dimension of the general phenomenon of the dependency of the "Province" on "Paris." The decision-making apparatus at the center helps reinforce this dependency relationship. France is the only country in Europe to be so heavily dominated by its capital city. Clientelism in these conditions must be viewed as a persistently pragmatic response to a system in which centralization and dependency have become self-perpetuating phenomena.

NOTES

1. We define political clientelism as a phenomenon involving a relation of personal dependency based on a reciprocal exchange of favors between two persons, the patron and the client, each controlling unequal resources. Political patronage refers to the distribution of public resources in return for political services. For further elaboration, see Médard (1976).

2. Our critique here borrows in part from the argument advanced by Jeanne Becquart-Leclercq (1976).

3. The term "notabilism" is roughly synonymous with what Grémion refers to as "*le système notabiliaire*." See Grémion (1976), 243 ff.

4. The distinction between "cadre" and "mass parties" is borrowed from Duverger (1958); see also Charlot (1968).

5. A situation best exemplified by the case of Raymond Marcellin, who, while serving as Minister of Interior, also held the office of mayor of Vannes and that of Chairman of the *Conseil Général* of Morbihan.

6. See for example Yves Agnes (1980).

REFERENCES

AGNES, Y. (1980). "The Giscardocracy: All the President's Men," the *Guardian*, 9 March 1980.

AGULHON, M. (1970). *La République au Village*. Paris: Plon.

ALAIN, (1952). *Politique*. Paris: Presses Universitaires de France.

AMIOT, M. and FONTMICHEL, H. (1971). "Nice: un exemple de monarchie élective au XXème siècle," *Ethnologie Française*, 1(2): 49-64.

BARRAL, P. (1968). *Les Agrariens Français de Méline à Pisani*. Paris: Armand Colin.

BECQUART-LECLERCQ, J. (1976). *Paradoxes du Pouvoir Local*. Paris: Fondation Nationale des Sciences Politiques.

BERGER, S. (1972). *Peasants Against Politics*. Cambridge, Mass: Harvard University Press.

BLEITRACH, D. and CHENU, A. (1974). "Notables et technocrates," *Cahiers Internationaux de Sociologie*, (56): 159-74.

BOIS, P. (1971). *Paysans de l'Ouest*. Paris: Flammarion.

BURON, R. (1963). *Le Plus Beau des Métiers*. Paris: Plon.

CAYROL, R., PARODI, J. L. and ISMAL, C. (1971). "L'image de la fonction parlementaire chez les députés français," *Revue Française de Science Politique*, 21(6): 1173-1206.

CHARLOT, J. (1968). *Les Partis Politiques*. Paris: Armand Colin.

CLESSIS, C., PREVOST, B. and WASJMAN, P. (1972). *Jacques Chirac ou la République des Cadets*. Paris: Presses de la Cité.

DELIGNY, H. (1977). *Chirac ou la Fringale du Pouvoir*. Paris: Moreau.

DENIS, P. M. (1979). "Piston: les petites faveurs du pouvoir," *Le Point*, 328, 1-7 January.

DULONG, R. (1978). *Les Régions, l'Etat et la Société Locale*. Paris: Presses Universitaires de France.

DUVERGER, M. (1958). *Les Partis Politiques*. Paris: Armand Colin.

ESCARRAS, IMPERIALI, and PINI, R. (1971). *Courrier Parlementaire et Fonction Parlementaire*. Paris: Presses Universitaires de France.

ESTIER, R. (1976). "Le temps des dépressions," in J. P. Houssel, ed., *Histoire des Paysans Français du XVIIIème siècle à nos jours*. Roanne: Editions Horvath.

FAURE, M. (1966). *Les Paysans dans la Société Française*. Paris: Armand Colin.

GOUAULT, J. (1954). *Comment la France est devenue Républicaine*. Paris: Armand Colin.

GRAZIANO, L. (1973). "Patron-Client Relationships in Southern Italy," *European Journal of Political Research*, 4(2): 149-74.

GRAZIANO, L. (1976). "A Conceptual Framework for the Study of Clientelistic Behavior," *European Journal of Political Research*, 4(2): 149-74.

GREMION, P. (1976). *Le Pouvoir Periphérique: Bureaucrates et Notables dans le Système Politique Français*. Paris: Le Seuil.

HALEVY, D. (1930). *La Fin des Notables*. Paris: Grasset.

KESSELMAN, M. (1967). *The Ambiguous Consensus*. New York: Alfred Knopf.

LAGROYE, J. (1973). *Chaban Delmas à Bordeaux*. Paris: Pedone.

LONGPIERRE, P. (1971). *Le Conseiller Général dans le Système Administratif Francais*. Paris: Cujas.

MARCHAND, M. H. (1970). *Les Conseillers Généraux depuis 1945.* Paris: Armand Colin.

MARTINET, G. (1973). *Le Système Pompidou.* Paris: Le Seuil.

MEDARD, J. F. (1971). "Les structures politico-administratives de l'agglomération de Bordeaux," *Revue Géographique des Pyrennées et du Sud-Ouest,* (42): 441-29.

MEDARD, J. F. (1972). "La recherche du cumul des mandats par les candidats aux elections legislatives sous la Cinquième République," in *Les Facteurs Locaux de la Vie Nationale.* Paris: Pedone.

MEDARD, J. F. (1976). "Le rapport de clientèle: du phénomène social à l'analyse politique," *Revue Française de Science Politique,* 26(1): 103-30.

MENDRAS, H. (1972). "Un schema d'analyse de la paysannerie occidentale," *Peasant Newsletter.*

MENDRAS, H. (1977). "Y a-t-il encore un pouvoir au village? Trois réflexions à propos du Rapport Guichard et des élections municipales," *Futuribles,* 10: 131-48.

MONTALDO, J. (1977). *La France Communiste.* Paris: Albin Michel.

NEVERS, J. Y. (1975). *Système Politico-Administratif Communal et Pouvoir Local en Milieu Urbain.* Thèse de Troisième Cycle. Toulouse.

PINI, R. (1971). "Essai d'analyse sur la fonction parlementaire," in Imperiali Escarras and R. Pini, *Courrier Parlementaire et Fonction Parlementaire.* Paris: Presses Universitaires de France.

POMPONI, F. (1976). "Pouvoir et abus des maires corses au 19ème siècle," *Etudes Rurales,* (6) 1: 153-70.

RAVIS-GIORDANI, G. (1976). "L'alta politica et la bassa politica: valeurs et comportements politiques dans les communautés villageoises corses (19ème-20ème siècles)," *Etudes Rurales,* (6)1: 171-89.

SCHIFFRES, M. (1973). "Le Midi Pyrénées où les Radicaux ne sont plus si tranquilles," *Le Monde,* 31 January.

SIEGFRIED, A. (1915). *Tableau Politique de la France de l'Ouest.* Paris: Armand Colin.

SIEGFRIED, A. (1965). *De la Troisième à la Quatrième République.* Paris: Grasset.

SOUCHON, M.-F. (1968). *Le Maire Elu Local dans une Société en Changement.* Paris: Cujas.

SOUCHON, M.-F. (1976). "Maires ruraux et problèmes communaux," *Etudes Rurales,* 63-4.

TARROW, S. (1977). *Between Center and Periphery: Grassroots Politicians in Italy and France.* New Haven: Yale University Press.

THOENIG, J. C. (1973). *L'Ere des Technocrates: Le Cas des Ponts et Chaussées.* Paris: Les Editions d'Organisation.

THOENIG, J. C. (1975). "La relation entre le centre et la péripherie en France," *Bulletin de l'Institut International d'Administration Publique,* 3: 77-124.

TUDESQ, J. (1973). *Le pouvoir local en France au 19ème siècle. Communication à la journée d'Etudes sur le Pouvoir Local.* Paris: Fondation Nationale des Sciences Politiques.

WILLIAMS, P. (1971). *La Vie Politique sous la IVième République.* Paris: Armand Colin.

WORMS, J. C. (1966). "Le préfet et ses notables," *Sociologie du Travail,* 8(3): 249-75.

6

Poland:
Patrons and Clients in
a Planned Economy

Jacek Tarkowski
University of Warsaw, Poland

Virtually all political scientists and sociologists in Poland accept that a planned economy is not free from the effects of spontaneous haphazard processes and of informal relationships and mechanisms. Much is already known about the origins of these phenomena in the system, and their development and influence on the functioning of the whole system. Up until now, however, little attention has been paid to the anatomy, or make-up, of these phenomena, their internal structure, and the motives which guide the participants in these processes.

Interviews carried out with economic managers and local leaders are full of references to such terms as "pull," connections, friendships, covert relationships and so on. Economic and political activists emphasize the importance of informal relationships with actors located at the top of the power structure.

The present paper is an attempt to apply the client-patron relationship concept to the Polish situation. The progress made by anthropology and political science in this area allows us to use previously-tested tools of analysis, as well as to formulate assumptions and hypotheses concerning the question of patronage in a centralized planned economy. A further advantage in employing this concept is to obtain a comparative perspective. Applying the already existing conceptual framework, we can determine firstly to what extent in Poland "accesses" and "connections" exhibit the same characteristics of client-patron relationships as can be observed in other societies. Secondly, we can suggest to what extent these features are unique and specific for the system of which they are a product and in which they operate.

A review of the relevant literature in this field reveals that there are two somewhat differing approaches to the question of patronage. For anthropologists the relations between patrons and clients have served as a traditional subject of inquiry. They have carried out research on such relations in small traditional communities, and have viewed client-patron relationships as a particular type of social relations between two individuals taking the form of a contract or exchange in dyad (Scott, 1972). In contrast political scientists have regarded patronage as an attribute of the system and show less interest in the internal structure of these relations. Weingrod serves as an illustration of this second tendency. He argues that "patronage needs to be explored not only in community context, but also as a kind of association, a network of communication, and as a means of political organization and control that operates throughout society" (Weingrod, 1968: 400). Political scientists focus primarily on political machines and party-directed patronage as their units of analysis. Here clients are no longer individuals but social or territorial groups which trade off their votes for the goods and services the party machine provides. The traditional patron, for instance, the head of a clan, a landlord, or a landed aristocrat, gave in return for a given service provided by an individual goods which were his private property. In contrast the modern form of patronage is characterized by the fact that the "individual can approach the patron . . . only as a member of the group, and the patron then acts as power broker relating the entire group to the institutional framework outside of it" (Wolf, 1966: 18).

The differences in approach between anthropologists and political scientists led to the general belief that we were dealing either with two completely contrasting phenomena, or at least with qualitatively different phenomena. As it is, however, both approaches may prove useful when analyzing patronage in Poland. As I argue later, the links between patron and client in Poland are generally very personal and individual, regardless of whether the client happens to be an individual or a group. Motives for acting, especially for patrons, display a very personal character. As a result the individualistic perspective employed by anthropologists to analyze patronage appears to be very useful here. On the other hand we also want to capture client-patron relationships in a system perspective, describing the influence of the system on patronage and indicating at least some of the effects of patronage on the whole system. Ultimately Polish patrons are closer to "modern patrons" since the goods that they dispense do not belong to them personally but constitute public property.

This paper is not based on any systematic empirical data; it represents rather some reflections connected with research carried out on the functioning of local power in Poland. For this reason some of the observations we make are of a speculative nature. The empirical material serves rather as a series of illustrations and not as a systematized body of data.

Patronage may take various forms, and the Polish case is no exception. We know of numerous kinds of classic traditional patronage in which patrons occupying high positions in the system of power or in economic management provide clients with desired goods and assure them of protection and support. In return these patrons are furnished with other kinds of goods and services. Such instances of mutual corruption are not very interesting from a theoretical or a cognitive point of view. We are also familiar with a purely political kind of patronage. By dispensing services, protection and support, strategically-located patrons acquire political support, either mobilized for them by clients or deriving from the very positions held by clients. Research into this type of relationship would undoubtedly prove fascinating but at the same time it would be very difficult to carry out. For this type of patronage is particularly commonplace at the highest levels of the power structure, and these are not very accessible to the investigator. It is worth drawing attention to the existence of such client-patron relationships, but in this paper I shall be concerned with those relationships in which either an entire community, or local leaders representing local interests, appears in the role of clients.

Polish local communities, or more precisely local authorities, possess a very restricted amount of autonomy. This is the logical outcome of a centralized system and of the general principle in force in Poland that national interests have priority over local ones. This principle is clearly stated in the People's Councils Act, article 4.2, which says that "People's Councils aim at the development of their communities as coherent socialist organisms whose existing and potential resources should be utilized for the further development of the country." In recent years the increasing centralist tendency has reduced the role of local authorities to that of agents for carrying out decisions of the higher tiers in the hierarchical administrative structure of the country. Communities receive prepared versions of their budgets and plans from provincial authorities. The right to allocate resources received from above is also limited by directives prescribing how assigned funds are to be invested. At the same time effective channels to articulate local interests are lacking. This state of affairs creates a powerful demand for alternative, informal channels of interest articulation, such as obtaining an influential patron.

The results of various studies of local power in Poland agree on one point. In spite of all the limitations local leaders are able to overcome, at least partially, such hindrances with which they are confronted, and effectively articulate and realize the interests of their localities. As we have mentioned, any organization within the system is supposed to direct its activities toward the common good, and subordinate its interests to national ones. But when it comes to practical solutions, an important question arises: how to divide up general national tasks into specific ones for various subdivisions of the system in such a way that these tasks if added together again, continue to reflect the national interests? Generally we can say that there exists *contradiction between macro and micro-rationality*. When making decisions the center takes into account the system as a whole and a longer time perspective. Operational units, be it a factory or a commune, are motivated by more immediate needs and particular interests — wages, bonuses, investments, etc. At times it happens that the decisions of the center sharply contradict the interests of a given unit. For example, the over-investment in heavy industry that took place in the Polish economy during the last couple of years induced the center to curtail it sharply. This decision, perhaps rational from the point of view of the system as a whole, is regarded by the individual communes, which require schools, roads, communal facilities, etc., as harmful and contradictory to their interests.

There is an antinomy in the role of the local leader. He is expected to unite local needs with nationwide tasks. But while local interests are for local leaders clearly defined, and the ways to satisfy them are easy to establish, the nationwide tasks are a more abstract matter. From their limited, local perspective, community leaders cannot grasp the tasks and policies pursued by the center in all their complexity and mutual interrelationship. They do not perceive nationwide tasks as a complex whole, but rather as particular items which come to them in the form of orders, accompanied by limited means for their implementation.

An important psychological factor should also not be overlooked. No matter to which local organization they belong local leaders are inhabitants of the community and naturally identify themselves with its interests. If we add to this the contradiction between macro and micro-rationality mentioned earlier, it is no wonder that these leaders pursue rather parochial, particular goals.

In a hierarchical system it is of extreme importance to have a friendly person strategically located at the higher rungs of the ladder, who can either directly supply desired goods and services or deliver information, secure connections with other influentials, or serve as a broker between the community and the upper-level divisions of the system.

What exactly is the basis of client-patron relationships? In what way do they differ from other types of social relations? According to Kaufman, who conducted an analysis of the literature in this field, what we are dealing with is a special type of dyadic exchange characterized by the following qualities:

(1) the relationship occurs between actors of unequal status and power;
(2) it is based on the principle of reciprocity, that is, a self-regulating form of interpersonal exchange, the maintenance of which depends on the return that each actor expects to obtain by rendering goods and services to the other and which ceases once the expected rewards fail to materialize;
(3) the relationship is particularistic and private, anchored only loosely in public law or community norms (Kaufman, 1974: 285).

It is generally agreed that client-patron relationships thrive particularly in a sharply stratified society where they are able to reduce social distances and barriers created by hierarchical divisions. Specialists dealing with patronage usually consider stratification to mean social stratification. There is no reason, however, to assume that the conventional hypotheses regarding patronage do not apply to a centralized, hierarchical, multitiered form of organization. Both in societies sharply divided along class lines, and in those organized according to hierarchical systems, patronage may play the role of "a kind of intervening mechanism between the local community and the nation" (Weingrod, 1968: 398) as well as serving as "a system of communication which is parallel to the official channels of government" (Boissevain, 1966: 25).

The motives which prompt clients — treated either as local communities or as their leaders — to seek out patrons are clear. Patrons are to ensure that schools, kindergartens and roads are built, a water supply is established, materials and equipment in short supply are furnished, and construction capacity (that is, building resources) to finish off local projects is achieved. In this respect they do not differ very much from clients in other countries, especially those in countries having a centralized power structure. On the basis of research carried out in local communities in France, J. Becquart-Leclercq concluded that "in order to obtain amenities and services (policy outputs), components of centralized environments (here municipalities with little autonomy) must effect informal relations with higher echelons (here state officials). Municipal leaders are therefore confronted with this dilemma: play a game of covert relationships or handicap your community" (Becquart-Leclercq, 1978: 254). This conclusion may equally apply to the Polish system of local power.

The question of patrons displays somewhat different features, however. As I shall point out later, their motives for entering into client-patron relationships are not as clear and obvious as those of clients.

Who are these patrons, then, and what type of ties do they have with local communities?

Patrons can be found everywhere, at all levels of the hierarchical structures in the economic, political and administrative spheres. They are party officials and functionaries, bureaucrats and economic managers. They are found at the central and provincial levels as well as at the lowest echelons, in communes and factories. In multitiered hierarchies, furthermore, the same person can play both roles and act as patron and client. The same actor can provide goods and services to his subordinates and at the same time extract similar favors from his superiors.

The most common type of relationship is based on *personal ties with the community as a whole*. The basis of the relationship may be the fact that the patron was born there, that some of his family live there, or that he went to school there. Patrons may also include central decision-makers who used to work in a given community. This is particularly true of persons who once occupied an important post in the locality, for example, head of the local administration, secretary of the local party committee, and so on. But there are also many examples of directors of local enterprises who, after having been transferred to more central posts, still maintain loyalty to their former place of work. Recently a new type of patron has appeared — the owner of a summer cottage located in a given community.

Personal links with local leaders may be just as strong a form of relationship with a local community. The basis of such relations can be attendance at the same school or work at the same place for patron and local leader, family bonds between them, or comradeship during wartime. Research has uncovered many instances of patronage that stemmed from the intermediary role played by a local leader. The popularity of this type of patronage, in Poland and elsewhere, has been confirmed by Boissevain's study of Sicily: "Patrons can be seen to link entire villages to the structure of government, for the personal networks of village leaders, while manipulated primarily for personal ends, also provide the lines of communication along which village business moves upward, and provincial, regional and national funds flow downward" (Boissevain, 1966: 29).

A third kind of relationship linking patrons with communities is *personal ties resulting from formal contacts*. A classic example of this kind of patron is the Sejm deputy, elected by a locality who performs an important function in a central institution. We are justified in describing Sejm deputies as patrons since their importance for their locality lies not so much in their representing local interests in the national parliament, as in their exerting the influence which their position in a central institution gives them. They are able either to furnish desired goods directly, if their position supplies them with such goods, or they can provide necessary contacts and generally create a favorable climate towards "their" community. A good example is contained in the report of the meeting between the authorities of the town of Sieradz and the editor of the popular weekly *Polityka,* who was standing as candidate for the Sejm in that constituency. The report said:

> Sieradz needs help. It is necessary to create a suitable climate towards us in Warsaw . . . Such an editor knows various people in Warsaw and when dealing with our affairs he should know whom to sound out. They are giving him his first assignment — to obtain six and a half million zlotys so as to begin the construction of a commercial and catering complex (Krall, 1976).

Obviously not all deputies, who serve as functionaries in central institutions, take on the role of patrons. But to judge by the material we have gathered, this occurs very often. Sometimes the role of patron lasts longer than the term of office.

Persons linked formally with one of the local institutions may also act as patrons. Ministers or directors of industrial corporations, for example, may be responsible for factories and offices located in a given community. In these instances, directors of local enterprises usually perform an intermediary role, furnishing local authorities with connections to their superiors. In time these contacts become more or less permanent and the community acquires yet another patron.

Regardless whether the origin of the ties with the community derives from private or formal contacts, or from the fact that the patron is linked to the community as a whole or only indirectly, through an intermediary, the relationship always displays a personal, private quality characteristic of all client-patron relationships. Patrons utilize the resources available to them from their formal roles and exploit them for the benefit of the community, and in so doing they overstep the boundaries of their formal roles.

In general, therefore, the nature of the relationship between patrons and communities rather resembles the ties characteristic of the traditional form of patronage. This is due to the personal nature of the relationship. At the same time, however, the dominant feature of the traditional form of patronage is the strong permanent link of the client to one patron, who furnishes the client with the goods and services he has at his disposal. In this respect client-patron relationships in present-day Polish society are in fact more similar to the modern form of patronage. Here, to quote from Wolf,

> Patronage takes the form of sponsorship, in which the patron provides connections with the institutional order. In such circumstances, his stock-in-trade consists less of relatively independent allocation of goods and services than of use of influence. Correspondingly, however, his hold on the client is weakened, and in place of solid patron-client ties we may expect to encounter diffuse and cross-cutting ties between multiple sponsors and multiple clients, with clients often moving from one orbit of influence to another (Wolf, 1966: 18).

Our discussion so far leads us to conclude that the relations between persons performing important functions at the central level and local communities are characterized by traits typical of all client-patron relationships:

1. asymmetry in the position of the partners, who are located at opposite ends of the organizational hierarchy;

2. a private individual character to the ties linking patrons with clients (either individuals or groups);

3. a particularistic, unaggregated character to the demands made on the patrons, and a particularistic, partisan character to the decisions taken by patrons regarding distribution.

There is, however, one trait missing in this schema, a trait sometimes regarded as the most fundamental one in the client-patron relationship. According to L. Graziano,

> There is in fact an element in clientelism which unifies all aspects — social as well as political, "traditional" and "modern" — of the phenomenon of exchange. Clientelism as an interpersonal relationship and clientelism as party-directed patronage are both based on the direct exchange of favors (Graziano, 1975:17).

An analysis of Polish client-patron relationships runs into serious difficulties on this issue. If, consistent with our assumptions, we disregard the relations between clients and patrons characterized by a mutual desire to gain personal advantages, or to mobilize or obtain political support through the use of patronage, then the question arises: what kind of goods and services can patrons, located at the top echelons of the organizational hierarchy, provide to local communities? It seems likely that the great distance separating the participants in such relationships in terms of their location in the organizational hierarchy, as well as the modest resources which local clients have available, precludes the kind of exchange typical of the traditional form of patronage. On the other hand, in a system in which there exists no free interplay of political power, party-directed patronage involving the repayment of goods and services rendered through electoral votes is out of the question. It appears, therefore, that Polish patrons do not obtain any real tangible advantages from the benefits they confer upon a local community.

At the same time research into patronage in other countries reveals that

> the offerings of the patron are more immediately tangible. He provides economic aid and protection against both legal and illegal exactions of authority. The client pays back in more intangible assets, such as information, esteem and political support (Wolf, 1966: 16).

Wolf's remarks concern primarily the traditional form of patronage since his research was focussed on Latin America and the Mediterranean countries of Europe. Still, a study of patronage in France produced similar findings. In the process of exchange (or bartering) between local leaders and the prefect, "local political leaders offer information and symbolic support in exchange for amenities and services" (Becquart-Leclerc, 1977: 21). Nevertheless, apart from such symbolic benefits as loyalty or esteem, patrons usually acquire more tangible advantages, too, such as effective political support, material goods, or support shown for the patron through the use of force. The scope of these tangible benefits obtained by the patron is in the Polish case very limited. The motives inclining patrons to act on behalf of a community are mainly found in the psychological make-up of the patrons and in the cultural norms of society. I shall not even attempt to present a tentative typology of such motives, at the most I wish to point out some potential psychological factors, cultural determinants and system conditioning which may persuade persons holding high political or economic positions to adopt the role of patrons.

1. PSYCHOLOGICAL REWARDS

These involve displays of respect, recognition and gratitude paid by local leaders or the inhabitants of a community to their patron. This respect may take the form of conferment of honorary titles on patrons which recognize the services they have given to the town or province, honorary citizenship, receptions given in their honor — generally the red carpet treatment which the patron gets from a community. At times patrons are given gifts, usually articles produced by local industry. It would be erroneous, however, to treat such gifts as repayment for goods and services rendered. For example, it is difficult to regard a tea set or a carpet presented to the patron as appropriate remuneration for his having arranged to have a school built, water supply provided, or cultural center put up in the community. I would be inclined to consider these as symbolic tokens, in much the same way as a box of chocolates or a bottle of cognac is given to doctors for their care and attention. In these cases it is not the gift but the sentiment that counts.

2. "INTERNAL" PSYCHOLOGICAL REWARDS

We may assume that many central decision-makers obtain psychological satisfaction from performing the role of patrons, regardless whether they receive rewards from their clients. In his classic work *Essai sur le don*, Marcel Mauss writes that "giving is to display one's superiority, to become something higher, to be the master; receiving without giving back, or without giving back more, is to subordinate oneself, to turn into a client, a servant, to become small, to fall lower" (Mauss, 1973: 317). In this way the role of patron gives one the opportunity to demonstrate one's capabilities, power and influence, to reinforce one's ego. Patronage in this sense can be considered as "ego massage."

3. CULTURAL FACTORS

The importance of factors such as family, tribal or clan loyalty, or loyalty to the place of one's birth, in traditional societies is generally well known. It is even pointed out sometimes that the strength of such loyalty, the strength of norms demanding the giving of unconditional and disinterested help to members of the family, tribe or local inhabitants, represents one of the main brakes on the process of modernization in underdeveloped countries. The popular view is that the intensive industrialization, migration and social mobility which occurred in Poland over the last 30 years helped completely break this type of tie. The analysis of client-patron relationships and the role that the personal links of the patron with the community play in these relations requires caution in formulating any categorical judgments on this issue. The norm prescribing the proferring of help to one's community continues to be significant in Poland, but in a weakened and modified way.

In his sketch on norms of reciprocity, Gouldner writes about "special mechanisms which compensate for or control the tensions which arise in the event of breakdown or reciprocity. Among such compensatory mechanisms there may be culturally shared prescriptions of one-sided or unconditional generosity, such as the Christian notion of 'turning the other cheek' . . ., the feudal notion of 'noblesse oblige' or the Roman notion of 'clemency' " (Gouldner, 1960: 164). Aron Guriewicz emphasizes the role of norms of generosity in medieval societies, indicating that "the most important of the positive traits charcterizing the feudal lord was generosity. The seigneur is therefore a person surrounded by courtiers, by a retinue, by vassals who serve him, support him and carry out his wishes . . . The most typical style of life for the seigneur was based on a generous distribution and squandering of his wealth" (Guriewicz, 1976: 253). It appears that persons who serve as central decision-makers in present-day Poland share the belief, though they may not be fully conscious of it, that "noblesse oblige", or rather that "my role obliges me." This norm not only precludes the possibility of refusing to give help to individuals or groups with whom he is in personal contact, but in fact prescribes showing generosity. In the course of my research I found that many of the visits paid to communities by persons of high central standing involved the approval of some large project, such as the building of a school, a factory, a housing estate, and so on. It is true that these are not typical examples of client-patron relationships since the contact and relationship is short term and ad hoc. But such examples show very clearly that the principle of generosity is adhered to. There is no permanent link between donor and the community, but in spite of this we observe the typical form of patronage based on personal contact as of an asymmetrical character, with allocation carried out according to particularistic criteria. This kind of relationship and of material support is an extraordinary phenomenon in the Polish form of patronage. Research carried out in two cities, one situated on the Polish border, the other located near a well-known health resort, showed that local authorities regarded their geographical setting as an important source of influence. The possibility of even passing contact with central leaders crossing the border or resting at the health resort could result in additional investment funds, equipment and material in short supply, above and beyond those specified in the plan. It is difficult to identify the motives producing such a form of behavior by ad hoc patrons other than the need to act in a way consistent with the norm of generosity.

In his survey of budgets of American cities, Terry Clark found that those in which a large part of the population was of Irish origin tended on average to have larger budgets. In trying to discover the reasons for this relation, Clark concluded that the basic determinant is the Irish ethic. This ethic is highly particularistic, leans more toward personal contacts for guidance than toward values and norms. It results in a distinctive style of political leadership, one heavily dependent on patronage (Clark, 1975). In his article Clark cites the remarks of a leading police executive in Chicago, reported in Wilson's study: "the most striking fact about the Irish Catholic command officers is the extent to which they rely on personal loyalties and exchange of personal favors as a way of doing things. If there is a perfectly legal, routine way of doing something, you can almost be certain that many of your Irish Catholic officers will prefer to do it through some informal means instead" (Clark, 1975: 322). These observations are equally relevant to the Polish case. It seems that the Irish as well as the Polish ethic have many features in common. The origins of the Polish ethic lie in history. Obviously a full analysis of the problem is beyond the scope of this paper. But we may note that for many centuries the Polish republic dominated by the nobility was characterized by the priority of the nobility's right to autonomy over considerations of the general interest or of the authority of the state and king. As a second factor we may single out the cultural inheritance of Poland under the partitions. During this period opposition to the foreign state apparatus and the legal system imposed by the partitioning powers was regarded as a patriotic duty. The absence of autonomous institutional structures forced social interaction to take the form of private non-institutional contacts. The German occupation in the last war reinforced this tendency.

Also important is the experience of the last 30 years. A centralized economy tends to produce a proliferation of directives which sometimes retard economic activity and limit the freedom of maneuver possessed by actors in the economic process. The ground rules undergo frequent alterations depending on the actual preferences of the central plan. Often actors located at the level where the plan is executed come under the crossfire of mutually contradictory directives and orders. They feel very strongly the pressure resulting from the contradictions of the macro-rational central plan and their own micro-rationality. The result is the well-known feature of "speculation with regulations" — manipulation with different rules, interpretation of ordinances and orders, and so on. A "parallel economy" develops, that is, a state of informal exchange transactions and a tendency to seek support through the system of patronage. This 30 year period is sufficiently lengthy to establish the Irish ethic as a permanent feature, given also that it is reinforced by historical tradition, and it has been transformed into a cultural norm which affects the economic culture of the country.

4. STRUCTURAL FACTORS

In this context an important question arises: how it is possible in a centralized, hierarchically organized system that patrons can

deliver goods and services to their communities? There are at least
four explanations for these kinds of activities:

1. The system tries to counteract its own centralization. The decisions made by the center or at the higher levels of the organizational hierarchy cannot take into account all the nuances and
specificities of the lower, subordinate units. Some departure from
the general line must be allowed. The "exception principle," once
introduced, has a tendency to multiply. The problem becomes to
decide when a given case is the exception. The "exception principle" opens a variety of loopholes by which "patrons" can push
forward the interests of their communities.

2. In a situation where demand greatly exceeds supply, patronage
is an additional criterion determining distribution. It is obvious
that a person in charge of distribution, having to choose between
two communities equally deserving allocation of some scarce
goods, will grant them to the one with which he has some personal
ties. One can say that patronage gives a human touch to the otherwise impersonal system of distribution. But once personal criteria
are introduced and semi-legitimized, the temptation arises to
always make allocation on a simply partisan basis. Because patrons
usually do not have direct access to the resources sought after, they
have to appeal to persons who are in charge of distribution. This
creates a network of mutual obligations. Patrons who once got
needed resources are expected to pay them back with the resources
they are in charge of. On the one hand, therefore, the network of
client-patron relationships takes in ever larger areas of social life
because of the great utility of such relations for clients. On the
other hand, the development of this network is speeded up by the
establishment of mutual dependencies and obligations among
patrons.

3. Multicentrism in the system is another factor which gives local
leaders chances to gain support at the higher levels of the system.
The structure of an institutional system of society is functionally
differentiated. This is not only because of the size, but also because
of the variety of functions performed by the system. The party,
ministries, state administration, each with their corresponding
agencies at the lower levels of the system, perform different functions and have their own spheres of activity. At the same time that
they are part of the same centralized supersystem, their spheres of
activity are not clearly demarcated, their competences often
overlap. Because of its leading position in the system, the party has

a right to interfere in the activities of economic and administrative organizations. Local authorities have certain rights with respect to the economic organizations which operate in their territory. Economic ministries make decisions affecting the local economy. This multiplicity of organizations gives local leaders some choice. They can appeal to the decisional centers where they can expect support. The mass character of local interests articulation cannot take place without having some effect on the functioning of the system as a whole. The system is not prepared to absorb spontaneous pressure alien to the logic of the system. Spontaneous local activities usually evoke the only possible counteraction: further limitation of local autonomy and tightening of central control. Much of the decisional capacity of the center is engaged in repressing uncontrolled pressures from below. The operation of the system is the result of center preferences on the one hand, and spontaneous actions of subordinate units on the other. In this way the scattered, unaggregated activities of local leaders and managers of industrial organizations influence not only the operation of the communities and factories, but also the operation of the system as a whole.

As I have already mentioned, patronage can be regarded as a substitute for blocked, inefficient channels of interest articulation. But it is not a totally satisfactory substitute. According to Almond and Powell, this form of interest articulation is characteristic of anomic groups and non-associational interest groups, that is, "kinship and lineage groups, and ethnic, status and class groups which articulate their interests intermittently through individuals, cliques, family and religious heads and the like" (Almond and Powell, 1966: 76). The diffusion of this form of articulation brings about serious disruptions and stresses in the economic and political systems, and in particular in the central planning system. Patronage disrupts the criteria regulating distribution already in force, it reduces the predictability of the behavior of actors, and it seriously weakens the steering system.

We suggested that the diffusion of client-patron relationships was caused by an over-centralized system of economic management and planning. The particularistic principles of management and distribution may, however, endure long after the conditions which brought them about have disappeared. These principles may become a permanent component of the set of attitudes which we may call the economic culture, an analogous term of political culture used by political scientists. This economic culture may end up becoming ripe for corruption and the privatization of public life.

REFERENCES

ALLUM, P. (1973). *Power and Society in Postwar Naples*. Cambridge: University Press.
ALMOND, G. and POWELL, G. (1966). *Comparative Politics: A Developmental Approach*. Boston: Little, Brown.
BECQUART-LECLERCQ, J. (1977). "Relational Power and Center-Periphery Linkages in a French Local Polity," *Sociology and Social Research*, 62 (1): 18-31.
BECQUART-LECLERCQ, J. (1978). "Relational Powei and Systemic Articulation in a French Local Polity," in L. Karpik, ed., *Organization and Environment: Theory, Issues and Reality*. London: Sage Publications.
BOISSEVAIN, J. (1966). "Patronage in Sicily," *Man* (NS), 1: 18-33.
CACIAGLI, M. et al. (1977). *Democrazia Cristiania e Potere Nel Mezzogiorno: Il Sistema Democrastiano a Catania.* Florence: Guaraldi Editore.
CLARK, T. (1975). "The Irish Ethic and the Spirit of Patronage," *Ethnicity*, (2): 305-59.
GOULDNER, A. (1960). "The Norm of Reciprocity: A Preliminary Statement," *American Sociological Review*, 25 (2): 162-69.
GRAZIANO, L. (ed.) (1974). *Clientelismo e Mutamento Politico*. Milan: Franco Angeli Editore.
GRAZIANO, L. (ed.) (1975). "A Conceptual Framework for the Study of Clientelism," *European Journal of Political Research*, 4 (2): 149-74.
GURIEWICZ, A. (1976). *Kategorie kultury sredniowiecznej* (Categories of medieval culture). Warsaw: PIW.
KAUFMAN, R. (1974). "The Patron-Client Concept and Macro-politics: Prospects and Problems," *Comparative Studies in Society and History*, 16 (3): 290-320.
KRALL, H. (1976). "Bagaz dla posla" (Luggage for a deputy), *Polityka*, No. 12, 20 March.
MAUSS, M. (1973). *Sociology and Anthropology*. Warsaw: PWN.
SALADINO, G. (1973). "Guardando dentro la DC siciliana," *l'Ora*, 23 July.
SCOTT, J. (1972). "Patron-Client Politics and Political Change in Southeast Asia," *American Political Science Review*, 66 (2): 91-113.
WEINGROD, A. (1968). "Patrons, Patronage and Political Parties," *Comparative Studies in Society and History*, 10 (3): 377-400.
WOLF, E. (1966). "Kinship, Friendship and Patron-Client Relations in Complex Societies," in M. Banton, ed., *The Social Anthropology of Complex Societies*. London: Tavistock.

III
The View from the Third World: Mexico, Peru and Turkey

—7—
Mexico: Clientelism, Corporatism and Political Stability

Susan Kaufman Purcell
University of California at Los Angeles, USA

Throughout Mexican history, the decentralization of political power has been associated with political instability at the national level. In the absence of a strong state, locally-based strongmen and their followings have engaged in fierce competition among themselves, at best to expand their clienteles and perhaps ultimately capture control of the central government, or at worst, to maintain the independence of their particular geographically-defined "fiefdoms."

Author's note: I especially would like to thank John F. H. Purcell for his many excellent suggestions and ideas. I have also benefited greatly from the comments of Douglas A. Chalmers, Jorge I. Domínguez, S.N. Eisenstadt, Fred Estévez, René Lemarchand, Daniel J. Levy, Kevin Middlebrook and Ezra N. Suleiman. The research on which this paper is partially based was carried out in Mexico between September 1975 and October 1976, and was supported by a fellowship from the Joint Committee of the American Council of Learned Societies and the Social Science Research Council. Many of the ideas in this paper were developed while I was a Fellow at the Woodrow Wilson International Center for Scholars, Washington, DC, between November 1976 and August 1977. Finally, I am grateful to the Academic Senate of the University of California, Los Angeles for its financial support.

Only during three periods of its history has Mexico enjoyed political stability, and during the longest of these (1519-1822) the country was not yet independent from Spain. Since Independence, Mexico has experienced stable rule only under the dictatorship of Porfirio Díaz (1876-1910) and in the post-revolutionary era, beginning approximately with the formation of the "single-party" system of government in 1929. In all three periods, centralization of political power was achieved by resorting to some form of authoritarian rule.[1] This is probably related to the essentially authoritarian nature of clientelist forms of social organization.[2] When people are dependent on local strongmen, democracy will only serve to reinforce the power of these local elites. A more feasible way to control locally-based strongmen, therefore, is through the creation of a national strongman who is even more powerful.

The three periods of stable authoritarian rule each overcame the potentially decentralizing impact of locally-based clientelist structures in somewhat different ways. Both the Spanish monarchs and the revolutionary political elites attempted to create a separate and distinct political base that would compete with those of the local strongmen or *caciques*. Their strategy involved organizing large numbers of individuals into corporatist entities that would be tied directly to the central government, thereby removing them from the control of the local bosses.[3] For reasons that will be discussed, Díaz did not have this option available to him and, instead, used the resources from a rapidly expanding national economy to buy the cooperation of the *caciques*. No matter which strategy was employed, however, the establishment of centralized authoritarian rule implied a modification of the behavior and, sometimes, the structure, of the local clientelist networks. In some cases, the impact was extreme enough to destroy such networks.

One purpose of this paper, therefore, is to examine in historical and comparative perspective the impact of centralized, authoritarian rule on local clientelist networks as well as the impact of such networks on the supposedly countervailing corporatist structures. A second purpose is to consider whether some form of nationalized corporatist infrastructure is required for the attainment of political stability in countries such as Mexico where political power is fragmented among locally-based strongmen and their clienteles. A final purpose is to consider whether a nationally-based corporatism and a locally-based clientelism can co-exist in dynamic balance, or whether one form of organization must necesarily supplant and eradicate the other.

CLIENTELISM, CORPORATISM AND STABILITY IN HISTORICAL PERSPECTIVE

The authoritarian political systems that have characterized Mexico's periods of stability have differed in the extent to which they have attempted to control or transform the nature of locally-based clientelist structures. Of the three periods of stable rule since the 16th century, the Porfiriato made the least alteration to the underlying clientelist social structure. The current political system has made the most deliberate and, to date, successful attempt to restructure patron-client relations. The Spanish colonial system falls somewhere in between, in that the Crown did try to offset the decentralizing potential of clientelism, but ultimately failed to do so.

Despite the supposedly "divine right of kings," the thousands of miles separating Spain from its colony and the poor state of communications within Mexico produced an erosion of royal authority in the New World. To help offset this situation, the Spanish monarchy availed itself of a two-pronged strategy. First, as part of a highly personalistic system of bureaucratic rule that has been labeled "bureaucratic patrimonialism," the Crown distributed patronage, wealth and privileges among the landowners, essentially to "buy" their loyalty and cooperation.[4] The other strategy involved the creation of a countervailing system of power that can be called corporatism. Realizing that access by landowners to vast numbers of Indians posed a potential threat to royal control, the Crown promulgated a series of laws that removed the Indian masses from the control of the *hacendado* and tied them directly to the Crown. To state it somewhat differently, Spain bestowed upon the Indians a corporate identity, sanctioned by a specific body of laws pertaining only to them and establishing for them a special and direct relationship with the Crown. The king's goal, simply put, was to deprive the landed patrons of their clients.

Unfortunately for the Spanish monarch, the countervailing corporate structures could not be institutionalized. Spain's periodic involvement in European wars caused financial problems that made her representatives in the New World susceptible to the influence of the local landed elites. These developments also undermined the ability of the Spanish Crown to protect its Indian subjects. The corporate organization of the Indians, therefore, remained more formal than real, as the landowners appropriated and divided among themselves the massive Indian labor force.

The Spanish colonial system was disbanded by the Mexican War of Independence in the early 19th century, and was followed by a chaotic period that lasted from the 1820s until the 1870s. During these years, the power of local landed elites was reinforced. This was partially due to the fact that the breakdown of the colonial system unleashed the centrifugal potential inherent in a system of locally-based clientelist structures. Also significant, however, was the outcome of the Wars of the Reform (1858-61). Won by the Liberals, who opposed corporate privilege in general and corporate landholding in particular, the wars effectively destroyed the corporate Indian communities. The intended target of the Liberals had been the Catholic Church, whose vast landholdings were quickly divided up among the most powerful landlords of the period. But the lands of the Indians also became subject to the anti-corporate legislation, with the result that these too were absorbed into the existing system of private *latifundia*. When political order was next achieved at the end of the 19th century, therefore, it would by necessity involve a coming to terms with a reinforced landed elite.

The man who eventually succeeded in winning the support of the *hacendados* was Porfirio Díaz, a military hero who had initially supported the Liberals in the Wars of the Reform. By means of his military prowess and a system known as *"pan o palo"* (bread or the stick), Díaz bought off or destroyed his competitors. His old and newfound supporters were then incorporated within a political system somewhat reminiscent of the Spanish colonial period, in that power was organized from the top down and centered in a single person, but with important differences as well.

The first contrast between the two periods of authoritarian rule involves the nature of central authority. The Spanish king represented traditional authority and, as a result, received obedience and deference without necessarily having to perform to the satisfaction of the governed. Díaz's authority, in contrast, was based on military victory. Allegiance to the supreme *caudillo* was therefore not automatic and unconditional but derived exclusively from a kind of cost-benefit analysis. Díaz's supporters demanded both larger and more tangible benefits than are usually expected from traditional leaders. Foreign investment was consequently welcomed into Mexico to help develop the economy and provide the economic wherewithal to keep supporters happy, while the bureaucracy was continually expanded so that patronage could be liberally distributed. The system thus took on the appearance of a huge distributive machine. Allegiant potential competitors got the most of what there was to get, distributing a portion of their payoffs to their immediate subordinates, and so on down the line. Access depended on *"amistad personal"* or personal contacts. Those unwilling or unable to play the game were eliminated.

In some ways, the game was not that different under Díaz than it had been during the preceding 50 years of political instability. This is because Díaz allowed the local landed elites to retain substantial control over their respective territories, provided that they did nothing to undermine his authority at the national level. The bargain represented a coming to terms with reality on the part of both Díaz and the local powerholders. Díaz could not destroy or ignore the power of the *hacendados* and they could not dislodge him. And as long as there was a commonality of interests or a kind of quid pro quo, neither Díaz nor the landed elites had sufficient motive to break with the system.

Had the Wars of the Reform not abolished corporate landownership, thereby destroying the corporate Indian communities, Díaz might have availed himself of corporate forms of political organization in order to offset the decentralizing impact of locally-based clientelist networks. Although the use of corporatism as a countervailing power against clientelism had not been totally successful during the colonial period, there was no obvious reason why it could not be experimented with in order to make it more serviceable. Díaz, however, never tried to resurrect the corporatist idea, perhaps because anti-corporatist forces and sentiments were still too strong during the Porfiriato.

Instead, Díaz came to terms with the local elites and their followings. But in order to assure that the balance of power lay with the center rather than with the localities, he encouraged the growth of the national economy, principally, as was noted, by encouraging high levels of foreign investment. As a result, the local strongmen were put in a position in which greater economic gain accrued from association with Díaz than from opposition to him. During most of the Porfiriato, therefore, a rich and expanded national economy served as the functional equivalent of the corporatism of the colonial period.

Although the Díaz dictatorship had many elements that are usually associated with machine politics, such as the lavish distribution of wealth and patronage, it had no organizational infrastructure. Distribution was not filtered through a political party and politics never became institutionalized. The entire system depended on Díaz's ability to maintain personalistic linkages with the locally-based landholding elites and their clienteles. The system originated as, and never evolved beyond, a personalistic dictatorship. As a result, when Díaz fell, the patron-client ties that came together in his person, and constituted the underpinnings of the system, abruptly unraveled.

The reasons for the fall of Díaz are directly related to the low level of political institutionalization that characterized the Porfiriato. First, Díaz had failed to build into his vast patronage system a process for the circulation of elites. Interests that had been spawned by the economic growth of the late 19th and early 20th centuries had not been incorporated into the upper levels of the political system, where they believed they belonged by virtue of their economic power. Second, Díaz had allowed the rural masses to be mercilessly exploited and repressed by the *hacendados*. Whereas the Spanish monarchy had tied the Indians directly to the Crown, in part to afford them a minimal amount of protection from the exploitation of the landowning elites, Díaz offered the masses no such protection. They consequently became available for mobilization by the dissatisfied counter-elites.

Once the masses became mobilized, the weak institutionalization of the Porfirian system caused it to collapse quickly. In the course of the civil war that ensued and eventually became the Mexican Revolution, the landed elites were supplanted by a new class of "men on horseback," who created a political system that bore a striking resemblance to the Porfirian system.[5] Like its predecessor, it was authoritarian and elitist. The Revolution had been a struggle among military men and their respective followings, and the revolutionary armies had related to their leaders less in terms of ideology than of personalistic loyalties. When the fighting ended, the victorious generals set up a political system that ratified the hierarchical leader-follower relationships established during the course of the Revolution. Power was concentrated in their hands and flowed from the top down rather than from the bottom up.

The peasant masses continued to be viewed as subjects whose demands had to be limited for elite survival. The principle of control was once again *"pan o palo,"* although the phrase, so prominent during the Porfiriato, could not be used. Cooperation and compliance with the revolutionary leadership was rewarded through the distribution of money, power, status, patronage and the like, while failure to play by the rules of the game resulted in punishment or repression.

One obvious difference between the Porfirian system and the arrangement favored by the revolutionary leaders, however, was the absence of a supreme *caudillo*. In place of Díaz there were now numerous power-holders. This was initially the result of circumstance rather than choice. Despite approximately a decade of civil war following the fall of Díaz in 1910, none of the revolutionary leaders had been able to establish his hegemony over all the others. Power was so fragmented that it had not been possible even to forge a winning coalition that would have definitively eliminated a particular revolutionary group. The fighting finally stopped only when the stalemated revolutionary leaders became persuaded that a continuation of the civil war would prove costly to all of them. By means of an informal agreement, therefore, they pledged themselves to mutual toleration and a division of the spoils that would reflect the then existing balance of power among them. Instead of a Díaz, therefore, there was a kind of governing committee.

The establishment of the distributive balance-of-power agreement among the revolutionary elites apparently was not regarded as a definitive solution by some of the more popular revolutionary leaders. Two of them in particular, Plutarco Elías Calles and Alvaro Obregón, conspired to wrest control from the others. Obregón served as President of Mexico from 1920 to 1924, and Calles, from 1924 to 1928. They used their control of the presidency to win over a substantial number of revolutionary chiefs to their side and to eliminate those who opposed their plan. They then amended the Constitution so that a president could be reelected after sitting out a term, and Obregón was elected in 1928 to succeed his ally Calles.

If Obregón had actually been allowed to serve a second term, it is unlikely that the Mexican political system would have evolved the way it did. As it happened, he was assassinated prior to assuming office. Calles then decided to retain his dominant position by establishing, in 1929, a single governing party. The party was to decide the order in which the various revolutionary leaders would succeed each other in the presidency, and the constitutional prohibition against the reelection of the president, consecutively or otherwise, was reinstated. Apparently convinced that the only alternative to the party was the breakdown of the elite bargain, Calles's plan was accepted.

The creation of an official political party was, therefore, a second important difference between the Díaz regime and the post-revolutionary system. Without the party, the new political system might have remained as incapable of dealing with popular participation as the Díaz dictatorship had been. With the party, there was at least a formal mechanism available for solving the need or demands for political participation that might arise.

At its creation, however, the official party was little more than a facade that ratified the political status quo. This consisted of a countryside divided among a number of regional strongmen. If the party had retained its original structure, the similarities between the new political system and the Porfirian one would have been accentuated. Both would have represented national systems that accommodated to essentially local bases of political power, although the Revolution had replaced the *hacendados* with revolutionary heroes possessing new regional power bases. Furthermore, both systems would have remained characterized by low levels of institutionalization at the center. Without additional modifications, the new system eventually would have been unable to manage or control the behavior of the local elites toward the rural masses, and Mexico would once again have been plunged into political chaos.

Perhaps recognizing this potential weakness, President Lázaro Cárdenas (1934-40) undertook a series of reforms aimed at strengthening the central government at the expense of the local strongmen. In a sense, he resurrected and modified the unsuccessful corporatist system of the Spanish monarchs. The party was restructured along corporatist lines in order to provide the national political elites with a power base that was separate from and more powerful than those of the local *caciques*. Peasants and workers were organized from above and incorporated into newly-created sectors of the party designated only for them. Sectors were also created for the middle class and the military. By virtue of their membership in the party's sectoral organizations, each of these groups, and especially the workers and peasants, was encouraged to regard itself as a corporate entity with interests that were distinct from, and often in conflict with, those of the locally-based strongmen.

The changes introduced by Cárdenas have endured into the present. Part of the explanation for their continued viability involves the modifications made by Cárdenas in the original Spanish system. First, by the time of Cárdenas presidency, corporately organized groups could not be attached to the Mexican president himself, since a president's term of office was limited. Unlike the Spanish monarchs, therefore, the newly-organized peasants and workers were tied to an institution, the official party, rather than to the ruler. This further institutionalized both the party and the national political system. Second, the Spanish monarchs had offered the Indians little more than intangible or symbolic benefits in their attempt to separate the Indians from the large landowners. As a result, the Indians remained dependent on the landowners for their survival. Cárdenas, in addition to bestowing symbolic rewards upon the workers and peasants, also provided them with the wherewithal to remain relatively independent of the local *caciques.* To the peasants, who during the Revolution had rallied to the slogan "land and liberty," he gave property expropriated from formerly powerful rural strongmen. For the workers, he reorganized and strengthened the union movement and collective bargaining system, and reinforced their right to strike. The use of corporatist organization as a countervailing force against locally-based clientelist structure thereby was made operative.

At the same time, however, the manner in which the peasants and workers were incorporated made them extremely dependent on the national leaders. Both groups had been organized before they had a strong sense of class identity that would have enabled them to define their true interests, select their own leaders, and enter the political system on their own terms. As a result, the price they paid for the "gifts" of organization, resources and rights was high. Having entered the national system from a position of relative weakness, they would find it difficult, if not impossible, to increase their power over their new national patrons.

To summarize, Mexico's three periods of stable authoritarian rule can be compared in terms of the mix of clientelism and corporatism. During the colonial period, the Indians were provided with a corporate identity but were not given a resource base to allow them to remain independent of the landed elites. Under Porfirio Díaz, corporatist organization to offset the power of local elites was not even attempted, due to the historical circumstances of the time. As a result, the local power bases remained relatively intact and no limits could be set to the exploitation of the rural masses by the *hacendados*. At the national level, the political system remained uninstitutionalized and dependent on a single individual. When aspiring elites mobilized the dissatisfied masses, the dictatorship was easily overthrown. The post-revolutionary political system represents the first successful attempt to offset and control the power of the rural bosses and their followings by creating a competing national power base consisting of government-sponsored and nurtured corporatist organizations incorporating both rural and urban masses. The political stability that has resulted from such an arrangement is due in great part to the fact that a dynamic balance seems to have been created between the centralizing force of corporatism and the decentralizing force of locally-based clientelism. To date, neither form of organization has been able to eradicate the other, while the interaction between them appears to be responsible for endowing the current political system with its much touted flexibility and adaptability. It is to an analysis of this dynamic interaction between centralized corporatist organizations and local clientelist structures that we now turn.

CLIENTELISM AND CORPORATISM
IN CONTEMPORARY MEXICO

As a result of the reforms introduced by Cárdenas, there are today essentially two clientelist systems operating in Mexico. The first is the chain of vertical, personalistic ties that originate in the presidency. The other is exemplified by the networks of patron-client relationships that are manipulated by *caciques* with as yet relatively autonomous local power bases. The two forms of clientelism differ not only in terms of whether they originate at the national or local level of the political system. The essence and quality of clientelist relationships in the two systems are also profoundly dissimilar.

The patron-client ties characteristic of the locally-based networks are basically stable.[6] A particular *cacique* often maintains control of his following for decades. There are even examples of *cacicazgos* that remain in the same family for generations. In the best of such cases, the *cacique* is respected, admired and obeyed by his grateful clients. In the worst, he is hated (and sometimes even killed) for the ways in which he exploits them.[7]

The clientelism that permeates the national political institutions, in contrast, is extremely unstable and fluid.[8] The explanation for this difference is the prohibition against the reelection of the Mexican president. Because the president cannot succeed himself, patron-client relations throughout the national system must adapt to a situation in which the supreme patron is replaced every six years. And given the fact that the authoritarian structure of the Mexican political system concentrates the power of appointment in the presidency, the assumption of that office by a new individual means that every six years a new group of people who are personally loyal to the new president are promoted to high-level positions. This is, however, only the tip of the iceberg. Just about all positions in Mexico are appointive, even those that are supposedly elective. This is because in a political system in which a single party is dominant, nomination is tantamount to election. This is not to say that the Mexican president is responsible for all appointments, for such is not the case, although he probably does have a final veto. But with the exception of the cabinet ministers, the heads of the most important state agencies, the presidency of the party and the state governorships, his power of appointment is usually shared with varying levels of subordinates. Such sharing of appointment power constitutes one of the tangible goods that the president's subordinates, in their role as patrons to individuals still lower in status, are able to distribute to their own clients.

Given the authoritarian structure of power, therefore, a change in the person occupying the presidency means a massive shift in the personnel of the entire system. Frank Brandenburg (1964: 157) estimated that every six years 18,000 elective positions and 25,000 appointive positions must be filled anew. Although comparable figures for the late 1970s are not available, there is no doubt that the number of elective and appointive positions that must now be filled following a presidential election is considerably greater. Since bureaucratic expansion is one way of increasing the political patronage available for distribution to supporters and potential supporters, the Mexican bureaucracy expands at a tremendous rate. One recent study (Godau, 1975: 137), for example, found a 144% increase in the number of department heads between 1956 and 1972. Measured in monetary terms, the expansion of government is even more spectacular. In 1970, for example, the old Department of Agrarian Affairs and Colonization had a budget of 125,000,000 *pesos;* in 1976, after the department had been transformed into the Secretariat of Agrarian Reform, its budget totaled 1,164,000,000 *pesos* (*El Universal,* 3 August 1976: 7).

Until recently, the issue of whether the massive turnover produced by a presidential election was merely a game of musical chairs, or whether a substantial portion of the appointments went to individuals who had not previously held public office office was a matter of some debate. As a result of the studies of Peter H. Smith (1976; 1979), however, it now appears that a significant number of individuals are definitely retired from the political arena with each presidential election. More specifically, Smith found a rate of continuity at the upper levels of the government of only 35%. This means that every three *sexenios* (six-year presidential terms), 90% of the officeholders are renewed. To state it differently, after every eighteen years, the individuals holding the more important public offices constitute an almost totally different group from that which held those positions during the previous eighteen years.

The impact of a presidential succession would be minimized if there was a decipherable career pattern that vastly increased one's chances of reaching the presidency. An ambitious individual could then either pursue such a career trajectory himself or align himself with individuals whose chances of becoming president or close subordinates of a president looked strong. But as Smith (1974) has concluded, based on his extensive study of patterns of political recruitment and political mobility in Mexico, "from almost any location in the political system, one could reasonably hope to move to almost any other location." Until 1958, however, there did seem to be a kind of pattern, in that all Mexican presidents starting with Lázaro Cárdenas had served either as Secretary of Defense or of the Interior prior to becoming president. The selection of the Secretary of Labor, Adolfo López Mateos, in 1958, introduced some variety into the recruitment process, and the nomination in 1976 of the Secretary of the Treasury, José López Portillo, opened still other possibilities.

There is an additional element of unpredictability that stems not only from the particular manner in which the institutionalization of presidential succession manifests itself, but also from the nature of the governing coalition. As Robert Scott (1959: 101) has noted, the

Mexican Revolution meant and means "everything to everybody and something different to each." In the same way that there was no agreement regarding goals during the Revolution, there is no agreement on goals today. The heterogeneous elite coalition contains leftists and rightists, people of socialist persuasion and staunch private enterprise capitalists, collectivists and individualists, liberals and authoritarians. Consequently, the accession of a new individual to the presidency often brings to prominence a new ideological slant or orientation.

The patron-client infrastructure in Mexico therefore has to adjust regularly to a change in the supreme patron (the Mexican president), a resulting massive turnover in the personnel occupying political positions at all levels of the political system, and a fluctuating ideological environment. Aside from being able to predict that these changes will occur every six years, the rest is essentially unpredictable.

The fact that the only thing that is predictable is change itself makes clientelist relationships in the national system highly tentative, conditional, pragmatic and opportunistic. Loyalty to one's patron, for example, cannot be carried to an extreme, since a patron who is well placed in the current *sexenio* could just as easily be without a job in the subsequent one if the "wrong man" is chosen to be president. It is, therefore, important to show loyalty to one's patron, "but not too much."[9] This is because individuals too closely identified with an incumbent president will be the first targets for demotion or removal by his successor. In a sense, then, the goal is to maintain sufficient flexibility so that you can easily transfer your loyalty from downwardly mobile to upwardly mobile individuals. That this goal is often attained is illustrated by the following anecdote, which is true:

> While Mr. X was Director of Credit, he played squash every week with Mr. Y. After Mr. X had left his post as Director of Credit, the squash game ceased. Then one day the ex-Director of Credit ran into his former squash partner and asked what had happened to their squash game. The man replied, "Oh, I still play golf every week with the Director of Credit."

On the other hand, it is unwise ever to break off ties completely with anyone. Because of the high degree of elite circulation in the Mexican political system, and the fact that appointments are generally made as a result of personal contacts, failure to retain or receive a position during one *sexenio* is no guarantee that the same thing will occur during the subsequent administration. As one informant observed, "Mexican politicians are like the phoenix; they rise from the ashes." The López Portillo administration is a good example of this adage, since several people who received high level appointments had been important politicians during the presidency of Adolfo López Mateos (1958-64) and had been consigned to oblivion by supporters of Presidents Gustavo Díaz Ordaz (1964-70) and Luis Echeverría (1970-76).

While too strong or too weak a personal relationship puts one in a vulnerable position, having too few personal contacts is equally undesirable. Since there are multiple routes to the presidency, it is important to keep one's options for political mobility as numerous as possible by knowing as many potential high-ranking *politicos* as possible. To a great extent, the high rate of turnover characteristic of the Mexican political system provides ample opportunities to meet and establish ties with a large number and wide variety of individuals. This is because a typical political career often includes short stints in various parts of the bureaucracy. The current president of Mexico, for example, served in the Ministries of National Patrimony, the Presidency, the Treasury, and also headed the National Electricity Commission prior to his appointment as the presidential candidate of the PRI (Partido Revolucionario Institucional). The individuals he named to his cabinet reflect his mobile background. The Secretaries of Labor, Industry and Commerce, and Tourism had served with López Portillo in National Patrimony; the Secretary of the Presidency served with him in the Treasury; and the Secretary of Public Health was a friend from his days in the Secretariat of the Presidency under President López Mateos.[10]

The preceding discussion of the mobility that is possible within the national clientelist system refers only to the elites or individuals enjoying the status of patron at all levels of the vertical linkage structures. The situation of their followers remains relatively unchangeable. This is true of all clientelist systems. Patron-client ties generally cut across class lines and make difficult the formation of horizontal class alliances. They therefore tend to perpetuate the social status quo. This does not mean that societies organized into clientelist networks are immune from breakdown or even revolution. Mexico, for example, is a country that, despite its clientelism, has experienced both. Clientelism, however, generally thrives in situations in which there is an inequitable distribution of political and economic resources. The disadvantaged attempt to make the best of their situation by entering into a personal relationship with a higher-placed individual who can reduce their vulnerability. From the perspective of the patron, such relationships reinforce his superior position and keep the disadvantaged in their place.[11]

The uniqueness of the national clientelist system of Mexico, therefore, is not the fact of elite mobility but rather, the extreme degree of such mobility. One can find in Mexico all the same relationships that are present in other systems organized along clientelist lines. There are one-to-one relationships between a patron and his client, as well as political cliques, known as *camarillas* in Mexico, composed of patrons of more-or-less equal rank who have joined forces to increase their opportunities for advancement.[12] But whereas such relationships are relatively stable in other countries, in Mexico they are highly ephemeral. They are stable only if viewed at a fixed point in time. Over the long run, they are fluid and constantly changing. They form and reform, with the *camarillas* in particular always adding and removing individuals. They are continuously in the process of redefinition, as their members attempt to maximize their opportunities and minimize their losses in a political system that is forever redistributing power and status from the top.[13] The Mexican political system can therefore be conceptualized as a rigid-looking authoritarian facade that overlays a hyperfluid clientelist interior composed of multistatus elites who are in perpetual motion.

The fluidity of clientelist relationships in the national system is intimately linked to the existence of the corporate organizations of peasants and workers. As permanent power bases of the national governing coalition, the corporate organizations both facilitate and minimize the risks inherent in elite circulation because they are permanently available for temporary appropriation by all who reach the top levels of the political system. This frees the circulating elites from having to devote their energies to building, and possibly mobilizing, ever larger individual followings. Such activities, after all, could ultimately destabilize the political system by increasing competition among the elites (thereby fragmenting them) and encouraging dangerously high levels of mobilization. Instead, the provision of permanent corporate power bases to the pool of circulating elites encourages the elites to spend their time constructing and improving relationships with other elites, so as to increase their chances of profiting from each others' promotions. The result is that the elitist nature of the national political coalition is reinforced and elite solidarity is enhanced.

The constant availability of these corporate power bases to the high-level political elites is explained, in turn, by the clientelist infrastructure of the corporate organizations. Organized into vertical chains of patron-client relationships, the head of each corporate organization can keep the entire membership in line by working only with those subordinates who function as patrons at the various levels of the corporate hierarchy. The patrons, in turn, will deal directly with their followings, thereby freeing the sector leader from the necessity of working directly with the mass membership of his organization. The lower level elites have a strong incentive to cooperate with the sector head, since the latter has the power to accelerate or block their entry into the pool of high-level circulating elites. The sector leader, in turn, cooperates with the Mexican president and his immediate subordinates because he receives, in return, the power to control patterns of advancement within his sector as well as the power to decide who gains access to the highest levels of the elite structure. In many cases, in fact, he can avail himself of this power to promote his own upward mobility.

Additional insight into the relationship between fluid clientelism and corporatism can be gained by contrasting the situation of the head of the labor sector with that of the leader of the peasant sector. In the case of labor, the workers have been led by the same individual for more than four decades. The leadership of the peasant sector, however, is in constant flux. The explanation is that the position of supreme patron of the labor movement brings with it real power, while that of supreme patron of the peasantry does not. The result is that individuals occupying the latter position must move up in order to achieve the satisfaction they seek. More specifically, the head of labor is powerful because he has control over the distribution of jobs (through the closed shop provisions of the Labor Law), as well as authority to negotiate wages, salaries and other benefits that affect every member of his corporate structure. This enables him to keep his followers in line for the benefit of the governing coalition, and also, to mobilize the support of his membership should he need to confront the Mexican president over a particular issue.

The head of the peasant sector, in contrast, has no real power because he has little to distribute. The issue of most interest to the peasants is the distribution and use of land. Both are decided by government ministries rather than by the leader of the peasant organizational hierarchy. The head of the organized peasantry, therefore, cannot "deliver" his followers in any consistent fashion to the governing coalition; nor can he mobilize them in order to extract concessions or benefits from the ruling elites, so as to consolidate his hold over his subordinates. All that the supreme patron of the peasants can do is "keep the peasants quiet" by using the patron-client infrastructure of his organization to fragment his following as much as possible. If he is successful, he will be granted access to the circulating pool of high-level elites.

The importance attributed by the elites to keeping the membership of the various corporate organizations under control derives from the nature of the corporate organizations themselves. Once a group is given a corporate label or identity, its members are at least implicitly, and sometimes explicitly, encouraged to think in collective terms. This is potentially very dangerous to Mexico's political elites, because the corporate organizations essentially reflect the class structure. If the various control mechanisms employed by the elites should malfunction, therefore, the corporate organizations could become effective spokesmen for the class interests of their members. To state it somewhat differently, in the absence of elite control, the corporate power bases of the current political system, particularly the peasant and labor organizations, could spearhead a movement aimed at radically restructuring Mexican society along lines that would be more congenial to the real interests of the peasants and workers.

In summary, therefore, clientelism and corporatism are both essential components of the centralized national political system established in the aftermath of the Revolution. By locating the apex of the national clientelist structure in the presidency, and limiting the tenure of all individuals who occupy the office, patron-client ties were made fluid, and a pool of circulating elites was created. The preemptive incorporation of peasants and workers into corporately defined sectoral organizations provided a permanent power base for the pool of circulating elites. And the permeation of these corporate structures by clientelist linkage mechanisms worked to undermine the potential threat inherent in collectivist groupings which, in the Mexican case, correspond to the underlying class structure of the society.[14]

The above discussion focusses entirely on the national political system that was created to offset the decentralizing impact of locally-based *caciques* and their followings. It is now generally conceded that political power in Mexico has achieved an impressive degree of centralization, particularly in comparison to the situation that prevails in other developing countries. What still remains to be analyzed, however, is the way in which this national system dealt with and continues to deal with the autonomous locally-based *caciques* and their clienteles.

The centralized, fluid clientelist structure did not require the eradication of the older, more stable local patron-client structures. It was sufficient, at least initially, to use the former to hold the latter in check. This proved feasible since the local *caciques* were fragmented among themselves and could be defeated in any confrontation with the national elites and their massive power base of organized workers and peasants. As long as the centralized system was dominant, therefore, the national political leaders were willing to tolerate the coexistence of two clientelist structures, the first originating in the presidency and extending down into the organized labor and peasant movements, and the second, originating at the local level and encompassing the unorganized masses living in the immediate vicinity of a rural *cacique*.

From the point of view of both the revolutionary elites and the relatively autonomous local strongmen, there were, and continue to be, several advantages to allowing the continued existence of the local bosses. First, by not incorporating all rural masses into the new national political structures, the national government keeps the number of demands made upon it to a minimum. Discontent among the unincorporated peasants remains focussed on the local *cacique,* and not on the central government. Second, by keeping large numbers of individuals out of the corporate structures, the central government can also exclude them from the system of payoffs and rewards that are regularly distributed among the organized workers and peasants. Third, the coexistence of two clientelist systems increases the flexibility of the national political system. Corporative *caciques* can adapt inappropriate policies formulated at the national level to the realities of the local level. Fourth, the local *cacique* can identify more rapidly and efficiently political problems in his domain than can lower level bureaucrats who are part of an extended bureaucratic chain of command originating in Mexico City. In addition, if repressive action must be taken against individuals or groups, the local strongman, rather than the national government, can be blamed.

There is a further advantage to allowing local *caciques* to continue their relatively independent existence. Numerous local studies have shown that the national government, and the official party in particular, do not have an identifiable structural presence in many localities throughout the country.[15] Frequently, the party is merely a local political boss who formalizes his high status by assuming a formal party post or title. Party membership, in such situations, is also more formal than real. This is because the local *cacique* who assumes a formal title automatically inscribes his clients as party members. By virtue of these kinds of practices, therefore, the institutions of the national political system are made to appear strong and omnipresent when, in reality, they are sometimes neither.

Present day Mexico therefore includes numerous local "fiefdoms" of patron-client relationships that have withstood destruction or incorporation into the corporate structures of the nationalized clientelist system. Sometimes these islands of relative autonomy continue to exist because the national political elites are unable to undermine them. But very frequently the continued survival of apparently anachronistic forms of patron-client relations can be explained by the fact that there is a symbiotic relationship between the local *caciques* and the national political system. The national government continues to tolerate the *caciques* because it has much to gain and relatively little to lose by doing so, while the local *caciques* can continue to enjoy power and relative autonomy at the local level by cooperating with the national political elites.

There are, however, some important disadvantages that result from the continued existence of *caciques* with relatively independent local power bases. When the interests of the national government and a local *cacique* conflict, "policy erosion" occurs and it becomes difficult to implement policies at the local level. Persistent difficulty in this regard can produce results that are politically or economically detrimental to the continued viability of the national political system.

There are two basic strategies for solving the problem of a *cacique* who has become a political and economic liability. The first involves replacing the unwanted individual with one who is willing to work with the national political elites. Such an individual may already exist. There are many regions, for example, where a number of *caciques* are in competition with each other, and by a shrewd distribution of resources from the national level, the balance of power among them can be changed to favor the one who appears most able and willing to work with the national political elites. During the Echeverría administration (1970-76), for example, a campaign was waged against unproductive *caciques* and attempts were made to identify and support those who possessed more modern entrepreneurial values (Esteva, 1975; Pereyra, 1975). It was hoped that the result would be increased productivity in the countryside. When there is no obvious alternative to an existing *cacique,* however, the national political elites can create such a person, again through the well-planned distribution of resources and patronage.

A more drastic solution involves the expansion of the state into economic areas and activities from which it had heretofore been absent. The dramatically increased involvement of the Echeverría government in the sugar, tobacco and coffee industries, for example, was produced mainly by growing dissatisfaction and unrest among the relevant peasantry or small producers and, in the case of sugar, by declining levels of production that had serious repercussions on domestic consumption and the country's balance of trade situation.[16]

When the state enters a new industry, it often results in the weakening and even displacement of the local *cacique.* This is particularly true when the government increases its involvement in the agricultural sector of the economy. The peasants, workers or small producers who were formerly under the *cacique's* control are placed under the authority of a government official. The state thereby becomes their new patron, and the membership of the labor, peasant or "popular" (middle class) sectors of the party is expanded.

It should be pointed out, however, that the government does not always have control over which masses enter the corporate structures and under whose leadership their entry is negotiated. Frequently, ambitious individuals who wish to enter the national pool of circulating elites mobilize a following or assume the leadership of an already mobilized movement. They then agree to demobilize the movement as the price for entry into the corporate organizations in a leadership capacity. Furthermore, individuals who already enjoy elite status are always on the lookout for opportunities to expand their followings. In both cases, the result is usually the expansion of the corporate organizations, as ambitious politicians "negotiate the passivity" of their followers by incorporating them into the functional sectors of the party. This process occurs not only in rural areas, but also in urban ones, particularly where large numbers of newly-arrived migrants from rural areas constitute an "available" following for an astute and upwardly-mobile individual.[17]

To summarize, a symbiotic relationship has developed between the national political elites and the remaining locally-based *caciques*. In some ways, it is similar to the arrangement that existed between Porfirio Díaz and the local strongmen during the Porfiriato. The principal difference, however, is that while Díaz had only the rapidly expanding economy as a means for inducing cooperation with the national government, the current political system has an official party divided into corporately defined sectors that serves as a power base for the coalition of ruling elites. The existence of this national power base is usually sufficient to encourage locally-based strongmen to cooperate. When it is not, the national government can use its political and economic resources to undermine the uncooperative individual.

CLIENTELISM, CORPORATISM AND THE FUTURE OF THE POLITICAL SYSTEM

It is always easier to predict that a stable political system will endure than it is to question its continued viability. In the case of the Mexican political system, the attraction of predicting "more of the same" is particularly strong because it has weathered a number of serious economic and political crises with apparent success. Many serious problems remain, of course, which could impact negatively on the political system if they are not resolved. These problems have been discussed elsewhere and will not be repeated here.[18] What does require some discussion, however, is whether the unique interrelationship between clientelism and corporatism described in the preceding pages can continue to function in the future as it has done in the past.

The wedding of corporatism and clientelism at the national level has enabled the political system to tame the decentralizing potential of locally-based *caciques* and their followings. In fact, there has been a clear, if not always consistent, trend toward increased centralization. The expansion of the national political system, however, has produced a series of problems that only now are becoming apparent. The expansion of the national political system has increased the complexity, as well as the size, of the heterogeneous elite coalition. As a result, it has become ever more difficult to make decisions regarding the course of public policy. When decisions are finally taken, they often cannot be implemented due to a lack of enthusiasm on the part of many high-level elites, some of whom may work diligently behind the scenes to undermine the decision. Raymond Vernon touched on this problem in the early 1960s when he concluded that the Mexican president was in a "straightjacket" produced by a need to achieve unanimity on all major policy decisions. Although subsequent events proved him incorrect in the short run, he may well be proved accurate by future developments. Unanimity is not the issue. The ability of the government to act when political and economic realities require it to do so, however, may become increasingly difficult as the state continues to expand.

The second potential problem involves the countervailing impact of corporately-organized national power bases. The system of countervailing power worked adequately when the central government entered into confrontation with a fragmented group of locally-based *caciques* and their followers. It was a match between a unified center and a fragmented periphery. But the years of political stability have also been accompanied by rather spectacular levels of economic growth, and the concomitant rise of new, basically urban, industrial and commercial interests. These interests, which form part of the so-called "private sector" of the economy, are considerably more integrated and powerful than were the rural *caciques*. Furthermore, with the expansion of commercial agriculture into the Mexican countryside, private agricultural interests are better integrated among themselves than were the old-style *caciques*. Finally, there are growing signs of integration between the urban industrial and agricultural private sector interests.

While the urban and rural business interests have increased in strength, the ability of the government to utilize the corporately-organized peasants and workers as a countervailing power has undergone a slow but steady decline. Part of the problem involves the non-expansion in recent years of the organized labor movement. Of the three sectoral organizations into which the party is divided, only labor has been capable of being quickly mobilized in support of government initiatives. As was explained earlier, this is related to the real authority that the head of the labor sector enjoys over his subordinates and their followings. The leader of the peasant sector has never possessed such authority.

If the system of countervailing power is to continue to function, and it must if the ruling elites hope to constrain the behavior of the private sector and retain the support of the rural and urban masses, two courses of action must be pursued by the government. First, the membership of the peasant and labor sectors of the party must be expanded. This implies a government-sponsored campaign to organize and incorporate those peasants and workers who still remain outside of the official organizations. Second, the leaders of the sectoral organizations must be given more real power. This is particularly true with regard to the leader of the organized peasantry. In the absence of an ability to distribute land and decide whether those with land are using it adequately, the head of the organized peasantry has little to "give" to his subordinates and their followings in return for their support.

If significant authority is not delegated to the sectoral leaders, all they can do is continue to divide and rule their membership. On one level, this is a desirable course of action from the point of view of the elites, since it avoids mobilization of the lower classes, particularly the peasantry, along class lines. From another perspective, however, the fragmentation caused and perpetuated by divide-and-rule tactics (which are facilitated by the clientelist infrastructure that permeates the corporate facades), undermines the ability of the ruling elites to maintain the delicate balance of power that until now has enabled the Mexican political system to endure. Whether Mexico's political elites are willing and able to delegate the required authority to the leaders of the corporate organizations is a question that lacks an easy answer.

NOTES

1. For analyses of authoritarian rule in Mexico see particularly Reyna and Weinert (1977); Purcell (1975); Hansen (1971); and Stevens (1974).

2. Two recent collections of essays on clientelism are Gellner and Waterbury (1977) and Schmidt et al. (1976). See also the extensive bibliography on patron-client relations by S.N. Eisenstadt and L. Roniger included in the present volume.

3. For discussions of corporatism in Latin America see especially Malloy (1977); Pike and Stritch (1974); and Wiarda (forthcoming).

4. The concept "Spanish bureaucratic-patrimonialism" is from Sarfatti (1966). See also the discussion of patrimonialism in Roth (1968).

5. The similarities between the Díaz system and the contemporary Mexican political system are discussed in Meyer (1977).

6. For a detailed analysis of such stable, essentially traditional relationships see Foster (1967).

7. An interesting study of a particular *cacicazgo* is that of Friedrich (1970). See also his article, "The Legitimacy of a Cacique" (Friedrich, 1968).

8. The following description of the "fluid clientelism" of the national political system was first published in Purcell and Purcell (1980).

9. This and all subsequent unattributed quotations are from personal interviews conducted by John F.H. Purcell and the author in Mexico City between September 1975 and October 1976. All translations are the authors'.

10. For case studies of such behavior see Glade (1975) and Grindle (1977).

11. Kaufman (1974). See also Tarrow (1967) and Wolf (1955: 465) for a discussion of patron-client relations and the existence of scarce resources.

12. *Camarillas* are discussed in greater detail in Padgett (1976: 69-70); Johnson (1971: 72-76); Camp (1977); and Grindle (1977).

13. In the words of Grindle (1977: 51), "implicit understandings of mutual advantage bind the members together, and therefore, when anyone is unable to continue supplying valuable resources to the other members, he may be excluded."

14. The mutually supportive relationship between clientelism and corporatism in the current Mexican political system is also discussed in the excellent article by Kaufman (1977).

15. For a more detailed discussion of this point see Purcell and Purcell (1976).

16. For a detailed study of the expansion of the state into the sugar industry, see Purcell (1979).

17. For an interesting case study of this process see Cornelius (1975: Chapter 6).

18. See particularly Purcell (1977).

REFERENCES

BRANDENBURG, F. (1964). *The Making of Modern Mexico*. Englewood Cliffs, NJ: Prentice-Hall.

CAMP, R. A. (1977). "Losers in Mexican Politics: A Comparative Study of Official Party Precandidates for Gubernatorial Elections, 1970-1975," pp. 23-33, in J. W. Wilkie and K. Ruddle, eds., *Quantitative Latin American Studies: Methods and Findings* (Statistical Abstract of Latin America Supplement No. 6). Los Angeles: UCLA Latin American Center Publications.

CORNELIUS, W. A. (1975). *Politics and the Migrant Poor in Mexico City*. Stanford: University Press.

ESTEVA, G. (1975). "La agricultura en México de 1950 a 1975: el fracaso de una falsa analogía," *Comercio Exterior*, diciembre de 1975: 1311-22.

FOSTER, G. M. (1967). "The Dyadic Contract," pp. 212-53, in G. M. Foster, *Tzintzuntzan: Mexican Peasants in a Changing World*. Boston: Little, Brown.

FRIEDRICH, P. (1968). "The Legitimacy of a Cacique," pp. 243-69, in M. J. Swartz, ed., *Local Level Politics: Social and Cultural Perspectives*. Chicago: Aldine.

FRIEDRICH, P. (1970). *Agrarian Revolt in a Mexican Village*. Englewood Cliffs, NJ: Prentice-Hall.

GELLNER, E. and WATERBURY, J. (1977). *Patrons and Clients in Mediterranean Societies*. London: Duckworth.

GLADE, W. P. (1975). "Entrepreneurship in the State Sector: CONASUPO of Mexico." Revised version of a paper prepared for a seminar on "The Economic Anthropology of Investment Behavior in Latin America," School of American Research, Santa Fe, New Mexico, 4-8 August 1975.

GODAU, R. H. (1975). "Mexico: A Bureaucratic Polity." Unpublished MA thesis, University of Texas at Austin.

GRINDLE, M. S. (1977). "Patrons and Clients in the Bureaucracy: Career Networks in Mexico," *Latin American Research Review*, XII(1): 37-66.

HANSEN, R. D. (1971). *The Politics of Mexican Development*. Baltimore: Johns Hopkins.

JOHNSON, K. F. (1971). *Mexican Democracy: A Critical View*. Boston: Allyn and Bacon.

KAUFMAN, R. R. (1974). "The Patron-Client Concept and Macro-politics," *Comparative Studies in Society and History*, 16(1): 284-308.

KAUFMAN, R. R. (1977). "Corporatism, Clientelism, and Partisan Conflict," pp. 109-48, in J. M. Malloy, ed., *Corporatism and Authoritarianism in Latin America*. Pittsburgh: University Press.

MALLOY, J. M. (ed.) (1977). *Corporatism and Authoritarianism in Latin America*. Pittsburgh: University Press.

MEYER, L. (1977). "Historical Roots of the Authoritarian State in Mexico," pp. 3-22, in J. L. Reyna and R. S. Weinert, eds., *Authoritarianism in Mexico*. Philadelphia: ISHI Press.

PADGETT, L. V. (1976). *The Mexican Political System* (2nd edn.). Boston: Houghton Mifflin.

PEREYRA, C. (1975). "Contradicción interna del PRI: Caciques hidalguenses," *Excélsior* (Mexico City), 24 November 1975: 7.

PIKE, F. and STRITCH, T. (eds.) (1974). *The New Corporatism: Social and Political Structures in the Iberian World*. Notre Dame, Indiana: University Press.

PURCELL, S. K. (1975). *The Mexican Profit-Sharing Decision: Politics in an Authoritarian Regime*. Berkeley: University of California Press.

PURCELL, S. K. (1977). "The Future of the Mexican Political System," pp. 173-91, in J. L. Reyna and R. S. Weinert, eds., *Authoritarianism in Mexico*. Philadelphia: ISHI Press.

PURCELL, S. K. (1979). "Politics and the Market in Mexico: The Case of the Sugar Industry." Paper presented at meeting of the Latin American Studies Association, Pittsburgh, Pennsylvania, April 1979.

PURCELL, J. F. H., and PURCELL, S. K. (1976). "Machine Politics and Socioeconomic Change in Mexico," pp. 348-66, in J. W. Wilkie et al., eds., *Contemporary Mexico: Papers of the IV International Congress of Mexican History*. Berkeley, Los Angeles and México, DF: University of California Press and El Colegio de México.

PURCELL, S. K. and PURCELL, J. F. H. (1980). "State and Society in Mexico: Must a Stable Polity be Institutionalized?" *World Politics*, 32: 194-227.

REYNA, J. L. and WEINERT, R. S. (eds.) (1977). *Authoritarianism in Mexico.* Philadelphia: ISHI Press.

ROTH, G. (1968). "Personal Rulership, Patrimonialism and Empire-Building in the New States," *World Politics,* 20: 194-206.

SARFATTI, M. (1966). *Spanish Bureaucratic-Patrimonialism in America.* Berkeley: Institute of International Studies, University of California.

SCHMIDT, S. W. et al. (1976). *Friends, Followers and Factions.* Berkeley: University of California Press.

SCOTT, R. E. (1959). *Mexican Government in Transition.* Urbana: University of Illinois Press.

SMITH, P. H. (1974). "Making it in Mexico: Aspects of Political Mobility since 1946." Paper presented at the annual meeting of the American Political Science Association, Chicago, Illinois, 29 August-2 September 1974. Cited in M. S. Grindle (1977), "Patrons and Clients in the Bureaucracy: Career Networks in Mexico," *Latin American Research Review,* XII(1): 40.

SMITH, P. H. (1976). "Continuity and Turnover within the Mexican Political Elite, 1900-1971," pp. 167-86, in J. W. Wilkie et al., eds., *Contemporary Mexico: Papers of the IV International Congress of Mexican History.* Berkeley, Los Angeles, and México, DF: University of California Press and El Colegio de México.

SMITH, P. H. (1979). *Labyrinths of Power: Political Recruitment in Twentieth Century Mexico.* Princeton: University Press.

STEVENS, E. P. (1974). *Protest and Response in Mexico.* Cambridge, Mass.: MIT Press.

TARROW, S. (1967). *Peasant Communism in Southern Italy.* New Haven: Yale University Press.

WIARDA, H. J. (forthcoming). *The Other Great "ISM": Corporatism and National Development, Studies in Theory and Practice.*

WOLF, E. R. (1955). "Types of Latin American Peasantry: A Preliminary Discussion," *American Anthropologist,* 3(1): 452-71.

===8===

Clientelism In Decline: A Peruvian Regional Study

Laura Guasti
Purdue University, USA

Before 1968 clientelism was the major underlying political structure in Peru.[1] The political parties, the national bureaucracy, and the regional and local governments had all been penetrated by clientelistic networks.[2] By 1968 clientelism had undergone modifications that made it relatively less effective as a means for lower-class clients to acquire political resources. The clientelistic structure had experienced an uneven decrease in personalism, reduced diffuseness, centralization and wider extension into the society, and a change in the importance of resources and in the locus of their control from the private commercial sector to the public sector (Guasti, 1977: 432).

From the time the present military regime was established in Peru in October 1968, clientelism appeared to be in outright decline. It served to structure interactions among individuals considerably less than it had in the past, and functioned inadequately as a means of access to resources. Specific actions taken by the military regime helped to accelerate the deterioration of clientelism as the basic political mode within the society.

This chapter will examine the decline in clientelism that occurred in Peru after 1968. Its purpose is twofold: first, to examine the impact of the decline on a marginalized section of the peasantry, and

The research for this study was supported by a grant from the Henry L. and Grace Doherty Foundation.

second, to examine the impact of the decline on inter-class relationships. The focus is the regional society of the Department of Cusco, a largely agrarian area located in the Peruvian Andes. The chapter first discusses the larger political changes initiated by the military regime that furthered the decline of clientelism. It then examines changes in the agrarian sector carried out by the regime, and briefly describes the government agencies responsible for the changes. The chapter then turns to an examination of the nature and consequences of the decline for a relatively isolated independent peasant community, and for inter-class interactions, here focussing additionally on a larger commercial town and the regional capital. The conclusions reached are that the deterioration of clientelism occurred particularly via the breakdown of patron-client relationships, and that the major consequences were reduced access to public resources for more marginalized rural populations and the class demarcation of personalistic interactions, with exchanges occurring mostly among individuals at the same socioeconomic level. The final section considers whether clientelism is likely to continue in decline or to resurge if the military regime, as it has indicated, permits a return to civilian government by 1980.

LARGER POLITICAL CHANGES UNDER THE MILITARY REGIME

The military government had as its central purpose the achievement of rapid social, economic and political development in Peru. During its first four years the government attempted to carry out major structural changes in the society. Within this, two political changes initiated by the regime particularly served to weaken clientelism. Both changes followed directly from the military leaders' developmental aims in assuming political power. The first was the exclusion of the civilian political parties from government activity, and the second was the effort to rationalize the national bureaucracy.

The sidelining of the political parties was the consequence of the military leaders' decision to remain in power to carry out a national development program, and to exclude the parties from participating in the implementation of the program. The military leaders criticized the parties for being clientelistic, and for being ineffective in providing political leadership and channels for popular participation (McClintock, 1977:16). National elections were not held and the parties were barred from government decision-making. The effect of these actions was to eliminate the parties' access to public resources for distribution to their clientelistic followings, and therefore to reduce the effectiveness and extensiveness of the parties' clientelistic networks.

The effort to rationalize the national bureaucracy was a necessity resulting from the particular development program the regime initiated. The major goal of the regime was the rapid restructuring and industrialization of the Peruvian economy.[3] As a counterpart to the military leaders' decision to sideline the political parties, the leaders determined that the rapid developmental effort would be carried out under the direction and stimulus of the national government itself.

As a result, the primary responsibility for the success of the rapid industrialization effort fell to the centralized national bureaucracy. The bureaucracy was given the dual functions of planning and overseeing all economic changes and activities, and assuming a direct entrepreneurial role within key economic sectors and activities. As the economic changes progressed, additional bureaucratic responsibilities arose, in particular that of controlling the political mobilization that resulted from the economic changes.

Thus, the industrialization aims of the regime required the rapid expansion of bureaucratic capability and improvement of bureaucratic performance to carry out the augmented distributive and regulatory roles. Improved bureaucratic capability and performance became all the more imperative because the rapid industrialization effort was being attempted in a society with limited technical and financial resources and expertise. These limitations increased the need for a carefully planned distribution and efficient use of resources by the bureaucracy in order for the development effort to succeed.

By nature, the new demands on bureaucratic capability and performance were opposed to the continued existence of personalistic dynamics within the bureaucracy. As a result, the regime's major goals required that clientelism in the bureaucracy be displaced.

The regime undertook a series of changes to rationalize the national bureaucracy. Several reorganizations were carried out and new agencies and ministries were created. A more careful examination of personnel was conducted, resulting in the hiring of some younger, more technically trained individuals. Increased surveillance of and checks on bureaucratic activities also were attempted. Simultaneously, "moralization" campaigns were begun that sought to set new standards of behavior and change bureaucrats' attitudes by emphasizing the impersonal enforcement of laws and carrying out of responsibilities. Training courses for bureaucrats also sought to inculcate the new standards.[4] Corruption, the use of personalistic criteria, and the use of bureaucratic positions for personal gain were repeatedly and strongly discouraged.

The campaign against personalistic behavior was carried into the larger society as well. Education against "bad functionaries" was conducted in newspapers and in the many leadership and occupational training courses offered to citizens by government agencies. The courses and campaigns served to create expectations among some of the citizenry that impersonal bureaucratic behavior should and would occur, and led over time to growing numbers of citizen denouncements of "bad bureaucrats."

Thus, the attack by the military regime on the use of clientelistic relationships was both overt and forceful, creating multiple pressures on bureaucrats to end personalistic behavior. This occurred at the same time that bureaucrats experienced demands to take on increased, multiple responsibilities and extend bureaucratic oversight to all parts of the society.

THE BUREAUCRACY AND CHANGES IN THE AGRARIAN SECTOR

Within the Peruvian economy, the agrarian sector underwent the most radical changes during the military government. The regime's development goals gave high priority to a large-scale agrarian reform. Between 1969 and 1975, over 22 million acres held in large landholdings (the sierra *haciendas* and coastal plantations) were expropriated and given to the peasants and laborers who worked them. The holdings were reorganized into agrarian production cooperatives (CAPs) that were structured to be self-management enterprises. Simultaneously the independent peasant communities were reorganized to have the same internal political structure as the CAPs. This was a preliminary step to organizing the communities into self-managed cooperative enterprises, or to incorporating them into larger cooperative structures that combined CAPs with communities.[5] While the reorganization into self-management enterprises was largely accomplished in the former *haciendas* and plantations, the majority of peasant communities did not become cooperative enterprises or become incorporated into the larger cooperative structures. They did, however, continue with their new internal political structure.

Beginning in 1972, the regime also focussed on restructuring political participation in the rural areas. The new participatory structure followed corporatist lines. The local units of participation were the self-management enterprises, which would communicate their interests to the government via a newly created government agency responsible for popular mobilization, and through a new agrarian confederation that would be organized by the government agency. Through these channels, organized and controlled by the government, rather than through political parties or rural unions, the peasantry would participate in the planning of national policies for the development of the agrarian sector, as well as express their demands (Bourque and Palmer, 1975: 186; McClintock, 1977: 16).

Two government agencies were responsible for implementing most of the changes in the agrarian sector, the Ministry of Agriculture and SINAMOS (the National System for the Support of Social Mobilization). The Ministry of Agriculture was responsible for the land expropriations and the creation of the CAPs, as well as the creation of the larger cooperative structures that combined CAPs and peasant communities. It was also responsible for carrying out the political restructuring of the peasant communities, and encouraging and organizing cooperative commercial enterprises in the communities. In addition, the Ministry was directly involved in the administration and production activities of the CAPs.

SINAMOS was the government agency created in 1972 to organize popular participation and mobilize popular support for the military regime. The rural population was only one of SINAMOS' many target groups,[6] but it was a priority group. The question of what SINAMOS' specific functions were to be was never definitively resolved within the military government, resulting in conflict and not inconsiderable confusion over SINAMOS' purposes.

In practice, SINAMOS developed a number of responsibilities in the agrarian sector. Among the most important were to promote and expand the participation of the rural population via the self-management enterprises and other local units. Rural participation was to be channeled particularly through the National Agrarian Confederation (CNA), organized by SINAMOS and officially established in 1974. The CNA was made the only legally recognized representative of agrarian interests.

In addition to providing support and assistance to the CNA, SINAMOS was responsible for working directly with the CAPs, peasant communities, and other local units. SINAMOS conducted leadership and ideological training courses for the new CAP members and leaders, as well as for the new peasant community office holders, provided additional technical, administrative and other assistance in the operation of the CAPs, supervised the CAPs' financial activities, and encouraged and assisted in the development of peasant communal improvement projects or cooperative enterprises.

As can be seen, the functions of the two government agencies in the rural areas were multiple and varied, and almost all were intended to be completed within five years after the agrarian reform was initiated in 1969. The implementation of the functions was further complicated by the fact that the jurisdictions of the two agencies frequently overlapped. This was intentional, for SINAMOS had been created as much to check on the Ministry of Agriculture (and other Ministries) as to assist it.

From the perspective of the independent peasant communities, the sidelining of political parties meant that the two government agencies and the government-created CNA became the key channels for expressing communal demands and for acquiring needed assistance and government resources. In addition, the Ministry of Agriculture and SINAMOS became the key channels for the extension of governmental regulatory activities into the communities.

The distributive functions of the government agencies were the most important to the impoverished independent communities. However, the communities and their economic and political transformation were among many responsibilities assigned to the agencies. The assignment of multiple responsibilities to the agencies affected the agencies' ability to carry out those related to the independent communities, and the communities' ability to acquire needed public assistance and resources.

In addition, because of the military leaders' strong emphasis on rationality and efficiency, explicit priorities were established within the industrialization program for allocating resources to the various economic sectors. The agrarian sector received the lowest priority among the four major sectors.[7] Further, within the agrarian sector highest priority was given to the capital, personnel and other resource needs of the land expropriations and new agrarian cooperatives. Thus, the independent peasant communities faced a dual disadvantage in acquiring government resources, being assigned low priority within a lower priority sector.

Nevertheless, resources were explicitly allocated for peasant community needs and development. At the same time, new regulations that increased governmental supervision of the peasant communities were established. The next section examines the impact of the decline in clientelism within this context on an independent peasant community.

IMPACT OF THE DECLINE ON
AN INDEPENDENT PEASANT COMMUNITY

Cancha is an independent peasant community located in the more isolated, less fertile, high mountain province of Paucartambo in the Department of Cusco.[8] Cancha and its neighboring communities are among the most isolated villages within the province, having no major roads passing near or through them, and no major market town nearby. In 1971 Cancha was reorganized into the new communal political structure decreed by the military regime. The community experienced no other major changes as a result of the regime's reforms. Cancha received no land from the agrarian reform, and was not incorporated into larger cooperative structures. Nor did it establish a communal cooperative enterprise. By 1974, Cancha was incorporated into the CNA, having an elected representative to the Agrarian League of the province.

Clientelism and the Community

Until 1968, there were two available areas of political clientelism by which Cancha, like other independent peasant communities, could seek access to governmental resources: through the political parties and electoral process (when elections were being held), and through the bureaucracy. For the peasants of Cancha, the political parties never became a means of access to resources. The physical isolation of the community, and its high illiteracy level (illiterates could not vote) resulted in Cancha being ignored by the political parties and their local organizations. While from the early 1940s Cancha had a two-grade school, and so had a small, but slowly growing number of literate persons eligible to vote, no Cancha member was affiliated with a political party, or had been approached by a party campaigner. As a result, no members of Cancha were included in the clientelistic networks of the political parties or had access to public resources via this means.

The channel that remained to the community and its individual members to gain access to public resources was the national bureaucracy. Regular efforts to gain needed resources and assistance from the national government for the community did not begin until the late 1950s. From this time until 1968, patron-client relationships were used on a limited basis for two purposes: to gain information about laws and procedures before entering a government office, and to get initial introductions to individual bureaucrats in the relevant offices. Patron-client relationships were employed to get public resources for the community only by the head of the community,[9] were used by him almost entirely to gain the resources for communal rather than personal use, and were not employed by other communal members to get governmental resources for private needs.

The manner in which patron-client ties were used to gain public resources for the community was not by establishing patron-client relationships with bureaucrats themselves. As of 1975, no community member had had a government employee as a patron, whether through *compadrazgo*[10] or via a less formalized clientele relationship. Although some community members said in general terms that bureaucrats would be good persons to have as *compadres*, they never had asked a bureaucrat to be their *compadre*. Other community members indicated that bureaucrats were undesirable as *compadres* because bureaucrats frequently were transferred to other posts, and therefore would be available to ask for favors only for a limited time.

Instead, the head of the community, Celestino Sayri, used *compadre* patrons outside the bureaucracy to assist him in getting resources for the community from government offices. He used one patronage relationship in particular, with Antonia Venero, a middle-class teacher who had been the first to teach in the community's school, and who later taught in the regional capital. This patron assisted Sayri in every community project for which he succeeded in getting governmental resources.

The most important resource for which he used this *compadrazgo* relationship was to acquire information: which offices to go to, whom to approach in the offices, how to approach the officials, and perhaps most importantly, the relevant laws and regulations on which to base his request for resources. His patron also occasionally accompanied Sayri when he first went to an office, to introduce him to a bureaucrat who was the patron's relative or friend. This occurred only in a few cases during the early years of Sayri's headship. According to both Sayri and Venero, the brokerage role was performed very infrequently because both patron and client perceived that Sayri was often as successful in getting resources from government offices when "armed" only with the information provided by his patron and persistence, returning to the offices time and again to pursue the request.

Sayri stated that he never sought to establish a patron-client relationship with a bureaucrat. Nor did he bring gifts, do work, or provide other services for the officials with whom he dealt.[11] The question that arises is, if Sayri did not engage in patronage exchanges with bureaucrats, what enabled him to receive their discretionary help? For it was through the personal discretion of the bureaucrats that Sayri was able to get public resources for the community. If the bureaucrats had decided not to help, requests for resources could have been excessively delayed or never processed.

In the cases where Sayri's patron acted as a broker and requested an official's help on Sayri's behalf, Sayri did not need to return the personalistic favor directly to the official. The official helped him the first time as a favor to Venero. This was a favor exchanged within a friendship relationship, and the official expected to be repaid at some later time by Venero, not by Sayri. Similarly, Sayri repaid the patronage assistance to his existing patron, not to a new one.

In the majority of cases, however, in which brokerage did not occur, or in return encounters with officials with whom brokerage occurred only initially, no personal exchanges were asked of Sayri, and none were offered. When asked why the bureaucrats helped him if he gave nothing in return, Sayri said it was because he knew the laws, and because "they knew me." What this seemed to imply was that he had established quasi-friendship relationships with government officials. Apparently his informational advantage, and his legal status as community representative served to diminish some of the status inequality between him and white-collar, hispanic public employees, thereby enabling him to take some advantage of the personalism that existed in bureaucratic activity without the need for a direct unequal exchange or a structured patron-client tie.

The absence of patron-client exchange, however, did not mean that taking advantage of bureaucratic personalism was costless for

Sayri. The costs to him were in lengthy negotiations and frequent travel, resulting in considerable expenditures of time, money and other economic losses. These were borne solely by Sayri. Therefore, to a certain degree Sayri was able to take advantage of personal discretion in the bureaucracy, but had to pay a cost for not directly reciprocating in a personal exchange.

Nevertheless, that he was able to take advantage of bureaucratic personalism for Cancha's benefit was apparent in the fact that he did get the government assistance and resources requested when other communities of the region could not get public assistance or experienced much greater delays in getting it. Cancha was the first peasant community in the area to build a road connecting it to the district capital, with tools, tractors and driver provided by the government. It was the first to get a five-grade school, with materials, equipment usually supplied by students' families, and additional teachers provided by the government. Sayri also succeeded in stopping the obligatory provision of produce and personal services to the district and provincial authorities by the Cancha communal authorities. Again, Cancha was the first community in the area to do so. Although it is clear that Sayri did not get major amounts of assistance and materials from the government, he succeeded in getting resources during a time when government resources were not earmarked for communal needs, and when peasant interests received little attention or priority from the national government.

Regime Changes: Decline in Clientelism and Reduced Access to Resources

In 1970 the military government decreed the political restructuring of the independent peasant communities, changing from the traditional *varayoq* hierarchy of communal authorities to a committee system of government whose members would be elected by all communal inhabitants.[12] Cancha elected Celestino Sayri to be the first president of the Administration Committee, the major communal committee.

During his two-year tenure as president, Sayri succeeded in getting considerably more governmental resources allocated to Cancha than Cancha previously had received, and again, more than the other area communities received in this period. This included an important financial allocation to improve the road and extend it to connect Cancha to a major market town, and the authorization, planning and financing of additional schoolrooms, a paramedical office, a police station and a children's park.

At first glance, Cancha's increased access to public resources might not seem surprising. By this time, the military government had specifically earmarked resources for peasant communities, and openly taken pro-peasant and pro-communal development positions. In addition, the military leaders already had initiated measures to reduce personalistic behavior within the bureaucracy. Both factors could have been expected to result in increased access to public resources for Cancha.

However, the two presidents and communal administrations that succeeded Sayri's in the following four years did not have comparable achievements. They did not get additional projects for Cancha authorized and financed and, moreover, succeeded in losing every project Sayri had initiated during his administration. If Sayri succeeded in getting resources for the community both before and during the military regime without entering into patron-client relationships with bureaucrats, why then, during the years when additional resources were made available for communities, and actions were being taken at the national level to reduce clientelism in the bureaucracy, could not later communal leaders also succeed in getting resources?

A number of factors appear to be involved. First, there were differences in individual abilities. Sayri was an active individual willing to spend considerable amounts of his own time and money for communal interests. From the accounts of the later community leaders and other community members, the later leaders were not willing or were not able to make equivalent expenditures of time and money. Since it was clear that without persistent returns to the provincial and regional offices communal projects could not be carried out, the later leaders' lack of persistence, resulting from their unwillingness or inability to pay the costs of persistence, hindered the completion or acquisition of community projects.

Beyond these individual differences, however, lay factors that affected the earlier and later communal leaders' ability to secure resources for the community. During Sayri's tenure as community president in the first years of reform, military regime pressures on bureaucratic performance were only beginning. From accounts by bureaucrats and others in the regional capital, it appears that the pressures to change bureaucratic behavior away from personalism did not filter down to the regional and provincial levels quickly enough to greatly affect bureaucratic behavior during Sayri's presidency.[13] It is likely, then, that Sayri did not witness a change in bureaucratic behavior away from personalism during the final two years of his leadership. It may, therefore, have been the combination of greater government resources earmarked for peasant communities, and the continuation of bureaucratic personalism, not its elimination, that were the important factors enabling Sayri to get the many projects approved and initiated. In addition, his many years experience interacting with government officials, and well-established personal relationships of trust with individual bureaucrats may also have contributed to Sayri's success in gaining additional public resources in the early years of reform.

The later two presidents and their fellow committee members faced a more problematic bureaucratic environment. It was an environment in which personalistic behavior was increasingly under attack, and it was a fluid environment, with laws, regulations and bureaucratic structure undergoing major changes. Such an environment created limitations for the later leaders in gaining equal or greater access to public resources.

None of the later committee members had experience in dealing with government offices for community matters, and almost all had never dealt with a bureaucratic office for any purpose. They therefore began with a disadvantage in not having well-established personal relationships with bureaucrats on which they could rely, nor prior knowledge of laws and bureaucratic procedure.

Further, the increasingly hostile atmosphere toward personalism made it difficult to establish new personal relationships with bureaucrats. Interviews indicated that none of the later committee members, including the presidents, succeeded in establishing regular contacts with individual bureaucrats. Nor did the brokerage role performed for them by Sayri help to establish regular bureaucratic contacts. Sayri accompanied his successors to government offices to introduce the new committee members to officials and give the members information on bureaucratic procedure. This brokerage did not succeed in facilitating the later committee members' interactions with government offices to complete or initiate communal projects. The bureaucrats were not as responsive to the later members as they had been to Sayri.

Therefore, the increasing pressures at the national level against bureaucratic personalism, combined with the absence of prior relations with bureaucrats that might have been made the latter still willing to use personal discretion for known, trusted peasants,

resulted in the newer leaders being unable to use personalistic relationships, either in clientele or neo-friendship form, to facilitate access to resources for the community.

A third factor worked against the later committee members' success in getting resources through the bureaucracy. The deterioration in clientelism was occurring not only within the bureaucracy.
Patron-client relations were deteriorating within the regional society as a whole. One of the consequences of the government's attack
on personalism was to increase the difficulty of exercising personal
influence in dealing with government offices, and to raise the risk
and, therefore, the cost of doing so. This made actual and potential
patrons and brokers from the regional middle class more reluctant
to exercise influence with bureaucrats on behalf of clients.[14] At the
same time, the governmental attack was being accepted by some
lower-class members, leading them to reject the use of clientele
relationships in dealing with government offices.

The consequence of this larger decline for the later Cancha communal leaders was reduced access to information about laws and
bureaucratic procedure, and reduced access to contacts with
bureaucrats provided by non-bureaucratic middle-class patrons.
None of the later committee members received assistance from
non-bureaucratic patrons in their dealings with government agencies. The committee members carried out all interactions with
government offices "on our own."

Some of the later communal leaders also absorbed government
pronouncements against the use of personal influence and in favor
of direct, impartial contacts with bureaucrats. These leaders were
told by SINAMOS and Ministry of Agriculture "promoters" that
they, the leaders, could go directly to bureaucratic offices, ask for
resources, and receive them by simply following procedure. These
leaders apparently acted on the new model of behavior, for they
stated they did not seek out higher-class *compadres* for help in their
official activities, even to gain information or advice about laws
and procedures. A few, including the third president, expressed
skepticism about the possibility that middle-class persons had any
useful information to offer.

The loss of this means to get important personal resources in
dealing with government agencies was the more deleterious because
the legal and bureaucratic structures were in considerable flux during this period. Laws and regulations were changed frequently,
while new bureaucratic agencies and procedures were created and
old ones reorganized or eliminated. It was a more confusing time

for community leaders to be dealing with government agencies than when Sayri had first become community head. The later community leaders, therefore, had a greater need for access to information about laws and procedures in order to acquire resources from the government. Yet it was at this time that access to needed information via non-governmental patrons was reduced.

The cumulative result of the above factors was that the later community leaders were placed in weaker positions from which to get public resources for the community. They did not interact successfully with government agencies and officials to complete the communal projects already initiated, or to initiate new projects. The political environment created by the military regime that made the establishment and use of personalistic contacts increasingly difficult, while making the legal and bureaucratic framework increasingly complex, worked against the leaders' accomplishment of their communal functions. Cancha never had adequate access to assistance from government offices during earlier regimes. Nevertheless, clientelistic relationships in the past had provided the community with an important, albeit limited means to get needed public resources. The military regime's reforms displaced clientelism as a primary means of political resource distribution. The reforms, however, failed to replace clientelism with an adequate new means for the distribution of resources.

Regime Changes: Increased Regulation

The impact of the military regime's changes on the independent peasant community was not limited to the breakdown of clientelistic relations and reduced access to public resources. While the distributive capability of the bureaucracy decreased in relation to the community, its regulatory capability increased.

Under the military regime, regulatory activities of the national government for the first time reached the independent peasant communities on an extensive and regular basis. Communities experienced a considerable increase in contacts with government officials, in regulations to which they were subject and which were enforced, and a considerable complication of the political responsibilities and activities of peasant community leaders.

The restructuring of the communal political structure, decreed in 1970, was implemented throughout Peru during the following year by Ministry of Agriculture employees who went to all communities to inform them of, and quickly carry out the change. In Cancha, from this time forward communal meetings had to be held at least once a month and attendance was obligatory; fines were charged for absence. Communal account books had to be kept by the newly-created office of the treasurer, and accounts of the meetings by the secretary. Both sets of records had to be relayed to the district Ministry of Agriculture office (to the district SINAMOS office, after the latter was created).

While Cancha was being restructured, the members experienced frequent visits by the Ministry of Agriculture employees responsible for carrying out the change. This was a considerable difference from past experience, where provincial authorities and regional office bureaucrats rarely entered the community. In addition, after SINAMOS was created Cancha experienced frequent visits from the SINAMOS "promoter," the district level official responsible for providing assistance to the CAPs and communities of the area. The promoter visited Cancha every one to three months to attend communal assemblies. The Cancha members' accounts of his activities were that he came to tell them that they had to develop projects to better the community and the kind of projects they should develop, but gave little assistance in actually developing or carrying out projects; told them about major changes the government was making; and "indoctrinated" them about the aims of the government, what actions the government was taking to help them, and the kind of behavior and attitudes they now had to have as citizens.[15]

During this period the activities and responsibilities of the community leaders were complicated to a considerable extent. The responsibility for explaining, and getting the community members accustomed to the new communal political structure fell in practice not to the Ministry of Agriculture employees, but to the first communal president and committee administration. In the first two years after the restructuring, it was the communal leaders who explained the procedures and meaning of the changes at the frequent communal meetings, and carried out the changes. In addition, the communal leaders were required to attend training courses to learn about the new changes and how to carry out their new responsibilities. They and later communal administrations also had to attend courses on community leadership, courses that explained the major changes being made in the agrarian sector (and later changes in those changes), courses that gave more intensive instruction in the regime's ideology, and courses that provided ideas for communal development. The number of courses the communal leaders were required to attend increased over time, while all were held in distant locations, usually requiring half a day's travel to reach. All these activities were added to the communal leaders' trips to the provincial and regional capitals to attempt to further the community's projects.

The extension of governmental presence in the peasant communities through regulatory activities created costs for the Cancha peasants in time, economic positions and modifications of behavior that held no intrinsic value for them. The changes and new regulations made necessary greater expenditures of time in frequently held communal assemblies with obligatory attendance, regardless of the season. Added to these were the extra assemblies held when changes had been decreed and governmental promotors came to the community to initiate them. All required time that had to be taken from the peasants' farming and other economic activities, adding difficulties to their ability to maintain their economic level above the survival margin.

The costs in time and economic position were greater for the communal leaders. Meeting the greater demands on their time either made it impossible for the leaders to adequately tend their fields, or made it necessary for them to hire workers when they could afford to do so. In addition, the communal leaders individually had to pay the travel, food and lodging costs of all the required trips outside the community. They received little financial compensation from the community and none from government offices.[16]

Of equal importance, the greater demands on communal leaders' time and finances resulting from increased government regulation created an additional impediment to the leaders' ability to get public resources for the community. The time and finances spent by the leaders to carry out these new activities reduced the time and finances available for the many outside trips needed to pursue the demands for resources.

Conclusions

In accordance with the military regime's requirements the national bureaucracy did succeed in extending its capabilities in the case of the community of Cancha, but did so primarily via regulation rather than distribution or both. In consequence, the increased national government penetration of the community created new costs but provided no compensating benefits to the peasant community, for the new mode of interaction did not result in equal or greater access to needed governmental resources than in the past. The overall result of bureaucratic rationalization and the deterioration of clientelism for this marginalized population was reduced access to public resources, reduced ability to fulfill communal needs and decreased likelihood that in the short to medium run the community would develop needed economic and social infrastructure or make advances in its agricultural activities.

IMPACT OF THE DECLINE ON
INTER-CLASS RELATIONSHIPS

In the region of Cusco the attempts by the military regime to displace clientelism as the basic mode of political interaction also affected personalistic interactions outside the national bureaucracy and class relations. This section will examine the character of friendship and patron-client relationships in the three major classes of the Cusco region: the middle class, *mestizo* class[17] and peasant class. The evidence indicates that in this period vertical relationships had deteriorated while horizontal relationships had increased, thereby reinforcing class divisions.

Regional Middle-Class Clientelistic
Relationships

The potential patronal group within the regional society was the urban middle class of the regional capital.[18] Within this class, friendship relationships[19] continued to be important during the military government in dealing with most aspects of life, and particularly in attending to matters with government agencies. Middle-class members frequently volunteered the statement that it was essential to have friends in government offices in order to get one's needs attended to, whether personal or professional, while friendships in general were important to have.

There was considerable variation in the frequency of use and the effectiveness of friendships. The strongest bases for effective friendship relations were related to the degree of affectivity in the relationships. The most effective were, in descending order, friendships with select relatives, schoolmates and work colleagues. These were the most frequently used and most reliable types of friendships. Where possible, they were called upon to satisfy more important needs, and to carry out more "delicate" (risk-laden) intercessions with third persons. Friendships established on these bases also were the most enduring.

In addition, there were friendships with all others with whom one was acquainted. Such friendships were used intermittently. Usually these were mobilized when a specific need arose, and were allowed to lapse once the need was fulfilled. Normally they did not involve contact or exchange beyond the particular favor needed. The effectiveness of an intermittent friendship relationship in getting the assistance requested was closely related to the status (determined by occupational position and prestige) of the individual requesting the favor.

The creation of a new intermittent friendship to attend to a particular problem or need also was facilitated by the holding of higher status. This was particularly noticeable among political authorities, as in, for example, favors done by one judge for another with whom he was previously unacquainted, when the latter judge had a personal lawsuit in the courts. There was, however, a second means available to create and use friendships, regardless of the relative status of the middle-class member. One could establish a viable friendship relation with a previously unknown person from whom one desired personal assistance by the simple expedient of inviting the individual to eat or, preferably, to drink. The fact of having food or drink paid for, and the camaraderie established during this sharing, de facto placed the recipient under an obligation to repay the offerer in some form. Continued invitations could solidify the friendship and establish a stronger basis of affect and trust. This, in turn, expanded the levels at which the friendship could be called upon for assistance.

As a result of the flexibility with which friendships could be established and used, all members of the regional urban middle class were potentially available for mobilization into friendship relationships according to desirability and individual need. The variety in methods for establishing viable friendship relationships had the effect of increasing the individual middle-class member's actual and potential access to the resources cumulatively held or controlled by the regional middle class.

Four functions of regional middle-class friendship relationships were apparent. The first, and most prevalent, was to expedite individual matters, particularly with government offices, in the face of delays and inefficiencies existing in bureaucratic procedure. A second function of friendship relationships was to enable individuals who did not meet legal requirements or qualifying criteria to obtain governmental benefits. A third function was to avoid the more severe penalties of legal infringements. And a fourth function of friendships was to acquire scarce material and non-material resources. This occurred both with private and public resources. There were numerous examples of middle-class members using friendship connections to get foods that had become scarce. This was done via friends (or friends acting as brokers with other friends) who were merchants or producers saving their particular scarce commodity for sale to "special" customers. Different examples were the cases of teachers who successfully enlisted the help of friends in the regional office of the Ministry of Education to obtain transfers from their jobs in distant peasant communal schools to schools in the regional capital. Because of the scarcity of city teaching jobs in relation to demand, proper qualifications and experience were insufficient to obtain these positions.[20]

It can be seen that the functions of middle-class friendships in Cusco were partly or wholly performed in relation to the government bureaucracy and the distribution of publicly controlled benefits. This in itself is not surprising. From well before the period of the military regime, the national government had become involved in the supervision and control of many aspects of economic, social and political life in Peru. The military regime further extended the areas of governmental control and direct involvement. What the connection of friendship functions to government activity serves to indicate, however, is that the military leaders' pressures to end clientelistic behavior within the national bureaucracy would have a direct impact on the conduct of many aspects of private citizens' lives, and therefore would have an impact on clientelistic behavior in the society that extended well beyond the national bureaucracy itself.

Changes in Middle-Class Clientelistic Relationships

Although friendship relationships were flourishing within the Cusquenian middle class in the mid-1970s, one of the consequences of the regime's pressures against clientelism was the development of an apparent resistance or reluctance on the part of at least more prominent regional bureaucrats and public authorities to give personalistic assistance to individuals who fell greatly below legally set qualifying criteria, or who had grossly violated laws and regulations. When a municipal councillor who interceded to get a driver's license for a son's friend discovered that she had used her influence to get a license for an incapable driver, she chastized the son for having requested that she intercede. In this case she indicated her concern that she would be associated with a flagrant case of favoritism and that this would prejudice her in keeping her appointed municipal position. Similarly, a dean at the public university refused the request of a cousin to help the latter's son gain admission to the university after the son had done poorly on the entrance examination. The university recently had undergone a government-ordered reorganization that had included the firing of many faculty members who had not met new professional and political criteria set by the military regime. After the reorganization, the university continued under close ministerial surveillance. The dean, who succeeded in keeping his position during the reorganization, was unwilling to risk losing his job for not adhering to the newly-set standards.

Such reluctance to use personal influence was an indication of a larger phenomenon that had developed within the middle class, the view of personal influence itself as a scarce resource. This appeared to be increasingly associated with the use of personal influence, where it did occur, largely only for the benefit of equals or near equals. In other words, what seemed to have occurred was the class demarcation of the use of personal influence and scope of personal influence networks.

The view and use of personal influence as a scarce resource could be seen more clearly in the deterioration of patron-client relationships between regional middle-class and lower-class persons. The primary data used here give no indication of when the deterioration began. Secondary data for the pre-military period indicate that, by 1968, patron-client relationships within Peru had begun to be less diffuse and affective (Guasti, 1977). One might infer that such changes had occurred by this time in the Cusco region as well. What the primary data do evidence is that by the mid-1970s, a serious deterioration in patron-client relationships had occurred in the region. There was considerable variation in the willingness of middle-class persons to recognize the implicit obligations of reciprocity in patronage relationships and to comply with requests by clients for favors or intercessions on their behalf.

For the urban regional middle class, the functions that patron-client relationships with lower-class persons performed in this period largely were to acquire additional foods and, to a lesser extent, to insure that jobs requiring skilled labor were carried out. However, the degree to which middle-class patrons were willing to act on obligations of reciprocity, and the degree to which they were willing to use personal influence as the means to reciprocate varied considerably. The question of the degree to which personal influence was used is particularly important in relation to the brokerage role that patrons can perform for clients to associate the latter with middle-class networks and resources.

Some middle-class patrons continued to recognize and fulfill reciprocity obligations to clients through exchanges of material goods (gifts of food and services by the client reciprocated with gifts of food, clothing and medicine by the patron), or exchanges of material goods for limited non-material resources (the patron suggesting or taking the client to a doctor or lawyer when one was needed; information on how to get legal papers processed or which government office to go to). Other middle-class patrons had reduced the definition of reciprocal obligation to commercial terms and paid for food or services provided by their clients. They considered the monetary payment sufficient to met the reciprocity obligation, and were unwilling to provide services or information to the clients that could not be paid in monetary terms by the clients as well.[21]

No cases appeared where patrons reciprocated by using personal influence to intercede for clients with other middle-class persons. While it is possible that such brokerage still occurred to some degree, no evidence of it appeared in the data collected. There were, however, examples of patrons refusing to use personal influence on their clients' behalf. For instance, a university official refused to intercede for a client to get a janitorial job at the university; a judge refused to accompany his client to court or intercede for him in a criminal complaint the client was presenting. It is notable that both examples involved actions in government-controlled areas. However, it was the same university official who was willing to use a friendship relationship with the head of a state bank office to have a debt on which the former's son had defaulted removed from the son's credit record (an illegal action), and the same judge who was willing to intercede for a relative with another judge to avoid a severe sentence for default on alimony payments. It appears, therefore, that it was not the circumstance that personal intercession had been requested in a government-controlled area per se that determined that the middle-class person would refuse to intercede, but that the intercession had been requested by a lower-class person. Such contrasting examples are further indications of a perception by the regional middle class of personal influence as a scarce resource and the limitation of its use, particularly in the political realm, to actions for the benefit of other middle-class persons.

Mestizo Class Clientelistic Relationships

The experience with patron-client relationships of the lower-class populations of the town of San Miguel[22] and the community of Cancha provide additional indications that a class demarcation in the use of personal influence had occurred. In the *compadrazgo* relationships of the San Miguel *mestizo* population, the type of persons selected as patrons had changed, over a 30 year period, from local middle-class persons and political authorities to middle-class individuals living in the regional capital. By 1975 the majority of the San Miguel *mestizo* population had one or two city professionals among their *compadres*. Lawyers and doctors were especially desired.

For the San Miguelians, the function of patron-client relationships was not to acquire professional services or information gratis or by unequal exchanges. The San Miguel clients expected to pay for the services as would regular customers. The function of patron-client relationships for them was to guarantee the availability of services and expertise when needed.

However, almost all the persons interviewed indicated that their patrons had rarely or never assisted them with any matter. Exchanges at all levels were fairly reduced between these patrons and clients. The 30 kilometer distance from the city to some extent contributed to the reduced exchanges, although there was a regular bus service between the two locales. However, there also appeared to be a reluctance on both sides to maintain the relationships. The San Miguelians perceived that their city patrons were unwilling to take time with them, or saw the clients as "nuisances." On their part, San Miguel clients were increasingly reluctant to expend time, effort, goods and services to attempt to maintain the patron-client relationships. Further, despite the perceived purposes of the relationships, they seemed unwilling to ask their patrons for assistance. Those few who had asked their patrons for personal assistance had received mixed responses, while most said they never had asked their patrons for help.

What was distinctive about the situation of patron-clientage in San Miguel was that, although the San Miguelians interviewed had not received much useful assistance from their middle-class patrons and largely had not asked for any, they continued to perceive that personalistic assistance from middle-class persons, and access to middle-class expertise, influence and other resources, was important and necessary. One person interviewed volunteered the statement that in order to get a laborer's job in SINAMOS it was necessary to have a *compadre* who worked there. He did not know of specific examples or evidence of this. The important point was that he considered it credible. It was for this reason that San Miguelians continued to include middle-class persons in their *compadrazgo* relationships, creating at least the possibility of future help.

However, the San Miguelians established most of their *compadrazgo* relationships with persons of equal socioeconomic standing, and they obtained most of the assistance they needed from friendship relationships, with or without the formal bond of *compadrazgo*. Economic assistance, assistance and advice in commercial activities, and assistance in family and health problems were acquired primarily from friends, with whatever resources the latter had available to them. Assistance in dealing with government offices was more frequently acquired by seeking an equal or near equal who had had experience in dealing with the office involved. Brokerage within friendship, recommending a friend to another friend for assistance or services, was common. The Cusquenian middle-class method of establishing friendships by inviting to eat or drink was also used by the San Miguel *mestizo* population to establish new friendship connections within and outside San Miguel. Brokerage within friendship and the flexible method of creating new friendships expanded the total amount of resources available to the *mestizo* individual which were held or controlled by the *mestizo* population. Friendship, not patronage, was the more prevalent and more important type of personalistic relationship for the San Miguel inhabitants in acquiring needed material and nonmaterial resources.

Peasant Class Clientelistic Relationships

The experiences of the Cancha community members also reinforce
the evidence of changes in patron-clientage and the use of personal
influence. While in the past the members of this isolated community had established *compadrazgo* relationships primarily among
themselves, a number of *compadrazgo* relationships had been
established with persons outside the community. These mostly were
patron-client relationships, with authorities or "prestigious"
citizens in the district and provincial capitals. Only a very few were
friendship relationships with peasants living in other communities
and areas.

By the mid-1970s Cancha members continued to establish some
patron-client *compadrazgo* relationships with outside individuals,
although the preferential choices in patrons no longer were district
or provincial authorities but middle-class persons located in the
regional capital. However, the number of friendship relationships
established with peasants outside the community, both within and
outside *compadrazgo*, had increased. The most common of these
were with peasants living in or near market towns who were involved in commercial activities.

Those Cancha members who had chosen middle-class persons as
compadre patrons indicated they had done so to have access to
help, information and the influence of the patron if needed.
However, like the San Miguelians, most indicated that they never
had received material or non-material assistance from their
patrons. An age difference existed between the few who said they
had received patronal help and the majority who said they had not.
The few community members who had received help from patrons
were over 50 years of age. In addition, the instances of help had
almost all taken place ten or more years in the past. None of the
community members who were under 40 indicated they had received any form of assistance from their patrons. What these experiences indicate is that, however limited patronal help had been
in the past, with one exception it had ceased entirely by the mid-
1970s.[23]

The Cancha members' most important sources of assistance in
their activities, including their slowly expanding commercial activities, were friendship relationships. Friendship relationships
within the community were used largely for exchanges of labor in
the fields and for disseminating information acquired outside the
community. Friendship relationships with outside peasants were

useful to the Cancha peasants particularly for assistance in initiating individual commercial activities. The approximately ten families in Cancha who were growing barley under contract with the beer factory in the regional capital[24] had been introduced to this activity by a member of one of the families. He in turn had learned of the existence of such contracts and how to acquire them via a friendship with a peasant from a community located near the regional capital. The Cancha member had then acquired a contract for himself, had given the information to his friends in the other families, and had helped them to acquire contracts. Another Cancha member had a friend in a town in the neighboring Department of Puno from whom he had learned where and how to purchase some quantities of manufactured items to bring back to sell in Cancha. Friendship relationships with outsiders also were used to insure that Cancha members had a place to lodge in or near a market town or the regional capital when they wanted to sell produce and buy other items, as well as to have guaranteed access to types of food not produced in Cancha, by exchanging produce with outside peasant friends.

While in the past the few friendship relationships with outsiders had been formed almost entirely within *compadrazgo*, viable outside friendships were increasingly being established on a more flexible basis without the formal bonds of *compadrazgo*. This was being done primarily by the younger community members who were under the age of 40. Their means of establishing friendships had become as flexible as the means used by the Cusco middle class and San Miguel *mestizo* class to establish friendships. The younger Cancha members established friendships by initiating conversations with others in market places or while traveling, and sealing the new friendship with an invitation to food or an offer to be lodged in the other's house. These members also considered their outside friendships as valuable as other personalistic relationships. When asked from whom they received the greatest help in their activities, the under-40 members frequently answered that they received it from friends outside the community.

Thus, in Cancha, as in San Miguel, friendship relationships were prevalent and expanding, and were the most useful for the needs and activities of the community members. More, the wider range of friendship relationships that the Cancha peasants were establishing were increasing their access to material and non-material resources outside the community held or controlled by other peasants. Such resources, while not considerable when compared to those held by the middle and *mestizo* classes, were a meaningful addition to individual and communal resources for the independent community members.

Conclusions

From the evidence available it appears that friendship relationships were flourishing within the regional communal peasant, *mestizo* and urban middle classes in Cusco, while patron-client relationships had deteriorated. The behavior of middle-class individuals within friendship and patron roles, and the experiences and perceptions of the *mestizo* and peasant class members as clients, indicated that the regional middle class had come to view personal influence as a scarce resource and to utilize it primarily for their own and other middle-class members' benefit. At the same time, *mestizos* and peasants had increasingly turned to personalistic relationships with members of the same class as the means of access to needed resources and assistance. What these changes represented was the demarcation of the use of personal influence and scope of personalistic networks along class lines.

The primary data do not indicate clearly whether the class demarcation began before or because of the military regime's pressures against clientelistic behavior within and outside the national bureaucracy. It is clear that the demarcation paralleled the military government's actions to rationalize the bureaucracy for developmental purposes. The data also give evidence that the regime's explicit pressures increased the risk involved in engaging in personalistic behavior, and thereby the scarcity of personal influence as a resource. As a result, the regime's actions appear to have been a contributory factor in the restructuring of personalistic relationships along class lines.

The class demarcation of personalistic relationships within the region had a larger consequence. The demarcation had the effect of individually cutting off lower-class members from the material and non-material resources, including governmental resources, controlled by the regional middle class. It is evident from the data that personalistic behavior had not been eliminated within the national bureaucracy. Rather, it occurred between bureaucrats and other members of the middle class. Therefore, personalistic behavior continued, and continued to benefit the regional middle class. The impact of the military regime's pressures and actions against clientelistic behavior in the bureaucracy primarily fell on the regional lower classes, whose members now had less individual access to government resources, in addition to other middle-class controlled resources, and, when living in communities that did not contain a middle-class population, had less group access to governmental resources as well.

The demarcation of personalistic relationships contains a number of implications for class relationships and their polarization. One of the larger effects of the existence of patron-client relationships and of clientelism as an underlying political structure within a society is to lessen the possibility that class-based organization will develop among the lower classes or that class-oriented conflict will arise. This occurs through the creation of important, individualized cross-class cleavages. The deterioration of clientelism as an underlying political structure in the manner experienced in the region of Cusco has broken down cross-class networks of individual linkages, and fortified intra-class networks of individual linkages. This has reduced the level of positive interactions between members of the different classes, and one of the bases on which deferential attitudes and individualized material dependency in the lower classes were maintained. At the same time, the deterioration of clientelism has increased the level of positive interactions and exchanges between members of the same class, augmenting the possibility of later group organization. Such changes alone hardly provide the necessary dynamics for movement toward class consciousness or class polarization. They do, however, serve as preconditions for such movement. Whether or not the classes do move from the existing conditions toward greater polarization and conflict is likely to depend more on whether, when, and in what manner further agricultural commercialization and industrialization come to the region.

RESURGENCE OR CONTINUED DECLINE OF CLIENTELISM?

An election for a national constituent assembly was held in Peru on 18 June 1978. The election was called by the military leaders as the first step leading to the return of civilian government by 1980. At this point in time, therefore, it is possible to speculate about whether or not the deterioration in clientelism that was promoted by the military regime and evidenced in the region of Cusco is a permanent change in Peruvian politics.

The two overtly political measures taken by the regime that helped further the decline were the efforts to rationalize the bureaucracy and the sidelining of the political parties. The regime succeeded in extending the capabilities of the bureaucracy, particularly in the area of regulation, and in decreasing personalistic bureaucratic behavior, although it was seen that this occurred primarily in relation to lower-class members. Whether the decrease in personalism and clientage in the national bureaucracy progresses or is reversed will depend to an important degree on the type of civilian governments that replace the military, as well as on the orientation of the governments toward economic and bureaucratic rationalization; in short, it depends on which political parties come to power.

The civilian parties that existed at the time of the military coup were to varying degrees clientelistic in their electoral and legislative behavior. After the military came to power, these parties were separated from political power and access to national political resources for over a decade, but were not outlawed by the military regime. They remained free to maintain their memberships and organizations, or to reorganize, as best they could in the absence of decision-making power and direct access to public resources. The more important of these parties continued in reduced existence and ran in the constituent assembly election.[25] Two of the parties, APRA and the *Partido Popular Cristiano*, together won over half the constituent assembly seats. With the continued existence of these older clientelistic parties, and their apparent opportunity to gain national power, the period of the military regime may only be an interlude, after which clientelistic politics will resurge with the return to elections and party government.

However, as a result of the military regime's industrialization policies, a number of important economic changes were initiated in Peru. Most of the changes have not had a direct impact on the Cusco region but have had important economic and political ramifications within the larger society.[26] The further industrialization of the economy has caused changes in economic relationships, occurring particularly in the manufacturing, mining and fishing sectors. One of the consequences of this has been the rise of politically important class-oriented labor syndicates and federations since 1970. The labor organizations have been affiliated with reformist political parties, such as the Peruvian Communist Party, or created their own party organizations to run in the constituent assembly election. The class-oriented labor syndicates and their electoral organizations provide a new, different means of access to public decision-making and resources for the working class and peasantry from that provided by the older clientelistic parties, or by the national bureaucracy under the military government. The labor-affiliated electoral organizations together won 27% of the vote in the assembly election. As a result, they represent an important challenge to the acquisition of national power by the clientelistic parties.

Barring further repression of the labor organizations, two major types of parties will therefore exist in Peru with the return to civilian government: the older, clientelistic parties that have not disbanded, and the newer, class-oriented parties focussed on the organization of labor and class conflict. Whether the clientelistic parties continue to be influential in electoral politics and public resource distribution, become the most important political organizations, or ultimately are displaced by the class-oriented political organizations again will depend fundamentally on the pace and extent of further industrialization of the economy, and its impact on the continued realignment of class relations.

NOTES

1. Clientelism is defined as the structure of dyadic relationships, including patron-client, broker and friendship relationships, connected into networks that extend from the local to the national level, and from lower to upper class.

2. For more detail, see Bourricaud, 1966; Larson and Bergman, 1969; Quijano, 1968; Astiz, 1969; Benton, 1970; Stein, 1961; Kleymeyer, 1973; and Guasti, 1977.

3. During the first four years of the regime, this was defined to mean: (1) increase mining and petroleum production and expand domestic refining and processing capabilities; (2) stimulate intermediate and capital industrial goods production and create linkages between manufacturing and extractive industries; (3) acquire government control over the financial sector and reorient credit distribution to support industrial growth; and (4) stimulate growth in agricultural production and redistribute income in the agrarian sector.

4. Interviews with officials of the Centro de Capacitación e Investigación de Reforma Agraria (CENCIRA), and the Instituto Nacional de Administración Publica (INAP).

5. These were the Agrarian Social Interest Societies (SAIS), Integral Rural Settlement Projects (PIAR) and Integral Development Projects (PID). For a detailed description of the structures, see Bourque and Palmer, 1975: 187-89.

6. SINAMOS' other target groups were the squatter settlements, youth organiza-

tions, worker organizations, cooperative and self-directed organizations, and professional and cultural organizations. For a detailed discussion of SINAMOS' activities, see Malloy, 1974: 65-70.

7. The agrarian sector followed after the mining/petroleum, manufacturing and fishing sectors.

8. The data for the following two sections are taken from interviews and observation conducted in the research sites between February 1974 and October 1975. With the exception of the regional capital, the names of places and persons have been changed.

9. The head of the community was called the *personero* and was the community representative legally recognized by the national government. Before the communal political reorganization, the political offices of the community were the *varayoq* and the *personero*. The *varayoq* were the traditional hierarchical communal authority positions through which men passed until reaching the highest position of mayor. The mayor was selected by the community members, who gave great weight in the selection to the opinion of the elders, the former mayors. The mayor then filled the rest of the *varayoq* positions by appointment. The *personero*, also selected by the community members, was a position created by the national government, and had no intrinsic connection to the *varayoq*. Only the *personero* had the legal right to deal with the national government for communal matters.

10. *Compadrazgo* was the relationship between the parents and godparents of a child. The most important *compadres* were the baptismal godparents. Other *compadres* were the godparents of confirmation and marriage. For a discussion of *compadrazgo*, see Wolf and Mintz, 1967.

11. Interview with Celestino Sayri. No evidence from other community members or from Antonia Venero contradicted this.

12. The new communal government consisted of an Administration Committee and a Vigilance Committee. Each had a president, vice-president, and secretary. The Administration Committee in addition had a treasurer and two other members. The Vigilance Committee had one other member. The Administration Committee was responsible for all communal affairs, and its president was the highest communal political authority. The Vigilance Committee served as an oversight group to the Administration Committee and as a grievance committee for any community member with a complaint against the Administration Committee or one of its members.

13. Conversations with employees of SINAMOS, the regional office of the Ministry of Industry and Tourism, the Banco Industrial and others.

14. See the section on inter-class relationships, below, for further discussion of this change.

15. The SINAMOS promoter and district office provided very little assistance to Cancha in getting resources from the government. The single exception was the help the promoter provided in acquiring some building materials for an addition to the communal school. More frequently, the promoter served to hinder Cancha's access to public resources. In particular, the Cancha members considered the promoter responsible for the loss of the important budgetary allocation for the road. The promoter told the second communal president that he, the promoter, would help the president acquire the road by filing for him the papers needed to get the budgetary allocation released. The papers never were filed. By the time the Cancha communal administration discovered this, the allocation had been lost.

The CNA and its provincial unit, the Agrarian League of Paucartambo, also did not become a channel for acquiring public resources for Cancha. Most Cancha members did not know what the CNA or the Agrarian League were, nor that the community had an elected representative to the Agrarian League. The few who recognized the terms CNA and Agrarian League had only a vague idea of the organizations' purpose. None of the community members, including the Cancha representative to the Agrarian League, saw the League and the CNA as a possible channel for specific interests and resource requests, or for registering complaints against problematic procedures and government officials. The representative viewed the CNA largely as an organization that promoted peasant interests in broad and ideological, rather than concrete terms.

16. The communal leaders were fed and lodged without cost when attending the obligatory training courses, but received no travel stipend or compensation for their time away from work.

17. *Mestizos* are peasants who have improved their economic status, are employed mostly as commercial middlemen, although they continue to farm their fields, and have begun to adopt modern dress and customs.

18. Cusco, the Department capital, has a population of 150,000. It has a rapidly growing laborer population, and a large middle class that represents the highest class in the region. The regional middle class is composed of professionals (legal, medical, academic, etc.), white-collar employees, including government regional office staff, and independent businessmen, involved in commerce, tourism and some manufacturing. Former *hacendados* (the large landowners of the region) and their families also live in the regional capital, and for the most part already had acquired middle-class occupations before their landholdings were expropriated.

19. Friendship relationships are defined as dyadic, personalistic relationships among equals or near equals.

20. Brokerage was used frequently within friendship relationships, thereby creating networks of friendships and increasing the efficacy with which the functions of friendships were carried out. By being introduced to an unknown middle-class person with the necessary resources or occupational position, by an intermediary who had friendships with both, a middle-class individual could expand his personal access to resources and assistance. Brokerage also served to increase the reliability of the means of access, by enabling the individual to utilize the affect and trust in another friendship relationship that he could not readily develop himself with the person whose resource or assistance was needed.

21. There were two cases observed where patrons accepted gifts from clients and did not reciprocate in any form. Such complete non-reciprocity toward clients appeared to still be exceptional at this time.

22. San Miguel is a *mestizo* town with a population of 10,000, located 30 kilometers from Cusco, the regional capital, on a main commercial road. The town has a small middle class and a large *mestizo* population, as well as a small laborer and artisan population. Because of its location, San Miguel has received the direct impact of urban influence, and experiences regular commercial interaction with Cusco, the cities and towns to the south, and Lima.

23. The exception was Celestino Sayri, who still received personal assistance from his patron.

24. The beer factory was the largest industrial enterprise in the region.

25. The exception was Accion Popular, the party of former president Fernando Belaunde Terry who was deposed by the coup that initiated the military government.

Accion Popular decided not to submit candidates for the constituent assembly election, but said it would participate in the future presidential and congressional elections.

26. The changes included major allocations of state resources to mining and industry to promote their rapid development; the nationalization of the largest mines, the petroleum companies, basic industries, the fishmeal industry and the major commercial banks, and the creation of state enterprises to operate these activities; the creation of the Industrial Communities, which were to be worker self-management enterprises in the manufacturing sector; and the expropriation and adjudication to cooperative peasant enterprises of over 22 million acres of farming and grazing land. Only the latter change directly affected the Cusco region.

REFERENCES

ASTIZ, C. (1969). *Pressure Groups and Power Elites in Peruvian Politics*. Ithaca, NY: Cornell University Press.

BENTON, K. (1970). "Peru's Revolution from Above," *Conflict Studies*, (2): 1-12.

BOURQUE, S. C. and PALMER, D. S. (1975). "Transforming the Rural Sector: Government Policy and Peasant Response," pp. 179-219, in A.F. Lowenthal, ed., *The Peruvian Experiment*. Princeton: University Press.

BOURRICAUD, F. (1966). "Structure and Function of the Peruvian Oligarchy," *Studies in Comparative International Development*, 2(2): 17-31.

GUASTI, L. (1977). "Peru: Clientelism and Internal Control," pp. 422-38, in S.W. Schmidt et al., eds., *Friends, Followers and Factions: A Reader in Political Clientelism*. Berkeley: University of California Press.

KLEYMEYER, C. (1973). "Social Interaction Between Quechua Campesinos and Criollos." Unpublished PhD dissertation, University of Wisconsin-Madison.

LARSON SARFATI, M., and BERGMAN, A. (1969). *Social Stratification in Peru*. Berkeley: Institute of International Studies.

MALLOY, J.M. (1974). "Authoritarianism, Corporatism and Mobilization in Peru," pp. 52-84, in F. B. Pike and T. Stritch, eds., *The New Corporatism*. Notre Dame: University Press.

McCLINTOCK, C. (1977). *Self-Management and Political Participation in Peru 1969-1975: The Corporatist Illusion*. Beverly Hills: Sage Professional Papers, Contemporary Political Sociology Series.

QUIJANO OBREGON, A. (1968). "Tendencies in Peruvian Development and in the Class Structure," pp. 289-328, in J. Petras and M. Zeitlin, eds., *Latin America: Reform or Revolution?* Greenwich, Conn.: Fawcett Publications.

STEIN, W. (1961). *Hualcan: Life in the Highlands of Peru*. Ithaca, NY: Cornell University Press.

WOLF, E. and MINTZ, S. (1967). "An Analysis of Ritual Co-Parenthood (Compadrazgo)," pp. 185-99, in J. Potter et al., eds., *Peasant Society*. Boston: Little, Brown.

9

Turkey: The Politics of Political Clientelism

Ergun Özbudun
University of Ankara, Turkey

Political parties in Turkey have had a history of almost 70 years, not counting earlier secret revolutionary societies. For more than three decades, a competitive multi-party system has been in operation with only a brief and partial interruption in 1960-61. Furthermore, Turkish political parties display a high degree of functional saliency in the Turkish political system. "Turkish politics," as Frey rightly said, "are party politics . . . It is perhaps in this respect above all — the existence of extensive, powerful, highly organized, grass roots parties — that Turkey differs institutionally from the other Middle Eastern nations with whom we frequently compare her" (Frey, 1965: 391).

In the slowly growing literature on Turkish political parties, the emphasis has generally been either on their formal structures and ideologies (Tunaya, 1952; Erogul, 1970; Kili, 1976; Landau, 1974 and 1976), or on social background characteristics of their parliamentary representatives and local leaders (Frey, 1965; Tachau, 1966, 1973a, 1973b). Surprisingly, scant attention has been paid to the clientelistic features of Turkish party politics and to the related phenomena of patronage, corruption, factionalism and party machines (one notable exception is the work by Sayari, 1975, 1977, and n.d.; see also Ozbudun, 1976). In fact, such concepts have been gaining increasingly wider currency in the study of political parties in developing countries, and have proven themselves extremely useful as tools of analysis (Scott, 1969 and 1972; Bienen, 1970 and 1971; Weiner, 1962; Lemarchand, 1972; Lande, 1973). Our purpose here is to explore further some of the clientelistic features of Turkish politics and to present them in a developmental context. The first section is an attempt to define the nature of patron-client ties and the conditions necessary for their maintenance with special reference to the Turkish case; the second deals with what are often called "traditional" patron-client ties; the third focusses on a more modern manifestation of clientelism, namely party machines, or as Weingrod (1968) called it, "party-directed patronage." In conclusion we try to analyze the developmental implications of clientelism in contemporary Turkey.

I. THE NATURE OF PATRON-CLIENT
RELATIONS

All definitions of patron-client ties stress at least three core elements: inequality, reciprocity and proximity (Powell, 1970: 412; Weingrod, 1968: 378-79; Lemarchand, 1972: 69; Scott, 1972: 92-95; Lande, 1973). They are unequal in that they develop between two parties unequal in status, wealth and influence. They are reciprocal in that the formation and maintenance of the relationship depends on reciprocity in the exchange of goods and services. Finally, proximity indicates that they are based on diffuse, personal, face-to-face relationships which often create feelings of affection and trust between the partners. Thus, we may define patron-client ties as "a more or less personalized relationship between actors (i.e., patrons and clients), or sets of actors, commanding unequal wealth, status, or influence, based on conditional loyalties, and involving mutually beneficial transactions" (Lemarchand, 1972: 69). Scott (1972: 92) stresses the same elements when he defines the patron-client relationship

as a special case of dyadic (two-person) ties involving a largely instrumental friendship in which an individual of higher socioeconomic status (patron) uses his own influence and resources to provide protection or benefits, or both, for a person of lower status (client) who, for his part, reciprocates by offering general support and assistance, including personal services, to the patron.

These definitions are broad enough to encompass a wide variety of phenomena, while at the same time they distinguish patron-client ties from a number of similar influence relationships. They encompass, on the one hand, traditional forms of clientelism in which the patron's superiority is based on some sort of traditional influence, often stemming from landownership or religious status. They include, on the other hand, such more modern phenomena as party-directed patronage commonly referred to as machine politics (Lemarchand, 1972: 69; Weingrod, 1968: 381). True, as Scott (1972: 95-96) has pointed out, the role of patron should theoretically be distinguished from those of party broker or boss. He admits, however, that "it is quite possible for a single individual to act both as a broker and a patron," just as "a boss may often function as a patron . . . Such a role combination is not only possible, but is empirically quite common." Whether of a traditional or modern variety, a relationship can be designated as a patron-client relationship, as long as it displays the elements of inequality, reciprocity and proximity.

These same attributes distinguish patron-client ties from certain other types of relationships which, like clientelism, may also result in the political mobilization of large numbers of people. Kinship ties are among such mechanisms for mobilized political participation. But they do not qualify as patron-client ties, since (1) they are based on affective, not instrumental, bonds, and (2) they do not typically bring together parties of unequal wealth and status.[1] Similarly, if the authority of a religious leader is based chiefly on the affection and deference of his followers, their relationship hardly qualifies as a patron-client tie, which presupposes elements of instrumentality and reciprocity. It will be shown below, however, that some such reciprocity is often observed in religious orders or brotherhoods. On the other hand, relationships based principally on coercion are obviously different from patron-client ties, even if they bind parties unequal in status and proximate in space. Coercive elements may be present in the patron-client pattern, but if they come to be dominant, the tie is no longer a patron-client relationship (Powell, 1970: 412; Scott, 1972: 99-100). Finally, such ties, dependent as they are on close, personal, face-to-face contact, ought to be distinguished from legal contractual relationships which, again, may be binding parties of unequal status, wealth and influence. In this regard, interesting borderline cases may be observed in the relationships between large capitalist farmers and their hired labor, between town merchants and their peasant customers, etc.

Turkey provides a fertile ground for the formation and maintenance of a wide variety of clientelistic relationships. In fact, she meets almost all the conditions necessary for the widespread presence of such relationships. First, clientelism is likely to flourish in periods of rapid socioeconomic change, as a result of which traditional patterns of deference weaken and "vertical ties can only be maintained through a relationship of greater reciprocity. Competition among leaders for support, coupled with the predominance of narrow, parochial loyalties, will encourage the widespread use of concrete, short-run, material inducements to secure cooperation" (Scott, 1969: 1146). With further socioeconomic modernization, however, new loyalties will emerge that will increasingly stress horizontal class or occupational ties. In other words, clientelistic patterns are more likely to be found in transitional societies than in either traditional or modern ones.

Turkey is presently in the midst of rapid socioeconomic change. Traditional authority patterns have considerably weakened, but have not yet been fully replaced by modern (i.e., rational-legal) authority patterns. Parallel to economic growth, material incentives have rapidly gained in importance, but class and occupational ties have not yet developed to the same extent. Extended families have become smaller and increasingly unable or unwilling to perform their social security functions, but modern social security organizations have not yet evolved to encompass the entire population or even a major part of it. Furthermore, Turkey displays great regional diversity with respect to the level of socioeconomic modernization. One can, therefore, simultaneously observe many varieties of clientelism associated with varying degrees of modernization.

The second general condition for the maintenance of patron-client relationships is inequality in the control of wealth, status and power, since such relationships develop, by definition, between unequal parties. Turkey also satisfies this condition with her high degree of socioeconomic inequality. While the country has had sustained economic growth in the last three decades and while all major social groups (probably with the exception of civil servants) have more or less benefited from it in absolute terms, disparities in wealth and income seem to have, if anything, become more marked.[2]

Thirdly, the extent of clientelistic relations is associated with the scope of governmental activities. When the functions of government are comparatively limited ones, the government does not control rich or considerable resources, hence a more limited role for patrons mediating between government and their clients (Weingrod, 1968: 393). Conversely, when such scope is broader and when, in particular, the government is involved in extensive development programs, the role of patron takes on new and more significant dimensions, since a much greater share of their clients' lives comes to be affected by governmental decisions (Scott, 1969: 1153-54). In Turkey, the scope of government has always been broader than in most countries in the same bracket of socioeconomic modernization, probably because of the long and strong tradition of statehood under the Ottoman Empire. Such scope has been further broadened under the Republic. Some government activities provide sectoral or sub-sectoral inducements, such as agricultural price supports, minimum wages, labor legislation, etc., which clearly cannot be manipulated by patrons' mediations. Some other programs, however, provide either pork-barrel inducements (roads, drinking water, schools, mosques, electricity, irrigation projects, community development projects, licenses for growing certain agricultural products, etc.) or entirely individual benefits (agricultural credits, employment, bureaucracy, choice of a factory or road location, etc.). The last two types of inducements can often be obtained through the services of a patron and, consequently, they tend to broaden the scope of clientelistic relationships.

Finally, electoral politics have an impact on patron-client ties. While such ties can also be observed in non-competitive systems, electoral competition transforms patron-client relations in some important ways. First, it improves the client's bargaining position with a patron by adding to his resources. Second, it tends "to promote the expansion of patron-client ties and the politicization of existing bonds. Knowing that an electoral victory is important, a local patron with a modest following will probably try to obligate more clients to him in order to strengthen his electoral position" (Scott, 1972: 109-10). The impact of electoral politics on patron-client ties will be analyzed in greater detail below. Suffice it to say that the presence of electoral competition in Turkey for more than three decades provided another favorable condition for the expansion of clientelistic patterns.

While all four favorable conditions mentioned above operate on a nationwide basis, some regions display still more favorable circumstances. This is particularly true for the Eastern region for historical, geographical, social, economic, ethnic, linguistic, religious and cultural reasons. Historically, this is a part of Turkey where state penetration has been much more superficial than in other regions. Geographically, it is the region most distant from the center (capital), and its mountainous terrain makes transportation and communication still more difficult. Economically, it is much less developed than the other regions, and within-region distribution of wealth and income is much more unequal. Socially, it displays a high degree of segmentation among numerous tribal groups and religious orders and communities. Linguistically, a substantial portion of its population speak Kurdish or Zaza with little or no knowledge of Turkish. Culturally, the gap between the Westernized legal systems of the nation and the customary law and morality of local society is also widest in this region. "It is essential for small villagers in their dealings with government officials to utilize intermediaries who understand the intricacies of the administration as well as the language of its officals" (Yalman, 1971: 190-91). If patron-client relations thrive on the communication gaps between government and low-status individuals (Weingrod, 1968: 382-85), then one can hardly imagine a more fertile ground for development of such relations than Eastern Turkey. Since this region is so different from the rest of the country, the nature of its clientelistic pattern is also, understandably, different from those dominant in the other regions. Such differences will be discussed in greater detail when we distinguish between two types of clientelism in Turkey.

II. TRADITIONAL CLIENTELISM

Lemarchand (1972: 72-75) distinguishes four different types of traditional political clientelism in Tropical Africa: the patrimonial, the feudal, the mercantile, and the "saintly" type. With the obvious exception of the patrimonial type, where the king doles out political and administrative offices to client-chiefs in exchange for service and support, all three types can be observed in some form in contemporary Turkey.

The feudal type is the one most commonly found, especially in the less developed parts of the country. It should be stressed that the term "feudal" is not used here to suggest any formal political hierarchy. It simply refers to "an interpersonal bond between a superior and a subordinate . . . involving an exchange of protection, economic security and a position in the society in return for loyalty, obedience and service from the subordinate'' (Lemarchand, 1972: 73). In this type of relationship, the patron's superiority stems chiefly from his ownership of large estates, and his clients are typically his tenants, sharecroppers and others who are dependent upon the patron's land for their livelihood.

Landowner-patrons in Turkey are commonly referred to as *agas*. However, there does not seem to exist a single, consistent concept of *aga* among Turkish villagers. Kiray (1964: 60-61) notes, for example, that in a Black Sea town she studied, town merchants were also addressed as *agas* by neighboring villagers. Similarly, Meeker (1972: 244-45, 259) describes the *agas* in an Eastern Black Sea village without emphasizing their landowning status. *Agas*, in his words, ''can be described as leaders of unstable and informal alliances, whose composition is based largely, but not exclusively, on kinship ties, whose purposes are mainly political, and whose cohesion is marginal and often fleeting.'' He further observes that the *agas'* source of legitimacy derives from their popular support, their use of coercion and their government connections. This description is more reminiscent of a factional leader or a boss than a patron proper (see Scott, 1972: 96).

Most of the available studies on Turkish village power structure, however, identify *agas* as large landowning patrons (Yalman, 1971; Ozankaya, 1971). Even in this case, *aga*'s relations with his clients are based not only on a mutually beneficial exchange relationship, but they also often contain some elements of coercion. Yalman (1971: 189, 213-14), for example, while drawing attention ''to the importance of constant generosity and benevolence'' of the *aga* to maintain his position with his clients, also observes that ''the law is weak and distant. Only tough men can survive the ruthlessness of the struggle. The landlord who is weak loses all he has and may, indeed, have to write off very considerable and valuable property as a total loss. On the other hand, there are great opportunities for effective and intelligent, albeit ruthless, persons in the shifting land situation.'' Similarly, Ozankaya (1971: 68-74) points out that the authority of landlord *agas* over peasants is based mainly on fear and physical coercion or threat of coercion. At the same time, however, he mentions a variety of services *agas* perform for the villagers, services commonly associated with the role of patron, such as mediation with administrative authorities; protection from police interrogations and gendarme harrassments; lending seeds, flour, hay, oxen, or tractors; credit sales from their shops in nearby towns; standing as surety for agricultural credits, etc.

Even though most *agas* appear to be large landowners, land-ownership is not the sole basis of their authority. They are also aided by such factors as having a large family, occupying or controlling the office of village headman (*muhtar*), monopolizing contacts with administrative agencies, controlling the few non-political associations which exist in some villages, e.g., agricultural cooperatives, mosque-building or village development associations (Ozankaya, 1971: 70, 72-73). They frequently enter into horizontal alliances with other patrons through such mechanisms as friendship or fictive kinship (*kirvelik*), which expand their power base. The fact that an *aga*'s direct dependents may themselves be embedded in a variety of other networks also tends to have a multiplier effect on his political influence. "Without these branching capabilities even the largest land owning *agas* would be unable to assemble significant political support" (Kudat, 1975: 75-76). Finally, just as the *aga*'s economic power over a number of clients gives him political significance, the reverse also is true: his membership in political party organizations greatly increases his influence on his clients because of his access to party-controlled resources. We will return to this point when we analyze party patronage below.

A second type of traditional clientelism corresponds to what Lemarchand (1972: 74) has called "mercantile clientelism." Very little work has been done on the clientelistic relationships between town merchants and their peasant customers. But Kiray (1964: 60-63) observes that the merchant and the villagers are involved in a highly personalized, diffuse social relationship. The merchant not only provides the villager with all his necessary supplies, but also purchases his products, extends him credit, mediates in his dealings with governmental authorities and acts as a friend and counselor. "Sometimes a whole village is involved with a single merchant. In such cases, the merchant has more influence upon the villagers than the headman, gendarmerie commander, and even the county governor." Sometimes, the mercantile-patron may be the same person, or belong to the same family, as the landowning patron who has a shop in the nearby town (Besikci, 1968: 67-69, 83-84; Ozankaya, 1971: 37, 74). Such a combination clearly expands the resource base of patronage and increases the influence of the patron over his clients.

A third type of traditional clientelism which exists in Turkey is the religious or "saintly" clientelism observed most conspicuously within *Sufi* brotherhoods (Lemarchand, 1972: 74). Nur Yalman (1969), who studied an *Alevi* community in Eastern Turkey, noted that the *Alevi sheikh* (*mursid*) of the area was "a well-known and very highly respected man" and that he had about 500 villages under his jurisdiction. The typical transaction in the saintly type is salvation for the clients (followers) in exchange for obedience and service offered to the *mursid*. In the particular case described by Yalman, a more instrumental element is also involved in the exchange relationship. Thus, the *mursid* performs a peace-making or dispute-settling function during his yearly visit to the village; and the villagers collect funds for him from every household every year, part of which goes to the local representative of the *mursid* (*Pir* or *Dede*) in charge of several villages. Sometimes, the status of *sheikh* or *mursid* is combined with large landownership. In this case, the roles of saintly and landowning patrons mutually reinforce each other, and the overall influence of the patron increases commensurately (Besikci, 1968: 179-80, 184).

What is the political significance of such traditional clientelistic patterns? Clearly, they constitute mechanisms for "mobilized" political participation, "vote-banks" ready to be delivered as the patrons see fit (Ozbudun, 1976: 5-6). One way to measure the extent of such mobilization is to study independent candidacies. To be sure, patrons may, and often do, mobilize their clients in the service of a political party rather than running as independents. Conversely, not all instances of mobilized voting display the characteristics of patron-client relationships. For example, tribes can often be mobilized electorally by their leaders; but such mobilization, being based on kinship ties, does not qualify as clientelistic mobilization. Nevertheless, there is an overall correlation between independent votes and the prevalence of patron-client ties. Without the help of such networks, independent candidates have very little chance of success. In fact, independents perform much better precisely in regions where traditional patron-client ties are strongest and most pervasive. In 1969, of the nineteen provinces where independents received more than 10% of the total valid votes cast, thirteen were in Eastern Turkey; and out of thirteen successful candidacies, nine were again from Eastern provinces and three more from bordering ones. In 1973, out of six independent deputies, five were elected from Eastern provinces. In 1977 all four successful independent candidates represented Eastern constituencies. Percentage of votes for independent candidates is found to be negatively correlated with the indicators of socioeconomic modernization (Ozbudun, 1976: 138-42; 1977a: 291-304). A more detailed analysis of successful independent or party candidates in Eastern Turkey in the 1969 elections showed that a great many of them were, indeed, *sheikhs*, large landowners, or tribal chiefs (Kudat, 1975: 83-85).

III. PARTY PATRONAGE

The transition from an authoritarian one-party rule to a competitive multi-party system in 1946 has affected clientelistic patterns in Turkey in two different ways. One is the transformation of traditional patron-client ties through the introduction of party patronage as an additional resource base for the patrons. The other is the emergence of new party-directed patronage patterns independent of such traditional patron-client ties.

As already implied in the foregoing analysis, traditional patrons often rose to important positions in the local organizations of political parties. Many students of Turkish politics have pointed out that, since the advent of a competitive party system, rural party organizations tend to be based on already existing groups and networks, and that the initial party choices are frequently determined by rivalries among them. Stirling (1965: 281-82; see also Meeker, 1972: 243, 251, 259; Rustow, 1966: 123; Beeley, 1970: 492-93; Sayari, 1975: 123-26) has observed, for example, that in most rural communities two sharply defined rival factions existed when the transition to a multi-party system took place.

> The reigning faction had necessarily already identified itself with the existing government, so that the headman and his supporters were automatically RPP. Those who opposed them were thus committed to the DP. . . . This conversion of existing local factions into local sections of the national parties made possible the very rapid establishment of a two-party political system in full-scale activity . . . This analysis implies that the DP in fact captured the support of most of the local oppositions which existed in every town and village in Turkey.

Such politicization of existing patron-client ties led to an increase in the overall influence of patrons. By assuming leadership roles in local party organizations, they gained access to new sources of party patronage and to new channels of mediation, which they could then use to bolster their authority over their clients. At the same time, their significance for national party leaderships also increased greatly, because of their capability to deliver blocs of votes at election times. Many among them became mayors, municipal council members, or even members of parliament (Yalman, 1969: 54; and 1971: 193; Ozankaya, 1971: 73; Besikci, 1968: 220). However, the multiplicity of party-connected patrons in the multi-party era gave their clients some bargaining power in exchange for their votes. Consequently, the trend in the less developed Eastern Turkey is from purely deferential patterns of influence to more typical patron-client ties in which elements of reciprocity and instrumentality play a much greater role.

Such trends were obviously more visible in the more developed regions of Turkey. There, a greater degree of state and market penetration (for a discussion of these factors, see Scott, 1972: 107-109; Powell, 1970: 413-14; Weingrod, 1968: 382-98) had already laid the basis for a transformation from traditional clientelism, from patrons in the conventional sense to party brokers. This process was also greatly aided by the mechanics of the multi-party system. As Sayari (1977: 108-109) notes,

> the replacement of notable clientelism with . . . "party-directed patronage" is one prominent aspect of this change . . . (T)he political influence of the notables at present depends more on their roles as party functionaries than on their control of traditional patronage resources . . . (T)he replacement of notable clientelism with party patronage is related to the weakening of the deferential political culture of the countryside as a result of socio-economic change.

The process of change in clientelistic patterns has not been limited to the transformation of the traditional (chiefly landowning) patrons into party brokers. A twin process has been the emergence of additional brokers to compete with the former for followings on the local level (Powell, 1970: 414). These are local party leaders who did not come from a traditional patron background. Few available studies of local politicians in Turkey reveal that a major part of them are businessmen, traders and professionals (Ozbudun, 1977b; Tachau, 1966 and 1973a; Kiray, 1964:

179-180). But through their control of the flow of party patronage, as well as their possession of greater political information and skills, they can often successfully compete with traditional patrons for local followings.

Such new party patronage patterns became particularly evident after the DP came to power in 1950. If a party machine is defined as "a non-ideological organization interested less in political principle than in securing and holding office for its leaders and distributing income to those who run it and work for it" (Scott, 1969: 1144), then the DP indeed displayed many of the characteristics of a political machine. The local cadres of the DP, consisting in large part of local traders, businessmen and professionals, were better able than the older, more elitist and more bureaucratic cadres of the rival Republicans to play a brokerage role. Under the DP rule, party patronage was usually "distributed through typical pork-barrel grants in the form of roads, waterways, mosques and various public works. These were rewarded to rural communities which had either hitherto supported the DP or appeared willing to make a switch" (Sayari, 1975: 129). Prior to elections, construction machines were often sighted near hotly contested or electorally important villages, waiting for a favorable electoral outcome to start or to continue their work. Larger communities such as towns or provinces were sometimes rewarded with factories, which were called "election factories" by the opposing Republicans for their usually non-economic locations. In addition to such pork-barrel grants, party patronage also included a wide variety of individual inducements ranging from cash payments to agricultural credits, from employment to solving some bureaucratic difficulty. The continued electoral success of the DP and its successor the JP (Justice Party) for two decades can, at least partially, be attributed to their efficiency as rural machines.

Machine characteristics were also observable in urban party organizations, but to a lesser extent and with considerably less success. In the urban settings, the DP/JP efforts were mainly directed towards the new urban migrants. Sherwood (1967) notes, for example, that "a typical villager arriving in Ankara or Istanbul goes immediately to that district populated by people from his own village. The local Justice Party man helps him settle, aids in the problems with authorities, and functions as an employment agency or a marriage bureau as the case may be." A former JP mayor of one of the largest cities is reported to keep a record of the votes for his party in each precinct and to allocate municipal services on the basis of their party loyalties (Keles, 1972: 199-200). A particularly powerful weapon in the hands of the party controlling the municipal government is to tolerate, or even legalize, the illegal squatter houses (*gecekondu*) of new urban migrants, or to demolish them by strictly implementing the laws. There is considerable evidence that such decisions were often made on the basis of political considerations. It has been observed, for example, that in the weeks preceding national or local elections, *gecekondu*-dwellers were given at least verbal assurances of legalization, and that such times were the most intense period of construction.

Such machine tactics, no doubt, contributed to the electoral success of the DP and the JP in the cities, as revealed by the fact that their urban superiority was largely based on their exceptionally strong showing in the low-income, migrant-populated *gecekondu* areas (Ozbudun, 1976: 201-206). More specifically, Karpat (1975: 116) has found that a large percentage of urban migrants who voted for the RPP in their villages switched their votes to the JP or the TLP (Turkish Labor Party) in the city. It is conceivable that part of the switch to the JP was a favorable response to the short-term, concrete, material benefits offered by the JP machine. I think, however, that the above pictures of the DP/JP urban organizations functioning like well-oiled, efficient American urban political machines are somewhat exaggerated. While these organizations evidently displayed certain machine-like characteristics, both their efficiency and long-term electoral success were much more limited than their American counterparts. An analysis of the changing urban voting patterns clearly indicates that, despite all the party-directed patronage it disposed, the JP's superiority in the big cities and particularly in the low-income migrant neighborhoods came to an end in the early 1970s. Although the JP held a two-to-one to three-to-one edge over the RPP in the squatter precincts of Istanbul, Ankara and Izmir in the 1960s, the situation was reversed in the 1973 elections, when the RPP gained an almost two-to-one superiority (Ozbudun, 1977a: 288-91). The 1977 parliamentary elections, as well as the municipal elections of 1973 and 1977, also showed that the JP's loss of support and the RPP's ascendancy in the urban areas were not a temporary aberration but were the manifestation of a long-term trend of realignment. We will return to the implications of this new trend in the concluding section of this paper.

Table 1

Patronage Activities of Local Party Organizations in Izmir (in percentages)

Services performed		JP			RPP			TLP	
		Often	Rarely	Never	Often	Rarely	Never	Often	Rarely	Never
Credits	Urban	7	34	59	5	21	70	—	—	93
	Rural	69	—	31	15	23	62	10	—	90
	Total	29	22	49	9	22	66	3	—	92
Employment	Urban	45	38	17	30	44	26	7	37	52
	Rural	69	19	13	23	31	46	—	20	80
	Total	53	31	16	28	39	33	5	32	59
Licenses	Urban	14	17	69	9	21	67	—	4	93
	Rural	50	—	50	23	19	58	10	10	80
	Total	27	11	62	14	20	64	3	5	89
Aid with the police	Urban	14	24	62	19	23	53	—	15	81
	Rural	44	13	44	12	8	81	10	10	80
	Total	24	20	56	16	17	64	3	13	81

Table 2
Voters' Expectations of Patronage Services from Local Party Organizations
as Perceived by Party Leaders (in percentages)

Services	JP			RPP			TLP		
	Urban	Rural	Total	Urban	Rural	Total	Urban	Rural	Total
Employment	28	25	27	29	15	24	13	—	9
Aid with govt. authorities (police, courts, licenses)	19	17	18	22	28	24	10	8	9
Social welfare (credits, cash payments, medical care)	17	31	22	18	18	18	7	25	12
Community projects (pork-barrel benefits)	28	19	24	16	26	20	10	17	12
Political education	—	—	—	1	—	1	20	50	29
Uncertain	9	8	9	13	13	13	40	—	29
Total (%)	101	100	100	98	100	100	100	100	100

Some data on the patronage activities of local party organizations were provided by my survey of party leaders in the province of Izmir carried out in 1968. The survey included a total of 152 local leaders of three parties (JP, RPP, and TLP). They were the members of the provincial (*il*) committees and of six county (*ilce*) committees of their respective parties. Of the six counties covered by the survey, three were urban (Merkez, Karslyaka, Bornova) and three were rural (Kiraz, Kinik, Karaburun) counties. Thus, it was hoped that the survey data would enable us to make urban-rural, as well as inter-party, comparisons.

Table 1 reveals that patronage services were provided much more frequently by the JP organizations than by the RPP or the TLP organizations. This can, no doubt, be partly attributed to the fact that the JP was in power at the time of the survey, and therefore had much greater patronage resources to dispense. But it may also support the above-mentioned impressionistic observation of many students of Turkish politics that the JP is better adapted than the RPP to play the role of a machine-type party. Among the patronage services, interestingly, employment came first for both the JP and the RPP. The JP (particularly its rural organizations) was also heavily involved in securing credits (apparently agricultural credits from the State Agricultural Bank) for its followers. Another important finding emerging from the Table is that the JP's rural organizations were much more frequently engaged in patronage distribution than its urban organizations, while there was no such clear urban-rural difference for the RPP. This also supports our impressionistic conclusion that party patronage is much more a rural phenomenon than an urban one.

Table 2 shows the local leaders' perceptions of the voters' expectations for patronage services. Here, we do not observe significant differences between the JP and the RPP, or between urban and rural areas. It is interesting, however, that according to the perceptions of the local leaders of both major parties, voters almost always expect some sort of patronage benefits from their party organizations. Again, employment came first for both major parties. The leaders of the TLP seemed to differ significantly in this regard. In their perceptions, their voters were much less interested in patronage benefits and definitely more interested in political education. This may be explained by the more ideological orientations of the TLP voters, as well as by their realistic understanding that their party is in no position to distribute patronage anyway.

IV. CLIENTELISM AND POLITICAL
DEVELOPMENT

What are the implications of clientelism for political development in Turkey? If, following Huntington (1968) we define political development as "institutionalization of political organizations and procedures," then the institutionalization of political parties becomes a very important, maybe the crucial, element in political development. The question can then be posed: how has clientelism affected the institutionalization of political parties in Turkey?

As was pointed out above, patron-client ties explain the rapid spread of party organizations throughout the countryside after the transition to a multi-party system in 1946. In many localities, party organizations were based on already existing factional oppositions and clientelistic networks. In this sense, clientelism can be said to have been functional for the development of political parties in Turkey.

By the same token, however, parties based essentially on a myriad of patron-client networks are bound to lack in elements of political institutionalization, namely autonomy, coherence and stability. Lande's (1973) account of the fluid and unstable Philippine party system is a good case in point. Party politics in Eastern Turkey, based as they are on more traditional types of patron-client relations, also suggest a very low level of party institutionalization compared to the rest of the country. In the Eastern provinces, party organizations display extremely personalistic features. "Influential patrons frequently switch parties which results in the wholesale transfer of the political loyalties of their personal followings" (Sayari, 1977: 110; 1976: 198). This is reflected in sudden and erratic fluctuations in party votes from one election to the next. Another indication of the personalistic nature of politics in Eastern Turkey is the much greater support received by independent candidates as mentioned above.

Machine politics or party-directed patronage, on the other hand, may not necessarily be incompatible with highly institutionalized national parties. They may even be functional in the sense that, being less interested in policies and principles, they may leave a measure of autonomy to the center to create new institutions or initiate new policies. In other words, by insulating the center and the periphery from each other, they may permit the accumulation of political power at the center (Lemarchand, 1972: 88). Without such mechanisms it would be inconceivable for the cross-class based Turkish political parties to have functioned adequately in the 1950s and the 1960s.

Even party-directed patronage, however, seems to be on the eclipse at present. As the changing voting patterns in the 1970s indicate, horizontal class and occupational ties apear to be gaining in importance as the basis of party loyalties (Ozbudun, 1976 and 1977a). If the trend in Eastern Turkey is from deferential influence patterns to patron-client ties involving greater reciprocity and instrumentality, the trend in the more developed regions of the country is from party patronage involving concrete, short-run, material individual and communal inducements to a more modern type of party politics based on horizontal ties and loyalties.

While clientelism may have served some useful functions regarding party institutionalization in Turkey, its impact on popular attitudes toward authority and on the institutionalization of the legislature seems to have been largely negative. With respect to the first, clientelism and the related phenomenon of political corruption led to a marked popular cynicism and distrust towards politicians. In the popular image, politicians are often portrayed as unprincipled, self-serving wheeler-dealers. With regard to the second, the pervasive clientelistic political culture led to an excessive preoccupation on the part of the legislators with constituency services. As Ozankaya (1971: 158-59) has shown in his study of political culture in four villages, a majority of Turkish rural voters expect their parliamentary representatives to render them local or personal services. Consequently, a very major part of a typical legislator's time is spent on such services, assisting his constituents to find a job, to obtain credits, to secure preferential treatment from a governmental agency, to be placed in a hospital, etc. While such activity is evidently appreciated by the benefactors, it also hinders the institutionalization and the proper functioning of the legislatures. At a time when broad sectoral issues are gaining in importance, this may be a factor negatively affecting the prestige of the parliament as an institution.

NOTES

1. Powell (1970: 416) makes the same distinction when he says that "a local political worker may pull together voters on the basis of kinship ties, fictive kinship or caste ties, or through a variety of relationships, including patron-client ties."

2. This seems to be the consensus emerging from a recent series of studies on public policies affecting income distribution in Turkey.

REFERENCES

BEELEY, B. W. (1970). "The Turkish Village Coffeehouse as a Social Institution," *The Geographical Review,* 60 (4): 475-93.

BESIKCI, I. (1969). *Dogu Anadolu'nun Duzeni: Sosyo-Ekonomik ve Etnik Temeller.* Istanbul: E. Yayinlari.

BIENEN, H. (1970). "One-party Systems in Africa," pp. 99-127, in Samuel P. Huntingdon and Clement H. Moore, eds., *Authoritarian Politics in Modern Society: The Dynamics of Established One-Party Systems.* New York: Basic Books.

BIENEN, H. (1971). "Political Parties and Political Machines in Africa," pp. 195-213, in Michael F. Lofchie, ed., *The State of the Nations: Constraints on Development in Independent Africa.* Berkeley and Los Angeles: University of California Press.

EROGUL, C. (1970). *Demokrat Parti: Tarihi ve Ideolojisi.* Ankara: AUSBF Yayini.

FREY, F. W. (1965). *The Turkish Political Elite.* Cambridge, Mass.: MIT Press.

HUNTINGTON, S. P. (1968). *Political Order in Changing Societies.* New Haven and London: Yale University Press.

KARPAT, K. H. (1975). "The Politics of Transition: Political Attitudes and Party Affiliation in the Turkish Gecekondu," pp. 89-119, in Engin D. Akarli and Gabriel Ben-Dor, eds., *Political Participation in Turkey: Historical Background and Present Problems.* Istanbul: Bogazici University Publications.

KELES, R. (1972). *100 Soruda Turkiye'de Sehirlesme, Konut ve Gecekondu.* Istanbul: Gercek Yayinevi.

KILI, S. (1976). *1960-1975 Doneminde Cumhuriyet Halk Partisinde Gelismeler.* Istanbul: Bogazici Universitesi Yayinlari.

KIRAY, M. (1964). *Eregli: Agir Sanayiden Once Bir Sahil Kasabasi.* Ankara: DPT Yayini.

KUDAT, A. (1975). "Patron-Client Relations: The State of the Art and Research in Eastern Turkey," pp. 61-87, in Engin D. Akarli and Gabriel Ben-Dor, eds., *Political Participation in Turkey: Historical Background and Present Problems.* Istanbul: Bogazici University Publications.

LANDAU, J. M. (1976). "The National Salvation Party in Turkey," *Asian and African Studies,* 11(1): 1-57.

LANDE, C. (1973). "Networks and Groups in Southeast Asia: Some Observations on the Group Theory of Politics," *American Political Science Review,* 67 (1): 103-27.

LEMARCHAND, R. (1972). "Political Clientelism and Ethnicity in Tropical Africa: Competing Solidarities in Nation-Building," *American Political Science Review,* 66 (1): 68-90.

MEEKER, M. E. (1972). "The Great Family Aghas of Turkey: A Study of a Changing Political Culture," pp. 237-66, in Richard Antoun and Iliya Harik, eds., *Rural Politics and Social Change in the Middle East.* Bloomington: Indiana University Press.

OZANKAYA, O. (1971). *Koyde Toplumsal Yapi ve Siyasal Kultur.* Ankara: AUSBF Yayini.

OZBUDUN, E. (1976). *Social Change and Political Participation in Turkey.* Princeton: University Press.

OZBUDUN, E. (1977a). "1973 Turk Secimleri Uzerine bir Inceleme," pp. 265-311 in *Bulent Nuri Esen Armagani*. Ankara: AUHF Yayini.

OZBUDUN, E. (1977b). "Izmir' de Siyasal Parti Yoneticilerinin Sosyo-Ekonomik Nitelikleri," pp. 629-65 in *Osman Fazil Berki Armagani*. Ankara: AUHF Yayini.

POWELL, J. D. (1970). "Peasant Society and Clientelist Politics," *American Political Science Review*, 64 (2): 411-25.

RUSTOW, D. A. (1966). "The Development of Parties in Turkey," pp. 107-33, in Jopseph LaPalombara and Myron Weiner, eds., *Political Parties and Political Development*. Princeton: University Press.

SAYARI, S. (1975). "Some Notes on the Beginnings of Mass Political Participation in Turkey," pp. 121-33, in Engin D. Akarli and Gabriel Ben-Dor, eds., *Political Participation in Turkey: Historical Background and Present Problems*. Istanbul: Bogazici University Publications.

SAYARI, S. (1976). "Aspects of Party Organization in Turkey," *Middle East Journal*, 30 (2): 187-99.

SAYARI, S. (1977). "Political Patronage in Turkey," pp. 103-13 in Ernest Gellner and John Waterbury, eds., *Patrons and Clients in Mediterranean Societies*. London: Duckworth.

SAYARI, S. (n.d.). "Parties, Patronage, and Political Corruption: The Turkish Case." Unpublished manuscript.

SCOTT, J. C. (1969). "Corruption, Machine Politics, and Political Change," *American Political Science Review*, 63 (4): 1142-58.

SCOTT, J. C. (1972). "Patron-Client Politics and Political Change in Southeast Asia," *American Political Science Review*, 66 (1): 91-113.

SHERWOOD, W. B. (1967). "The Rise of Justice Party in Turkey," *World Politics*, 20 (3): 54-65.

STIRLING, P. (1965). *Turkish Village*. New York: Wiley.

TACHAU, F. (1966). "Local Politicians in Turkey," pp. 91-132 in *Regional Planning, Local Government, and Community Development in Turkey*. Ankara: Turkish Society for Housing and Planning.

TACHAU, F. (1973a). "Turkish Provincial Party Politics," pp. 282-316 in Kemal H. Karpat, ed., *Social Change and Politics in Turkey: A Structural-Historical Analysis*. Leiden: E. J. Brill.

TACHAU, F. (1973b). "The Anatomy of Political and Social Change: Turkish Parties, Parliaments, and Elections," *Comparative Politics*, 5 (3): 551-73.

TUNAYA, T. Z. (1952). *Turkiye'de Siyasi Partiler*. Istanbul: Dogan Kardes Yayinlari.

WEINER, M. (1962). *The Politics of Scarcity*. Chicago: University Press.

WEINGROD, A. (1968). "Patrons, Patronage, and Political Parties," *Comparative Studies in Society and History*, 10 (3): 376-400.

YALMAN, N. (1969). "Islamic Reform and the Mystic Tradition in Eastern Turkey," *Archives Européennes de Sociologie*, 10 (1): 41-60.

YALMAN, N. (1971). "On Land Disputes in Eastern Turkey," pp. 180-218 in G. L. Tikku, ed., *Islam and its Cultural Divergence*. Urbana: University of Illinois Press.

Conclusion

The Study of Patron-Client Relations and Recent Developments in Sociological Theory

S. N. Eisenstadt

Hebrew University of Jerusalem, Israel

and

Luis Roniger

Hebrew University of Jerusalem, Israel

I

The study of patronage and of patron-client relations has come lately to the fore in anthropology, political science and sociology, and has exerted a great fascination for scholars in these disciplines. From a topic of relatively marginal concern it has become a central one, closely connected to basic theoretical problems and controversies in all the social sciences.

In the late 1950s and early 1960s the study of patron-client relations was in a rather marginal position in most of the social sciences: anthropology, sociology and political science. It dealt with types of social relations or organizations that were seen as differing widely both from the "corporate," kinship and territorial groups so strongly emphasized in anthropological literature and from the universalistic-bureaucratic or market frameworks usually portrayed in sociology or political science as the epitomes of modernity and rationality. Patron-client relations, although fascinating, were seen as somewhat marginal in their respective societies and were studied in the framework of traditional concepts and concerns of these disciplines.[1] Since then the study of patronage and patron-client relations has burgeoned into central importance.

This change came first of all from the extension of the objects of these studies from relatively limited, dyadic, interpersonal, semi-institutionalized relations between a single patron and one or several clients to a broader variety of social relations and organizations. These ranged from semi-institutionalized personal dyadic or tryadic relations in small communities or in more organized settings, like various bureaucratic agencies to relatively loose, less rigidly prescribed social relations, often organized in complex networks and connected by brokers, as well as to loose cliques and factions in political machines. In all of these a less structured exchange of diverse services and resources took place, in which the element of solidarity between patron and client was much weaker.[2]

Second, these studies encompassed a wide range of societies throughout the world, in the Mediterranean, the Near East, Africa, Latin America, India and Southeast Asia among others.[3]

Third, the centrality of these studies sprang from the growing awareness that patron-client relations were not destined to remain on the margins of society nor to disappear with the development and establishment of democracies with well-functioning political and economic systems marked by economic development and modernization, or with the growth of class consciousness among the lower strata. It was also seen that, while any single type of patronage, as for instance semi-institutionalized kinship-like personal dyadic patron-client relationship, may disappear under such conditions, new types may appear, and that they can be found in a variety of forms in many societies, cutting across different levels of economic development and political regimes, and seemingly performing important functions within these more highly developed modern frameworks.[4]

Fourth, and most important from the point of view of our analysis, the growing centrality of these studies was due to the fact that they became closely related to major theoretical developments and controversies in the social sciences and thus became an important focus for theoretical debates.

At the most general level, in all social science disciplines, the analysis of patronage has become closely connected with outcries against "functionalist," systemic and "developmentalist" evolutionary emphases in anthropology, sociology and political science in general, and against the assumptions of the classical studies of modernization and development that were, as is well known, so closely related to the structural-functional school in sociology, in particular.[5] But the study of patron-client relations was not only related to these theoretical developments and controversies; it has also made contributions to the resolution of some of the problems which arose out of these controversies.

II

The central focus or starting point of most of these controversies was the criticism of the structural-functional school in sociology and of the functional school in (especially English) anthropology, which began to be very vocal in the mid-1960s and which comprised, in addition to the structuralists, such schools as the "conflict" school represented by Dahrendorf, Bendix and Collins; the exchange school, as developed by Homans, Blau and Coleman; the "symbolic interactionist" and ethnomethodology models with their stress on the construction by individuals in their social interaction of the meanings of the definition of situations in which they interact (Blumer, Goffman, Garfinkel, Cicourel); the Marxist model or models which became revived in the late 1960s; and the "systems" or "secondary cybernetic" approach to the analysis of social systems — developed above all by Walter Buckley, Margoroh Maruyama and Karl Deutsch.[6]

The discussions around these various models and counter-models, the continuous confrontation of these counter-models with the structural-functional model, and with each other, constituted the focus of theoretical discussions and controversies in sociology from the middle or later 1950s on.

Perhaps the theme most common to all these approaches has been the non-acceptance of the "natural" givenness of any single institutional order in terms of its organizational needs or prerequisites. Any given institutional arrangement — be it the formal structure of a factory or a hospital, the division of labor in the family, the critical definition of deviant behavior, or the place of a ritual in a given social setting — was no longer taken for granted, as given and derivable from its functional place in the broader social systems; and the different patterns of behavior that developed in connection with it were no longer examined only or mainly in terms of their contribution to the working of such setting. Instead, or in addition to, the former emphasis, the very setting up and continuity of such institutional arrangements was transposed from a given into a problem to be studied.

The various models differed in their proposals as to how to cope with this problem of how to explain any concrete institutional order. One such approach stressed that any institutional order develops, is maintained, and is changed through a process of continuous interaction, negotiation and struggle among those who participate in it. Within this broad approach the conflict and exchange schools emphasized the elements of power and bargaining over resources in such negotiations, while the symbolic-interactionists and ethnomethodologists focussed on the definition of the meaning of these situations and especially on the basic codes of the language of social interaction.

In contrast, the (symbolic) structuralists and to some degree the Marxists gave here a seemingly contradictory answer. They stressed the search for some principles of "deep" or "hidden" structure of social structure akin to the kind that, according to linguists such as Chomsky, provide the deep structure of language. In attempting to identify the principles of this structure the Marxists stressed a combination of structural and symbolic dimensions — such as the dialectic between forces and relations of production; alienation; class-struggle and class-consciousness — as providing the principles of the deep structure of societies which explain their crucial institutional features and dynamics.

The structuralists, on the other hand, stressed the importance of the symbolic dimension of human activity, of some inherent rules of the human mind.

Lévi-Strauss' own emphasis on the autonomous characteristics of the symbolic sphere and on its inherent internal structure was to no small degree derived from a dissatisfaction with the derivation or development of Durkheim's work in (above all English) social anthropology which tended to explain the symbolic sphere in terms of contributions to the working of the social system. Instead, he stressed the very high degree of autonomy and dimension of human nature, culture and also of social order.

But structuralism as developed by Lévi-Strauss goes beyond the mere emphasis on the autonomy, importance, or even predominance of the symbolic dimension in the construction of culture and society. The crux of the structuralist claim is, first, that there exists within any society or culture some "hidden structure" which is more real, permeating the overt social organization or behavioral patterns; second, that the rules which govern such structure are not concrete rules of organization and are not derived from organizational or institutional needs or problems but are crystallized code-wise in the rules of the human mind; third, that these rules are the constitutive element of culture and society, and they provide for deeper ordering principles of the social and cultural realms; fourth, that the most important of these rules (according, at least, to Lévi-Strauss and his followers) are those of binary-opposition, which are inherent givens in all perceptions of the world by the human mind, and the rules of transformation which govern the ways in which the contradictions which are supposedly inherent in the working of human minds are resolved; and fifth, that these principles constituted the real models of the society — that is, the models according to which society is structured — while they need not be identical with the conscious models represented in the minds of its participants or symbolized in various concrete situations.[7]

But these controversies, and especially the confrontation between these controversies and various research programs, have also pinpointed the weak points of each of those approaches — points which call for further elaboration and analysis.

The common denominator of all these weak points has been the lack of specification, by the respective theoretical approaches, of the mechanisms through which those aspects of social activity which they emphasize are institutionalized.

Thus, for instance, those who insist on the autonomy or privacy of the symbolic dimensions have to specify the nature of the exact institutional loci and mechanisms and social carriers through which the symbolic dimensions of human activities impinge on institutional life and on the working of social systems.

They also must specify in detail the nature of those aspects of institutional structure and interpersonal relations which are shaped by such symbolic orientations and their relations to various other aspects of institutional structure, as well as the conditions and mechanisms of their institutionalization, maintenance and change.

At the same time those like the conflict and exchange theorists — who emphasize the organizational or power dimensions of social life — have to explain both the ubiquity of such a symbolic dimension as well as the ways in which different symbolic orientations are selected or created by different individuals in different social settings.

III

The study of patron-client relations, closely interwoven as it was with the different controversies, has indeed made important contributions to some of these problems — especially to the identification of different levels and types of negotiation in the structuring of the institutional format of a society, of the relation of these levels to what may be called deep structure of a society and of the interweaving in such deep structure of elements of power and of the symbolic dimension of human activities.

A good starting point for the understanding of these contributions of the study of patron-client relations to the more general theoretical problems is the identification of the major characteristics of patron-client relations as patterns of interaction and exchange — an emphasis which in itself grew out of the criticism of the systemic emphasis of the functional schools.[8]

The most important of these core analytical characteristics of patron-client relations, as types of social interaction and exchange are

1. Patron-client relations are usually particularistic and diffuse.

2. The interaction on which they are based is characterized by the simultaneous exchange of different types of resources, above all instrumental, economic, as well as political ones (support, loyalty, votes, protection) on the one hand and promises of solidarity and loyalty on the other.

3. The exchange of these resources is usually effected by a "package-deal,"; i.e., neither resource can be exchanged separately but only in a combination that includes both types.

4. Ideally, a strong element of unconditionality and of long-range credit and obligations is built into these relations.

5. As a corollary there is a strong element of solidarity in these relations — an element often couched in terms of interpersonal loyalty and attachment between patrons and clients — even though these relations may often be ambivalent. The element of solidarity may be strong, as in the restricted primary relationship of the classical type of patronage, or, as in many of the more modern political machines, very weak, but to some degree it is to be found in all of them. Solidarity is often closely related to conceptions of personal identity, especially of personal honor and obligations, and it is also evident that some, even if ambivalent, personal "spiritual" attachment may exist between patron and clients.

6. At the same time, the relations established are not fully legal or contractual; they are often opposed to the official laws of the country and are based more on informal — although tightly binding — understandings.

7. Despite their seemingly binding, long-range and, in their ideal portrayal, almost life-long endurance, patron-client relations are entered into voluntarily, at least in principle, and can, officially at least, be abandoned voluntarily.

8. These relations are undertaken between individuals or networks of individuals in a vertical fashion (the simplest kind is a strong dyadic one) rather than between organized corporate groups. They seem to undermine the horizontal group organization and solidarity of both clients and patrons, but especially of clients.

9. Last and not least, patron-client relations are based on very strong elements of inequality and power differences. Even at this stage of our discussion it should be evident that the crucial element of this inequality is the monopolization by the patrons of certain positions that are of vital importance for the clients; especially, as we shall see in greater detail later, of the access to the means of production, major markets and centers of the society.

These characteristics indicate that the exchange effected in patron-client relations takes place on several levels and that it does create paradoxical situations that are the major feature of the patron-client nexus. The most important contradictions are: first, a peculiar combination of inequality and asymmetry in power with seeming mutual solidarity expressed in terms of personal identity and interpersonal sentiments and obligations; second, a combination of potential coercion and exploitation with voluntary relations and compelling mutual obligations; third, a combination of the emphasis on these obligations and solidarity with the somewhat illegal or semi-legal aspect of these relations.

These characteristics and paradoxical features of patron-client relations can be found in societies at various levels of social differentiation, technological development and political regimes and in different types of concrete organization (i.e., in dyadic relations, in broader networks, as parts of broader bureaucratic organization and the like). These core characteristics and their crystallization around these contradictions provide the clue to the nature of patron-client relations as a specific type of social relation in general and as a macro-societal phenomenon in particular.

First of all they indicate that the crux of patron-client relations is indeed the organization or regulation of exchange or flow of resources between social actors. But second, contrary to what seems to be implied in parts of the literature, they indicate that patron-clients do not denote a special type of simple, specific, market-like or power exchange as envisaged by the theories of individualistic exchange, best represented in the work of George C. Homans and Peter M. Blau.[9] Rather, like other modes of regulation of the flow of societal resources, patron-client relations constitute a special combination of specific exchange with what has been denoted in sociological and anthropological literature as generalized exchange.

IV

The term generalized exchange, probably coined by Marcel Mauss, was elaborated and somewhat changed by C. Lévi-Strauss in his earlier works on kinship. It is also related to the analysis of generalized media of exchange, as elaborated from a structural-functional perspective by T. Parsons and from an individualistic one by J. S. Coleman.[10]

The problems with which the term generalized exchange is concerned were first defined in Mauss' analysis of the gift. As is well known, he has shown that gift-giving constitutes an exchange with special yet highly structured characteristics. The exchange of gifts is distinct from the usual "specific" market exchange in that it is seemingly non-utilitarian and disinterested. But at the same time it is highly structured, being based on elaborate rules of reciprocity, which nevertheless differ from those of utilitarian specific market exchange.[11]

These differences are closely related to the purposes or functions of these two types of exchange. The latent purpose of the exchange of gifts is to establish conditions of solidarity, the "pre-contractual" elements of social interaction which include the obligation to engage in social interaction and to uphold one's obligations; or in other words generalized exchange, if successful, helps to establish the conditions of basic trust and solidarity in society, to uphold what Durkheim has called the pre-contractual elements of social life.

The basic paradigm of such relations can be found in kinship systems — in what Meyer Fortes has designated as the core of kinship, namely amity — which implies unconditional obligations rooted in some basic components of personal and collective identity and upheld by moral sanctions.[12] Most of these characteristics and especially the pronounced emphasis on unconditional relations as based on certain attributes, whether primordial, sacred or civil, is shared by kinship with other socially ascriptive collectivities or orders, such as communities, strata, nations and the like. In all such frameworks the setting up of unconditionalities takes place first through the institutionalization of various titles, i.e., of ascriptive (often hierarchical, power-based) specifications of limitations on institutional interaction or exchange and on access to positions.[13] Second, limitation on exchange of resources is effected through the establishment of public goods provided by the collectivity (e.g., the government), such as defence or health services. These benefits are so set up that if one member of a collectivity receives them, they cannot be denied to other members; and they establish the prices taken — directly or indirectly through taxation — from different groups for this purpose.[14] Third, structuring of the flow of resources is manifest in the public distribution of private goods, that is, the direct allocation of services and rewards to groups of the population according to criteria that differ widely from those of pure exchange. The flow of relations in the specific patterns of generalized exchange is structured in all these ways which distinguishes it from the routine "market" type of specific interpersonal or institutional interrelations and exchange. The institutionalization of generalized exchange need not be egalitarian. It often contains strong elements of power and hierarchy, but here they are structured in ways that differ from direct power relations or market-like exchange.

V

A crucial aspect of any social structure is the relation of the institutional links between generalized and specific exchange and especially of the degree of linkage between, first, membership in major ascriptive categories and sectors of a society on the one hand and access to the centers of power, to positions of control or production, and to the major markets on the other; and second, between such access and the relative standing of different groups or categories in the major institutional markets, that is, between ownership of resources and the ability to control their use in broader settings. Such linkages generate relations between in-equalities in the different aspects of social order enumerated above: between inequalities in the ascriptive sectors; in access to the major centers of power and institutional markets; and inequality within these markets. In this way they shape the structure of crucial aspects of social hierarchies in a society.

It is from the point of view of the relations between generalized and specific exchange that some of the major characteristics of patron-client relationships stand out.

VI

The clientelistic model of structuring relations between generalized and specific exchange is predicated on the existence of some tension between potentially broad, sometimes even latent, universalistic or semi-universalistic, premises; and on the free flow of resources and relatively broad scope of markets derivable from these premises on the one hand and continued attempts to limit such free flow on the other. These premises are evident in societies or sectors thereof in the fact that, unlike societies in which the hereditary ascriptive model is predominant, the members of various strata may in princi-ple be able to obtain direct access to the means of production, to the major markets and to the centers of power. They may organize themselves for such access and for the ensuring of their own control of the use of their resources in broader settings; concomitantly the centers of these societies may develop autonomous relations to the broader strata for which the clients and brokers are recruited.

But at the same time continuous attempts are make to circum-vent these potentialities; to limit, first, the free access of broader strata to the markets and centers by the monopolization by poten-tial patrons and brokers of those positions that control such access; and second, of the use and conversion of their resources. It is the combination of potentially open access to the markets with con-tinuous semi-institutionalized attempts to limit free access that is the crux of the clientelist model.[15]

In the clientelistic model the structuring of relations between generalized and specific exchange is characterized above all by a special constellation of the two types of institutional linkages. The first such linkage is one between the respective standing of the potential patrons and clients in the semi-ascriptive hierarchical sub-communities or sub-sectors of the society on the one hand, and the control of access — to the center or centers of the society, to the bases of production, to the major institutional markets, to the setting up of most public goods and to the public distribution of private goods — on the other. The second linkage is between access to markets and centers and the use and conversion of potentially free resources in these markets.

The crucial aspect of these two linkages in the clientelistic model is that they are very strong, yet not fully legitimized. They are based on the clients' abdication of their potentially autonomous access to major markets, to positions of control over use of resources or to the center and to the setting-up of public goods and services except through the mediation of some patron (whether person or organization, i.e., party or trade union). Such mediation is contingent on the clients having entered into a relation of exchange with the patron. The exchange has many of the aspects of the routine exchange of goods or services within the various institutional markets and necessarily limits the scope and convertibility of resources freely exchanged there.

VII

Thus we see that the structuring of patron-client relations, especially in so far as they constitute the major institutional nexus of a society or sector thereof, involves two aspects of societal interaction or exchange — the generalized and specific exchange.

The level of concrete exchange is related to the exchange of different concrete services, goods or resources. Here indeed there may be, as a result of the changing positions of patrons or of clients in the markets of specific exchange, wide variability and change in the concrete terms of such exchange.

But in all such relations between patrons and clients there is another level of exchange connected to certain crucial aspects of generalized exchange. On this level the client "buys," as it were, protection against the exigencies of the markets or of nature or of the arbitrariness or weakness of the center, or against the demands of other powerful groups or individuals. The price he pays for it is not just a specific service but the acceptance of the patron's control of his (the client's) access to markets and to public goods, as well as of his ability to convert fully some of his resources. But this limitation, as against the one found in societies where the hierarchical-ascriptive model if prevalent, cannot be derived from the full institutional premises of the society, and its acceptance is potentially precarious.

Hence the relations of generalized exchange here are not, as they are in the ascriptive models, fully prescribed or subject to special (ritual and power) negotiations different from those undertaken with respect to specific market exchange. In the clientelistic model these relations constitute a focus of struggle, marked by continuous negotiations about specific exchange. Also these features mean that the patrons are indeed willing to accept, in principle at least, some of the limitations that patronage may entail, even though they do of course always try to secure the best possible terms for themselves.

The numerous case-studies of patron-client relations which have been studied in the literature — and some of which have been also collected in this volume — indicate that while the details of the specific exchange undertaken in such relations may vary greatly from case to case it is the pattern of generalized exchange analyzed above that is more enduring. Thus the principles of generalized exchange may be seen as concomitant with the deep structure of society — those very principles which were sought for, as we have seen, by some of the approaches in the recent controversies in sociology, and which set up the boundaries of any social system and define its relations to its respective internal and external environments.

These principles of deep structure do not, however, only specify the broad contours of the possible boundaries of the social systems. At the same time, by specifying the ways in which the basic societal functions — of allocation, integration and the like — are taken care of, they also influence the range of a society's systematic sensitivities. They influence the ways in which different systems cope with the range of problems to which they are exposed; the specific types of conflicts to which such organizations are especially sensitive, the types of conditions under which the potentialities for such conflicts become articulated into more specific boiling points which may threaten any society. Thus they influence the nature of the crises which may be generated within them, especially their differential sensitivity to those different crises as well as the possible outcome of such crises — especially the modes of incorporation of different types of demands, the range of flexibility or of rigidity in response to them and the relative importance of regressive — as against expansive — policies in coping with them; and the potential direction of change within them.

VIII

The setting up of these principles of deep structure, of generalized exchange does also contain very strong elements of power and negotiation as does specific, routine exchange.

Common to both of them, to the specific and generalized exchange, is the reduction, distribution and consumption of resources, be they material or more symbolic ones. They differ, however, in the ways in which they regulate or structure the flow of such exchange of resources; in the nature of the actors who engage in these respective activities and in the "tempo" or pacing of their respective activities.

The more "routine" specific exchange and interaction is mostly undertaken by individuals acting in their private capacity or as representatives of existing collectivities with their specific goals and interests and who engage in ad hoc or continuous exchange of the "simple," "basic" resources, be they wealth (services), power or esteem, relatively free resources. As against this, generalized exchange is focussed on potential long-range commitments, and on readiness to forego some of the benefits and risks inherent in the more direct exchange or interaction.

Because of this, the setting up of such premises of generalized exchange involves not only the exchange of the "simple," "basic", relatively free resources — but above all the interchange and connecting of these resources with symbolic orientations; the combination of the structuring of control over relatively long-range distribution of the major types of resources with the construction of the meaning of the situations of social interchange.

It is also activated by special types of actors, by different social elites and is closely related to certain types of cultural orientations and political ecological formations.

These factors are brought out, in the context of the analysis of patron-client relations, in the specification of the broader societal conditions which generate the tendency to the emergence of patron-client relations as well as to maintain them — and which we have analyzed in greater detail elsewhere[16] and shall only briefly recapitulate here.

Such conditions refer to the structure of major social groups and elites, and cultural orientations. The most important characteristic of the broader groups in society that has been stressed in the literature has been internal weakness, evident above all in a relatively low degree of internal solidarity and of symbolic, and sometimes also of organizational, autonomy, especially of the lower groups of the society.[17] A closer look at the evidence indicates, however, that it is not only the lower groups, but also as a rule all the major societal actors — the center or centers, the broader periphery and the major elites — who evince these characteristics. All these social actors show, in those societies in which the clientelistic model is predominant, a relatively low degree of autonomous access to the major resources needed to implement their goals, and to the control, in broader settings, of their own resources.

Such a relatively low level of autonomy is evident in the centers of the societies in which the clientelistic model is predominant, not necessarily in the amount of resources at their disposal or even in their ability to penetrate the periphery administratively, although in many of these societies (such as early modern Italy or Greece, or many African societies) the centers were very weak. But even when the centers were much more compact and able to establish relatively wide administrative frameworks, their structural weakness was seen in their inability to act autonomously, distinct from the mode of use of resources found in the periphery, and to penetrate the periphery in an independent way. Of crucial importance here is the fact that in most of these societies there were few symbolic-institutional differences between center and periphery, and that the differentiation that existed was based mainly on ecological distinctiveness, symbolic articulation and on a greater concentration of population. [18]

The resources and symbols of the centers have not been structured and organized through autonomous channels but rather through channels either embedded in the power domains of the periphery or structured according to principles very similar to those of the periphery and are carried by elites who also indicate a relatively low level of autonomy and solidarity. In most of these societies, the distinctiveness of the center and its elites was not connected with attempts to transform the periphery structurally and ideologically, to effect far-reaching changes in the periphery's basic conception of social order. Accordingly, there were rather weak autonomous linkages between center and periphery, links that created but few basic structural changes within either sectors or strata of the periphery or within the center itself.

Parallel manifestations of relatively low levels of broader corporate symbolic or organizational autonomy can be identified in these societies in the different units of the periphery on all ladders of the social hierarchy.[19] The major societal units usually do not exhibit a strong collective consciousness and self-identity based on symbols of kinship, territoriality, class or strata, or on other principles of social organization, whether community, country or sector-wide. Similarly, the units of the periphery have few mechanisms through which to control corporately access to outside resources and loci of decisions that affect them or autonomous control over the conversion of their own resources. Accordingly, the units of periphery in these societies have relatively little capacity to influence the center either with respect to policy-making and allocation of resources or to the construction of the center's own symbols.

There is a relative weakness of corporate kinship units in general and of unilineal kinship groups in particular; a tendency to bilateral kinship with a strong emphasis on matrilineal descent; a relatively high predilection to narrow and unstable, cross-cutting kinship networks and alliances, with a marked tendency to lack clear boundaries of the kinship unit or network,[20] beyond some of the minimal demarcation of exogamous units.

IX

These societies were also characterized by the prevalence within them of symbolic orientations or images, among which maternal religious ones, an emphasis on mediators[21] and the various conceptions of honor mentioned above have been singled out in the literature as most clearly related to patron-client relations. However, in order to understand the full importance of these specific cultural idioms as they apply to patron-client relations, it is important to see that they are related to the basic conceptions of cosmic and social order prevalent in these societies.[22]

The most important of such orientations have been first, certain conceptions of tension between a higher transcendental order and the mundane order, especially in the religious sphere proper, together with the absence or weakness of the need to overcome tensions through some "this-worldly" activity (political, economic or scientific) oriented to the shaping of the social and political order or its transformation. In other words in these societies strong other-worldly orientations tend to develop. Second, cultural and social order was seen as given; the perception of active autonomous participation of any of the social groups in shaping its contours was weak. The major groups and elites of these societies rarely conceived of themselves as actively responsible for the shaping of those contours. Third, this was closely related to a relatively low level of commitment to a broader social or cultural order, to a perception of this order as something to be mastered or adapted to but not as commanding a high level of commitment from those who participated in it or were encompassed by it. Fourth, and closely related, was the relatively weak emphasis on the autonomous access of the principal groups or strata to the major attributes of these orders or of salvation. Such access was usually seen as mediated by various actors — mostly ascriptive groups or ritual experts who represented the "given" order — and mediating symbols and supernatural powers were stressed. These cultural orientations were carried by elites who exhibited some of the forementioned characteristics — and above all a relatively low level of solidarity, of (especially symbolic) autonomy, and a high level of embedment in broader, ascriptive strata.[23]

Between these cultural orientations, a certain continuous reinforcement, through which the specific characteristics of the deep structure generate the tendency to the clientelistic mode of relations with all its variations develop.

X

Such conditions may, as indicated briefly in the beginning of this chapter, cut across different levels of economic development and structural differentiation or political organization, and the specific characteristic of patron-client relations — whether for instance they are organized in small interpersonal relations or in large scale organizational networks — does greatly depend on such conditions.

The preceding analysis of patron-client relations as a specific relation between generalized and specific exchange and which is activated under specific social conditions by special social actors and mechanisms, has thus not only thrown some light on the characteristics of the nature of this institutional pattern, but also on some of the central problems which arise out of the recent developments and controversies in sociological theory. Above all it has indicated, in line with some other analyses,[24] those institutional areas which can be identified as the loci of the deep structure of a society; the actors and mechanisms which activate and maintain these areas; and the way in which symbolic and power elements are interwoven in such activation.

NOTES

1. Thus, in anthropology, they were connected with the study of such phenomena as ritual kinship or friendship, and anthropologists tended to concentrate on the more institutionalized types of personal patron-client relationship, to be found above all in tribal settings or in small rural communities. Among the best known studies are Mintz and Wolf (1950), Tegnaeus (1952), Ishino (1953), Pitt-Rivers (1954, 1958), Kenny (1966), Hutchinson (1957), Freed (1963), and Foster (1953, 1961, 1963). In sociology, it was closely related to the study of "primary" groups and relations as they developed and functioned in more formalized settings such as bureaucracies. See the Hawthorne Studies in the 1930s, Roethlisberger and Dickson (1970), Warner and Lunt (1941), Whyte (1960), Shils (1975a, 1975b) and Katz and Lazarfeld (1955).

In political science the study of patronage was initially concentrated on the studies of political "machines" and "bossism" in more developed societies, gradually extending to the study of corruption in developing countries. See for instance Carmen and Luthin (1943), Sorauf (1959), Wilson (1961), Mandelbaum (1965), Banfield and Wilson (1963). Among the literature on those phenomena at this stage of inquiry see Wraith and Simkins (1963), Smith (1964), Greenstone (1966), Nash (1963, 1965) and Landé (1965).

2. For illustrations of these developments in the conceptualization of patron-client relationships since the late 1960s see for instance Wolf (1966a), Weingrod (1968), the issue of *Sociologische Gids* that deals with patron-client relations (1969), Lemarchand and Legg (1972), Stuart (1972), Kaufman (1974), Graziano (1975), La Fontaine (1975), Gellner and Waterbury (1977), especially the following papers: Gellner (1977), Scott (1977), Weingrod (1977) and Waterbury (1977); Davis (1977), Schmidt et al. (1976).

3. The wide geographical and cultural occurrence of patron-client relationships encompassed a great variety of links. For details of those ties throughout the world and research done on them see Eisenstadt and Roniger (1980). The bibliography presented in this volume includes references of works on clientelism in the major geographical areas of patron-client relations.

4. See for instance Ike (1972), Galjart (1976), Weingrod and Morin (1971), Blok (1969), Allum (1973), Bax (1970) and Khalaf (1977). For a broad treatment of the above-mentioned adaptability of patron-client relations see Powell (1970), Scott (1969, 1972), Lemarchand and Legg (1972), Landé (1973), Schneider et al. (1972), and Legg (n.d.).

5. These controversies are analyzed in great detail in Eisenstadt and Curelaru (1976) especially chapters 8 and 9; and in idem (1977), especially chapters II and III.

6. Illustrative of the approach of "classical" functionalist anthropology on this point are Radcliffe Brown (1952) and Gluckman (1955). On the structural-functional approach see for instance Parsons and Shils (1951), Parsons (1964), and Parsons and Smelser (1965).

On the "conflict" approaches see Dahrendorf (1959), Bendix (1968) and Collins (1975). For the exchange theories see Homans (1961), Blau (1964b) and Coleman (1966, 1970). On symbolic interactionism and ethnomethodology see Blumer (1969), Goffman (1959), Garfunkel (1967) and Cicourel (1973). On systems approaches see Buckley (1967), Maruyama (1968) and Deutsch (1963).

7. On structuralism see Lévi Strauss' works, Macrac (1968) and Goddard (1965).

8. The exposition on patron-client relations that follows is elaborated in greater detail in Eisenstadt and Roniger (1980).

9. See Homans (1961), Blau (1964a, 1964b). A treatment of these different orientations in social exchange theory can be found in Ekeh (1964). See also Turner (1974), pp. 211-320.

10. See Mauss (1954), Lévi-Strauss (1969), Parsons (1963a, b, c) and Coleman (1970).

11. Durkheim (1933). For further treatments of the pre-contractual elements of social life see for instance Parsons (1937) especially pp. 301-38, 460-70 and 708-14; Davis (1963) and Befu (1966/67). See also Parsons (1963).

12. Fortes (1965). On the societal significance of this aspect of reliability as connected to the "moral" realm of kinship see Bloch (1973).

13. On unconditionalities and titles see Eisenstadt (1971a) and idem (1968), pp. 62-103.

14. On public goods see Kuhn (1963), Olson (1968), Williamson (1973a and 1973b). See also Eisenstadt and Curelaru (1976), pp. 364 ff.

15. For some examples of the limitation in the scope and convertibility of the free flow of resources in these societies see Aya (1975), Campbell (1968), Sayari (1977). For illustrations of the pressures on patronalistic arrangements derived from the latent premises of these societies see Boissevain (1966), Tarrow (1969, 1974). For a general treatment of this subject see Eisenstadt (1978), pp. 273-310.

16. Eisenstadt and Roniger (1980).

17. This point can be found among others in Banfield (1958), Wolf (1966b), Schneider (1971), Alavi (1973), Powell (1970), Blok (1973), Johnson (1977) and Lynch (1964).

18. On the distinction between strong and weak centers see Eisenstadt (1971b), idem (1971a) especially chapter 8; and idem (1973). Further elaboration can be

found in idem (1978), especially chapters IV and V. The description of the weak structural character of those centers was a recurrent theme in the literature. See for instance Tarrow (1974, 1976), Silverman (1965), Landé (1973), and Scott (1972).

On the symbolical institutional characteristics of center and periphery in some of these societies see Roth (1968), Zolberg (1971), Riggs (1966), Schrieke (1957), Van Lear (1955), Whitmore (1970), Heine-Geldern (1956), Hanke (1967), Sarfatti (1966), Haring (1947).

19. See for instance Landé (1973), Boissevain (1966), and Meertens (1975).

20. On the low degree of community cohesion and solidary corporate organization of social units see for example Powell (1970), Aya (1975), Waterbury (1970) and Tarrow (1967). In Sicily and other regions, the enormous overlapping and intermingling of occupational roles and identities can hamper the formation of broad, categorical commitments; for Sicily see Schneider (1969) and Blok (1974). On the structure of kinship in "clientelistic" societies see Eisenstadt and Roniger (1980).

21. Wolf (1969).

22. For a broad treatment of these concepts see Eisenstadt and Curelaru (1976, 1977). On the above mentioned conceptions see Hanna and Gardner (1969), Matz (1966), Gallagher (1966, 1976), Worcester (1969), Silvert (1969), Evers (1964), Sarkisyanz (1965), Peacock (1968) and Milton (1965).

23. See Eisenstadt and Roniger (1980) for a broader treatment of this problem.

24. Eiesenstadt (1978), especially chapters IV, V and IX. See also idem (1977, 1980).

REFERENCES

ALAVI, H. (1973). "Peasant Classes and Primordial Loyalties," *Journal of Peasant Studies*, 1 (1): 23-62.

ALLUM, P.A. (1973). *Politics and Society in Postwar Naples*. Cambridge: University Press.

AYA, R. (1975). *The Missed Revolution. The Fate of Rural Rebels in Sicily and Southern Spain, 1840-1950*. Amsterdam: Amsterdam University Papers on European and Mediterranean Societies, No. 3.

BANFIELD, E. (1958). *The Moral Basis of a Backward Society*. Glencoe: Free Press.

BANFIELD, E. and WILSON, J.Q. (1963). *City Politics*. Cambridge, Mass.: Harvard University Press and the MIT Press.

BAX, M. (1970). "Patronage Irish Style: Irish Politicians as Brokers," *Sociologische Gids*, 17: 179-91.

BEFU, H. (1966/67). "Gift Giving and Social Reciprocity in Japan," *France-Asia/Asie*, 188: 161-77.

BENDIX, R. (1968). *State and Society*. Boston: Little Brown.

BLAU, P. (1964a). "Justice in Social Exchange," *Sociological Inquiry*, 34 (1-2): 193-206.

BLAU, P. (1964b). *Exchange and Power in Social Life*. New York: Wiley.

BLOCH, M. (1973). "The Long Term and the Short Term: The Economic and Political Significance of Kinship," pp. 75-89, in J. Goody, ed., *The Character of Kinship*. Cambridge: University Press.

290   *Political Clientelism, Patronage and Development*

BLOK, A. (1969). "Peasants, Patrons and Brokers in Western Sicily," *Anthropological Quarterly*, 42 (3): 155-70.

BLOK, A. (1973). "Coalitions in Sicilian Peasant Society," pp. 151-65, in J. Boissevain and C. Mitchell, eds., *Network Analysis Studies in Human Interaction*. The Hague: Mouton.

BLOK, A. (1974). *The Mafia of a Sicilian Village, 1860-1960. A Study of Violent Peasant Entrepreneurs*. Oxford: Blackwell.

BLUMER, H. (1969). *Symbolic Interactionism*. Englewood Cliffs, NJ: Prentice-Hall.

BOISSEVAIN, J. (1966). "Poverty and Politics in a Sicilian Agrotown," *International Archives of Ethnography*, 50: 198-236.

BUCKLEY, W. (1967). *Sociology and Modern System Theory*. Englewood Cliffs, NJ: Prentice-Hall.

CAMPBELL, J.K. (1968). "Two Case-Studies of Marketing and Patronage in Greece," pp. 143-54, in J.G. Peristiany, ed., *Contributions to Mediterranean Sociology*. Paris/The Hague: Mouton.

CARMEN, H.J. and LUTHIN, R.J. (1943). *Lincoln and the Patronage*. New York.

CICOUREL, A. (1973). *Cognitive Sociology*. Harmondsworth: Penguin.

COLEMAN, J.S. (1966). "Foundations for a Theory of Collective Decision," *American Journal of Sociology*, 71(6): 615-27.

COLEMAN, J.S. (1970). "Political Money," *American Political Science Review*, 64(4): 1074-87.

COLLINS, R. (1975). *Conflict Sociology: Toward an Explanatory Science*. New York: Academic Press.

DAHRENDORF, R. (1959). *Class and Class Conflict in Industrial Society*. Stanford: University Press.

DAVIS, J.A. (1963). "Structural Balance, Mechanical Solidarity, and Interpersonal Relations," *American Journal of Sociology*, 68(4): 444-62.

DAVIS, J. (1977). *People of the Mediterranean. An Essay in Comparative Social Anthropology*, chapter 4. London: Routledge and Kegan Paul.

DEUTSCH, K. (1963). *The Nerves of Government*. New York: Free Press.

DURKHEIM, E. (1933). *On the Division of Labor in Society*. New York: Macmillan.

EISENSTADT, S.N. (1968). "Prestige, Participation and Strata Formation," pp. 62-103, in J.A. Jackson, ed., *Social Stratification*. Cambridge: University Press

EISENSTADT, S.N. (1971a). *Social Differentiation and Stratification*. Glenview, Ill.: Scott Foresman.

EISENSTADT, S.N. (1971b) *Political Sociology*. New York: Basic Books.

EISENSTADT, S.N. (1973). *Traditional Patrimonialism and Modern Neopatrimonialism*. Beverly Hills: Sage Research Papers in the Social Sciences.

EISENSTADT, S.N. (1977). "Sociological Theory and an Analysis of the Dynamics of Civilizations and of Revolutions," *Daedalus*, Vol. II: 59-78.

EISENSTADT, S.N. (1978). *Revolution and the Transformation of Societies. A Comparative Study of Civilizations*. New York: Free Press.

EISENSTADT, S.N. (1980). "Cultural Orientations, Institutional Entrepreneurs, and Social Change: Comparative Analysis of Traditional Civilizations," *American Journal of Sociology*, 85(4): 840-69.

EISENSTADT, S. N. and CURELARU, M. (1976). *The Form of Sociology. Paradigms and Crises*. New York: Wiley.
——(1977). "Macrosociology: Theory Analysis and Comparative Studies," *Current Sociology*, 25(2).
EISENSTADT, S.N. and RONIGER, L. (1980). "Patron-Client Relations as a Model of Structuring Social Exchange," *Comparative Studies in Society and History*, 22(1): 43-78.
EKEH, P. (1964). *Social Exchange Theory. The Two Traditions*. Cambridge, Mass.: Harvard University Press.
EVERS, H.D. (1964). *Kulturwandel in Ceylon*. Baden-Baden: Lutzeyer.
FORTES, M. (1965). *Kinship and the Social Order*. Chicago: Aldine.
FOSTER, G.M. (1953). "Cofradia and Compadrazgo in Spain," *Southwestern Journal of Anthropology*, 9: 1-28.
FOSTER, G.M. (1961). "The Dyadic Contract: A Model for the Social Structure of a Mexican Peasant Village," *American Anthropologist*, 63(6): 1173-92.
FOSTER, G.M. (1963). "The Dyadic Contract in Tzintzuntzan II: Patron-Client Relations," *American Anthropologist*, 65(6): 1280-94.
FREED, S.H. (1963). "Fictive Kinship in a North Indian Village," *Ethnology*, 2: 86-104.
GALJART, B. (1967). "Old Patrons and New: Some Notes on the Consequences of Patronage for Local Development Projects," *Sociologia Ruralis*, 7: 335-46.
GALLAGHER, C.F. (1966). "Contemporary Islam, A Frontier of Communalism. Aspects of Islam in Malaysia," *American Universities Field Staff Reports, Southeast Asia Series*, 14(10).
GALLAGHER, C.F. (1976). "The Shaping of the Spanish Intellectual Tradition," *American Universities Field Staff Reports*, 9(8).
GARFUNKEL, H. (1967). *Studies in Ethnomethodology*. Englewood Cliffs, NJ: Prentice-Hall.
GELLNER, E. (1977) "Patrons and Clients," pp. 1-6, in E. Gellner and J. Waterbury, eds., *Patrons and Clients*.
GELLNER, E. and WATERBURY, J. (1977) (eds.). *Patrons and Clients in Mediterranean Societies*. London: Duckworth.
GLUCKMAN, M. (1955). *Custom and Conflict in Africa*. Oxford: Blackwell.
GODDARD, D. (1965). "Conceptions of Structure in Levi-Strauss and in British Anthropology," *Annual Review of Anthropology*, 1: 329-49.
GOFFMAN, E. (1959). *The Presentation of Self in Everyday Reality*. New York: Doubleday.
GRAZIANO, L. (1975). *A Conceptual Framework for the Study of Clientelism*. New York: Cornell University Western Societies Program Occasional Papers, 4.
GREENSTONE, J.D. (1966). "Corruption and Self-Interest in Kampala and Nairobi," *Comparative Studies in Society and History*, 8(1): 199-210.
HANKE, L. (1967) (ed.). *History of Latin American Civilization* (2 vols.). Boston: Little, Brown.
HANNA, S.A. and GARDNER, G.H. (1969) (eds.). *Arab Socialism*. London: E.J. Brill.
HARING, C.H. (1947). *The Spanish Empire in America*. New York: Oxford University Press.

HEINE-GELDERN, R. (1956). "Conception of State and Kinship in Southeast Asia". Ithaca, NY: Cornell University Press, *Southeast Asian Program Data Paper*, 18: 1-13.

HOMANS, G.C. (1961). *Social Behavior: Its Elementary Forms.* New York/ Harcourt, Brace and World.

HUTCHINSON, H. (1957). *Village and Plantation Life in Northeast Brazil.* Washington: University Press.

IKE, N. (1972). *Japanese Politics: Patron-Client Democracy.* New York: A. Knopf (1967).

ISHINO, I. (1953). "The Oyabun-Kobun: A Japanese Ritual Kinship Institution," *American Anthropologist*, 55(1): 695-707.

JOHNSON, M. (1977). "Political Bosses and their Gangs: Zuiama and Qabadayat in the Sunni Muslim Quarters of Beirut," pp. 207-24, in E. Gellner and J. Waterbury, eds., *Patrons and Clients.*

KATZ, E. and LAZARFELD, P.F. (1955). *Personal Influences.* Glencoe, Ill.: Free Press.

KAUFMAN, R. (1974). "The Patron-Client Concept and Macropolitics: Prospects and Problems," *Comparative Studies in Society and History*, 16(3): 284-308.

KHALAF, S. (1977). "Changing Forms of Political Patronage in Lebanon," pp. 185-206, in E. Gellner and J. Waterbury, eds., *Patrons and Clients.*

KENNY, M. (1966). *A Spanish Tapestry: Town and Country in Castile.* New York: Harper and Row.

KUHN, A. (1963). *The Study of Society. A Unified Approach.* Hamerwood, Ill.: Dorsey.

LA FONTAINE, J.S. (1975) "Unstructured Social Relations," *West African Journal of Sociology and Political Science*, 1(1): 51-81.

LANDE, C.H. (1965). *Leaders, Factions and Parties: The Structure of Philippine Politics.* New Haven: Yale University Press, Southeast Asian Studies.

LANDE, C.H. (1973). "Networks and Groups in Southeast Asia: Some Observations on the Group Theory of Politics," *American Political Science Review*, 67(1): 103-27.

LEGG, K.R. (n.d.). *Patrons, Clients and Politicians. New Perspectives on Political Clientelism.* Beverly Hills: Institute of International Studies, Working Papers on Development, No. 3.

LEMARCHAND, R. and LEGG, K.R. (1972). "Political Clientelism and Development: A Preliminary Analysis," *Comparative Politics*, 4(2): 149-78.

LEVI-STRAUSS, C. (1963). *Structural Anthropology.* New York: Basic Books.

LEVI-STRAUSS, C. (1966). *The Savage Mind.* London: Weidenfeld and Nicolson.

LEVI-STRAUSS, C. (1969). *Totemism.* Boston: Beacon.

LEVI-STRAUSS, C. (1969). *The Elementary Structures of Kinship.* Boston: Beacon (1949).

LEVI-STRAUSS, C. (1968, 1971). *Mythologiques* (3 vols.). Paris: Plon.

LYNCH, F. (1964). *Four Readings in Philippine Values.* Quezon City: Altener de Manda Press, Institute of Philippine Culture, Papers No. 2.

MACRAC, D.G. (1968). Introduction to R. Bouchon, *The Uses of Stucturalism.* London/ Heinemann.

MANDELBAUM, S. (1965). *Boss Tweed's New York.* New York: Wiley.

MARUYAMA, M. (1968). *The Second Cybernetics: Deviation-Amplifying Mutual Causal Processes*, pp. 304-13, in W. Buckley, ed., *Modern Systems Research for the Behavioral Scientist*. Chicago: Aldine.

MATZ, A.J.D. (1966). "The Dynamics of Change in Latin America," *Journal of Inter-American Studies*, 9(1): 66-76.

MAUSS, M. (1954). *The Gift-Forms and Functions of Exchange in Archaic Societies*. London: Cohen and West (1925).

MEERTENS, D. (1975). "South from Madrid: Regional Elites and Resistance," pp. 65-74, in J. Boissevain and J. Friedl, eds., *Beyond the Community. Social Process in Europe*. Amsterdam: European-Mediterranean Study Group of the University of Amsterdam.

MILTON, R.N. (1965). "The Basic Malay House," *Journal of the Royal Asiatic Society, Malay Branch*, 29(3): 145-55.

MINTZ, S.W. and WOLF, E.R. (1950). "An Analysis of Ritual Coparenthood (Compadrazgo)," *Southwestern Journal of Anthropology*, 6(4): 341-68.

NASH, M. (1963). "Party Building in Upper Burma," *Asian Survey*, 3(4): 197-202.

NASH, M. (1965). *The Golden Road to Modernity*. New York: Wiley.

OLSON, M. (1968) *The Logic of Collective Action*. New York: Schocken.

PARSONS, T. (1937). *The Structure of Social Action*. New York: Macmillan.

PARSONS, T. (1963a) "On the Concept of Influence," *Public Opinion Quarterly*, 27: 37-62.

PARSONS, T. (1963b). "Rejoinder to Baver and Coleman," *Public Opinion Quarterly*, 27: 83-92.

PARSONS, T. (1963c). "On the Concept of Political Power," *Proceedings of the American Philosophical Society*, 103(3): 232-62.

PARSONS, T. (1964). *The Social System*. New York: Free Press.

PARSONS, T. (1973). "Durkheim on Religion Revisited: Another Look at the Elementary Forms of Religious Life," pp. 156-81, in Ch. Y. Clock and Ph. E. Hammond, eds., *Beyond the Classics: Essays in the Scientific Study of Religion*. New York: Harper and Row.

PARSONS, T. and SHILS, E. (1951) (eds.). *Towards a General Theory of Action*. Cambridge, Mass.: Harvard University Press.

PARSONS, T. and SMELSER, N.J. (1965). *Economy and Society*. New York: Free Press.

PEACOCK, J. (1968). *Rites of Modernization: Symbols and Social Aspects of Indonesian Proletarian Drama*. Chicago: University Press.

PITT-RIVERS, J. (1954). *The People of the Sierra*. London: Weidenfeld and Nicolson.

PITT-RIVERS, J. (1958). "Ritual Kinship in Spain," *Transactions of the New York Academy of Sciences*, Series 2, 20: 424-31.

POWELL, J.D. (1970). "Peasant Society and Clientelistic Politics," *American Political Science Review*, 64(2): 411-25.

RADCLIFFE BROWN, A.R. (1952). "On the Concept of Function in Social Science" and "On Social Structure," pp. 178-204, in idem, *Structure and Function in Primitive Society*. London: Cohen and West.

RIGGS, F.W. (1966). *Thailand: The Modernization of a Bureaucratic Polity*. Honolulu: East West Center Press.

ROETHLISBERGER, F.J. and DICKSON, W.J. (1970). *Management and the Worker: An Account of a Research Program, conducted by the Western Electric Co., Hawthorne Works.* Cambridge: Harvard University Press (1939).

ROTH, G. (1968). "Personal Rulership, Patrimonialism and Empire-Building in The New States," *World Politics*, 20(2): 194-206.

SARFATTI, M. (1966). *Spanish Bureaucratic Patrimonialism in America.* Berkeley: University of California, Institute of International Studies.

SARKISYANZ, R. (1965). *Buddhist Backgrounds of the Burmese Revolution.* The Hague: M. Nijhoff.

SAYARI, S. (1977). "Political Patronage in Turkey," pp. 103-13, in E. Gellner and J. Waterbury, eds., *Patrons and Clients.*

SCHMIDT, S.W., SCOTT, J.C., LANDE, C.H. and GUASTI, L. (1976) (eds.). *Friends, Followers and Factions.* Berkeley: University of California Press.

SCHNEIDER, J. (1969). "Family Patrimonies and Economic Behaviour in Western Sicily", *Anthropological Quarterly*, 42(3): 109-29.

SCHNEIDER, J. (1971). "Of Vigilance and Virgins. Honour, Shame and the Access to Resources in Mediterranean Societies," *Ethnology*, 10(1): 1-24.

SCHNEIDER, P., SCHNEIDER, J. and HANSEN, E. (1972). "Modernization and Development: The Role of Regional Elites and Noncorporated Groups in the European Mediterranean," *Comparative Studies in Society and History*, 14: 328-50.

SCHRIEKE, B. (1957). *Indonesian Sociological Studies.* The Hague/Bandung: Van Hoeve.

SCOTT, J.C. (1969). "Corruption, Machine Politics, and Political Change," *American Political Science Review*, 63(4): 1142-58.

SCOTT, J.C. (1972). "Patron-Client Politics and Political Change in Southeast Asia," *American Political Science Review*, 66(1): 91-113.

SCOTT, J.C. (1977). "Patronage or Exploitation?," pp. 21-40, in E. Gellner and J. Waterbury, eds., *Patrons and Clients.*

SHILS, E. (1975a). "Primordial, Personal, Sacred and Civil Ties," pp. 111-26, in idem, *Center and Periphery.* Chicago: University Press.

SHILS, E. (1975b). "Primary Groups in American Army," pp. 384-405, in ibid.

SILVERMAN, S.F. (1965). "Patronage and Community-Nation Relationships in Central Italy," *Ethnology*, 4(2): 172-89.

SILVERT, K. (1969). "Latin America and its Alternative Future," *International Journal*, 24(3): 403-44.

SMITH, M.G. (1964). "Historical and Cultural Conditions of Political Corruption among the Hause," *Comparative Studies in Society and History*, 6(1): 164-94.

SOCIOLOGISCHE GIDS (1969), 16(6).

SORAUF, F.J. (1959). "Patronage and Party," *Midwest Journal of Political Science*, 3(2).

STUART, W.T. (1972). "The Explanation of Patron-Client Systems: Some Structural and Ecological Perspectives," pp. 19-42, in A. Strickon and S. Greenfield, eds., *Structure and Process in Latin America — Patronage, Clientage and Power Systems.* Albuquerque: New Mexico University Press.

TARROW, S. (1967). *Peasant Communism in Southern Italy.* New Haven: Yale University Press.

TARROW, S. (1969). "Economic Development and the Transformation of the Italian Party System," *Comparative Politics*, 1(2): 161-83.

TARROW, S. (1974). "Local Constraints on Regional Reform — A Comparison of Italy and France and France," *Comparative Politics*, 7(1): 1-36.

TARROW, S. (1976). *From Center to Periphery. Alternative Models of National-Local Policy Impact and an Application to France and Italy.* New York: Cornell University, Western Societies Program Occasional Papers, No. 4.

TEGNAEUS, H. (1952). *Blood Brother.* New York: Philosophical Library.

TURNER, J.H. (1974). *The Structure of Sociological Theory.* Homewood, Ill.: Dorsey.

VAN LEAR, J.C. (1955). *Indonesian Trade and Society.* The Hague/Bandung: Van Hoeve.

WARNER, L.W. and LUNT, P.S. (1941). *The Social Life of a Modern Community.* New Haven: Yale University Press.

WATERBURY, J. (1970). *The Commander of the Faithful. The Moroccan Political Elite. A Study in Segmented Politics.* London: Weidenfeld and Nicolson.

WATERBURY, J. (1977). "An Attempt to Put Patrons and Clients in Their Place," pp. 329-42, in E. Gellner and J. Waterbury, eds., *Patrons and Clients.*

WEINGROD, A. (1968). "Patrons, Patronage, and Political Parties," *Comparative Studies in Society and History*, 7: 377-400.

WEINGROD, A. (1977). "Patronage and Power," pp. 41-52 in E. Gellner and J. Waterbury, eds., *Patrons and Clients.*

WEINGROD, A. and MORIN, E. (1971). "Post-Peasants: The Character of Contemporary Sardinian Society," *Comparative Studies in Society and History*, 13: 301-24.

WHYTE, W.F. (1960). *Street Corner Society — the Social Structure of an Italian Slum.* Chicago: University Press.

WHITMORE, J.K. (1970). *Vietnamese Adaptations of Chinese Government Structure in the Fifteenth Century.* New Haven: Yale University Southeast Asian Studies.

WILLIAMSON, O.E. (1973a). "Market and Hierarchies: Some Elementary Considerations," *American Economic Review*, 63(2): 316-25.

WILLIAMSON, O.E. (1973b). "Some Notes on the Economics of Atmosphere." University of Pennsylvania: The Fels Center of Government, Fels Discussions Papers, No. 29.

WILSON, J.Q. (1961). "The Economy of Patronage," *Journal of Political Economy*, 69(4): 369-80.

WOLF, E. (1966a). "Kinship, Friendship, and Patron-Client Relationships in Complex Societies," pp. 1-22, in M. Banton, ed., *The Social Anthropology of Complex Societies.* London: Tavistock, ASA Monographs.

WOLF, E. (1966b). *Peasants.* Englewood Cliffs, NJ: Prentice Hall.

WOLF, E. (1969). "Society and Symbols in Latin Europe and in the Islamic Middle East: Some Comparisons," *Anthropological Quarterly*, 42(3): 283-301.

WORCESTER, D.E. (1969). "The Spanish-American Past: Enemy of Change," *Journal of Interamerican Studies*, 11(1): 66-75.

WRAITH, R. and SIMKINS, E. (1963). *Corruption in Developing Countries.* London: Allen and Unwin.

ZOLBERG, A.R. (1971). *Creating Political Order: The Party States of West Africa 1870-1960.* Cambridge: University Press.

Clientelism and Patron-Client Relations: A Bibliography

Luis Roniger
Hebrew University of Jerusalem, Israel

The subject of clientelism and patron-client relations is too closely interwoven with many other areas of research in the social sciences, such as stratification and social markets, kinship, exchange, political organization and participation, the structure of trust in society, cultural orientations, rural society and center-periphery relations. This fact imposes limitations in preparing a comprehensive bibliography on clientelism. However, we believe that the following bibliography can serve as a useful tool for the student and researcher interested in patron-clientelism.

The bibliography is divided into two sections. The first is devoted to theoretical works, while the second deals with the literature on the major geographical areas in which patron-client relations were reported.

For reasons of editorial format we had to reduce the bibliography in length, taking out the entries related to some central aspects of clientelism such as the societal conditions of emergence, the major frameworks of patron-client relations (rural society, political clientelism, urban patterns, etc.), cognate systems and processes of continuity and change. As these parts were built mainly on cross-references referring to the works in the second section of the bibliography, the number of entries was not affected severely. However, the reader interested in the theoretical aspects of clientelism will have to work his way through the bibliography by himself.

A. PATRON-CLIENT RELATIONS

1. General and Comprehensive Approaches

A1   ABERCROMBIE, N. and HILL, S. (1976). "Paternalism and Patronage," *British Journal of Sociology*, 27(4): 413-29.

A2   BALANDIER, G. (1969). "Les relations de dépendance personnelle. Présentation du thème," *Cahiers d'Etudes Africaines*, 9(35): 345-49.

A3   BLOK, A. (1969). "Variations in Patronage," *Sociologische Gids*, 16(6): 365-78.

A4   BLOK, A. (1970). "Man as Entrepreneur," *Sociologische Gids*, 17(3): 225-34.

A5   BOISSEVAIN, J. (1969). "Patrons as Brokers," *Sociologische Gids*, 16(6): 379-86.

A6   BOISSEVAIN, J. (1974). *Friends of Friends: Networks, Manipulators, and Coalitions*. Oxford: Basil Blackwell.

A7   BURKOLTER, V. (1976). *The Patronage System. Theoretical Remarks*. Basel: Social Strategies.

A8   DAVIS, J. (1967). *People of the Mediterranean. An Essay in Comparative Social Anthropology*. London, Henley and Boston: Routledge and Kegan Paul. Esp. chapter 4.

A9   EISENSTADT, S. N. and RONIGER, L. (1980). "Patron-Client Relations as a Model of Structuring Social Exchange," *Comparative Studies in Society and History*, 22(1): 43-78.

A10   FLYNN, P. (1974). "Class, Clientelism and Coercion: Some Mechanisms of Internal Control," *Journal of Commonwealth and Comparative Politics*, 12(2): 133-56.

A11   GALJART, B. (1967). "Old Patrons and New: Some Notes on the Consequences of Patronage for Local Development Projects," *Sociologia Ruralis*, 7: 335-46.

A12   GELLNER, E. (1977). "Patrons and Clients," pp.1-6, in E. Gellner and J. Waterbury, eds., *Patrons and Clients in Mediterranean Societies*. London: Duckworth.

A13   GRAZIANO, L. (1975). *A Conceptual Framework for the Study of Clientelism*. New York: Cornell University Western Societies Program Occasional Papers.

A14   GREENFIELD, S. M. (1969). "An Analytical Model of Patronage." Paper presented at the annual meeting of the American Anthropological Association. 20-22 November.

A15   HALL, A. (1974). "Concepts and Terms. Patron-Client Relations," *Journal of Peasant Studies*, 1: 506-509.

A16   KAHANE, R. (1980). "Patronage and Modernization: Comparison of the oyabun-kobun, the jajmani and the bapak-anak-buah Systems." The Hebrew University of Jerusalem, unpublished Ms.

A17   KAUFMANN, R. R. (1974). "The Patron-Client Concept and Macropolitics," *Comparative Studies in Society and History*, 16(3): 284-308.

A18   LA FONTAINE, J. S. (1975). "Unstructured Social Relations," *West African Journal of Sociology and Political Science*, 1(1): 51-81.

A19   LANDÉ, C. J. (1973). "Networks and Groups in Southeast Asia: Some Observations on the Group Theory of Politics," *American Political Science Review*, 67(1): 103-27.

A20   LEGG, K. (1972). "Interpersonal Relationships and Comparative Politics: Political Clientelism in Industrial Society," *Politics* (Australia), 7(1): 1-11.

A21   LEGG, K. (n.d.) *Patrons, Clients and Politicians. New Perspectives on Political Clientelism*. Berkeley: Institute of International Studies, Working Papers on Development No. 3.

A22   LEMARCHAND, R. (1972). "Political Clientelism and Ethnicity in Tropical Africa," *American Political Science Review*, 66(1): 68-90.

A23   LEMARCHAND, R. (1973). "African Power through the Looking Glass," *Journal of Modern African Studies*, 11(2): 305-14.

A24   LEMARCHAND, R. (1978). "Clientelism, Class and Ethnicity: The Informal Structuring of Community Boundaries." Paper presented to the Conference on Political Clientelism, Patronage and Development. Bellagio, August (hereafter, papers presented there will be referred as Bellagio Papers).

A25   LEMARCHAND, R. and LEGG, K. (1972). "Political Clientelism and Development: A Preliminary Analysis," *Comparative Politics*, 4(2): 149-78.

A26   LEMIEUX, V. (1977). *Le patronage politique: Une étude comparative*. Quebec: Les Presses de l'Université Laval.

A27   LEWIS, H. S. (1974). *Leaders and Followers: Some Anthropological Perspectives*. Addison-Wesley Modules in Anthropology No. 50.

A28   MAYER, A. C. (1967). "Patrons and Brokers: Rural Leadership in Four Overseas Indian Communities," pp. 167-88, in M. Freedman, ed., *Social Organization: Essays Presented to Raymond Firth*. Chicago: Aldine.

A29   MEDARD, J. F. (1976). "Le rapport de clientèle, du phènomène social à l'analyse politique," *Revue française de science politique*, 26: 103-31.

A30   PAINE, R. (1971). "A Theory of Patronage and Brokerage," pp. 3-21, in idem, ed., *Patrons and Brokers in the East Arctic*. Memorial University of Newfoundland, Institute of Social and Economic Research, Social and Economic Papers No. 2.

A31   POWELL, J. D. (1970). "Peasant Society and Clientelist Politics," *American Political Science Review*, 64(2): 411-25.

A32   SCHMIDT, S., SCOTT, J., GUASTI, L. and LANDÉ, C. (1976) (eds.). *Friends, Followers, and Factions*. Berkeley: University of California Press.

A33   SCOTT, J. C. (1969). "Corruption, Machine Politics, and Political Change," *American Political Science Review*, 63(4): 1142-58.

A34   SCOTT, J. C. (1972a). "Patron-Client Politics and Political Change in Southeast Asia," ibid, 66(1): 91-113.

A35   SCOTT, J. C. (1972b). "The Erosion of Patron-Client Bonds and Social Change in Rural Southeast Asia," *Journal of Asian Studies*, 32(1): 5-37.

A35a   SCOTT, J. C. (1977). "Patronage or Exploitation?," pp. 21-40, in E. Gellner and J. Waterbury, eds., *Patrons and Clients*.

A36   SHEFTER, M. (1977). *Patronage and its Opponents. A Theory and Some European Cases*. Ithaca, NY: Cornell University Western Societies Program Occasional Papers, No. 8.

A37   SILVERMAN, S. (1977). "Patronage as Myth," pp. 7-20, in E. Gellner and J. Waterbury, eds., *Patrons and Clients*.

A38   SOCIOLOGISCHE GIDS (1969). Issue 16(6).

A39   STUART, W. T. (1972). "The Explanation of Patron-Client Systems: Some Structural and Ecological Perspectives," pp. 19-42, in A. Strickon and S. Greenfield, eds., *Structure and Process in Latin America: Patronage, Clientage, and Power Systems*. Albuquerque: University of New Mexico Press.

A40   WATERBURY, J. (1977). "An Attempt to Put Patrons and Clients in Their Place," pp. 329-42, in E. Gellner and J. Waterbury, eds., *Patrons and Clients*.

A41   WEINGROD, A. (1968). "Patrons, Patronage and Political Parties," *Comparative Studies in Society and History*, 10: 376-400.

A42   WEINGROD, A. (1977). "Patronage and Power," pp. 41-52, in E. Gellner and J. Waterbury, eds., *Patrons and Clients*.

A43   WOLF, E. R. (1966). "Kinship, Friendship and Patron-Client Relationships in Complex Societies," pp. 1-22, in M. Banton, ed., *The Social Anthropology of Complex Societies*. London: Tavistock, ASA Monographs Vol. 4.

2. The Structure of Power Related to Patron-Client Relations. Networks and Exchange

A44   BAILEY, F. G. (1968). "Parapolitical Systems," pp. 281-94, in M. Swartz, ed., *Local-Level Politics*. Chicago: Aldine.

A45   BAILEY, F. G. (1969). *Stratagems and Spoils. A Social Anthropology of Politics*. Oxford: Basil Blackwell.

A46   BAILEY, F. G. (1971). *Gifts and Poison: The Politics of Reputation*. Oxford: Basil Blackwell.

A47   BARNES, J. A. (1968). "Networks and Political Processes," pp. 107-30, in M. J. Swartz, ed., *Local-Level Politics*. Chicago: Aldine.

A48   BEFU, H. (1974). "Power in the Great White Tower — A Contribution to Social Exchange Theory." Paper presented at the American Association for Advancement of Science annual meeting on "The Ethnography of Power". San Francisco, 25 February.

A49   BELSHAW, C. S. (1965). *Traditional Exchange and Modern Markets*. Englewood Cliffs, NJ: Prentice Hall.

A50   BOISSEVAIN, J. (1968). "The Place of Non-groups in the Social Sciences," *Man*, 3(4): 542-56.

A51   BOISSEVAIN, J. (1971). "Second Thoughts on Quasi-Groups, Categories, and Coalitions," *Man*, 6(3): 468-72.

A52   BOISSEVAIN, J. and MITCHELL, J. C. (1973) (eds.). *Network Analysis in Human Interaction*. The Hague-Paris: Mouton.

A53 COHEN, A. (1969). "Political Anthropology. The Analysis of the Symbolism of Power Relations," *Man* 4(2): 215-35.

A54 GOULDNER, A. W. (1960). "The Norm of Reciprocity: A Preliminary Statement," *American Sociological Review*, 25(2): 161-78.

A55 HEATH, A. (1971). "Exchange Theory," *British Journal of Political Science*, 1(1): 91-119.

A56 ILCHMAN, W. and UPHOFF, N. (1969). *The Political Economy of Change*. Berkeley: University of California Press.

A57 MAUSS, M. (1954). *The Gift: Forms and Functions of Exchange in Archaic Societies*. Glencoe, Illinois: Free Press.

A58 MAYER, A. C. (1966). "The Significance of Quasi-Groups in the Study of Complex Societies," pp. 97-122, in M. Banton, ed., *The Social Anthropology of Complex Societies*.

A59 NICHOLAS, R. W. (1965). "Factions. A Comparative Analysis," pp. 21-61, in M. Banton, ed., *Political Systems and the Distribution of Power*. London: Tavistock, ASA Monographs No. 2.

A60 NICHOLAS, R. W. (1966). "Segmentary Factional Political Systems," pp. 49-60, in M. J. Swartz et al., eds., *Political Anthropology*. Chicago: Aldine.

A61 NICHOLSON, N. (1972). "The Factional Model and the Study of Politics," *Comparative Political Studies*, 5(3): 291-314.

A62 PITT-RIVERS, J. (1974). "The Kith and the Kin," pp. 89-104, in J. Goody, ed., *Character of Kinship*. London: Cambridge University Press.

A63 SAHLINS, M. (1965). "On the Sociology of Primitive Exchange," pp. 139-236, in M. Banton, ed., *The Relevance of Models for Social Anthropology*. London: Tavistock, ASA Monographs No. 1.

A64 SOCIOLOGICAL INQUIRY (1972). Issue 42(3-4) on Exchange Theory.

A65 STRICKON, A. (1967). "Folk Models of Stratification, Political Ideology and Socio-Cultural Systems," *Sociological Review Monographs* No. 11.

A66 SWARTZ, M. J. (1968) (ed.). *Local-Level Politics: Social and Cultural Perspectives*. Chicago: Aldine.

A67 SWARTZ, M., TURNER, W. and TUDEN, A. (1966). *Political Anthropology*. Chicago: Aldine.

A68 WHITTEN, N. E. Jr. and WOLFE, A. W. (1973). "Network Analysis," pp. 717-46, in J. Honigmann, ed., *The Handbook of Social and Cultural Anthropology*. Chicago: Rand McNally.

3. The Structure of Trust in Society. Values and Patron-Client Relations

A69 ALAVI, H. (1973). "Peasant Classes and Primordial Loyalties," *Journal of Peasant Studies*, 1(1): 23-62.

A70 BAILEY, F. G. (1966). "The Peasant View of the Bad Life," *Advancement of Science*, 23: 399-409.

A71   EISENSTADT, S. N. (1974). "Friendship and the Structure of Trust and Solidarity in Society," pp. 138-45, in E. Leyton, ed., *The Compact — Selected Dimensions of Friendship*. Memorial University of Newfoundland, Institute of Social and Economic Research, Social and Economic Papers No. 6.

A72   FOSTER, G. M. (1965). "Peasant Society and the Image of Limited Good," *American Anthropologist*, 67: 293-315.

A73   FOSTER, G. M. (1966). "Foster's Reply to Kaplan, Saler and Bennett," *American Anthropologist*, 68: 210-14.

A74   FOSTER, G. M. (1972). "A Second Look at Limited Good," *Anthropological Quarterly*, 45(2): 57-64. Includes references on the subject.

A75   GLUCKMAN, M. (1963). "Gossip and Scandal," *Current Anthropology*, 4(3): 307-16.

A76   GREGORY, J. R. (1975). "Image of Limited Good, or Expectation of Reciprocity?," *Current Anthropology*, 16(1): 73-92.

A77   KAPLAN, D. and SALER, B. (1966). "Foster's 'Image of Limited Good': An Example of Anthropological Explanation," *American Anthropologist*, 68(1): 202-205.

A78   KENNEDY, J. G. (1966). "Peasant Society and the Image of Limited Good. A Critique," *American Anthropologist*, 68(5): 1212-25.

A79   PAINE, R. (1967). "What is Gossip About? An Alternative Hypothesis," *Man* (NS), 2(2): 278-85.

A80   PIKER, S. (1966). "The Image of 'Limited Good': Comments on an Exercise in Description and Interpretation," *American Anthropologist*, 68(5): 1202-11.

A81   PITT-RIVERS, J. A. (1965). "Honour and Social Status," pp. 19-78, in J. G. Peristiany, ed., *Honour and Shame*. London: Weidenfeld and Nicolson.

A82   PITT-RIVERS, J. A. (1968a). "Honor," in *International Encyclopaedia of the Social Sciences*. New York: Macmillan, 6: 503-11.

A83   PITT-RIVERS, J. A. (1968b). "The Stranger, the Guest and the Hostile Host: Introduction to the Study of the Laws of Hospitality," pp. 13-30, in J. G. Peristiany, ed., *Contributions to Mediterranean Sociology*. Paris-The Hague: Mouton.

A84   SCHNEIDER, J. (1971). "Of Vigilance and Virgins. Honor, Shame and Access to Resources in Mediterranean Societies," *Ethnology*, 10(1): 1-24.

A85   SELIGSON, M. A. and SALAZAR, J. M. (1979). "Political and Interpersonal Trust among Peasants: A Reevaluation," *Rural Sociology*, 44(3): 505-24.

A86   SINGELMANN, P. (1975). "The Closing Triangle: Critical Notes on a Model for Peasant Mobilization," *Comparative Studies in Society and History*, 17(4): 389-409.

B. MAJOR GEOGRAPHICAL AREAS OF PATRON-CLIENT RELATIONS

I. Southern Europe

1. General

B1   BLOK, A. (1972). "Reflections on City-Hinterland Relations in Mediterranean Europe," *Sociologische Gids*, 19: 115-25.

B2   CAUSI, L. (1976). "Antropologia e Ideologia: note sul 'patronage' nelle societa 'Mediterranea'," *Rassegna Italiana di Sociologia*, 17(1): 119-31.

B3   HOBSBAWM, E. J. (1965), *Primitive Rebels: Studies in Archaic Forms of Social Movement in the 19th and 20th Centuries*. New York: W. W. Norton.

B4   PERISTIANY, J. G. (1968) (ed.). *Contributions to Mediterranean Sociology: Mediterranean Rural Communities and Social Change*. Paris-The Hague: Mouton.

B5   PITKIN, D. S. (1963). "Mediterranean Europe," *Anthropological Quarterly*, 36: 120-29.

B6   SCHNEIDER, P., SCHNEIDER, J. and HANSEN, E. (1972). "Modernization and Development: The Role of Regional Elites and Non-Corporate Groups in the European Mediterranean," *Comparative Studies in Society and History*, 14(3): 328-50.

B7   WOLF, E. (1969). "Society and Symbols in Latin Europe and in the Islamic Near East," *Anthropological Quarterly*, 42(3): 287-301.

2. Spain

B8   AYA, R. (1975). *The Missed Revolution. The Fate of Rural Rebels in Sicily and Southern Spain 1840-1950*. Amsterdam University. Papers on European and Mediterranean Societies No. 3.

B9   BRANDES, S. H. (1973). "Social Structure and Interpersonal Relations in Navanogal (Spain)," *American Anthropologist*, 75: 750-65.

B10   CORBIN, J. (1979). "Social Class and Patron-Clientage in Andalusia: Some Problems of Comparing Ethnographies," *Anthropological Quarterly*, 52(2): 99-114.

B11   COSTA, J. (1967). "Oligarquía y caciquismo como la forma actual de gobierno en España," pp. 15-45, in idem, *Oligarquía y Caciquismo. Colectivismo agrario y otros escritos*. Madrid: Alianza.

B12   FOSTER, G. M. (1953). "Cofradia and Compadrazgo in Spain and Spanish America," *Southwestern Journal of Anthropology*, 9: 1-28.

B13   KENNY, M. (1960). "Patterns of Patronage in Spain," *Anthropological Quarterly*, 33: 14-23.

B14   KENNY, M. (1966). *A Spanish Tapestry: Town and Country in Castile.* New York: Harper and Row.

B15   KENNY, M. (1968). "Parallel Power Structures in Castile: The Patron-Client Balance," pp. 155-62, in J. G. Peristiany, ed., *Contributions to Mediterranean Sociology.*

B16   KERN, R. (1973). "Spanish Caciquismo: A Classic Model," pp. 42-55, in idem, *The Caciques.* Albuquerque: University of New Mexico Press.

B17   LISON-TOLOSONA, C. (1973). "Some Aspects of Moral Structure in Galician Hamlets," *American Anthropologist*, 75: 823-34.

B18   MALEFAKIS, E. (1970). *Agrarian Reform and Peasant Revolution in Spain.* New Haven: Yale University Press.

B19   MARTINEZ-ALIER, J. (1971). *Labourers and Landowners in Southern Spain.* London: George Allen and Unwin.

B20   MEERTENS, D. (1973). "South from Madrid: Regional Elites and Resistance," pp. 65-74, in J. Boissevain and J. Friedl, eds., *Beyond the Community: Social Process in Europe.* The Hague: Department of Educational Science of the Netherlands.

B21   PIKE, F. B. (1971). *Hispanismo 1898-1936.* Notre Dame: University of Notre Dame Press. Chapter 1.

B22   PITT-RIVERS, J. (1954). *The People of the Sierra.* New York: Criterion.

B23   PITT-RIVERS, J. (1958). "Ritual Kinship in Spain," *Transactions of the New York Academy of Sciences*, Series 2, 20: 424-31.

B24   PI-SUNYER, O. (1974). "Elites and Non-Corporate Groups in the Mediterranean: A Reconsideration of the Catalan Case," *Comparative Studies in Society and History*, 16: 117-31.

B25   ROMERO-MAURA, J. (1977). "Caciquismo as a Political System," pp. 53-62, in E. Gellner and J. Waterbury, eds., *Patrons and Clients.*

3. Portugal

B26   CUTILEIRO, J. (1971). *A Portuguese Rural Society.* Oxford: Clarendon.

B27/8   RIEGELHAUPT, J. F. (1972). "Peasants and Politics in Portugal." Paper presented to the annual meeting of the American Political Science Association, Washington. December.

4. Italy

a. General

B29   ANDERSON, G. (1956). "A Survey of Italian Godparenthood," *Kroeber Anthropological Society Papers*, 15: 1-110.

B30 BARNES, S. H. and SANI, G. (1974). "Mediterranean Political Culture and Italian Politics: An Interpretation," *British Journal of Political Science*, 4: 289-303.

B31 CAZZOLA, F. (1967). *Carisma e Democrazia nel Socialismo Italiano. Strutura e funzione della direzione del P.S.I.* Rome: V. Ferri.

B32 GRAZIANO, L. (1980). *Clientelismo e sistema politico. Il caso dell'Italia.* Milan: Franco Angeli.

B33 HASKELL, F. (1963). *Patrons and Painters. A Study in the Relations between Italian Art and Society in the Age of the Baroque.* London: Chatto and Windus.

B34 McHALE, V. and McLAUGHLIN, J. (1974). "Economic Development and the Transformation of the Italian Party System: A Reconsideration," *Comparative Politics*, 7(1): 37-60.

B35 SARTORI, G. (1971). "Proporzionalismo, frazionismo e crisi du partite," *Rivista Italiana di Scienza Politica*, 1: 629-55.

B36 SNOWDEN, F. (1972). "On the Social Origins of Agrarian Fascism in Italy," *Archives Européenes de Sociologie*, 13(2): 268-95.

B37 STERN, A., TARROW, S. and WILLIAMS, M. (1971). "Factions and Opinion Groups in European Mass Parties: Some Evidence from a Study of Italian Socialist Activities," *Comparative Politics*, 3: 529-61.

B38 STIRLING, P. (1968). "Impartiality and Personal Morality," pp. 49-64, in J. G. Peristiany, ed., *Contributions to Mediterranean Sociology.*

B39 TARROW, S. (1967). "Political Dualism and Italian Communism," *American Political Science Review*, 6(1): 39-63.

B40 TARROW, S. (1969). "Economic Development and the Transformation of the Italian Party System," *Comparative Politics*, 1(2): 161-83.

B41 TARROW, S. (1976a). "Local Constraints on Regional Reform: A Comparison of Italy and France," *Comparative Politics*, 7(1): 1-36.

B42 TARROW, S. (1976b). *From Center to Periphery. Alternative Models of National-Local Policy Impact and an Application to France and Italy.* New York: Cornell University Western Societies Program Occasional Papers No. 4.

B43 ZARISKI, R. (1962). "The Italian Socialist Party: A Case Study in Factional Conflict," *American Political Science Review*, 56(2): 372-90.

B44 ZARISKI, R. (1965). "Intra-party Conflict in a Dominant Party: the Experiences of Italian Christian Democracy," *Journal of Politics*, 27: 3-34.

B45 ZARISKI, R. and WELCH, S. (1975). "The Correlates of Intraparty Depolarizing Tendencies in Italy: A Problem Revisited," *Comparative Politics*, 7(3): 407-33.

B46 ZUCKERMAN, A. (1972). "Social Structure and Political Competition: The Italian Case," *World Politics*, 24(3): 428-33.

B47 ZUCKERMAN, A. (1975). *Political Clienteles in Power: Party Factions and Cabinet Coalitions in Italy.* Beverly Hills and London: Sage Publications. Sage professional paper in Comparative Politics, Vol. 5, Series No. 01-055.

B48 ZUCKERMAN, A. (1977). "Clientelist Politics in Italy," pp. 63-80, in E. Gellner and J. Waterbury, eds., *Patrons and Clients.*

b. Central Italy

B49   JONES, P. J. (1968). "From Manor to Mezzadria: A Tuscan Case Study in the Medieval Origins of Modern Agrarian Society," pp. 193-241, in N. Rubinstein, ed., *Florentine Studies*. London: Faber and Faber.

B50   SILVERMAN, S. (1965). "Patronage and Community-Nation Relationships in Central Italy," *Ethnology*, 4(2): 172-89.

B51   SILVERMAN, S. (1966). "An Ethnographic Approach to Social Stratification: Prestige in a Central Italian Community," *American Anthropologist*, 68: 899-921.

B52   SILVERMAN, S. (1967). "The Community-Nation Mediator in Traditional Central Italy," pp. 279-93, in J. M. Potter, M. N. Diaz and G. M. Foster, eds., *Peasant Society*. Boston: Little Brown.

B53   SILVERMAN, S. (1968). "Agricultural Organization, Social Structure and Values in Italy: Amoral Familism Reconsidered," *American Anthropologist*, 70: 1-20.

B54   SILVERMAN, S. (1970). "Exploitation in Rural Central Italy: Structure and Ideology in Stratification Study," *Comparative Studies in Society and History*, 12: 327-39.

B55   WADE, R. (1971). "Political Behaviour and World View in a Central Italian Village," pp. 252-80, in F. G. Bailey, ed., *Gift and Poison*. Oxford: Basil Blackwell.

c. Southern Italy

B56   ALLUM, P. A. (1973). *Politics and Society in Postwar Naples*. Cambridge: University Press.

B57   BANFIELD, E. C. (1958). *The Moral Basis of a Backward Society*. New York: Free Press.

B58   BROEGGER, J. (1971). *Montevarese. A Study of Peasant Society and Culture in Southern Italy*. Bergen: Universitets-forlaget.

B59   CACIAGLI, M. and BELLONI, F. P. (1978). "The New Clientelism in Southern Italy: The DC in Catania." Bellagio paper.

B60   CAIZZI, B. (1973) (ed.). *Nuova antologia della questione meridionale*. Milan: Edizioni di Comunitá.

B61   COLE, J. W. (1975). "On the Origins and Organization of Southern Italian Poverty," *Reviews in Anthropology*, 2(1): 84-91.

B62   DAVIS, J. (1969a). "Honour and Politics in Pisticci," *Proceedings of the Royal Anthropological Institute*, 68-81.

B63   DAVIS, J. (1969b). "Town and Country," *Anthropological Quarterly*, 43: 171-85.

B64   DAVIS, J. (1970). "Morals and Backwardness," *Comparative Studies in Society and History*, 12: 340-53.

B65   DAVIS, J. (1973). *Land and Family in Pisticci*. London: Athlone.

B66   DAVIS, J. (1975). "Beyond the Hyphen. Some Notes and Documents on Community-State Relations in South Italy," pp. 49-55, in J. Boissevain and J. Friedl, eds., *Beyond the Community*.

B67   GALT, A. H. (1974). "Rethinking Patron-Client Relationships: The Real System and the Official System in Southern Italy," *Anthropological Quarterly*, 47(2): 182-202.

B68   GRAZIANO, L. (1973). "Patron-Client Relationships in Southern Italy," *European Journal of Political Research*, 1(1): 3-34.

B69   LITTLEWOOD, P. (1974). "Strings and Kingdoms. The Activities of a Political Mediator in Southern Italy," *Archives Européenes de Sociologie*, 15(1): 33-51.

B70   MARSELLI, G. A. (1963). "American Sociologists and Italian Peasant Society: With Reference to the Book of Banfield," *Sociologia Ruralis*, 3: 319-38.

B71   PIZZORNO, A. (1966). "Amoral Familism and Historical Marginality," *International Review of Community Development*, 15(16): 55-66.

B72   ROSSI-DORIA, M. (1958). "The Land Tenure System and Class in Southern Italy," *American Historical Review*, 64: 46-53.

B73   TARROW, S. G. (1967). *Peasant Communism in Southern Italy*. New Haven: Yale University Press.

B74   WICHERS, A. J. (1964). "Amoral Familism Reconsidered," *Sociologia Ruralis*, 4(2): 167-81.

d. Sicily

B75   BLOK, A. (1969a). "Peasants, Patrons and Brokers in Western Sicily," *Anthropological Quarterly*, 42(3): 155-70.

B76   BLOK, A. (1969b). "Mafia and Peasant Rebellion as Contrasting Factors in Sicilian Latifundism," *Archives Européenes de Sociologie*, 10: 95-116.

B77   BLOK, A. (1969c). "South Italian Agro-Towns," *Comparative Studies in Society and History*, 11: 121-35.

B78   BLOK, A. (1973). "Coalitions in Sicilian Peasant Society," pp. 151-66, in J. Boissevain and C. Mitchell, eds., *Network Analysis in Human Interaction*. The Hague-Paris: Mouton.

B79   BLOK, A. (1974). *The Mafia of a Sicilian Village, 1860-1960: A Study of Violent Peasant Entrepreneurs*. Oxford: Basil Blackwell.

B80   BOISSEVAIN, J. (1966a). "Poverty and Politics in a Sicilian Agrotown," *International Archives of Ethnography*, 50: 198-236.

B81   BOISSEVAIN, J. (1966b). "Patronage in Sicily," *Man* (NS), 1: 18-33.

B82   BOISSEVAIN, J. (1971). "Democracy, Development and Proportional Representation: A Sicilian Case," *Journal of Development Studies*, 8(1): 79-90.

B83   D'ALESSANDRO, E. (1959). *Brigantaggio e mafia in Sicilia*. Messina/Florence: G. d'Anna.

B84   HESS, H. (1973). *Mafia and Mafiosi: The Structure of Power*. Westmead, Farnborough: Saxon House, 2nd. edition.

B85   HOBSBAWN, E. (1974). "Political Theory and the Mafia," *Cambridge Journal*, 7: 738-55.

B86   MÜHLMANN, W. E. and LLARYORA, R. J. (1968). *Klientschaft, Klientel und Klientel-system in einer Sizilianischen Agro-Stadt*. Tübingen: J. G. B. Mohr.

B87   MÜHLMANN, W. E. and LLARYORA, R. J. (1973). *Strumula Siciliana. Ehre, rang und soziale schichtung in einer Sizilianischen agrostadt*. Meisenheim a. Glan: A. Hain.

B88   PANTALEONE, M. (1962). *Mafia e politica: 1943-1962*. Turin: Einaudi (*Mafia and Politics*. London: Chatto and Windus, 1966).

B89   PONTIERI, E. (n.d.). *Il tramonto del baronaggio Siciliano*. Florence: Sansoni.

B90   ROMANO, S. F. (1952). *Momenti del Risorgimento in Sicilia*. Messina/Florence: G. d'Anna.

B91   SCHNEIDER, J. (1969). "Family Patrimonies and Economic Behaviour in Western Sicily," *Anthropological Quarterly*, 42(3): 109-29.

B92   SCHNEIDER, J. and SCHNEIDER, P. (1976). *Culture and Political Economy in Western Sicily*. New York: Academic Press.

B93   SCHNEIDER, P. (1969). "Honor and Conflict in a Sicilian Town," *Anthropological Quarterly*, 42(3): 130-54.

B94   SCHNEIDER, P. (1972). "Coalition Formation and Colonialism in Western Sicily," *Archives Européenes de Sociologie*, 13: 255-67.

e. Sardinia

B95   WEINGROD, A. and MORIN, E. (1971). "Post Peasants: The Character of Contemporary Sardinian Society," *Comparative Studies in Society and History*, 13: 301-24. See also WEINGROD (A41).

5. Greece

B96   ASCHENBRENNER, S. E. (1975). "Folk Model vs. Actual Practice: The Distribution of Spiritual Kin in a Greek Village," *Anthropological Quarterly*, 48(2): 65-86.

B97   CAMPBELL, J. K. (1964). *Honour, Family and Patronage: A Study of Institutions and Moral Values in a Greek Mountain Community*. Oxford: Clarendon Press.

B98   CAMPBELL, J. K. (1968). "Two Case Studies of Marketing and Patronage in Greece," pp. 143-58, in J. G. Peristiany, ed., *Contributions to Mediterranean Sociology*.

B99   LEGG, K. (1969). *Politics in Modern Greece*. Stanford: University Press.

B100   LEGG, K. (1973a). "Clientelism and Politics in Modern Greece." Paper presented to the Modern Greece Studies Association Symposium on Forces Shaping Modern Greece, Columbia University, November.

B101   LEGG, K. (1973b). "Political Change in a Clientelistic Polity: The Failure of Democracy in Greece," *Journal of Political and Military Sociology*, 1(2): 231-46.

B102   LEGG, K. (n.d.) "Retreat to the Barracks. Perspectives on the Collapse of the Military Regime in Greece." Unpublished Ms.

B103   MOUZELIS, N. (1978). "Class and Clientelistic Politics. The Case of Greece," *Sociological Review* (NS), 26(3): 471-97.

B104   McNALL, S. G. (1974a). *The Greek Peasant: Values in Conflict.*
Washington: American Sociological Association.

B105   McNALL, S. G. (1974b). "Value Systems that Inhibit Modernization:
The Case of Greece," *Studies in Comparative International Development*, 9(3): 46-63.

6. Malta

B106   BOISSEVAIN, J. (1962). "Maltese Village Politics and their Relation to
National Politics," *Journal of Commonwealth Political Studies*, 1(3):
211-22.

B107   BOISSEVAIN, J. (1964). "Factions, Parties, and Politics in a Maltese
Village," *American Anthropologist*, 66: 1275-87.

B108   BOISSEVAIN, J. (1965). *Saints and Fireworks: Religion and Politics in
Rural Malta*. London: Athlone Press.

B109   BOISSEVAIN, J. (1977). "When the Saints Go Marching Out: Reflections on the Decline of Patronage in Malta," pp. 81-96, in E. Gellner and
J. Waterbury, eds., *Patrons and Clients*.

7. Republican Rome

B110   BADIAN, E. (1958), *Foreign Clientelae (246-70 BC)*. Oxford: Clarendon
Press.

B111   GELZER, M. (1969). *The Roman Nobility*. Oxford: Basil Blackwell,
pp. 62-111.

B112   DE STE. CROIX, G. E. M. (1954). "Suffragium: From Vote to
Patronage," *British Journal of Sociology*, 5: 33-48.

B113   TAYLOR, L. R. (1971). *Party Politics in the Age of Caesar*. Berkeley:
University of California Press.

B114/5 WATSON, A. (1967). *The Law of Persons in the Later Roman Republic*.
Oxford: Clarendon Press. Esp. pp. 226-36.

II. Middle East

1. Turkey

B116   KUDAT, A. (1975). "Patron-Client Relations: The State of the Art and
Research in Eastern Turkey," pp. 61-88, in E. Akarli and G. Ben-Dor,
eds., *Political Participation in Turkey*. Istambul: Bogazici University
Publications.

B117   MAGNARELLA, P. G. (1973). "Descent, Affinity and Ritual Relations
in Eastern Turkey," *American Anthropologist*, 75: 1626-33.

B118   MEEKER, M. (1972). "The Great Family Aghas of Turkey: A Study of Changing Political Culture," pp. 237-66, in R. Antoun and I. Harik, eds., *Rural Politics and Social Change in the Middle East*. Bloomington: Indiana University Press.

B119   ÖZBUDUN, E. (1975). "Political Participation in Rural Turkey," pp. 33-60, in E. Akarli and G. Ben-Dor, eds., *Political Participation*.

B120   ÖZBUDUN, E. (1978). "Political Clientelism in Turkey." Bellagio paper.

B121   SAYARI, S. (1975). "Some Notes on the Beginnings of Mass Political Participation," pp. 121-33, in E. Akarli and G. Ben-Dor, eds., *Political Participation*.

B122   SAYARI, S. (1977). "Political Patronage in Turkey," pp. 103-14, in E. Gellner and J. Waterbury, eds., *Patrons and Clients*.

B123   SERTEL, A. K. (1971). "Ritual Kinship in Eastern Turkey," *Anthropological Quarterly*, 44(1): 37-50.

B124   SERTEL, A. K. (1972). "Derivative Analysis of Reputational Community Power Structure." Center for International Studies, Massachusetts Institute of Technology, Ms.

2. Morocco

B125   BROWN, K. (1976). *People of Salé. Tradition and Change in a Moroccan City, 1830-1930*. Manchester: University Press.

B126   BROWN, K. (1977). "Changing Forms of Patronage in a Moroccan City," pp. 309-28 in E. Gellner and J. Waterbury, eds., *Patrons and Clients*.

B127   BURKE, E. (1969). "Morocco and the Near East," *Archives Européenes de Sociologie*, 10: 70-94.

B128   GELLNER, E. (1969a). *Saints of the Atlas*. Chicago: University Press.

B129   GELLNER, E. (1969b). "The Great Patron: A Reinterpretation of Tribal Rebellions," *Archives Européenes de Sociologie*, 10: 61-69.

B130   HAGOPIAN, E. (1964). "The Status and Role of the Marabout in Pre-protectorate Morocco," *Ethnology*, 3: 42-52.

B131   HART, D. M. (1970). "Clan, Lineage, Local Community and the Feud in a Rifian Tribe," pp. 3-75, in L. E. Sweet, ed., *Peoples and Cultures of the Middle East*. New York: Natural History Press, Vol. 2.

B132   ROSEN, L. (1972). "Rural Political Process and National Political Structure in Morocco," pp. 214-36, in R. Antoun and I. Harik, eds., *Rural Politics and Social Change in the Middle East*.

B133   WATERBURY, J. (1967). "Marginal Politics and Elite Manipulation in Morocco," *Archives Européenes de Sociologie*, 8: 94-111.

B134   WATERBURY, J. (1970). *The Commander of the Faithful: The Moroccan Political Elite. A Study in Segmented Politics*. London: Weidenfeld and Nicolson.

B135   WATERBURY, J. (1973). "Endemic and Planned Corruption in a Monarchical Regime," *World Politics*, 25(4): 533-55.

3. Lebanon

B136   GUBSER, P. (1973). "The Zu'ama of Zahlah: The Current Situation in a Lebanese Town," *Middle East Journal*, 27(2): 173-89.

B137   HARIK, I. F. (1965). "The Iqta' System in Lebanon: A Comparative Political View," *Middle East Journal*, 19(4): 405-21.

B138   HOTTINGER, A. (1966). "Zuama in Historical Perspective," pp. 85-105, in L. Binder, ed., *Politics in Lebanon*. New York: John Wiley.

B139   JABBRA, J. G. and JABBRA, N. W. (1978). "Local Political Dynamics in Lebanon: The Case of 'Ain el-Qasis," *Anthropological Quarterly*, 51(2): 137-51.

B140   JOHNSON, M. (1977). "Political Bosses and their Gangs: Zu'ama and Qabadayat in the Sunni Muslim Quarters of Beirut," pp. 207-24, in E. Gellner and J. Waterbury, eds., *Patrons and Clients*.

B141   KHALAF, S. (1977). "Changing Forms of Political Patronage in Lebanon," pp. 185-206, in E. Gellner and J. Waterbury, eds., *Patrons and Clients*.

4. Others

B142   ABOU ZEID, A. (1965). "Honour and Shame among the Bedouins of Egypt," pp. 243-59, in J. G. Peristiany, ed., *Honour and Shame: The Values of Mediterranean Society*. London: Weidenfeld and Nicolson.

B143   ATTALIDES, M. (1977). "Forms of Peasant Incorporation in Cyprus during the Last Century," pp. 137-56, in E. Gellner and J. Waterbury, eds., *Patrons and Clients*.

B144   BAER, G. (1979). "Patrons and Clients in Ottoman Cairo." Jerusalem, unpublished Ms.

B145   BURSTEIN, P. (1976). "Political Patronage and Party Choice among Israeli Voters," *Journal of Politics*, 38: 1024-32.

B146   EL-MESSIRI, S. (1977). "The Changing Role of the Futuwwa in the Social Structure of Cairo," pp. 239-54, in E. Gellner and J. Waterbury, eds., *Patrons and Clients*.

B147   ETTIENE, B. (1977). "Clientelism in Algeria," pp. 291-308, in E. Gellner and J. Waterbury, eds., *Patrons and Clients*.

B148   FARRAG, A. (1977). "The Wastah among Jordanian Villagers," pp. 225-38, in E. Gellner and J. Waterbury, eds., *Patrons and Clients*.

B149   FAVRET, J. (1968). "Relations de dependence et manipulation de la violence en Kabylie," *L'Homme*, 8(4): 18-44.

B150   GUBSER, P. (1973). *Politics and Change in Al-Karak, Jordan. A Study of a Small Arab Town and its District*. London: Oxford University Press.

B151   LOIZOS, P. (1977). "Politics and Patronage in a Cypriot Village, 1920-1970," pp. 115-36, in E. Gellner and J. Waterbury, eds., *Patrons and Clients*.

B152   MOORE, C. H. (1977). "Clientelist Ideology and Political Change: Fictitious Networks in Egypt and Tunisia," pp. 255-74, in E. Gellner and J. Waterbury, eds., *Patrons and Clients*.

B153   PETERS, E. L. (1968). "The Tied and the Free (Lybia)," pp. 167-88, in J. G. Peristiany, ed., *Contributions to Mediterranean Sociology.*

B154   PETERS, E. L. (1977). "Patronage in Cyrenaica," pp. 275-90, in E. Gellner and J. Waterbury, eds., *Patrons and Clients.*

B155   POOL, D. (1972). *The Politics of Patronage: Elites and Social Structure in Iraq.* Princeton University, PhD Thesis.

B156   RASSAM, A. (1977). "Al-Taba'iyya: Power, Patronage, and Marginal Groups in Northern Iraq," pp. 157-66, in E. Gellner and J. Waterbury, eds., *Patrons and Clients.*

B157   SPERBER, D. (1971). "Patronage in Amoraic Palestine (c. 220-400): Causes and Effects," *Journal of the Economic and Social History of the Orient*, 14: 227-52.

B158   VINOGRADOV, A. (1974). "Ethnicity, Cultural Discontinuity and Power Brokers in Northern Iraq: The Case of the Shabak," *American Ethnologist*, 1(1): 207-18.

III. Southeast Asia

1. General

B159   ALAVI, H. (1974). "Rural Bases of Political Power in South East Asia," *Journal of Contemporary Asia*, 4(4): 413-22.

B160   LANDE, C. J. (1973). See A19.

B161   SCOTT, J. C. (1972a-b). See A34-A35.

B162   SCOTT, J. C. (1976). *The Moral Economy of the Peasant: Rebellion and Subsistence in Southeast Asia.* New Haven: Yale University Press.

B163   SCOTT, J. C. and KERKVLIET, B. J. (1973). "How Traditional Rural Patrons Lose Legitimacy: A Theory with Special Reference to Southeast Asia," *Cultures et Développement*, 5(3): 501-40.

B164   WERTHEIM, W. F. (1964). "Sociological Aspects of Corruption in Southeast Asia," *East-West Parallels: Sociological Approaches to Modern Asia.* The Hague: H. van Hoeve, pp. 103-31.

2. Burma

B165   HANKS, L. M. (1968). "Entourage and Circle in Burma," *Bennington Review*, 2(1): 32-46.

B166   SPIRO, M. E. (1968). "Factionalism and Politics in Village Burma," pp. 401-21, in M. Swartz, ed., *Local-Level Politics.*

3. Indonesia

B167   FEITH, H. (1962). *The Decline of Constitutional Democracy in Indonesia*. Ithaca, NY: Cornell University Press.

B168   GEERTZ, C. (1960). "The Javanese Kijai: The Changing Role of a Cultural Broker," *Comparative Studies in Society and History*, 2: 228-49.

B169   GEERTZ, C. (1965). *The Social History of an Indonesian Town*. Cambridge, Mass.: MIT Press.

B170   GREGORY, A. (1970). "Factionalism and the Indonesian Army. The New Order," *Journal of Comparative Administration*, 2(3): 341-54.

B171   JACKSON, K. D. (1974). *Urbanization and the Rise of Patron-Client Relations: The Changing Quality of Interpersonal Communications in the Neighborhoods of Bandung and the Villages of West Java*. Cambridge, Mass.: Center for International Studies, MIT.

B172   WERTHEIM, W. F. (1969). "From Aliran towards Class Struggle in the Countryside of Java," *Pacific Viewpoint*, 10(2): 1-17.

B173   WOLF, E. R. (1957). "Closed Corporate Peasant Communities in Mesoamerica and Central Java," reprinted in pp. 230-46, in J. M. Potter, M. N. Diaz and G. M. Foster, *Peasant Society*. Boston: Little Brown, 1967.

4. Philippines

B174   AGPALO, R. E. (1972). *The Political Elites and the People: A Study of Politics in Occidental Mindoro*. Manila: College of Public Administration.

B175   ANDERSON, J. N. (1969). "Buy-and-Sell and Economic Personalism — Foundations for Philippine Entrepreneurship," *Asian Survey*, 9(9): 641-68.

B176   GROSSHOLTZ, J. (1964). *Politics in the Philippines*. Boston: Little Brown.

B177   HOLLNSTEINER, M. R. (1963). *The Dynamics of Power in a Philippine Municipality*. Quezon: Community Research Development Council, University of the Philippines.

B178   KIEFER, T. M. (1972). *The Tausug: Violence and Law in a Philippine Moslem Society*. New York: Holt, Rinehart and Winston.

B179   LANDE, C. (1965). *Leaders, Factions, and Parties. The Structure of Philippine Politics*. New Haven: Yale University Southeast Asian Studies, Monograph No. 6.

B180   LYNCH, F. (1964). *Four Readings in Philippine Values*. Quezon: Ateneo of Manila Press, Institute of Philippine Culture Papers.

B181   MACHADO, K. G. (1974). "From Traditional Faction to Machine — Changing Patterns of Political Leadership and Organization in the Rural Philippines," *Journal of Asian Studies*, 33(4): 523-49.

B182   NOWAK, T. and SNYDER, K. A. (1970). "Urbanization and Clientelist Systems in the Philippines," *Philippine Journal of Public Administration*, 14. Quoted by B183.

B183   NOWAK, T. and SNYDER, K. A. (1974). "Clientelist Politics in the Philippines: Integration or Instability?", *American Political Science Review*, 68(3): 1147-70.

5. Thailand

B184   HANKS, L. M. Jr. (1962). "Merit and Power in the Thai Social Order," *American Anthropologist*, 64: 1247-61.

B185   HANKS, L. M. Jr. (1966). "The Corporation and the Entourage: A Comparison of Thai and American Social Organization," *Catalyst*, Summer.

B186   HANKS, L. M. Jr. (1968). "American Aid is Damaging Thai Society," *Transaction*, 5(10): 29-34.

B187   KAUFMAN, H. K. (1960). *Bangkhvad. A Community Study in Thailand*. Locut Valley, NY: Augustin, Monographs of the Association of Asian Studies No. 10.

B188   MILLAR, D. W. (1971). "Patron-Client Relations in Thailand," *Cornell Journal of Social Relations*, 6(2): 215-25.

B189   MOERMAN, M. (1968). *Agricultural Change and Peasant Choice in a Northern Thai Village*. Berkeley: University of California Press.

B190   NEHER, C. D. (1974). *The Dynamics of Politics and Administration in Rural Thailand*. Ohio University: Center for International Studies, Southeast Asian Series No. 30.

B191   PHILLIPS, H. P. (1965). *The Peasant Personality: The Patterning of Interpersonal Behaviour in the Village of Bang Chou*. Berkeley: University of California Press.

B192   RABIBHADANA, A. (1969). *The Organization of Thai Society in the Early Bangkok Period: 1782-1872*. Ithaca, NY: Cornell University Press.

B193   RABIBHADANA, A. (1975). "Clientship and Class Structure in the Early Bangkok Period," pp. 93-124, in G. W. Skinner and A. T. Kirsch, eds., *Change and Persistence in Thai Society. Essays in Honor of Lauristan Sharp*. Ithaca, NY and London: Cornell University Press.

B194   RIGGS, F. W. (1962). "Interest and Clientele Groups," pp. 153-92, in J. L. Sutton, ed., *Problems of Politics and Administration in Thailand*. Bloomington: Indiana University Press.

B195   RIGGS, F. W. (1966). *Thailand: The Modernization of a Bureaucratic Polity*. Honolulu: East-West Center Press.

B196   SHOR, E. (1960). "The Thai Bureaucracy," *Administrative Science Quarterly*, 5: 66-86.

B197   WILSON, D. A. (1962). *Politics in Thailand*. Ithaca, NY: Cornell University Press.

6. Others

B198   McCOY, A. W. (1973). "The Politics of the Poppy in Indochina: A Comparative Study of Patron-Client Relations under French and American Administrations." Paper presented to the annual meeting of the Association of Asian Studies, Chicago.
B199   MILNE, R. S. (1973). "Patrons, Clients, and Ethnicity: The Case of Sabah and Sarawak in Malaysia," *Asian Survey*, 13.

IV. Africa

1. General

B200   BERMAN, B. J. (1974). "Clientelism and Neocolonialism: Center-Periphery Relations and Political Development in African States," *Studies in Comparative International Development*, 9(2): 3-25.
B201   BIENEN, H. (1971). "Political Parties and Political Machines in Africa," pp. 195-213, in M. Lofchie, ed., *The State of the Nations: Constraints on Development in Independent Africa*. Berkeley and Los Angeles: University of California Press.
B202   COLSON, E. (1967). "Competence and Incompetence in the Context of Independence," *Current Anthropology*, 8(1-2): 92-111.
B203   GOODY, J. (1963). "Feudalism in Africa?," *Journal of African History*, 4(1): 1-18.
B204   GOODY, J. (1969). "Economy and Feudalism in Africa," *Economic History Review*, 22(3): 393-405.
B205   LEMARCHAND, R. (1972). "Political Exchange, Clientelism and Development in Tropical Africa," *Cultures et Développement* (Brussels), 4(3): 483-516. See also A22, A23, A24.
B206   LEYS, C. (1965). "What is the Problem About Corruption?," *Journal of Modern African Studies*, 3(2): 215-30.

2. West Africa

B207   APTER, D. (1960). "The Role of Traditionalism in the Political Modernization of Ghana and Uganda," *World Politics*, 13: 45-68.
B208   AUGE, M. (1969). "Statut, pouvoir et richesse: Relations lignageres, relations de dépendance et rapports de productier dans la société alladian," *Cahiers d'Etudes Africaines*, 9(35): 261-81.
B209   BARKER, J. S. (1971). "The Paradox of Development: Reflections on a Study of Local-Central Political Relations in Senegal," pp. 46-63, in M. Lofchie, ed., *The State of the Nations: Constraints on Development in Independent Africa*. Berkeley and Los Angeles: University of California Press.

B210 BEHRMAN, L. (1970). *Muslim Brotherhoods and Politics in Senegal.* Cambridge, Mass.: Harvard University Press.
B211 COHEN, A. (1965). "The Social Organization of Credit in a West African Cattle Market," *Africa,* 35: 8-20.
B212 COHEN, A. (1969). *Custom and Politics in Urban Africa.* London: Routledge and Kegan Paul.
B213 DARE, L. O. (1978). "Patron-Client Relations and Military Rule in Nigeria." Bellagio paper.
B214 DORJAHN, V. R. and FYFE, C. (1962). "Landlord and Stranger: Change in Tenancy Relations in Sierra Leone," *Journal of African History,* 3(3): 391-97.
B215 FOLTZ, W. J. (n.d.). *Social Structure and Political Behaviour in Senegalese Elites.* Yale Papers in Political Science No. 33.
B216 HILL, P. (1966). "Landlords and Brokers: A West African Trading System," *Cahiers d'Etudes Africaines,* 6(23): 349-66.
B217 LE VINE, V. T. (1968). "Political Elite Recruitment and Political Structure in French Speaking Africa," *Cahiers d'Etudes Africaines,* 8(31): 369-89.
B218 MORGENTHAU, R. S. (1964). *Political Parties in French Speaking West Africa.* Oxford: Clarendon Press. Pp. 336-58.
B219 NADEL, S. F. (1946). *A Black Byzantium. The Kingdom of Nupe in Nigeria.* London: Oxford University Press (c. 1942).
B220 O'BRIEN, D. C. (1969). "Le Talibé mouride: Etude d'un cas de dépendance sociale," *Cahiers d'Etudes Africaines,* 9(35): 502-507.
B221 O'BRIEN, D. C. (1971). *The Mourides of Senegal. The Political and Economic Organization of an Islamic Brotherhood.* Oxford: Clarendon Press.
B222 POST, K. (1972). " 'Peasantization' and Rural Political Movements in Western Africa," *Archives Européenes de Sociologie,* 13(1): 223-54.
B223 WHITAKER, C. S. (1965). "Three Perspectives on Hierarchy: Political Thought and Leadership in Northern Nigeria," *Journal of Commonwealth Political Studies,* 3(1): 1-19.
B224 WHITAKER, C. S. (1970). *The Politics of Tradition. Continuity and Change in Northern Nigeria 1946-1966.* New Jersey: Princeton University Press.

3. East Africa

B225 BOTTE, R. et al. (1969). "Les relations personnelles de subordination dans les sociétés interlacustres de l'Afrique centrale," *Cahiers d'Etudes Africaines,* 9(35): 350-401.
B226 BUXTON, J. (1967). "Clientship among the Mandari of the Southern Sudan," pp. 229-45, in R. Cohen and J. Middleton, eds., *Comparative Political Systems: Studies on the Politics of Pre-Industrial Societies.* Garden City, NY: Natural History Press.

B227   CHILVER, E. M. (1960). "Feudalism in the Interlacustrine Kingdoms," pp. 378-93, in A. I. Richards, ed., *East African Chiefs. A Study of Political Development in Some Uganda and Tanganyika Tribes*. London: Faber and Faber.

B228   CODERE, H. (1962). "Power in Rwanda," *Anthropologica*, series 2, 4(1): 45-85.

B229   FALLERS, L. (1955). "The Predicament of a Modern African Chief: An Instance from Uganda," *American Anthropologist*, 57: 290-305.

B230   FALLERS, L. (1965). *Bantu Bureaucracy: A Century of Political Evolution among the Basoga of Uganda*. Chicago: University Press.

B231   GRAVEL, P. (1967). "The Transfer of Cows in Gisaka," *American Anthropologist*, 69: 322-31.

B232   GRAVEL, P. (1968). *Remera: A Community in Eastern Ruanda*. The Hague-Paris: Mouton.

B233   LA FONTAINE, J. S. (1975). "The Mother's Brother as Patron," *Archives Européenes de Sociologie*, 16: 76-92.

B234   LEMARCHAND, R. (1966). "Power and Stratification in Rwanda. A Reconsideration," *Cahiers d'Etudes Africaines*, 6(24): 592-610.

B235   LEMARCHAND, R. (1968). "Les relations de clientèle comme agent de contestation: Le cas du Ruanda," *Civilizations*, 18(4): 553-78.

B236   LEMARCHAND, R. (1977) (ed.). *African Kingdoms in Perspective. Political Change and Modernization in Monarchical Settings*. London: F. Cass.

B237   LEYS, C. (1967). *Politicians and Policies: An Essay on Politics in Acholi Uganda 1962-1965*, Nairobi: East African Publishing House.

B238   LEYS, C. (1971). "Politics in Kenya: The Development of Peasant Society," *British Journal of Political Science*, 1(3): 307-37.

B239   LEYS, C. (1974). *Underdevelopment in Kenya. The Political Economy of Neo-Colonialism, 1964-1971*. Berkeley: University of California Press.

B240   MAIR, L. (1961). "Clientship in East Africa," *Cahiers d'Etudes Africaines*, 6: 315-25.

B241   MAQUET, J. P. (1961a). "Une hypothèse pour l'étude des féodalités africaines," *Cahiers d'Etudes Africaines*, 6: 292-315.

B242   MAQUET, J. P. (1961b). *The Premise of Inequality in Rwanda*. Oxford: International African Institute.

B243   MAQUET, J. P. (1969). "Institutionalization féodale des relations de dépendance dans quatre cultures interlacustres," *Cahiers d'Etudes Africaines*, 9(35): 402-14.

B244   MILLER, N. M. (1970). "The Rural African Party: Political Participation in Tanzania," *American Political Science Review*, 54(2): 548-71.

B245   SANDBROOK, R. (1972a). "Patrons, Clients and Unions: The Labour Movement and Political Conflict in Kenya," *Journal of Commonwealth Political Studies*, 10(1): 3-27.

B246   SANDBROOK, R. (1972b). "Patrons, Clients and Factions: New Dimensions of Conflict Analysis in Africa," *Canadian Journal of Political Science*, 5(1): 104-19.

B247   STEINHART, E. (1967). "Vassal and Fief in three Lacustrine Kingdoms," *Cahiers d'Etudes Africaines*, 7(28): 606-23.

B248 TROUWBORST, A. (1962). "L'accord de clientèle et organisation politique au Burundi," *Anthropologica*, 4: 9-43.
B249 VINCENT, J. (1971). *African Elite: The Big Men of a Small Town*. New York: Columbia University Press.

4. Southern-central and Central Africa

B250 BATES, R. H. (1971). *Unions, Parties and Political Development: A Study of Mineworkers in Zambia*. New Haven: Yale University Press.
B251 BRETTON, M. (1977). "Clients or Classes? Patterns of Resource Distribution in Rural Zambia." Unpublished Ms.
B252 EPSTEIN, A. L. (1968). "Power, Politics and Leadership: Some Central African and Melanesian Contrasts," pp. 53-68, in M. Swartz, ed., *Local-Level Politics*.
B253 GOULD, D. J. (1978). "Underdevelopment Administration: Systemic Corruption in the Public Bureaucracy of Mobutu's Zaire." Bellagio paper.
B254 LA FONTAINE (1975). See B233.
B255 REY, P. P. (1969). "Articulation des modes de dépendance et des modes de réproduction dans deux sociétés lignagères (Punu et Kunyi du Congo Brazaville)," *Cahiers d'Etudes Africaines*, 9(35): 415-40.
B256 WILLIAME, J. C. (1972). *Patrimonialism and Political Change in the Congo*. Stanford: University Press.

V. Latin America

1. General

B257 BRISK, W. J. (1973). "The New Caciquismo," pp. 151-63, in R. Kern, ed., *The Caciques. Oligarchical Politics and the System of Caciquismo in the Luso-Hispanic World*. Albuquerque: University of New Mexico Press.
B258 KAUFMAN, R. R. (1977). "Corporatism, Clientelism and Partisan Conflict. A Study of Seven Latin American Countries," pp. 109-48, in J. M. Malloy, ed., *Authoritarianism and Corporatism in Latin America*. University of Pittsburgh Press.
B259 KERN, R. (1973) (ed.). *The Caciques. Oligarchical Politics and the System of Caciquismo in the Luso-Hispanic World*. Albuquerque: University of New Mexico Press.
B260 LANDSBERGER, H. A. (1969). *Latin American Peasant Movements*. Ithaca, NY: Cornell University Press.
B261 LANDSBERGER, H. A. (1973). "The Problems of Peasant Wars. Review Article," *Comparative Studies in Society and History*, 15(3): 378-88.

B262 MALLOY, J. (1977) (ed.). *Authoritarianism and Corporatism in Latin America*. Pittsburgh: University of Pittsburgh Press.

B263 MITCHELL, S. (1978). *The Patterning of Compadrazgo Ties in Latin America*. Institute of Latin American Studies Occasional Papers No. 24.

B264 QUIJANO OBREGON, A. (1967). "Contemporary Peasant Movements," pp. 301-40, in S. M. Lipset and A. Solari, eds., *Elites in Latin America*. New York: Oxford University Press.

B265 RABINOVITZ, F. F. (1968). "Sound and Fury Signifying Nothing? A Review of Community Power Research in Latin America," *Urban Affairs Quarterly*, 3: 111-22.

B266 SCHWERIN, K. H. (1973). "The Anthropological Antecedents: Caciques, Cacicazgos and Caciquismo," pp. 5-17, in R. Kern, ed., *The Caciques*.

B267 SINGELMANN, P. (1974). "Campesino Movements and Class Conflict in Latin America: The Functions of Exchange and Power," *Journal of Inter-American Studies and World Affairs*, 16: 39-72.

B268 SINGELMANN, P. (1975). "The Closing Triangle: Critical Notes on a Model for Peasant Mobilization in Latin America," *Comparative Studies in Society and History*, 17(4): 389-409.

B269 STRICKON, A. (1965). "Folk Models of Stratification: Political Ideology and Sociocultural Systems," *Sociological Review Monographs* No. 11.

B270 STRICKON, A. and GREENFIELD, S. (1972) (eds.). *Structure and Process in Latin America: Patronage and Power Systems*. Albuquerque: University of New Mexico Press.

B271 WIARDA, H. J. (1973). "Towards a Framework for the Study of Political Change in the Iberic-Latin Tradition: The Corporative Model," *World Politics*, 25(2): 206-35.

B272 WIARDA, H. J. (1974) (ed.). *Politics and Social Change in Latin America*. Amherst: University of Massachusetts Press.

B273 WOLF, E. R. and HANSEN, E. C. (1967). "Caudillo Politics: A Structural Analysis," *Comparative Studies in Society and History*, 9(2): 168-79.

2. Brazil

B274 BRUMER, A. (1976). "O sistema paternalista no Brasil," *Revista do Instituto de Filosofia e Ciencias Humanas da Universidade Federal do Rio Grande do Sul*, Ano IV: 57-79.

B275 CARDOSO, F. H. (1961). "Tensoes Sociais no campo e reforma agraria," *Revista Brasileira de Estudos Politicos*, 12.10.61.

B276 FAORO, R. (1958). *Os Donos do Poder: Formaçâo do Patronato Politico Brasileiro*. Porto Alegre: Globo.

B277 FREYRE, G. (1964). "The Patriarchal Basis of Brazilian Society," pp. 155-73, in J. Maier and R. Weatherhead, eds., *Politics of Change in Latin America*. New York: Praeger.

B278 GALJART, B. (1964). "Class and 'Following' in Rural Brazil," *América Latina*, 7(3): 3-24.

B279   GALJART, B. (1965). "A Further Note on Followings," *América Latina*, 8(3): 145-52.

B280/1 GALJART, B. (1968). *Itaguaí: Old Habits and New Practices in a Brazilian Land Settlement*. Wagerningen: Center for Agricultural Publishing and Documentation.

B282   GREENFIELD, S. (1970). "Patronage Networks, Factions, Political Parties and National Integration in Contemporary Brazilian Society." Latin American Center, University of Wisconsin, Milwaukee, Discussion Paper No. 1.

B283   GREENFIELD, S. (1977). "Patronage, Politics, and the Articulation of Local Community and National Society in Pre-1968 Brazil," *Journal of Interamerican Studies and World Affairs*, 19(2): 139-72.

B284   HALL, A. (1970). "Social and Economic Obstacles to Agrarian Reform in North-East Brazil." MPhil. thesis, Glasgow University.

B285   HARRIS, M. (1956). *Town and Country in Brazil*. New York: Columbia University Press.

B286   HUTCHINSON, B. (1966). "The Patron-Dependent Relationship in Brazil: A Preliminary Examination," *Sociologia Ruralis*, 6: 3-30.

B287   HUTCHINSON, H. (1957). *Village and Plantation Life in Northeast Brazil*. Washington: University Press.

B288   LEAL, V. N. (1948). *Coronelismo, Enxada e Voto*. Rio de Janeiro: Livraria Forense.

B289   LEEDS, A. (1964). "Brazilian Careers and Social Structure: An Evolutionary Model and Case History," *American Anthropologist*, 66(6): 1321-47.

B290   LEWIN, L. (1979). "Some Historical Implications of Kinship Organization for Family-based Politics in Brazilian Northeast," *Comparative Studies in Society and History*, 21(2): 262-92.

B291   PANG, E. S. (1970). "The Politics of Coronelismo in Brazil: The Case of Bahia, 1889-1930." PhD thesis, University of California, Berkeley.

B292   PANG, E. S. (1973). "Coronelismo in Northeast Brazil," pp. 65-88, in R. Kern, ed., *The Caciques*.

B293   ROETT, R. (1972). *Brazil: Politics in a Patrimonial Society*. Boston: Allyn and Bacon.

B294   SCHMITTER, P. (1971). *Interest Conflict and Political Change in Brazil*. Stanford: University Press.

B295   SCHWARTZMAN, S. (1975). *Sao Paulo e o Estado Nacional*. São Paulo: DIFEL.

B296   STEPHEN, X. (1973) (ed.). *Authoritarian Brazil*. New Haven: Yale University Press.

3. Mexico

B297   ADIE, R. F. (1970). "Cooperation, Cooptation and Conflict in Mexican Peasant Organizations," *Inter-American Economic Affairs*, 24(3): 3-25.

B298   ANDERSON, B. and COCKROFT, J. D. (1966). "Control and Cooptation in Mexican Politics," *International Journal of Comparative Sociology*, 7: 11-28.

B299   BARTRA, R. et al. (1975). *Caciquismo y poder político en el México rural.* Mexico: Siglo XXI.

B300   BUVE, R. Th. (1974). "Patronaje en las zonas rurales de México," *Boletin de Estudios Latinoamericanos y del Caribe* (Amsterdam), 16: 118-56.

B301   BUVE, R. Th. (1975). "Peasant Movements, Caudillos and Land Reform during the Revolution (1910-1917) in Tlaxcala, Mexico," *Journal of Latin American and Caribbean Studies*, 18: 112-53.

B302   CARLOS, M. L. (1973). "Fictive Kinship and Modernization in Mexico: A Comparative Analysis," *Anthropological Quarterly*, 46(2): 75-91.

B303   CORNELIUS, W. A. Jr. (1973). "Contemporary Mexico: A Structural Analysis of Urban Caciquismo," pp. 135-50, in R. Kern, ed., *The Caciques.*

B304   DESHON, S. K. (1967). "Conpadrazgo in a Henequen Hacienda in Yucatan: A Structural Re-evaluation," *American Anthropologist*, 65(3): 574-83.

B305   FOSTER, G. M. (1961). "The Dyadic Contract: A Model for the Social Structure of a Mexican Peasant Village," *American Anthropologist*, 63(6): 1173-92.

B306   FOSTER, G. M. (1963). "The Dyadic Contract in Tzintzuntzan II: Patron-Client Relationships," *American Anthropologist*, 65(6): 1280-94.

B307   FOSTER, G. M. (1967). *Tzintzuntzan: Mexican Peasants in a Changing World.* Boston: Little Brown.

B308   FOSTER, G. M. (1969). "Godparents and Social Networks in Tzintzuntzan," *Southwestern Journal of Anthropology*, 25(3): 261-78.

B309   FRIEDRICH, P. (1965). "A Mexican Cacicazgo," *Ethnology*, 4(2): 190-209.

B310   FRIEDRICH, P. (1968). "The Legitimacy of a Cacique," pp. 243-69, in M. J. Swartz, ed., *Local-Level Politics.*

B311   FRIEDRICH, P. (1970). *Agrarian Revolt in a Mexican Village.* Englewood Cliffs, NJ: Prentice Hall.

B312   FURLONG, W. L. (1972). "Peruvian and Northern Mexican Municipalities: A Comparative Analysis of Two Political Systems," *Comparative Political Studies*, 5(1): 59-83.

B313   GIBSON, C. (1973). "Caciques in Postconquest and Colonial Mexico," pp. 18-26, in R. Kern, ed., *The Caciques.*

B314   GRAHAM, L. S. (1968). *Politics of a Mexican Community.* Gainsville: University of Florida Press.

B315   GRINDLE, M. S. (1977a). *Bureaucrats, Politicians, and Peasants in Mexico: A Case Study in Public Policy.* Berkeley: University of California Press.

B316   GRINDLE, M. S. (1977b). "Patrons and Clients in the Bureaucracy: Career Networks in Mexico," *Latin American Research Review*, 12(1): 37-65.

B317   HUIZER, G. (1969). "The Role of Patronage in the Peasant Political Struggle," *Sociologische Gids*, 16(6): 411-18.

B318   INGHAM, J. M. (1970). "The Asymmetrical Implications of Godparenthood in Tlayacapan, Morelos," *Man* (NS), 5: 281-89.

B319   LOMNITZ, L. (1978). "Mechanisms of Articulation between Shanty-town Settlers and the Urban System," *Urban Anthropology*, 7(2): 185-205.

B320   PARE, L. (1972). "Diseño teórico para el estudio del caciquismo en México," *Revista Mexicana de Sociología*, 34(2): 335-54.

B321   PARE, L. (1973). "Caciquisme et structure du pouvoir dans le Mexique rural," *Canadian Review of Sociology and Anthropology*, 10(1): 20-43.

B322/3 POITRAS, G. E. (1973). "Welfare Bureaucracy and Clientele Politics in Mexico," *Administrative Science Quarterly*, 18(1): 18-26.

B324   PRESS, I. (1969). "Ambiguity and Innovation: Implications for the Genesis of the Cultural Broker," *American Anthropologist*, 71: 205-17.

B325   PURCELL, S. Kaufman (1973). "Decision Making in an Authoritarian Regime: Theoretical Implications from a Mexican Case Study," *World Politics*, 26(1): 28-54.

B326/7 PURCELL, S. Kaufman (1978). "Clientelism and Development in Mexico." Bellagio paper.

B328   ROTHSTEIN, F. (1979). "The Class Basis of Patron-Client Relations," *Latin American Perspectives*, 6(2): 25-35.

B329   TORRES-TRUEBA, H. E. (1970). "Faccionalismo en un municipio mexicano," *América Indigena*, 30(3): 727-49.

B330   TUMOY, W. S. (1972). *Politics and Privilege in a Mexican City*. Stanford: University Press.

B331   UGALDE, A. (1973). "Contemporary Mexico: From Hacienda to PRI. Political Leadership in a Zapotec Village," pp. 119-34, in R. Kern, ed., *The Caciques*.

B332   VAN DEN BERGHE, G. and VAN DEN BERGHE, P. (1966). "Compadrazgo and Class in Southeastern Mexico," *American Anthropologist*, 68: 1236-44.

B333   WOLF, E. R. (1956). "Aspects of Group Relations in a Complex Society: Mexico," *American Anthropologist*, 58: 1065-78.

4. Peru

B334   ALBERTI, G. (1972). "The Breakdown of Provincial Urban Power Structure and the Rise of Peasant Movements," *Sociologia Ruralis*, 12: 315-33.

B335   AMERICAN BEHAVIORAL SCIENTIST (1965). "The Vicos Case: Peasant Society in Transition." 8(7).

B336   BOLTON, R. (1970). "El Fuete y el Sello: Patrones cambiantes de liderazgo y autoridad en pueblos peruanos," *América Indígena*, 30(4): 883-928.

B337   COLLIER, D. (1976). *Squatters and Oligarchs. Authoritarian Rule and Policy Change in Peru*. Baltimore: Johns Hopkins University Press.

B338   COTLER, J. (1970). "The Mechanisms of Internal Domination and Social Change in Peru," pp. 407-44, in I. L. Horowitz, ed., *Masses in Latin America*. New York: Oxford University Press.

B339   DEW, E. (1969). *Politics in the Altiplano: The Dynamics of Change in Rural Peru*. Austin: University of Texas Press.

B340   GUASTI, L. (1976). "Peru; Clientelism and Internal Control," pp. 422-38, in S. Schmidt et al., eds., *Friends Followers and Factions*.

B341   GUASTI, L. (1978). "Clientelism in Decline: A Peruvian Regional Study." Bellagio paper.

B342   JAQUETTE, H. L. (1973). "Revolution by Fiat: The Context of Policy Making in Peru," *Western Political Quarterly*, 25(4): 648-66.

B343   KARNO, H. L. (1973). "Julio Cesar Arana; Frontier Cacique in Peru," pp. 89-98, in R. Kern, ed., *The Caciques*.

B344   TULLIS, F. La Mond (1970). *Lord and Peasant in Peru: A Paradigm of Political and Social Change*. Cambridge, Mass.: Harvard University Press.

5. Venezuela

B345   BLANK, D. E. (1973). *Politics in Venezuela*. Boston: Little Brown.

B346   POWELL, J. D. (1971). *Political Mobilization of the Venezuelan Peasant*. Cambridge, Mass.: Harvard University Press. See also A31.

B347   RAY, T. F. (1969). *The Politics of the Barrios of Venezuela*. Berkeley and Los Angeles: University of California Press.

6. Others

B348   CRESPI, M. (1971). "Changing Power Relations: The Rise of Peasant Unions in Traditional Ecuadorian Haciendas," *Anthropological Quarterly*, 44(4): 223-40.

B349   DANDLER, J. (1971). *Politics of Leadership, Brokerage and Patronage in the Campesino Movements of Cochabamba, Bolivia (1935-1954)*. Ann Arbor, Mich.: University Microfilms.

B350   DIRKS, R. (1972). "Networks, Groups and Adaptation in an Afro-Caribbean Community," *Man*, 7(4): 565-85.

B351   GREGORY, J. R. (1975). See A76.

B352   GUZMAN CAMPOS et al. (1962, 1964). *La Violencia en Colombia*. Bogotá: Tercer Mundo. 2 Vols.

B353   HEATH, D. C. (1973). "New Patrons for the Old: Changing Patron-Client Relationships in the Bolivian Yungas," *Ethnology*, 12(1): 75-98.

B354   HERMITTE, E. and BARTOLOMÉ, L. (1977) (eds.). *Procesos de articulación social*. Buenos Aires: CLACSO and Amorrortu.

B355   HICKS, F. (1971). "Interpersonal Relationship and Caudillismo in Paraguay," *Journal of Inter-American Studies and World Affairs*, 13(1): 89-111.

B356   MINTZ, S. W. (1961). "Pratik: Haitian Personal Economic Relationships," *Proceedings of the annual meeting of the American Ethnological Society*, pp. 54-63.

B357   OSBORN, A. (1968). "Compadrazgo and Patronage: A Colombian Case," *Man* (NS), 3: 593-608.

B358   SCHMIDT, S. (1974a). "The Transformation of Clientelism in Rural Colombia." Paper presented at the annual meeting of the APSA. Chicago, September.

B359   SCHMIDT, S. (1974b). "Bureaucrats as Modernizing Brokers: Clientelism in Colombia," *Comparative Politics*, 6(3): 425-50.

B360   SCHMIDT, S. (1974c). "La Violencia Revisited: The Clientelist Bases of Political Violence in Colombia: The Case of Cali," *Journal of Latin American Studies*, 6(1): 97-111.

B361   SCHWARTZ, N. B. (1969). "Goal Attainment Through Factionalism: A Guatemalan Case," *American Anthropologist*, 71(6): 1088-1108.

B362   STRICKON, A. (1962). "Class and Kinship in Argentina," *Ethnology*, 1(4): 500-15.

VI. South Asia

1. India

B363   BAILEY, F. G. (1963). *Politics and Change: Orissa in 1959*. Berkeley and Los Angeles: University of California Press.

B364   BAYLY, C. A. (1973). "Patrons and Politics in Northern India," *Modern Asian Studies*, 7(3): 349-88.

B365   BEIDELMAN, T. O. (1959). *A Comparative Analysis of the Jajmani System*. New York: Association for Asian Studies, J. J. Augustin.

B366   BENSON, J. (1976). "A South Indian Jajmani System," *Ethnology*, 16(3): 239-50.

B367   BETEILLE, A. (1974). *Studies in Agrarian Social Structure*. New York: Oxford University Press.

B368   BRASS, P. (1965). *Factional Politics in an Indian State: The Congress Party in Uttar Pradesh*. Berkeley: University of California Press.

B369   BREMAN, J. (1974). *Patronage and Exploitation: Changing Agrarian Relations in South Gujarat, India*. Berkeley: University of California Press.

B370   CARRAS, M. C. (1972). *The Dynamics of Indian Political Factions: A Study of District Councils in the State of Maharashtra*. Cambridge: University Press.

B371   CARTER, A. T. (1974). *Elite Politics in Rural India: Political Stratification and Political Alliances in Western Maharashtra*. Cambridge: University Press.

B372   COHN, B. and McKIM, M. (1958). "Networks and Centers in the Integration of Indian Civilization," *Journal of Social Research*, 1: 1-9.

B373   ELDER, J. (1970). "Rajpur: Change in the Jajmani System of an Uttar Pradesh Village," pp. 105-27, in K. Ishwaran, ed., *Change and Continuity in India's Villages*. New York: Columbia University Press.

B374   FIRTH, R. (1957). "Factions in India and Overseas Indian Societies," *British Journal of Sociology*, 8: 291-94.

B375   GOULD, H. (1958). "The Hindu Jajmani System: A Case of Economic Particularism," *Southwestern Journal of Anthropology*, 14: 428-37.

B376   GRAHAM, B. D. (1968). "The Succession of Factional Systems in the Uttar Pradesh Congress Party," pp. 323-60, in M. Swartz, ed., *Local-Level Politics*.

B377   KOLENDA, P. M. (1963). "Toward a Model of the Hindu Jajmani System," *Human Organization*, 22: 11-31.

B378   LEWIS, O. and BARNOUW, V. (1967). "Caste and the Jajmani System in a North Indian Village," pp. 110-34, in J. M. Potter, M. N. Diaz and G. M. Foster, eds., *Peasant Society. A Reader*. Boston: Little Brown.

B379   MAYER, A. C. (1967). See A28.

B380   MILLER, D. F. (1965). "Factions in Indian Village Politics," *Pacific Affairs*, 38: 17-31.

B381   NICHOLAS, R. W. (1963). "Village Factions and Political Parties in Rural West Bengal," *Journal of Commonwealth Political Studies*, 2(1): 17-32.

B382   NICHOLAS, R. W. (1965). "Factions: A Comparative Analysis," pp. 21-61, in M. Banton, ed., *Political Systems and the Distribution of Power*. London: ASA Monographs No. 2.

B383   SRINIVAS, M. H. and BETEILLE, A. (1964). "Networks in Indian Social Structure," *Man*, 64: 165-68.

B384   WISER, W. and WISER, C. (1971). *Behind Mud Walls 1939-1940*. Berkeley: University of California Press.

2. Nepal

B385   BISTA, D. B. (1971). "The Political Innovators of Upper Kali-Gandaki," *Man* (NS), 6: 52-60.

B386   CAPLAN, L. (1971). "Cash and Kind: Two Media of 'Bribery' in Nepal," *Man* (NS), 6: 266-78.

VII. Japan

B387   ABEGGLEN, J. C. (1958). *The Japanese Factory*. Glencoe, Ill.: Free Press.

B388   BAERWALD, H. (1964). "Factional Politics in Japan," *Current History*, 60: 223-29.

B389   BEARDSLEY, R. K., HALL, J. W. and WARD, R. I. (1959). *Village Japan*. Chicago: University Press.

B390   BEFU, H. (n.d.). "Gift Giving in a Modernizing Japan," *Monumenta Niponica*, 23(3-4): 445-56.

B391   BEFU, H. (1966/67). "Gift-Giving and Social Reciprocity in Japan," *France-Asia/Asie*, 188: 161-77.

B392   BEFU, H. (1971). "Bribery in Japan: When Law Tangles with Culture." Paper presented at the Coloquium, Center for Japanese and Korean Studies, University of California, Berkeley.

B393   BEFU, H. (1974). "Power in Exchange: Strategy of Control and Patterns of Compliance in Japan," *Asian Profile* (Hong Kong), 2(6): 601-22.

B394   BENNETT, J. W. (1958). "Economic Aspects of a Boss-Henchman System in the Japanese Forestry Industry," *Economic Development and Cultural Change*, 7(1): 13-30.

B395   BENNETT, J. W. and ISHINO, I. (1963). *Paternalism in the Japanese Economy: Anthropological Studies of Oyabun-Kobun Patterns*, Minneapolis: University of Minnesota Press.

B396   CURTIS, G. L. (1971). *Election Campaigning, Japanese Style*. New York: Columbia University Press.

B397   DORE, R. P. (1958). *City Life in Japan. A Study of a Tokyo Ward*. London: Routledge and Kegan Paul.

B398   FLANAGAN, S. C. (1968). "Voting Behavior in Japan: The Persistence of Traditional Patterns," *Comparative Political Studies*, 1(3): 391-412.

B399   HALL, J. W. (1962). "Feudalism in Japan. A Reassessment," *Comparative Studies in Society and History*, 5: 15-51.

B400   IKE, N. (1957). *Japanese Politics. Patron-Client Democracy*. New York: Knopf.

B401   ISHINO, I. (1953). "The Oyabun-Kobun: A Japanese Ritual Kinship Institution," *American Anthropologist*, 55(1): 695-707.

B402   KURODA, Y. (1974). *Reed Town, Japan. A Study in Community Power Structure and Political Change*. Honolulu: University Press of Hawaii.

B403   MARUYAMA, M. (1963). *Thought and Behaviour in Modern Japanese Politics*. London: Oxford University Press.

B404   NAKANE, Ch. (1970). *Japanese Society*. London: Weidenfeld and Nicolson.

B405   ROHLEN, T. P. (1976). *For Harmony and Strength, Japanese White-Collar Organization in Anthropological Perspective*. Berkeley: University of California Press.

B406   SCALAPINO, R. A. and MASUMI, J. (1962). *Parties and Politics in Contemporary Japan*. Berkeley: University of California Press.

B407   THAYER, N. B. (1969). *How the Conservatives Rule Japan*. Princeton, NJ: University Press.

B408   WHITE, J. W. (1974). "Tradition and Politics in Studies of Contemporary Japan: Review Article," *World Politics*, 26(3): 400-27.

B409   YANAGA, Ch. (1968). *Big Business in Japanese Politics*. New Haven: Yale University Press.

VIII. China

B410   FEI, HSIA-T'UNG (1953). *China's Gentry: Essays in Rural-Urban Relations*. Chicago: University Press.

B411   FOLSOM, K. E. (1968). *Friends, Guests and Colleagues: The Mu-fu System in the Late Ch'ing Period*. Berkeley: University of California Press.

B412   FRIED, M. (1953). *Fabric of Chinese Society*. New York: Praeger.

B413   GALLIN, B. (1968). "Political Factionalism and its Impact on Village Social Organization in Taiwan," pp. 377-400, in M. Swartz, ed., *Local-Level Politics*.

B414   NATHAN, A. J. (1973). "A Factionalism Model for CCP Politics," *The China Quarterly*, 53: 34-66.

B415   PYE, L. W. (1971). *Warlord Politics: Conflict and Coalition in the Modernization of Republican China*. New York: Praeger.

B416   SKINNER, G. W. (1964/65). "Marketing and Social Structure in Rural China," *Journal of Asian Studies*, 24: 3-43, 195-228 and 363-99.

IX. Pacific Ocean

B417   BROWN, P. (1967). "The Chimbu Political System," *Anthropological Forum*, 2: 36-51.

B418   BROWN, P. (1970). "Chimbu Transactions," *Man* (NS), 5(1): 99-117.

B419   GOODENOUGH, W. H. (1955). "A Problem in Malayo-Polynesian Social Organization," *American Anthropologist*, 57: 71-83.

B420   SAHLINS, M. (1963). "Poor Man, Rich Man, Big-Man Chief: Political Types in Melanesia and Polynesia," *Comparative Studies in Society and History*, 5: 285-303.

B423   STRATHERN, A. (1966). "Despots and Directors in the New Guinea Highlands," *Man* (NS), 1(3): 356-67.

B424   STRATHERN, A. (1971). *The Rope of Moka: Big Men and Ceremonial Exchange in Mount Hagen, New Guinea*. Cambridge: University Press.

X. Eastern and Central Europe

1. USSR

B425   BRZEZINSKI, Z. and HUNTINGTON, S. (1964). *Political Power: USA/USSR*. New York: Viking.

B426   EISENSTADT, S. N. and RONIGER, L. (1981). "Clientelism in the Soviet Union. A Comparative Perspective." Jerusalem, unpublished Ms.

B427   FAINSOD, P. (1958). *Smolensk under Soviet Rule*. Cambridge, Mass.: Harvard University Press.

B428   FRANK, P. (1969). "How to Get On in the Soviet Union," *New Society*, 5 June: 867-68.

B429   IONESCU, G. (1977). "Patronage under Communism," pp. 97-102, in E. Gellner and J. Waterbury, eds., *Patrons and Clients*.

B430   WILLERSTON, J. P. et al. (1979). "Clientelism in the Soviet Union," *Studies in Comparative Communism*, 12 (2-3): 159ff.

2. Hungary

B431 FEL, E. and HOFER, T. (1969). *Proper Peasants: Traditional Life in a Hungarian Village*. Chicago: Aldine, Viking Foundation Publications of Anthropology No. 46.

B432 FEL, E. and HOFER, T. (1973). "Tanyakert-s, Patron-Client Relations and Political Factions in Atany," *American Anthropologist*, 75: 787-801.

XI. Northern Europe

1. Ireland

B433 BAX, M. (1970). "Patronage Irish Style: Irish Politicians as Brokers," *Sociologische Gids*, 17: 179-91.

B434 BAX, M. (1972). "Integration, Forms of Communication and Development: Centre-Periphery Relations in Ireland, Past and Present," *Sociologische Gids*, 19: 137-44.

B435 BAX, M. (1973). *Harpstrings and Confessions: An Anthropological Study of Politics in Northern Ireland*. Amsterdam: University Press.

B436 BAX, M. (1975). "The Political Machine and its Importance in the Irish Republic," *Political Anthropology*, 1(1): 6-20.

B437 SACKS, P. (1976). *The Donegal Mafia: An Irish Political Machine*. New Haven: Yale University Press.

B438 WHYTE, J. H. (1965). "Landlord Influence at Elections in Ireland: 1760-1885," *English Historical Review*, 80: 740-60.

2. Others

B439 GWYN, W. B. (1962). *Democracy and the Cost of Politics in Britain*. London: Athlone Press.

B440 MEDARD, J. F. (1978). "Le clientelisme politique sous la Vème République: Persistance ou renouveau?" Bellagio paper.

B441 MINGAY, G. E. (1963). *English Landed Society in the Eighteenth Century*. London: Routledge and Kegan Paul.

B442 NAMIER, Sir L. (1957). *The Structure of Politics at the Accession of George III*. London: Macmillan.

B443 PAINE, R. (1970). "Lappish Decisions, Partnership, Information Management and Sanctions. A Nomadic Pastoral Adaptation," *Ethnology*, 9: 52-68.

B444 PEHRSON, R. N. (1957). *The Bilateral Network of Social Relations in Konkama Lapp District*. Bloomington: Indiana University Research Center in Anthropology, Folklore and Linguistics.

B445 RICHARDS, P. G. (1963). *Patronage in British Government*. London: George Allen and Unwin.

B446   SCOTT, J. C. (1972). *Comparative Political Corruption*. Englewood Cliffs, NJ: Prentice Hall.

B447   THOMPSON, E. P. (1971). ''The Moral Economy of the English Crowd in the Eighteenth Century,'' *Past and Present*, No. 50.

B448   THOMPSON, F. M. L. (1963). *English Landed Society in the Nineteenth Century*. London: Routledge and Kegan Paul.

B449   THOENIGH, I. C. (1975). ''La relation entre le centre et le peripherie en France: une analyse systematique,'' *Bulletin de l'Institut International d'Administration Publique*, 36: 77-123.

B450   WORMS, J. P. (1966). ''Le prefet et ses notables,'' *Sociologie du Travail*, 3: 249-75.

B451   ZELDIN, T. (1958). *The Political System of Napoleon III*. London: Macmillan.

XII. North America

1. United States

B452   BANFIELD, E. C. and WILSON, J. Q. (1965). *City Politics*. Cambridge, Mass.: Harvard University Press.

B453   BURNHAM, W. D. (1967). ''Party Systems and the Political Process,'' pp. 277-307, in W. Nisbet Chambers and W. D. Burnham, eds., *The American Party Systems: Stages of Political Development*. New York: Oxford University Press.

B454   MANDELBAUM, S. (1965). *Boss Tweed's New York*. New York: John Wiley.

B455   OGBU, J. W. (1974). *The Next Generation. An Ethnography of Education in an Urban Neighborhood*. New York and London: Academic Press.

B456   POLLOCK, J. K. (1937). ''The Cost of the Patronage System,'' *The Annals*, 189.

B457   RIORDON, W. L. (1963). *Plunkitt of Tammany Hall*. New York: E. P. Dutton.

B458   SORAUF, F. J. (1959). ''Patronage and Party,'' *Midwest Journal of Political Science*, 3(2).

B459   TOLCHIN, M. and TOLCHIN, S. (1971). *To the Victor: Political Patronage from the Clubhouse to the White House*. New York: Random House.

B460   WILSON, J. Q. (1961). ''The Economy of Patronage,'' *Journal of Political Economy*, 49: 369-80.

B461   WOLFINGER, R. E. (1972). ''Why Political Machines Have Not Withered Away and Other Revisionist Thoughts,'' *Journal of Politics*, 34: 365-98.

B462   WOLFINGER, R. and FIELD, J. (1966). ''Political Ethos and the Structure of City Government,'' *American Political Science Review*, 60(2): 306-26.

2. *East Arctic — Canada*

B463   FREEMAN, M. (1971). "Tolerance and Rejection of Patron-Roles in an Eskimo Settlement," pp. 34-54, in R. Paine, ed., *Patrons and Brokers in the East Arctic.* Memorial University of Newfoundland, Newfoundland Social and Economic Papers No. 2.

B464   HENRIKSEN, G. (1971). "The Transactional Basis of Influence: White Men among Naskapi Indians," pp. 22-33, in R. Paine, ed., *Patrons and Brokers.*

B465   HILLER, J. (1971). "Early Patrons of the Labrador Eskimos: The Moravian Mission in Labrador, 1764-1805," pp. 74-97, in R. Paine, ed., *Patrons and Brokers.*

B466   LEMIEUX, V. (1971). "Patronage ou bureaucratie," pp. 225-35, in *Parente et Politique. L'Organisation sociale dans l'Ile d'Orléans.* Quebec: Les Presses de l'Université Laval.

B467   LEMIEUX, V. and HUDON, R. (1975). *Patronage et politique au Quebéc (1944-1972).* Sillery: Les Editions du Boreal Espress.

About the Contributors

Frank Belloni teaches at Virginia Commonwealth University. He has published several studies on political parties, factions and elections in Italy. He is co-author, with Dennis Beller, of *Faction Politics* (1978).

Mario Caciagli was educated at the University of Florence and since 1973 has taught at the University of Catania. He is the author of several works on political parties and electoral behavior. His most recent book is *Democrazia Cristiana E Potere Nel Mezzogiorno* (1978).

Judith Chubb is currently teaching at the College of the Holy Cross in Worcester, Massachusetts. She is the author of a forthcoming book-length study of machine politics in Naples and Palermo.

S. N. Eisenstadt is Professor of Sociology at the Hebrew University of Jerusalem. He has been awarded the McIver Award of the American Sociological Association (1964), the Rothschild Prize in Social Sciences (1969), the Kaplun Prize in Social Sciences (1969), and the Israel Prize in Social Sciences (1973). His most recent work is *Revolution and the Transformation of Societies* (1978).

Laura Guasti teaches at Purdue University. She is the author of several articles on issues of development in Latin America, and co-editor of *Friends, Followers and Factions* (1977).

René Lemarchand teaches at the University of Florida. He is the author of several books and articles on contemporary politics in Black Africa. His book on *Rwanda and Burundi* earned him the Herskovits Award of the African Studies Association (1971).

Jean-Francois Médard is Professor at the Institut d'Etudes Politiques of Bordeaux and has taught at the Institut des Relations Internationales in Yaounde (Cameroon). He is the author of several articles on French local politics. His research interests are now primarily focussed on African politics, especially the Cameroons and Nigeria.

Ergun Ozbudun is on the Political Science Faculty of the University of Ankara. He has written extensively on Turkish politics. He is the author of *Social Change and Political Participation in Turkey* (1976).

Susan Kaufman Purcell is an Associate Professor of Political Science at the University of California, Los Angeles. She currently is a member of the Policy Planning Staff, US Department of State, where she works on US policy toward Latin America and the Caribbean. She is the author of *The Mexican Profit-Sharing Decision: Politics in an Authoritarian Regime* and the editor of a forthcoming volume on *Mexico-US Relations*.

Luis Roniger was born in Argentina and is currently a research assistant in the Department of Sociology at the Hebrew University of Jerusalem.

Jacek Tarkowski is Associate Professor of Political Sociology at the University of Warsaw. He is the author of a score of articles on local politics in Poland, and of a major study of Polish local councillors. He is co-editor of *Studies in the Polish Political System* (1978).